social research

An International Quarterly of the Social Sciences

Vol 75 : No 3 : Fall 2008

THE NEW SCHOOL
A UNIVERSITY

EDITOR Arien Mack

EDITORIAL BOARD Arjun Appadurai, Alice Crary, Elzbieta Matynia, Corey Robin, Alan Ryan, Jamie Walkup

MANAGING EDITOR Cara N. Schlesinger

COPY EDITOR Bill Finan

MANAGING EDITORIAL ASSISTANTS Matthew Congden, Chris Crews, and Benjamin Marte

ENDANGERED SCHOLARS WORLDWIDE RESEARCH ASSISTANT John Clegg

WEB ASSISTANTS Elizabeth Hope Atkins, John Clegg, and John Giunta

COVER Jamie Prokell

BUSINESS & EDITORIAL OFFICE
Social Research, The New School for Social Research, 80 Fifth Avenue–7th Floor, New York, NY 10011. Email: socres@newschool.edu

SUBSCRIPTIONS

Print + Online: $45 per year individuals, $145 libraries and institutions. Online only: $40 individuals, $140 libraries and institutions. Single print issues available through our office. Agency discounts available. Subscribe online at <www.socres.org> or contact our office.

Social Research is published quarterly by The New School for Social Research, a division of The New School, 66 West 12th Street, New York, NY 10011.

Contributions should be no more than 8,000 words and typed double-spaced on 8.5" x 11" paper. Notes and references should be typed as separate documents, double-spaced and according to MLA style. Two copies of the manuscript and a stamped return envelope are required. Articles published in Social Research may not be reprinted without permission.

Reprints of back issues, if still available, may be ordered from Periodicals Service Co., 11 Main St., Germantown, NY 12526. Microfilm or microfiche copies of complete volumes of Social Research may be ordered from Bell & Howell Information and Learning/UMI, P.O. Box 1346, Ann Arbor, MI 48106. Complete volumes may be ordered by regular subscribers and copies of single issues, if out of print, may be ordered by any reader, in either microfilm or in print enlarged from microfilm.

Social Research is indexed in ABC POL SCI, ASSIA, Current Contents / Social & Behavioral Sciences, Public Affairs Information Service (PAIS), Research Alert, Social Sciences Citation Index, Social Scisearch, and United States Political Science Documents.

Copyright 2008 by The New School. All rights reserved. ISSN 0037-783X.
ISBN 978-1-933481-14-2

Periodicals postage paid at New York, NY and at additional mailing offices.

Postmaster: Send address changes to Social Research, 66 West 12th St., New York, NY 10011.

Contents

Disasters: Recipes and Remedies

Endangered Scholars Worldwide

We are distressed to report that once again, the most serious violations of academic freedom and free inquiry are occurring in Iran, where a professor of law, two AIDS researchers, and a physician have been imprisoned, all accused of acts against the state for which no evidence has been provided. The plights of all four are described below.

Given the seriousness of these violations, we urge you once again to act now on behalf of these scholars. In particular, we urge that you add your name to the petition demanding the release of Mehdi Zakerian, which you can do by visiting our website at <www.socres.edu/endangeredscholars>. Please also urge your colleagues to do so as well. The more voices of protest, the more effective it will be.

—Arien Mack
Information current, to the best of our knowledge, as of September 22, 2008.

IRAN

MEHDI ZAKERIAN, a prominent scholar of international relations and an assistant professor at Islamic Azad University in Tehran, was detained on August 15, 2008 in Tehran. There has been no statement of any charges against him, nor any information issued regarding his current location and condition. Dr. Zakerian, who is also chair of the International Studies Association of Iran and editor of the bilingual English/Farsi journal *International Studies,* was fired last year from his job at Tehran University. His detention has prevented him from attending the fall semester at the University of Pennsylvania Law School, where he had been awarded the position of visiting scholar.

DRS. ARASH and **KAMIAR ALAEI,** two brothers working on the prevention and treatment of HIV/AIDS, were detained by Iranian security forces on June 28, 2008. No charges have yet been brought against them, but a Tehran prosecutor has accused them of trying to "recruit individuals" to overthrow the Iranian government, according to the Associated Press. The brothers helped establish a series of advanced HIV/AIDS clinics and a national HIV prevention plan. They also participated in the first US-funded people-to-people exchange with postrevolutionary Iran in 2006, visiting Tufts–New England Medical Center and other medical-related sites with a group of Iranian doctors. Kamiar, who has a master's degree in public health from Harvard, was enrolled in a Ph.D. program at the State University of New York–Albany and was home in Iran for a summer break at the time of his arrest. The authorities have not released information about where the brothers are being held, but they are believed to be in Tehran's Evin prison.

DR. MOSTAFA ALAVI was sentenced to 15 years imprisonment by an Iranian court on August 22, 2008. Dr. Alavi is a doctor and researcher who ran a nongovernmental organization called the Iranian Elite Association that sought to boost interaction between educated Iranians and global academic centers. He has reportedly been held in Gohardasht prison since March 2007 and initially stood trial in January 2008, when he was charged with "plotting against the regime." Dr. Alavi suffers from numerous illnesses including diabetes and heart problems, and has been refused necessary medication whilst in prison.

Appeals to:

His Excellency Ayatollah Sayed   Tehran
'Ali Khamenei   Islamic Republic of Iran
Leader of the Islamic Republic   E-mail: info@leader.ir
The Office of the Supreme Leader
Islamic Republic Street—   Salutation: Your Excellency
Shahid Keshvar Doust Street

Ayatollah Mahmoud Hashemi
Shahroudi
Head of the Judiciary
Howzeh Riyasat-e Qoveh
Qazaiyeh/Office of the
Head of the Judiciary
Pasteur St., Vali Asr Ave.,
South of Serah-e Jomhouri
Tehran
Islamic Republic of Iran
E-mail: info@dadgostary-tehran.ir
(In the subject line write:
FAO Ayatollah Shahroudi)

Salutation: Your Excellency

Gholam Hossein Mohseni Ejeie
Minister of Intelligence
Ministry of Intelligence
Second Negarestan Street,
Pasdaran Avenue
Tehran
Islamic Republic of Iran

Salutation: Your Excellency

UPDATES

We are please to announce that two of the scholars we have featured in previous issues, HU SHINGEN and 'AREF DALILAH, have been released.

On the other hand, Professor EMADEDDIN BAGHI, who had previously been released on health grounds, has not only been returned to prison but his situation has worsened. Dr. Baghi suffers from serious heart and kidney ailments. On August 9, 2008, prison physicians declared his condition critical and asked that he be transferred to a hospital for specialist care. However, prison authorities instead ordered his transfer to section 209 of Evin prison for interrogations regarding his ongoing prosecution. Section 209 is a notorious section of the prison operated by the Intelligence Ministry. According to reports, Baghi's health continues to deteriorate.

The following scholars remain in prison: KO AUNG HTUN (Burma), IGOR SUTYAGIN (Russia), ZHENG YICHUN (China), XU ZERONG (China), EMADEDDIN BAGHI (Iran), USSAMA AL-MULLA (Iraq), ABDULLAH AL-HAMID (Saudi Arabia). Their details, as well as means to support them, can be found on our website: <www.socres.org/endangeredscholars>.

—*Written by John Clegg*

THE RELIGIOUS—SECULAR DIVIDE: THE US CASE

A SOCIAL RESEARCH CONFERENCE AT THE NEW SCHOOL

March 5 & 6 2009

As tensions sharpen, join distinguished scholars and intellectuals to explore the nature and future of religion, spirituality, and secularism in the United States, looking at their changing relations both historically and through contemporary debates. This conference will look backward at the religious secular divide and forward to what the future may have in store.

The keynote address will be delivered by Charles Taylor, Professor, Northwestern University.

Tickets
$50, $12/session
Nonprofits: $35, $8/sess
New School alumni: $15, $5/sess
New School students and faculty: Free
Other Students: $15, $5/sess

www.socres.org

Contact
socres@newschool.edu
212-229-5776 x3

This conference is made possible by generous support from Russell Sage Foundation, John Templeton Foundation, and Eugene Lang College, The New School.

Location
The New School
John Tishman Auditorium
66 West 12th Street, NYC

social research
AN INTERNATIONAL QUARTERLY OF THE SOCIAL SCIENCES

THE NEW SCHOOL FOR SOCIAL RESEARCH

Arien Mack
Editor's Introduction

THIS ISSUE CONTAINS PAPERS FROM THE SEVENTEENTH *SOCIAL RESEARCH* conference, Disasters: Recipes and Remedies, which took place at the New School in November 2007. We chose "Disasters" as our topic for a number of compelling reasons. First, there is clear evidence that disasters of many different kinds are becoming more frequent and their effects increasingly far-reaching as a result of growing globalization. In addition, as we all know, one of the dangerous effects of global warming is an increase in the number and magnitude of natural disasters. This makes it important for us to look at these events to learn what we can from them.

A third reason for choosing "Disasters" as our topic is that disasters, which grab media attention when they happen, are often quickly forgotten and disappear from the media long before their consequences have been adequately dealt with and well before we have been able to learn as much as we can from them. A case in point is Hurricane Katrina, which the media now rarely discusses and received not even a mention in President Bush's last State of the Union address. The papers in this issue make it painfully clear that more attention must be paid.

The conference, as this issue illustrates, looked at concerns surrounding preparedness and responsiveness to hurricanes and tsunamis as well as pandemics and bioterrorist attacks, all of which surely qualify as disasters. It examined the important public issues raised by disasters, such as the equitable distribution of resources and what often seem to be the inevitable inequalities of both the protection and treatment of populations with health or economic vulnerabilities. (The poor—a codeword in this country for immigrant and African-American populations—are always likely to suffer the most.) One needs to look no further than Katrina for the most recent painful example of this in the United States. It is the poor, whether on the Gulf coast or in Aceh, Indonesia, who have been the most seriously affected by the recent natural disasters, and it is the poor who will be most vulnerable to the effects of any pandemic.

The conference also explored the commonalities shared by all disasters—those that are conventionally considered "natural," such as hurricanes and tsunamis, and those that may be considered man-made like pandemics and large scale bioterrorist attacks. We recognize that the term "disaster" itself is a fuzzy one and the ways in which we think about disasters are the subject of the first section of this issue.

We asked the conference participants who are now the authors of this issue a series of questions. We asked them what we know about what makes us pay attention to disaster warnings or ignore them. We asked what are the most effective ways to communicate with the public once a disaster occurs or is about to. What makes us more or less vulnerable to disasters and how can we protect the most vulnerable? Who is responsible for preparation and who is responsible for responding, both in the short and long term?

The readers of this issue are bound to come away not only with a much sharper sense of the extent to which it is the poor and the already suffering who are doomed to be the most severely affected by any disaster, but also of how much needs to be done if we are to better protect ourselves from what are likely to be an increasing number of catastrophic events both man-made and natural, a distinction that is becoming increasingly difficult to make.

Part I
Definitions: What We Talk about When We Talk about Disasters

Jonathan Veitch

Introduction: What We Talk about When We Talk about Disasters

WHEN I WAS FIRST ASKED TO INTRODUCE THESE PAPERS, I IMMEDIATELY began to reflect on my own experience with disaster—which, as it turns out, is more substantial than I had imagined. In Los Angeles, the Rodney King insurrections took place a dozen blocks or so from where I lived and went to school (though in Los Angeles even the distance of a few blocks can put you on the other side of the moon). I recalled that I had lived through the Northridge earthquake and the fires in the Santa Monica Mountains, the most recent of which burned my parents' home. And later, after moving to New York, I came out of the subway on 14th Street one glorious autumn day to see the World Trade Center float to the ground like so much pixie dust.

In reflecting on all this, I came to the stunning realization that disaster was not just something that happened to other people, but rather, it was a phenomenon that had transpired—to a remarkable degree—in shocking proximity to the places I worked and lived. It was only fate or luck that made me a witness rather than a participant of these dramatic upheavals—and a witness so curiously inured to events of this sort that I could have hitherto imagined my life without them. That bears further reflection, but this is not the place for it.

As the lone humanist setting the stage for papers by so many distinguished scientists and social scientists, I find myself in circumstances that recall those of Emily Dickinson, when she described her position in the pecking order of Amherst society as a "kangaroo among the beauties." That characterization of herself was an admission of her clumsiness or awkwardness. I would like, if I may, to introduce these texts with a rather awkward question that might be useful to keep in mind.

The question begins with an extrapolation from Susan Sontag's famous essay, "The Imagination of Disaster." Sontag is, of course, anything but clumsy. She is one of the most provocative and elegant essayists of her generation. It is my question that is clumsy (though provocative, I hope). Briefly summarized, "The Imagination of Disaster" is a reflection on the science fiction movies of the 1950s in which Sontag explores the subtext of these "charming" and "naïve" films, which range from *Them* to *Godzilla* to the *Invasion of the Body Snatchers.*

In her essay, Sontag muses about the public appetite for and pleasure in the spectacle of destruction: "a panorama of melting tanks, flying bodies, crashing walls, awesome craters and fissures in the earth, plummeting spacecraft, colorful deadly rays." This orgy of destruction is always imagined in morally simplistic terms, accompanied by the nostalgia for the "Good War," a war without ambiguity and without the threat of collective destruction.

In her essay, Sontag also talks about America's deep ambivalence toward the scientist who is alternately portrayed as a Faustian character (bad) or a technician (good). I do not have space to go into the many interesting observations she makes along the way, but I do want to dwell on her conclusion. Sontag writes:

> Ours is indeed an age of extremity. For we live under continual threat of two equally fearful, but seemingly opposed,

destinies: unremitting banality and inconceivable terror. It is fantasy, served out in large rations by the popular arts, which allows most people to cope with these twin specters. For one job that fantasy can do is to lift us out of the unbearably humdrum and to distract us from terrors—real or anticipated—by an escape into exotic, dangerous situations which have last-minute happy endings. But another of the things that fantasy can do is to *normalize what is psychologically unbearable,* thereby inuring us to it. . . . . There is a sense in which *all these movies are in complicity with the abhorrent. They neutralize it* (emphasis added).

That neutralization takes many forms. One finds it in the touching banality of movie lines like "Come quickly, there's a monster in my bathtub"; "We must do something about this"; or perhaps more simply (and desperately) expressed, "Gosh, I hope it works!"

Of course, not every form of neutralization is as touchingly banal as the sci-fi movies I have just alluded to. And now, here comes the kangaroo's question: Could that same cultural work—the cultural work of neutralization—be performed by conferences like these, even conferences as well-intentioned, thoughtful, and sophisticated as this one?

How, for example, does one respond to what Eric Noji called "complex emergencies and the equally complex responses they require (from first responders, the military, the medical establishment, communications) without neutralizing disaster as simply another problem to be managed? (It is regrettable that Noji's thought-provoking paper, though presented at the conference on which this issue is based, could not be included here.) Or to borrow from Lee Clark, how do we keep the genuine horror of possibility (his term) from being submerged/neutralized/assimilated into the quotidian roar of statistical probability and its accompanying protocols? One might also turn the question around and ask, How we can avoid the paralysis that comes with dwelling too much on the horror of disaster?

This collection of papers is a good start, but we might do well to keep these questions in mind as we proceed.

Michael Oppenheimer
A Physical Science Perspective on Disaster: Through the Prism of Global Warming

THE ISSUE OF DISASTER AND THE PROBLEM OF GLOBAL WARMING intersect strongly in four ways. First, lay understanding of global warming is frequently built from images of disastrous hurricanes, heat waves, floods, and other recent climate trends and weather events. Second, some climate trends have been attributed in part to the atmospheric accumulation of greenhouse gases that is causing global warming. Third, such recent climatic disasters, whether or not attributable to GHGs, have provided useful and often surprising (and discouraging) insights into the human and societal responses to the sort of events that are expected to become more common in the future. Fourth, the increasing frequency or intensity of certain climate-related disasters is shedding new light on the question of disaster preparedness and response in general. It is also providing intriguing insights into the perception of disaster: What characteristics cause an episode to be viewed by policy makers and the public as a disaster?

This paper views disaster through the lens of global warming to elucidate these key questions: What is a disaster, Why do disasters matter so much, and How can we improve capacity to avoid and respond to disaster?

In using this particular lens, we shall consider events that have already occurred, and others that are expected to occur in the future. The global warming problem is useful as a model for thinking about disaster because, like the outcomes of global warming, any disaster is important beyond the direct individual and societal damage it causes in two ways: 1) anticipation of disaster drives far-reaching and costly government policy—good and bad; and 2) the traumatic effects of disaster have consequences that transcend in both in space and time its direct consequences for people and the immediate physical environment (for example, infrastructure that is immediately affected). Furthermore, much of the framing of public discourse about the global warming problem is in terms of disaster. Examining this framing makes it easier to understand why some events are characterized as disasters and some are not. Whether disaster is a representative description of the way most people will experience global warming has yet to be seen, but the idea or anticipation of disaster is certainly shaping public views and influencing public policy on this issue.

WHAT MAKES AN EVENT A DISASTER?

From a physical science perspective, three factors contribute to disaster:

- the intensity of the event: the damage to structures, or to the natural environment, or the levels of morbidity and mortality (what happens to people);
- the event's duration and timing: Does it play out over a long period of time or a short period? Did it occur recently or is it expected to occur in the future? If in the future, is it the distant future or soon? In the global warming context, an event could have happened already, or it could be expected with a certain probability to occur over the next few years, decades, centuries, or millennia;
- its geographic scale.

Beyond the physical factors lies the rich context of economic, political, and social factors that add to the making of the disaster, in part by ameliorating or exacerbating its consequences, and in part by influencing whether an event is ultimately viewed as a disaster. Such factors interact with a physical event to determine a state of *vulnerability*, the degree of susceptibility of the systems that are affected by the physical event. Vulnerability is not just a pre-existing state of affairs. For instance, if a settlement exists in a low-lying land area unprotected by a barrier beach and having not much wetland to absorb shock, a hurricane can cause substantial damage. Or, for example, an island unprotected by coral reefs or other natural structures would be vulnerable to a disastrous strike by a tsunami. These are essentially natural states of high vulnerability.

But of particular concern is the added or reduced vulnerability occurring as a result of an overlay of individual and government decisions that may either mitigate or exacerbate natural vulnerability. Consider the levees that were supposed to protect New Orleans. It has been argued that building those levies actually increased vulnerability in some respects by creating the expectation of safety and facilitating the growth of the city accordingly, making for a greater disaster when a hurricane finally struck. At least some people settled in the area having confidence in the ability of the levies to protect the area far exceeding the reality. One can construct counterexamples, of course, where the responses of people and government might actually have mitigated disaster. Government does work sometimes and people's decisions are sometimes constructive and forward-looking.

Again using New Orleans as an example, the delivered wisdom at least as of today (and we are not finished studying it by any means) is that government at all levels essentially failed: failed not only in the anticipation, but failed in real time as the event unfolded, and failed afterward to successfully remediate the consequences. The sociopolitical reality—how people and government respond to a hazard or to an event—is as important an element in making a disaster as the pre-existing physical vulnerability.

Perception is also important. Consider the fires in California in the fall of 2007. Were they a disaster? Very few people died. Using mortality as a metric of the magnitude of the events, it does not rank very highly; perhaps it does not rank at all. But in the age of television, perhaps it is perception that determines what is defined as a public disaster. On the other hand, if your home happened to be one of the ones that burned, it was certainly a personal disaster.

Another element is the particular group that is affected. In a classic case, one of the biggest physical disasters in recent times was the cyclone that struck the upper Bay of Bengal and killed as many as a million Bangladeshis in 1970. It should perhaps be in a class by itself. But how many people reading this paper have even heard of that event? A few have, but more probably have not. Globally, the significance of this disaster may not have left large footprints because those involved were largely poor and without an international voice. But locally, the cyclone had remarkable reverberations, including an element of legacy that is positive, which we will discuss later.

Finally, expectation and surprise have a lot to do with what is labeled a disaster. One of the largest disasters in the global warming context, forming a reference point for many subsequent studies, is the summer of 2003 in western Europe, when, it is argued, as many as 40,000 people succumbed to the direct and indirect effects of a persistent heat wave peaking in the last two weeks of August. A substantial influenza epidemic that occurred the previous February had caused a comparable number of deaths but is not viewed as a disaster. Why is this so? The heat wave was totally unexpected, including by experts in governments— who were supposed to protect people from this sort of occurrence. (It is fair to say that we do not yet understand why the mortality rates were so high in certain groups—why the demographic distribution occurred as it did). The label "disaster" partly results from the factor of surprise. On the other hand, few cataclysms were as widely anticipated as the strike of a strong hurricane on New Orleans. The surprise was not in the event itself but in the ineptitude of preparation and response.

PHYSICAL ELEMENTS AND PERCEPTION INTERACT

The physical elements and the element of perception cannot, however, be separated so easily. One of the largest risks associated with global warming is the release of ice from the major ice sheets that remain in Antarctica and Greenland. Antarctica is composed of two parts: the part called the West Antarctic ice sheet has the potential to add 5 meters to the level of the sea. The East Antarctic ice sheet has the potential to add about 60 meters: that's *Water World*. The Greenland ice sheet has the potential to add 7 meters. The East Antarctic ice sheet is thought to be more or less stable, while the West Antarctic ice sheet is believed to be relatively unstable. Greenland, because it is not actually so far north, may be directly melting away even as I write this paper. So there is a rather large sea-level rise of about 12 meters that could result from a sustained warming. Based on magnitude alone, that would count as a disaster.

But when one considers how long complete discharge of an ice sheet may take to happen, one gets a different answer. The ice sheets may deteriorate slowly, and the large anticipated sea-level rise could unfold gradually over a period of thousands of years. The rate of sea-level rise might be on the order of a foot per century (similar to the rate of 7 inches in the past century), which would present problems for many areas but generally not insurmountable ones (with a few exceptions). People would have plenty of time to withdraw from the coast, and planning for displacement of infrastructure to a different location would be relatively straightforward and would avoid premature destruction of capital stock. The potential for disaster from certain episodes that might occur anyway, like a strong hurricane, would increase because the combination of a hurricane and a higher sea-level significantly increases risk. But the risk would come from the gradual extension of an existing hazard, not one entirely new in kind or magnitude.

Losing a large amount of what is now the coastal zone would still involve an unprecedented (peacetime) destruction of cultural artifacts and traces of our current settlements, which would all gradually have to disappear. Even our current throwaway society does retain a memory a thousand years or more (consider Cathedral San Marco in Venice). An interesting question to consider is this: What difference would it make to you if you were around for onset of a rising sea level, knowing that various objects representing your culture were not going to be there in 500, 1,000, or 2,000 years? Many people would not categorize such losses as a disaster. Others would.

On the other hand, a large sea-level rise, as much as 40 feet if both the West Antarctic and Greenland ice sheets fully disintegrated rapidly, could play out over a few hundred years at a rate of about 10 feet per century. Such a global average rate of rise would be unprecedented in the history of civilization. Nothing even close to that has happened in the history of settlement. It is doubtful that an adequate response would be feasible. In my view, this would be a disaster. For instance, Florida would turn into a skinny nub of its former self. Still, while the process might be triggered within the next several decades if we do nothing about greenhouse gas emissions, the high rates of rise might not begin for another century of so. One has to ask oneself: How much do we care about what happens in the world of our great-grandchildren? I personally believe we have a responsibility to avoid such outcomes even in the far future. Yet some people might feel differently. Unfortunately, our great-grandchildren have no voice in the discussion.

Consider another example. There has been an observed increase in wildfire frequency in the western United States over the past 30 years, in terrain that is not influenced by human development. These are wildfires that did not occur because of proximity to places where people were located. Part of the increase is probably ascribable to changes in fire management practices. But it is also noteworthy that the temperature of those particular regions has increased at the same time. Earlier snow melts and longer fire season also characterize this region. Now consider that water availability 50 years from now is expected to decrease in the same region. Accordingly, disasters related to forest fires are expected to occur with greater frequency. In contrast to a large sea-level rise from the ice sheets, fires embody a potential for disaster right now, and this risk would grow under in a warmer climate. But as I noted earlier, most such fires are difficult to classify as disasters. Even if disastrous, are they in the same class as the loss of an ice sheet? Can one even analyze such disparate phenomena using a single category—

"disaster"? We may need a new language to deal with the fallout of climate change.

RESPONSES

In considering the future prospect of disaster, we need to consider the likelihood and efficacy of response. I have already pointed out that loss of the ice sheets would likely preclude an effective response, overwhelming the capacities of individual communities and in some cases, entire nations. But a more gradual sea-level rise is already under way due to the melting of mountain glaciers and the expansion of ocean water as it warms. In other words, vulnerability along the coast is gradually increasing even without large-scale mobilization of the major ice sheets. Yet governments and private actors seem largely (though not everywhere) oblivious to the threat. Consider Atlantic City, New Jersey for example. There has not been a strong hurricane along that section of the northeast coastline in a long time. But by any reasonable definition of the word, the area is being primed for disaster. Vulnerability is being increased rather than decreased, with government as a facilitator.

Similarly, sometimes when disasters do occur, governments respond in ways that increase rather than decrease future vulnerability. An example is provided by the follow-on to the great nor'easter of 1992: the barrier island at Westhampton Beach, New York, was severed, and houses and beachfront were lost to the sea. If you go back there today, you will notice that the barrier island has been reconstructed. Houses with similar vulnerability have been rebuilt, with a 30 year guarantee from the federal government. In this context, it is worth noting that sea level rise will move the flood levels for a storm of a given intensity inland. The 1992 storm penetrated the 100-year flood level in that area. As sea level rises, storms of a fixed intensity will breach successively higher flood levels. What is now a 50-year storm, and then a 30-year storm, and then a 10-year storm will penetrate the current 100-year flood level. It is possible that the 30-year guarantee will need to be redeemed with taxpayer money because of such an event. At that point, would the government encourage rebuilding and give yet another guarantee? This is clearly a case where the government has created a perverse incentive that increases, rather than decreases, vulnerability.

Adaptation is a complex thing. There is a limit to how far vulnerability can be reduced by it because there are physical limits on doing so. The previous example indicates that certain forms of adaptation (restoration and reimbursement) may actually heighten vulnerability. In addition, we do not all adapt in a coordinated fashion. One person's anticipation of vulnerability to disaster and preemptive adaptation may increase another person's risks. Certain adaptations abetted by government help one set of people at the expense of another. I like to use the case of Bangladesh to illustrate these points.

India built a dam across the Ganges near its border with Bangladesh to divert water to the fast-growing population of West Bengal, reducing the flow in the Ganges into southwestern Bangladesh. One result has been salinization of rice fields there and the disruption of the normal water cycle. Instead of two seasonal rice crops, there is now only one because of the reduced flow. The dam was an adaptation that in the end helped some people and hurt others. An interesting question is how to coordinate adaptation at levels higher than the local level to optimize outcomes.

Bangladesh is also in a precarious position because the land in that country is sinking. It is a delta which is undergoing compaction. Groundwater withdrawals are exacerbating the sinking of the land. Tectonism is contributing as well. In addition, sea level is rising. Taken together, these effects appear likely to cause the area of the country now below the 1 meter elevation to disappear into the sea sometime in this century if emissions are not abated soon. Over 8 million people now live in this area. It's not entirely clear where they, or others living there decades in the future, or others that would have moved there from elsewhere if the land had remained, will go.

On the positive side, this is precisely where the cyclone I referred to earlier made landfall. There has been a constructive response to that experience. The government built a reliable early warning system and many block houses on concrete stanchions so that people could evacuate effectively. Consequently, the death rates in similar cyclones, like the one that occurred in the fall of 2007, while still tragic, have been lower by a factor of a hundred or more compared to the 1970 event. Considerable learning has accord and policy makers reacted accordingly. Unfortunately, there is a limit to what can be done in this regard; I cannot imagine what Bangladesh would do in face of a 40-foot rise. I doubt that a sea wall could be constructed across the top of the Bay of Bengal.

THE ROLE OF LEARNING

Arien Mack, the editor of *Social Research*, has made the point that memory fades. Hurricane Betsy struck the Gulf Coast in 1965. Apparently the right lessons were not learned, and 40 years later, New Orleans paid for that lack of learning. If we are to thrive in the face of a warming planet, we must improve our ability to absorb the right lessons, and respond accordingly. To make the situation more complex, global warming is changing the statistics of disasters, making the extraction of lessons from the past all the more difficult. In particular, the likelihood of intense hurricanes occurring in the future is changing. As a result, our adaptation capabilities have a major blind spot in them already. There are many such holes in the climate-related safety net, in addition to the many things we do not do very well already, such as noted above. The large uncertainties about how the statistics may change further complicate adaptation to potential disasters. Combined with our history of not always learning the right lesson from disaster, and our limited ability to respond effectively when we have learned the right lesson, one ia less than optimistic about our ability to deal with climate change. My colleagues and I, as physical scientists, need to become much more skilled at prediction. But the users of the information we produce need to understand that our predictive capacities will not improve rapidly. In some sense, the climate may change faster than our predictive capacity. In the meantime, a strong emphasis needs to be placed on learning to improve the social and political response to disasters. Without such improvements, and without prompt reductions in GHG emissions, the future promises to be grim indeed.

Lee Clarke
Possibilistic Thinking: A New Conceptual Tool for Thinking about Extreme Events

IN SCHOLARLY WORK, THE SUBFIELD OF DISASTERS IS OFTEN SEEN AS narrow. One reason for this is that a lot of scholarship on disasters is practically oriented, for obvious reasons, and the social sciences have a deep-seated suspicion of practical work. This is especially true in sociology. Tierney (2007b) has treated this topic at length, so there is no reason to repeat the point here. There is another, somewhat unappreciated reason that work on disaster is seen as narrow, a reason that holds some irony for the main thrust of my argument here: disasters are unusual and the social sciences are generally biased toward phenomena that are frequent. Methods textbooks caution against using case studies as representative of anything, and articles in mainstreams journals that are not based on probability samples must issue similar obligatory caveats. The premise, itself narrow, is that the only way to be certain that we know something about the social world, and the only way to control for subjective influences in data acquisition, is to follow the tenets of probabilistic sampling. This view is a correlate of the central way of defining rational action and rational policy in academic work of all varieties and also in much practical work, which is to say in terms of probabilities. The irony is that probabilistic thinking has its own biases, which, if unacknowledged and uncorrected for, lead to a conceptual neglect of extreme events. This leaves us, as scholars, paying attention to disasters only when they happen and doing *that* makes the accumulation of good ideas about disaster vulnerable to issue-attention cycles (Birkland, 2007).

These conceptual blinders lead to a neglect of disasters as "strategic research sites" (Merton, 1987), which results in learning less about disaster than we could and in missing opportunities to use disaster to learn about society (cf. Sorokin, 1942). We need new conceptual tools because of an upward trend in frequency and severity of disaster since 1970 (Perrow, 2007), and because of a growing intellectual attention to the idea of worst cases (Clarke, 2006b; Clarke, in press). For instance, the chief scientist in charge of studying earthquakes for the US Geological Service, Lucile Jones, has worked on the combination of events that could happen in California that would constitute a "give up scenario": a very long-shaking earthquake in southern California just when the Santa Anna winds are making everything dry and likely to burn. In such conditions, meaningful response to the fires would be impossible and recovery would take an extraordinarily long time. There are other similar pockets of scholarly interest in extreme events, some spurred by September 11 and many catalyzed by Katrina.

The consequences of disasters are also becoming more severe, both in terms of lives lost and property damaged. People and their places are becoming more vulnerable. The most important reason that vulnerabilities are increasing is population concentration (Clarke, 2006b). This is a general phenomenon and includes, for example, flying in jumbo jets, working in tall buildings, and attending events in large capacity sports arenas. Considering disasters whose origin is a natural hazard, the specific cause of increased vulnerability is that people are moving to where hazards originate, and most especially to where the water is. In some places, this makes them vulnerable to hurricanes that can create devastating storm surges; in others it makes them vulnerable to earthquakes that can create tsunamis. In any case, the general problem is that people concentrate themselves in dangerous places, so when the hazard comes disasters are intensified. More than one-half of Florida's population lives within 20 miles of the sea. Additionally, Florida's population grows every year, along with increasing development along the coasts. The risk of exposure to a devastating hurricane is obviously high in Florida. No one should be surprised if during the next hurricane season Florida becomes the scene of great tragedy.

The demographic pressures and attendant development are widespread. People are concentrating along the coasts of the United States, and, like Florida, this puts people at risk of water-related hazards. Or consider the Pacific Rim, the coastline down the west coasts of North and South America, south to Oceania, and then up the eastern coastline of Asia. There the hazards are particularly threatening. Maps of population concentration around the Pacific Rim should be seen as target maps, because along those shorelines are some of the most active tectonic plates in the world. The 2004 Indonesian earthquake and tsunami, which killed at least 250,000 people, demonstrated the kind of damage that issues from the movement of tectonic plates. (Few in the United States recognize that there is a subduction zone just off the coast of Oregon and Washington that is quite similar to the one in Indonesia.) Additionally, volcanoes reside atop the meeting of tectonic plates; the typhoons that originate in the Pacific Ocean generate furiously fatal winds.

Perrow (2007) has generalized the point about concentration, arguing not only that we increase vulnerabilities by increasing the breadth and depth of exposure to hazards but also by concentrating industrial facilities with catastrophic potential. Some of Perrow's most important examples concern chemical production facilities. These are facilities that bring together in a single place multiple stages of production used in the production of toxic substances. Key to Perrow's argument is that there is no technically necessary reason for such concentration, although there may be good economic reasons for it.

The general point is that we can expect more disasters, whether their origins are "natural" or "technological." We can also expect more death and destruction from them. I predict we will continue to be poorly prepared to deal with disaster. People around the world were appalled with the incompetence of America's leaders and organizations in the wake of Hurricanes Katrina and Rita. Day after day we watched people suffering unnecessarily. Leaders were slow to grasp the importance of the event. With a few notable exceptions, organizations lumbered to a late rescue. Setting aside our moral reaction to the official neglect, perhaps we ought to ask why we should have expected a competent response at all? Are US leaders and organizations particularly attuned to the suffering of people in disasters? Is the political economy of the United States organized so that people, especially poor people, are attended to quickly and effectively in noncrisis situations? The answers to these questions are obvious. If social systems are not arranged to ensure people's well-being in normal times, there is no good reason to expect them to be so inclined in disastrous times.

Still, if we are ever going to be reasonably well prepared to avoid or respond to the next Katrina-like event, we need to identify the barriers to effective thinking about, and effective response to, disasters. One of those barriers is that we do not have a set of concepts that would help us think rigorously about out-sized events. The chief toolkit of concepts that we have for thinking about important social events comes from probability theory. There are good reasons for this, as probability theory has obviously served social research well. Still, the toolkit is incomplete when it comes to extreme events, especially when it is used as a base whence to make normative judgments about what people, organizations, and governments should and should not do. As a complement to probabilistic thinking I propose that we need *possibilistic thinking*.

In this paper I explicate the notion of possibilistic thinking. I first discuss the equation of probabilism with rationality in scholarly thought, followed by a section that shows the ubiquity of possibilistic thinking in everyday life. Demonstrating the latter will provide an opportunity to explore the limits of the probabilistic approach: that possibilistic thinking is widespread suggests it could be used more rigorously in social research. I will then address the most vexing problem with advancing and employing possibilistic thinking: the problem of infinite imagination. I argue that possibilism *can* be used with discipline, and that we can be smarter about responding to disasters by doing so.

EQUATING PROBABILISM WITH RATIONALITY

In many quarters, thinking probabilistically seems almost natural. But it is far from that. Indeed probabilism, as a set of concepts, theorems, or as an integrated logic, is only a few hundred years old (Hacking, 1990). Much of it had its beginnings in mathematicians' struggles to figure the probabilities of throwing a particular combination of dice. But their greatest accomplishment was to conceptualize causes and to decrease uncertainty about the social and physical worlds. In this quest they succeeded masterfully. There is no question that the slow accretion of ideas regarding probability constitutes one of the greatest advancements of modernity. Without it airplanes do not fly, bridges do not stay up, medicines do not work, and population surveys fail miserably.

The problem with probability is that over time it has come to be equated with rationality itself, rather than as a form of rationality, and this has stunted imaginations. Extreme events, "way out" phenomena, rare things are by its lights ruled to be exotic, deviant, strange, and, more to the point, so far out on the normal curve that there is little we can say about them that we know to be true. The presumption seems to be that if there is no pattern that fits a normally distributed probability distribution, or some reasonable facsimile thereof, then there is no pattern to be discovered, and no way to usefully theorize the events.

Using probability theory as the basis for rational thought is ubiquitous in scholarship, and most especially in sociology, psychology, and economics. Here I shall stay within the subfield of disaster studies and risk, using a few characteristic examples to demonstrate my point.

Wildavsky's writings on risk frequently referred to the ways that fears were out of proportion to their actual threat. In *Risk and Culture*, he and Douglas argued that concern about environmental hazards was on par with worrying about Satan (Douglas and Wildavsky, 1983; Wildavsky, 1997). Similar arguments issue from scholars, and others, regarding nuclear power and toxic chemicals. The acronym NIMBY— Not in My Backyard—is frequently used to dismiss the concerns of local populations when they complain about facilities that they fear might pose some risk to them.

Cognitive psychologists have provided a raft of work on how people use heuristics and other kinds of mental shortcuts in perceiving and making decisions about risk. The early and most fundamental contributions here were from Amos Tversky, Daniel Kahneman, and Paul Slovic (Kahneman, Slovic and Tversky, 1982; Kahneman and Tversky, 1972; Slovic, 1987; Slovic, Fischhoff and Lichtenstein, 1982; Tversky and Kahneman, 1974). This work is founded on the essential insight of Herbert Simon (1955) that people can only be boundedly rational because they cannot process all the information that might be relevant for a particular decision. Combs and Slovic (1979) and Lichtenstein et al. (1978), for instance, argued that individuals' risk assessments are systematically biased because they rely too heavily on newspapers and television as sources of information. Because of the volume and character of such sources, which themselves rely on sensational stories, people use mental heuristics as sense-making devices. This work is built on the notion that there is an objective distribution of events against which subjects' cognitive estimates are held for comparison. For example, Slovic et al. (1979) found that nonexperts consistently overestimate the risk of nuclear power plant accidents, as measured against a probability distribution of the hazard. An apparently obvious policy conclusion to draw from such research is that low-level risks should receive low levels of public resources in making allocative and regulatory decisions (Lave, 1984; Wildavsky, 1979).

Glassner has been a particularly effective proponent of probabilism in regard to risk. His book *Culture of Fear* (1999) provides an impor-

No Postage
Necessary
if Mailed
in the
United States

BUSINESS REPLY MAIL

First Class Permit No. 6083 Sec. 34.9 P.L. & R. N.Y., N.Y.

POSTAGE WILL BE PAID BY ADDRESSEE

SOCIAL RESEARCH

NEW SCHOOL FOR SOCIAL RESEARCH

66 WEST 12TH ST

NEW YORK NY 10114-0185

social research

80 FIFTH AVENUE · ROOM 715, NEW YORK, NY 10011

PLEASE ENTER MY SUBSCRIPTION TO *SOCIAL RESEARCH*, STARTING WITH THE CURRENT ISSUE.

(These rates for print only. For print + online or online only, please subscribe at www.socres.org.)

❋ **ONE YEAR**	Individual subscribers $40	Institutions $140
❋ **TWO YEARS**	Individual subscribers $72	Institutions $270
❋ **THREE YEARS**	Individual subscribers $99	Institutions $385

Foreign subscribers add $22 postage per year.

Agents and booksellers take 5% off institutional rates only.

❋ **CHECK ENCLOSED**   ❋ **BILL MY VISA/MASTERCARD**

CARD NUMBER/EXPIRATION _____

SIGNATURE _____

NAME _____

STREET _____

CITY _____ **STATE** ___ **ZIP** ___

TEL.: 212.229.5776x1 • FAX: 212.229.5746

75:3

tant, needed corrective to the usual view of many psychologists and economists: that people's biases, cognitive shortcuts, and passions interfere with sensible decision-making and so they ought to be excluded from important policy debates. Glassner demonstrates that there is a great deal to be gained by people being fearful, and it is to these issue-entrepreneurs to whom we should look for promoting disproportionate concern in the public. Newspapers sell and politicians are re-elected in false panics about illegal drug use, imagined crime waves, and the like. Glassner argues persuasively that American society wastes its resources on "mythical hazards" (210) such as road rage and crack-cocaine. But by what measure can Glassner come to the conclusion that "Americans are afraid of the wrong things"? He does not provide a formal definition, but claims that "we compound our worries beyond all reason" (xii), worry "disproportionately about [even] legitimate ailments" (xii) and that dangers are "blown out of proportion" (xvi). Clearly Glassner's comparative metric is a probability distribution of events or hazards; if intensity of worry does not match such a distribution, then it is disproportionate to the hazard.

There are also a large number of popular writings that criticize people's perceptions and decisions about risk because they are not based on probability theory. Laudan, a noted philosopher of science, puts forth that argument in *Danger Ahead: The Risks you Really Face on Life's Highway* (1997) and *The Book of Risks: Fascinating Facts about the Chances We Take Every Day* (1994). There are many other books with a similar message. In *Beating Murphy's Law,* Berger points out that "risk theory" is used widely in business and government, which helps to make those institutions more rational than individuals (Berger, 1994). If the public were to use such procedures, it would make smarter, more sensible, choices about how to live.

Probability theory is in general how modern societies frame rhetoric about risks. Scholars make the normative judgment that people ought make choices on the basis of probability. They take for granted that a probabilistic approach to the future prescribes a set of rational principles that should drive decisions, actions, and policies. Prominent institutions, too, either justify what they do in terms of probabilism or use probabilism to drive toward choices that can be defended on apparently objective grounds. Probabilistic thinking is clearly the chief rhetoric of rationality in the modern day.

THE UBIQUITY OF POSSIBILISTIC THINKING

Probabilistic thinking is not the only available rhetoric with which to make sense of risks, hazards, and disasters. I have proposed the idea of possibilistic thinking (Clarke, 2006b) as a complement to probabilistic thinking. Possibilistic thinking highlights consequences of events, slighting, to some degree at least, the likelihood that such events will occur. A possibilistic approach shifts our gaze away from the center of a normal distribution out to its tails. A possibilistic approach acknowledges that a civilian nuclear power plant is unlikely to melt down, but wonders what happens if a plant has a particularly bad day. From a possibilistic point of view, it can be entirely sensible to pay attention to events and phenomena even though they do not occur frequently enough to generate a probability distribution. As Sagan (1993:12) has written, "things that have never happened before happen all the time."

Various scholars and arguments, as I have noted, regard such logic as extremist, defeatist, and irrational. I would be remiss not to acknowledge that people cannot lead all aspects of their lives animated by possibilistic thinking. Similarly, organizations cannot run effectively nor societies be organized reasonably strictly on the basis of possibilistic thinking. When such happens mental and social paralysis ensue. Indeed, this is known as "analysis paralysis" in the decision-making literature in public policy and public management. It is the essential character of the paranoid to ignore probabilities. Erich Fromm once told the US Senate Foreign Relations Committee that "the paranoid person is so removed from reality that he bases his beliefs on mere possibility. The normal person bases his beliefs on a greater or lesser degree of probability" (Fromm, 1975).

My argument is not that we should jettison probabilistic reasoning but that possibilistic reasoning is not a simple emotional, irrational, senseless response to a hazard or perceived hazard. Rather, careful consideration of consequences along with likelihood of occurrence is often quite sensible.

Consider flying. From a probabilistic point of view, flying in modern jet aircraft is the safest way to travel, for two reasons. First, it is highly unlikely that someone will be hurt or killed traveling in such a manner. Second, flying is peculiarly safe relative to other modes of transportation, especially driving automobiles. Probabilistically speaking, people who worry about flying let their emotions get the better of them. These are the people who become visibly nervous when airplanes run into turbulence; they are the ones whose fears are out of proportion to the likelihood of a plane crash.

Their nervousness looks different, however, from a possibilistic point of view. Planes *do* occasionally lose power in all their engines. Sometimes they collide in midair. Modern jet liners *have* exploded in flight. None of these events—and it is not an exhaustive list—are likely and nearly all people who fly know that, which is one reason that more and more people fly every year. But when those kinds of events do happen, probability does not matter. If an airplane is 35,000 feet in the sky and there is an explosion on it, it makes no sense to talk about probabilities of survival. It is the possibilities that make people nervous when they run into turbulence.

In fact possibilistic thinking is more widespread than might first be apparent. As a moment of imagination, such thinking in fact permeates society, but lives an uncomfortable existence with probabilistic thinking. That possibilistic thinking *is* widespread suggests that individuals and social units can function effectively even while employing it. In other words, just because paranoia is characterized by possibilistic thinking does not mean that all possibilistic thinking is paranoid. Let us examine just a few other cases, across several levels of social organization.

At the individual level, consider life insurance. Imagine a 30-year-old person deciding whether or not to buy such insurance. Stipulate that our purchaser is sufficiently wealthy that s/he can afford it, although of course there are always opportunity costs. Let us complicate the scenario by adding children and a life partner to the mix. The decision is to buy or not to buy the insurance. If our decisionmaker buys the insurance, the choice will clearly be animated by possibilistic thinking. The purchaser is making the bet that s/he will die earlier than the life insurance company expects. In fact the purchaser is betting *against the odds* that death will come sooner than later. The decision is made completely on grounds of the consequences of dying; the probabilities of dying have nothing to do with it. For its part, the life insurance company is betting *with the odds* that the Grim Reaper will not visit the policyholder in the near future. Surely one reason that insurance companies make so much money is that they understand and invest on grounds of probabilities. But just as surely would society judge harshly the 30-year-old should s/he die prematurely without life insurance. We might even level the ultimate modernist epithet at our decisionmaker: irrationality.

Now consider an organizational example. After every major airline accident in the United States, the National Transportation Safety Board launches an intensive investigation. A "go-team" is dispatched to the site, sometimes even sent overseas, to sift through airplane parts and interview witnesses. The go-team can be comprised of experts from many specialty areas, including "structures, systems, power plants, human performance, fire and explosion, meteorology, radar data, event recorders, and witness statements" (NTSB, 2008). The go-team tries to discover causes and contributing factors of accidents. Their investigations are rigorous and thorough. They are undoubtedly expensive, although I could find no data on their cost.

The NTSB's investigations sometimes reveal problems that apply to other aircraft. One example involved TWA Flight 800. On July 17, 1996, the Boeing 747 exploded in midair soon after takeoff from New York's JFK airport, killing all 230 people aboard. Although initial fears were that terrorists had blown up the aircraft, the NTSB discovered that the most likely cause was a spark in the fuel-level probe in the center fuel tank. The tank was empty, or nearly empty, and was therefore filled with explosive gas that was further heated by the near constant operation of the adjacent air conditioning units on a hot July day. This created the opportunity for the spark to cause the vapors to ignite. The NTSB quickly recommended amelioration measures for other aircraft with similar designs (the flaw had already been discovered and repaired on the US president's *Air Force One*).

Yet such cases are relatively rare. Far more frequent is that the NTSB does its extensive research but learns little or nothing that would prevent future accidents. On October 31, 1999 a pilot for Egypt Air crashed a Boeing 767 into the Atlantic Ocean, killing all 217 people aboard. The NTSB's investigation was as extensive as any, and took two years to complete, which is not an extraordinary length of time. The case was politically sensitive because the Egyptian government refused to believe that suicide was possible. But every indication was indeed that the first officer deliberately crashed the plane, although the NTSB's final report repeatedly refers to Egypt Air Flight 990 as the "accident flight" (NTSB, 2002). In any case, the point is that there were no lessons learned from the investigation, or at least nothing that would prevent a future suicide attempt in a commercial aircraft.

But even when such lessons *are* learned, their overall contribution to saving lives is statistically trivial. There are so many miles flown without fatalities, and so many successful takeoffs and landings, that by any measure there can be little probabilistic argument in favor of continuing the NTSB's investigations. Yet few would argue that such investigations should stop. The logic for continuing them, however, is fully possibilistic.

It is exactly the possibilities that local protest groups are often most worried about. Such groups are often labeled NIMBYs by opponents who wish to rhetorically shift the terms of debate. By leveling at such groups an epithet that questions their motives and good sense, attention moves away from what from their point of view is protection of their interests. Consider the Indian Point nuclear power station. Constructed on the banks of the Hudson River about 30 miles north of New York City, the plant consists of three nuclear reactors, one of which is shuttered. People around Indian Point, including local governments, with assistance from New York state government, have complained for years that the plant is unsafe. Moreover, the emergency planning zone—a 10-mile radius around the plant—could not be evacuated effectively, critics charge, if a reactor's contents were to breach containment. Having evacuation plans for the emergency planning zone has been a legally necessary part of licensing since the 1979 accident at the nuclear power plant at Three Mile Island. The risks at Indian Point apparently increased (alternatively, arguments about the risks increased) after September 11 because the hijackers who flew from Boston, using the Hudson River Valley as a navigation tool to guide them to lower Manhattan, must have flown close to or over Indian Point. After that worst-case day, opponents of Indian Point wondered what might happen if a well-fueled Boeing 767 were to crash into a reactor at 500 miles per hour.

The response of the utility and other proponents of the Indian Point facility, such as the Nuclear Regulatory Commission, was predictable: the likelihood of a meltdown is trivial, the containment structure that is built around the reactors would likely withstand a direct strike, and the chance of a terrorist steering a plane directly into a reactor is, in engineering parlance, "vanishingly small." Rather than dwell on the response of Indian Point's supporters, I wish simply to point out that the epistemology of the opponents' logic is possibilistic, one that places higher value on the consequences than the probabilities of failure. Viewed this way, their argument is quite sensible and even rational.

Such examples abound. They demonstrate that probabilistic reasoning is not the only way to reason about potential futures. Of course it is entirely possible to misuse possibilistic thinking. The obvious instances of such abuse were the trumped-up claims by the Bush administration in the run-up to the Iraq invasion. The blunt talk, from the Bush administration, about mushroom clouds, anthrax, and weapons of mass destruction was all about the consequences, not probabilities, of Saddam Hussein having access to substances that can do great harm. The point of all this propaganda was, of course, to instill possibilistic fears in Americans so that going to war would seem like a good idea, or even a necessity. However, just because possibilistic thinking can be abused does not mean that it is inherently flawed. Probabilistic thinking, after all, can also be abused. The challenge is to develop ways to use possibilistic thinking with discipline, rather than to reject it out of hand.

Later in this paper I will propose some mechanisms to avoid abuses of possibilistic thinking. Here I just wish to emphasize the point that there is nothing *inherent* about possibilism that leads to such abuse. Note, too, that abuses of probabilistic thinking are never interpreted as indicating that something is inherently flawed about probabilism. As an example, consider the arguments of tobacco company executives. For years they claimed that there were numerous influences on people's chances of contracting lung cancer and other ailments which we now know (and they knew for a long time) are caused by smoking. Their argument was, essentially, a probabilistic one that served as a smokescreen, as it were, for what they knew to be true. They were abusing probabilism just as surely as the Bush administration was abusing possibilism in the Iraq case.

THE INTELLIGENT USE OF POSSIBILISTIC THINKING

How then can possibilistic thinking be used with intelligence and discipline? I do not have a complete answer to the question, which would be comprised of a set of principles, empirically grounded and logically sound, and that could be applied in a broad array of circumstances or scenarios. I do, however, have a few elements of the answer.

First, individuals and organizations can make fuller use of simulations, gaming, and the like—virtual worst-case thinking. For example, in June 2001 the Johns Hopkins Center for Civilian Biodefense, along with some similar agencies, ran a two-day exercise called Dark Winter. Dark Winter simulated a smallpox attack in the United States. The exercise had but 12 participants, although they were quite unusual: former Georgia Senator Sam Nunn played the President, former FBI Director

William Sessions played the FBI director, former CIA Director James Woolsey played the CIA director, and so on (O'Toole, Mair, and Inglesby, 2002).

In the simulation, 300 people were initially infected by three simultaneous smallpox outbreaks, which began in shopping malls in several cities. The researchers' assumptions were extrapolated from the available scientific literature—for instance, that 30 grams of smallpox were enough to cause 3,000 infections. Similarly they used data from an outbreak in Yugoslavia in 1972, which has been well studied, to set the infection rate of 11 infections per person. By the sixth (virtual) day, there were 2,000 smallpox cases in 15 states and the vaccine was running out. The scenario posited that political arguments about border controls would intensify and the country's health system would be overloaded. By day 13 there were 16,000 smallpox cases and a thousand deaths, with the expectation that there would be 17,000 additional cases over the following 12 days with 10,000 total deaths.

There is an argument among people who work on terror-related issues that spending scarce resources on smallpox is wasteful. After all, the risk of a smallpox epidemic *is* small, according to experts in bioterrorism. Weaponized smallpox is hard to manufacture, and hard to deliver. From another view, though, there are good reasons to be concerned about smallpox. Few doctors have ever seen a case of smallpox so it would likely be misdiagnosed at first (in the same way that SARS looks like flu). Ironically, Americans are at greater risk because the virus has been eradicated—very few Americans have been recently vaccinated (people from the third world, however, are often vaccinated against smallpox). Too, the Soviet Union maintained a 20-ton stockpile of smallpox, which has not been fully accounted for. The virus has a fatality rate of about 30 percent. Here again is a case where it seems sensible to worry about possibilities more than the probabilities.

Dark Winter was a productive virtual worst case, and the use of it suggests how possibilistic thinking can be used intelligently. The exercise's authors and players drew several important lessons from Dark

Winter. They learned that America's leaders do not understand bio-attacks or the policy issues that such attacks would entail. Dark Winter also threw into sharp relief how policy options would be constrained by an insufficiency of vaccine. They learned about the ways that medical and public health data would be important, and that the US lacks "surge capacity" in its health care system. The exercise highlighted how federal and state policies might conflict in a smallpox crisis. Finally, and unusually, Dark Winter showed that everyday people would be essential participants in a response, not just victims. "President" Sam Nunn said that "the federal government has to have the cooperation from the American people. There is no federal force out there that can require 300,000,000 people to take steps they don't want to take" (O'Toole, Mair, and Inglesby, 2002:982)

Though useful, simulations like Dark Winter must be used with caution. It is important to remember that they are unlikely to represent how events would actually unfold in a disaster or a terrorist attack. Virtual possibilistic thinking is not usually accompanied by much *ground truthing*. In remote sensing—mapping out a forest with a satellite, for example—ground truthing is when someone actually goes to the place for on-site observations. Real ground truthing, for disasters, would involve understanding very complex phenomena: the intricate histories of people's cultures, values, constraints, opportunities, and so on. To understand a smallpox terrorist attack, for instance, simulating official behavior is insufficient; one would also need to understand terrorist behavior: their goals, their aims, their methods, their frustrations, their strategies, their tactics. It is the lack of ground truthing that led to America's quagmire in Vietnam, and Iraq.

It may be that virtual possibilistic exercises are *least useful* when they are thought to approximate reality. Indeed their greatest virtue may be their *unreality*. As devices to stretch the imagination, they may be particularly useful when there is no experience with a particular kind of hazard. If experts want to plan for a disaster like the *Titanic*, there is a substantial empirical record of passenger ship disasters they can use. There are many precedents to use if they want to think through the problems of a large hurricane in a densely populated city. But what if they want to think through how an Ebola virus outbreak in Atlanta might play out? And what if planners are given the task of planning a response to a large increase in the world's temperatures? Without meaningful experience to draw on for such cases, simulations and models may be the best way to innovate and otherwise address remote possibilities.

An important challenge with using possibilistic thinking intelligently is the infinite possibilities problem: if nearly everything is possible, how do you know when to stop making up scenarios, considering new variables, inventing outrageous stories? In other words, by what standards can one distinguish a reasonable from an unreasonable set of possibilities?

We can use counterfactual analysis in our quest to discipline possibilistic thinking. Because hindsight is nearly perfect, counterfactual analysis must be employed carefully. Such analysis can be used intelligently and so can be used to help plan for extreme events.

Political scientists and historians, and to a lesser extent historical sociologists, have developed an extensive literature on using counterfactuals with discipline (Ferguson, 1999; Hawthorn, 1993; Tetlock and Belkin, 1996). Two rules, in particular, emerge from that literature that can be used to reign in the potential excesses of possibilistic thinking. One rule to follow when looking backward is called the "minimal rewrite-of-history" rule. The idea is to propose changing as few factors, events, or variables as is feasible to imagine a plausibly different past, or future. Unavoidably, there is a subjective judgment involved in deciding what minimal means. Still, imagine arguing that President Bill Clinton would have been our greatest president *if only* he had been faithful to his wife *and* he was not hounded by the political far-right *and* he had been more savvy about international politics *and* he had found a way to unite Americans on issues of poverty, racism, and health care. Too many conditions would have to be different for this to qualify as a good counterfactual.

Looking forward, is it reasonable to postulate, as do some astronomers, that a naturally occurring explosion from an asteroid could trigger a nuclear war? A careful look at the record of nuclear accidents suggests the plausibility of such a scenario. During the Cuban missile crisis, a bear climbed a fence in Minnesota, prompting an Air Force sentry to take a shot at it and to sound the alarm warning of sabotage. At an airfield in Wisconsin, an alarm rang, indicating that a nuclear war had begun. Pilots of nuclear armed interceptors got their planes ready. Although the planes never left the ground, they easily could have which would have importantly increased the opportunities for an accidental nuclear launch. There have, as well, been numerous instances in which American defense officials mistakenly thought that nuclear missiles had been launched against the United States (obviously, the mistakes were discovered in time) (Sagan, 1993). Finally, only a few countries have the technological sophistication to distinguish a nuclear explosion from a natural one in space. So a natural occurring explosion might be misinterpreted, say by India or Pakistan, as an attack and respond in kind.

A second rule from the literature on counterfactuals is called the "possible worlds" rule, which means that the action being imagined or proposed must have been, or be, possible for the actor to think about and act upon. By this prescription we would rule out as useless the question of how World War I might have turned out if Germany had nuclear weapons because it was a scientific impossibility for anyone to have nuclear weapons at the time. On this count, we would probably judge as reasonable the counterfactual prediction that a nuclear war *could* be started by a naturally-occurring atmospheric explosion. Confusion and ambiguity are quite likely among participants in a crisis situation. And it is a hallmark of strategic thinking about nuclear weapons that a first strike can be the most rational course of action for a combatant facing the prospect of nuclear war (Clarke, 2006a).

From one view, developing and using hypothetical scenarios and concentrating on possibilities is unproductive. But if these thought experiments can be conducted in a reasonably rigorous way, intelligence and imagination about extreme events can be enhanced. Judging useful from useless counterfactuals does not have to be mere speculation. The practical significance of this is that policymakers and managers could, should they choose to, make good use of experts skilled in building counterfactuals. That kind of imagining does not have to stay behind the doors of think tanks and esoteric departments in intelligence organizations.

EXTREME EVENTS AND POSSIBILISTIC THINKING

Extreme events are "focusing events," as Birkland has said about disasters more generally (Birkland, 2007). Focusing events are dramatic and sudden, and people organize around them, mobilizing their interests and passions. The meltdown at Three Mile Island was a focusing event, as it worked to galvanize anti-nuclear efforts and shook up the industry is other ways too.

The epistemologically and politically interesting paradox about disasters is that they are important practically, and interesting intellectually, but socially ignored and professionally unprofitable. Kathleen Tierney, a sociology professor but more relevantly the director of the Natural Hazards Center at the University of Colorado, has said that "disasters do not matter much in U.S. society" (Tierney, 2007a). Tierney means that there are no powerful institutional actors willing to shoulder the political and financial investments required for proper preparation. Hers is an overstatement, because the insurance and re-insurance industries care a great deal about disasters. But Tierney's judgment is correct in the main: individuals, families, and communities generally do not prepare for disaster or work to reduce exposure in the first place. At the organizational level, vulnerability reduction and response preparation are out of the revenue stream, or at the very least are always costly.

But individuals, organizations, and society more generally may reasonably be expected to pay more attention to large disasters in the future, because there are good reasons to think there will be more of them with increasingly severe consequences. To be prepared for that, social science needs to develop the conceptual tools with which to make sense of the myriad issues it will confront. I have suggested that the idea of possibilistic thinking is one such tool.

Clearly, probabilistic thinking cannot provide the full range of concepts necessary to understand extreme events. Nor can probabilistic thinking provide clear and unequivocal counsel for social policy regarding disaster. For if decisions were made and policy formulated only on the basis of probabilities, we would be pushed in the direction of committing resources to hazards only on the basis of their likelihood of occurrence. While that is a sensible way to approach resource allocation, it is not the only sensible way. Relying almost exclusively on a probabilistic approach leaves little room for a reasonable argument that we should also worry about nuclear plant meltdowns, train accidents involving toxic chemicals, increases in hurricane intensity from global warming, asteroid strikes, airplane crashes, or bird flu. It is in the nature of "extreme events" that they are statistically rare and that they do not provide us with a distribution of events to which we could attach probabilities. The idea of possibilistic thinking complements probabilistic thinking in the social scientific quest to understand how and why people behave as they do.

NOTES
* For commentary and support I thank Thomas Birkland, Charles Perrow, and Patricia Roos. Some of the material in this paper draws on Clarke (2006b).

REFERENCES
Berger, Bob. *Beating Murphy's Law*. New York: Delta, 1994.

Birkland, Thomas A. *Lessons of Disaster: Policy Change after Catastrophic Events*. Washington, D.C.: Georgetown University Press, 2007.

Clarke, Lee. "Mistaken Ideas and Their Effects." *Oxford Handbook of Contextual Political Analysis*. Eds. Robert Goodin and Charles Tilly. Oxford: Oxford University Press, 2006a: 297-315.

———. *Worst Cases: Terror and Catastrophe in the Popular Imagination.* Chicago: University of Chicago Press, 2006b.

———. "Foreseeing the Future: The Sociology of Worst Cases." *Sociological Inquiry* 78 (in press).

Combs, Barbara, and Paul Slovic. "Newspaper Coverage of Causes of Death." *Journalism Quarterly* 56 (1979): 837-849.

Douglas, Mary, and Aaron Wildavsky. *Risk and Culture: An Essay on the Selection of Technological and Environmental Dangers.* Berkeley: University of California Press, 1983.

Ferguson, Niall. *Virtual History.* New York: Basic Books, 1999.

Fromm, Erich. "Remarks on the Policy of Detente." US Senate Committee on Foreign Relations. Washington, D.C.: US Government Printing Office, 1975: 455-459.

Glassner, Barry. *Culture of Fear.* New York: Basic Books, 1999.

Hacking, Ian. *The Taming of Chance.* Cambridge: Cambridge University Press, 1990.

Hawthorn, Geoffrey. *Plausible Worlds: Possibility and Understanding in History and the Social Sciences.* Boston: Cambridge University Press, 1993.

Kahneman, Daniel, Paul Slovic, and Amos Tversky, eds. *Judgment under Uncertainty: Heuristics and Biases.* Cambridge: Cambridge University Press, 1982 .

Kahneman, Daniel, and Amos Tversky. "Subjective Probability: A Judgment of Representativeness." *Cognitive Psychology* 3 (1972):430-454.

Laudan, Larry. *The Book of Risks: Fascinating Facts about the Chances We Take Everyday.* New York: John Wiley and Sons, 1994.

———. *Danger Ahead: The Risks You Really Face on Life's Highway.* New York: John Wiley and Sons, 1997.

Lave, Lester. "Regulating Risks." *Risk Analysis* 4 (1984): 79-80.

Lichtenstein, Sarah, Paul Slovic, Baruch Fischhoff, Mark Layman, and Barbara Combs. "Judged Frequency of Lethal Events." *Journal of Experimental Psychology: Human Learning and Memory* 4 (1978):551-578.

Merton, Robert K. "Three Fragments from a Sociologist's Notebooks:

Establishing the Phenomenon, Specified Ignorance and Strategic Research Materials." *Annual Review of Sociology* 13 (1987):1-28.

National Transportation Safety Board (NTSB). "Egypt Air Flight 990, Boeing 767-366ER, SU-GAP, 60 Miles South of Nantucket, Massachusetts October 31, 1999." Washington, D.C.: NTSB, 2002.

———. "Major Investigations." NTSB, 2008 <http://www.ntsb.gov/Events/major.htm>.

O'Toole, Tara, Michael Mair, and Thomas V. Inglesby. 2002. "Shining Light on 'Dark Winter.'" *Clinical Infectious Diseases* 34: 972-983.

Perrow, Charles. *The Next Catastrophe: Reducing Our Vulnerabilities to Natural, Industrial, and Terrorist Disasters.* Princeton: Princeton University Press, 2007.

Sagan, Scott. *The Limits of Safety: Organizations, Accidents, and Nuclear Weapons.* Princeton: Princeton University Press, 1993.

Simon, Herbert A. "A Behavioral Model of Rational Choice." *Quarterly Journal of Economics* 69 (1955): 99-118.

Slovic, Paul. "Perception of Risk." *Science* 236 (1987): 260-285.

Slovic, Paul, Baruch Fischhoff, and Sarah Lichtenstein. "Rating the Risks: The Structure of Expert and Lay Perceptions." *Environment* 21 (1979):14-20.

———. "Why Study Risk Perception." *Risk Analysis* 2 (1982): 83-93.

Sorokin, Pitirim. *Man and Society in Calamity: The Effects of War, Revolution, Famine, Pestilence upon Human Mind, Behavior, Social Organization, and Cultural Life.* New York: Greenwood Press, 1942.

Tetlock, Philip E., and Aaron Belkin, eds. *Counterfactual Thought Experiments in World Politics.* Princeton: Princeton University Press, 1996.

Tierney, Kathleen. "Why We Are Vulnerable." *American Prospect* (June 18, 2007a).

———. "From the Margins to the Mainstream? Disaster Research at the Crossroads." *Annual Review of Sociology* 33 (2007b): 503-525.

Tversky, Amos, and Daniel Kahneman. "Judgment under Uncertainty: Heuristics and Biases." *Science* 185 (1974): 1124-1131.

Wildavsky, Aaron. "No Risk Is the Highest Risk of All." *American Scientist* 67 (1979):32-37.

————. *But Is It True? A Citizens Guide to Environmental Health and Safety Issues.* Cambridge: Harvard University Press, 1997.

John C. Mutter
Preconditions of Disaster: Premonitions of Tragedy

DISASTERS ARE NOT EVENTS; THEY ARE PROCESSES. TRUE, NEWS MEDIA inevitably focuses our attentions on the disaster singularity because it makes such compelling coverage. In the era of reality TV it is about as good as it gets. Buildings are torn apart as we watch, people are seen in abject distress; there are miraculous escapes and heroic rescues and, as the cameras follow rescue workers into the rubble of buildings or search houses as flood waters recede, we might even see an actual corpse. The only thing to compare is war reporting. Watching disaster coverage live on television is something akin to necro-voyeurism. But like wars and other forms of deadly conflict, disasters are anything but the singularities portrayed in news coverage. They have long portentous rehearsals and extended coda, little of which makes for entertainment like graphic scenes of destruction. In this essay I want to highlight the social conditions that lead to disaster, drawing on global and local lessons from natural disasters and deadly conflicts.

DISASTER AS PROCESS, DISASTER AS (MEDIA) EVENT

Disaster coverage depends very much on who is affected and where they live or have lived. Almost regardless of death toll, disasters in remote parts of the world hold media attention for only a short time unless, like the Indian Ocean tsunami in 2004 they affect tourist resorts. Then we can hear reports from returning survivors, people just like us, imagine ourselves there, and wonder if we too might have escaped, and had our own stories to tell. It was the tourists who had the video cameras and provided the only images of the tsunami's frightening arrival, giving rise to the initial illusion that the tsunami had struck only tourist resorts. To be fair, coverage of the 2004 tsunami was extensive and lasted many days to weeks after the event itself (depending on the news outlet) and continues from time to time even now with follow-up stories, especially on anniversary dates. No doubt this was because of the incomprehensible enormity of the event—almost an entire hemisphere—and because it was so utterly unique and phenomenal in almost everyone's experience. (No one in coastal Sri Lanka had any memory of a previous tsunami). In general, though disasters are far more devastating in human terms for the people who are not like us and live in remote countries (and do not have camcorders), they receive far less media attention than those nearby, especially those that directly impact the United States, even if the number of fatalities is small, as they usually are. As Gibbon noted, "Our sympathy is cold to the relation of distant misery."

The tragedy of a natural disaster is rehearsed over decades, with the cathartic event itself putting on garish display just how defenseless and susceptible some people are to harm. Live television coverage has, at least, given a human face to disasters, so we no longer merely hear estimates of property losses from insurance company spokesmen and see newspaper pictures of collapsed buildings; we also witness in a near firsthand way the plight of those caught up in the shock and chaos of disaster events and the efforts of those who try to respond. Images of disasters are at first shocking, then uncomfortably revealing. It must surely have struck most of us that survivors of Hurricane Katrina, so graphically documented in news coverage and later in Spike Lee's documentary *When the Levees Broke,* did not fit exactly with the media's typical portrayal of a slice of Americana, and that things had gone badly wrong for those people. Katrina was the first major natural catastrophe in the United States in which the plight of so many victims was recoded so relentlessly, in such close-up detail and so accessibly through television. Previous hurricanes in the United States had, of course, received media coverage but it is hard to recall an instance where cameras have focused so closely on the victim's pitiful circumstances and on the equally pitiful official efforts to provide for them.

Some of the most memorable, deeply disturbing, otherworldly images of the Katrina catastrophe were scenes of surviving victims who made it to the Superdome or the convention center in New Orleans. Why were so many people going to such places and why was their care so dreadful? We know that is not what happens when hurricanes makes landfall in Florida or the Carolinas or in a major snowstorm in New York. People from Miami did not crowd into public buildings during Hurricane Andrew in 1992, although that hurricane was the same strength as Katrina. Why was the expression of and response to Hurricane Katrina so different from that associated with other major hurricanes that typically occur in nearby regions of the Gulf coast and Florida? New Orleans has the extraordinarily dangerous physical geography of a city lying mostly below sea level, protected by levees that proved to be insufficient for the task. That situation is quite different from other parts of the Gulf coast, Florida, and the Carolinas and the levee failures were certainly a major contributor to the disaster moment. But appealing to New Orleans' unique physical setting to explain the catastrophe of Katrina provides an alibi for ignoring the role of dangerous social pre-conditions that made the deadly outcome almost unavoidable.

At the time of the New School conference at which this paper was presented, wildfires in California had just been brought under some measure of control and people were returning to discover whether they still had homes to live in. They too were displaced in massive numbers and many were temporarily housed at the Qualcomm stadium in Los Angeles. Their treatment was hardly the same as those who made it to the New Orleans Superdome. They arrived in SUVs to find masseuses, more than ample fine food (a call had to be put out asking that people stop sending food and drink—they had too much!), and entertainment by rock bands. President George W. Bush was just the most prominent commentator to take the opportunity to draw on the comparison of treatment to point the finger of blame for the catastrophe of Katrina at former Governor Kathleen Blanco, and praise his Republican partner in the governor's house in California for the good work done there (*New York Times,* 2007). Apparently we are to believe that had a Republican been in charge in Louisiana in the last days of August 2005, that the disaster would have been handled much better. The real difference lies in the social status of people who formed the population affected by the two events: in California they comprise some of the very wealthiest people in the country, in New Orleans, some of the very poorest. Those preconditions determine the vastly different outcomes in the two settings.

One truly unique expression of the Katrina catastrophe was the way in which scenes of the hurricane's work caused numerous commentators to remark that it made a part of the United States look like a "Third World country."[1] It is hard to recall that remark being made before about a disaster in the United States. It is not being said of the California fire disaster. What exactly did commentators mean when they made that remark? What does it mean to *look like* a Third World country?

Perhaps it was that the damage was so utterly complete? Biloxi after Katrina vies with Sri Lanka after the tsunami in their scenes of eradication of almost all evidence of human-made structures. In that sense parts of the Lower 9th Ward of New Orleans did *look like* a poor country. Perhaps it was the disturbing images of armed troops sent there to keep order and prevent looting because of the unfounded fear that the city would break down into lawlessness. Studies have consistently shown that large-scale looting in disasters is a myth (see Quarantelli in this issue; Tierney et al., 2006), yet the media still devotes exaggerated attention to those minor incidents that do occur. Troops patrolling deserted streets in New Orleans with automatic rifles in the ready position recall scenes of Port-au-Prince in Haiti, the poorest country in the western hemisphere, not an advanced US city.

Perhaps the Katrina disaster conjured up poor world analogies because of the disarming fact that the faces of the surviving victims bore such a chilling resemblance to the destitute in poor countries?

It would be all too easy to cut and paste images of Katrina victims into scenes of the tsunami in coastal Sri Lanka. The same confused, distressed expressions look pleadingly at the cameras, asking for help and for an explanation of why it has not arrived. They were sometimes likened to refugees, even before they were evacuated, and many were indignant at that description, and rightly so. Strictly, Katrina victims were Internally Displaced People (IDPs), but metaphorically use of the term "refugee" might have been appropriate. Many of Katrina's victims lived in the "nation within a nation," enclaves of concentrated poverty in New Orleans, and were unwillingly displaced from that nation to places they had only heard of before, but never seen. Though no one with explicit intent to harm actively persecuted them, they must have felt that having been harassed by nature, they were then persecuted by neglect.

In fact, those who commented at the time could not have guessed the most telling way in which the Katrina catastrophe resembled a disaster in a poor country. It was in the number of victims who did *not* survive. Katrina broke the rule that large death tolls are associated with poor countries. We now know that the death toll for Katrina places it among the largest in the history of the United States and ranks with some of the worst in the world. It might well exceed the number of victims of the terrorist attack of September 11, 2001. Katrina ranks next in deaths to the so-called Galveston Flood of 1900, also a hurricane that was probably the same strength as Katrina. In 1900 the Weather Channel did not exist, there were no weather satellites, and there were no ocean monitoring systems. There were no motorized means of evacuation except for trains. With no warning and no effective means of escape it should come as no surprise that perhaps 5,000 people died (see <http://hurricanes.noaa.gov/>). What accounts for Galveston-like mortality in 2005 is the social condition of those who suffered in Katrina, left behind as others have risen to prosperity and mobility, as ill-prepared for nature's extremes as people a century ago.

The dual catastrophes of armed conflict and natural disasters particularly burden the world's poorest people, causing large mortality and development consequences. Prosperity serves as a shield against outbreaks of conflict and outbreaks of nature; or perhaps, having learned to shield ourselves against such outbreaks, we have become prosperous. The shielding mechanism of prosperity is poorly understood though one thing is very clear—it cannot be thrown up at the time an extreme approaches, like the plywood sheets nailed to windows of houses in a storm's path, then stowed away until next time its needed. It is part of a society's fabric, acquired over centuries of development and fundamentally pre-determines outcomes in a disaster. Failure to acquire the shield means almost certain tragedy.

POVERTY: GUARANTOR OF DISASTER, NATURAL AND MAN-MADE

The earth today is host to a human population that experiences vastly different conditions of welfare. Citizens of Norway, ranking at the top of the UN Development Program (UNDP) Human Development Index (HDI)[2] have utterly different lifestyles, concerns, and expectations from citizens of Niger, currently ranked at the bottom. Every conceivable measure of material well-being differs so completely between top and bottom that it is difficult to understand how these two countries can exist on the same planet. A child born today in Norway can expect to live 79.6 years (in Japan its even higher at 82.2 years), while a child born in Niger will likely live 44.6 years; the literacy rate in Niger is 28.7 percent while in Norway it is effectively 100 percent; an adult Norwegian will have approximately 50 times the income of a person in Niger ($38,454 compared with $779, purchasing power parity adjusted).[3] The two countries have approximately the same population density, but Niger's population growth rate is triple that of Norway. For Niger and Norway economic development challenges and sustainability issues also have very little in common—Niger's challenge is to achieve development, Norway's is to achieve sustainability. These numbers are averages and describe an inequality in development status that has never existed in the world before. Differences at the extremes are more astonishing still; the three wealthiest people in the world have combined assets equal to the 550 million who live in sub-Saharan Africa (Serageldin, 2002). Extremes within countries can be almost as large as those from one country to another and some of countries that are poorest overall have some of the largest income inequities.[4] Even in the United States, state-to-state differences are large, with the average household income in Louisiana, for instance, being only two-thirds of that in California.[5]

As figure 1 shows, prosperity is not randomly distributed across the globe (Bloom et al., 2003: Gallop et al., 1999; Nordhaus, 2006; Sachs and Bloom, 1998; Sachs et al., 2001, Sachs, 2003). Norway, bordering the North Sea and Norwegian-Greenland Seas in a temperate region has a setting typical of developed economies, and landlocked Niger in the dry lands of sub-Saharan Africa has the typical setting of a poor country (Faye et al., 2004). The 22 countries bringing up the bottom of the ranking of HDI are mostly landlocked, and all are in sub-Saharan Africa, the region that is today host to the world's most extreme and refractory poverty. It is no accident that poverty thrives in these harsh settings where daily life can be a struggle to survive, a struggle lost by perhaps 30,000 people every day. To the daily burden faced by the poorest, the dual catastrophes of natural disasters and armed conflicts add an egregious load. These catastrophes arrest, suppress, or set back development and deeply erode development gains. We begin with conflict since, perhaps because it is the worst we can do to each other, has been given more attention than natural disasters—which is the worst that Nature can do to us.

POVERTY AND THE BURDEN OF CONFLICT

Nothing impedes progress in the acquisition of material welfare like armed conflict. The ongoing cathartic tectonism of the political landscape that resulted from the US intervention in Iraq has utterly consumed the financial, human, intellectual and emotional resources of the United States. That conflict may be responsible for more than 600,000 deaths including an excess of 100,000 among civilians (Burnham et al., 2006), has brought the Iraqi economy to a standstill, and is responsible for the acquisition of a vast US national debt. These

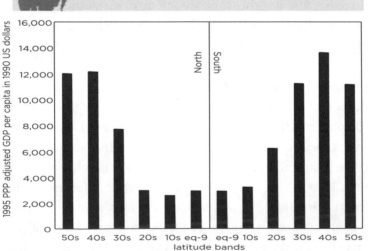

Figure 1. At right is a rendition of the gross distribution of income around the planet today from Worldmapper in which the size of countries is distorted in proportion to the value of the quantity being measured. Note that Africa all but disappears and the USA and Europe are bloated. At left are the zonal averages of GDP per capita from Sachs.

are just the direct consequences, and there are many others, including 50 percent unemployment among Iraqi youth (Brice et al., 2006).

The Iraqi conflict is challenged for media headline space by the desperate though seemingly very different tragedy in the remote Darfur region of western Sudan. Conflict in Afghanistan is less often on the front pages, but is no less tragic. The death toll in Darfur likely exceeds 200,000 (Hagan and Paloni, 2006), though claims have been made by advocacy groups like Save Darfur for numbers around 400,000. No one doubts that more than 2 million people have been displaced and 3.5 million are fully reliant on international aid. Then there is the internal struggle in the Democratic Republic of Congo (DRC) that may be the deadliest conflict of modern times. There are many others conflicts current today; those noted are the ones that have captured most media attention.

The great majority of conflicts occur in the very poorest countries (Brenard and Challet, 2007). These conflicts seldom pit trained, uniformed national armies against one another using technologically advanced weaponry. Conflicts in Darfur and the DRC evoke images of absolutely ancient forms of combat: replace the rifles in the hands of Darfur's Janjaweed horseman with spears or swords and the scenes could describe a centuries-old battle. "Battle," in fact, is hardly an appropriate term, as the violence has mostly been inflicted by raiding parties on unarmed civilians who endure rape, mutilation, and torture, and have their meager homes burned and livelihoods destroyed. The fighters are loosely organized into militias or rebel groups engaged in internal struggles, rather than cross-border wars fought by nation states for territorial acquisitions (Small Arms Survey, 2006). Many of the combatants, particularly those fighting in Africa, are minors who have not volunteered to fight but are the victims of forced abduction.[6]

Conflict mortality figures are notorious for huge associated uncertainties. They are always hard to obtain and often controversial and politicized; witness the debate over the civilian death statistics for Iraq (Burnham et al., 2007). Nevertheless, we can be fairly certain that the total death toll from armed conflicts in the early years of the century exceeds 1 million, and could be as high as 1.5 million. Since the end of World War II, conflict victims have shifted to a great majority being intentional civilian casualties. Most conflict casualties are not inflicted by sophisticated armaments, as seen in the massive spectacular displays of "shock and awe" aerial bombardments that began the Iraqi conflict, but by small arms and improvised weapons.

Analyzing conflict in poor countries, Collier and Hoefler (2004; see also Collier, 2007) have shown that "greed" (the ability to finance rebellion), considerably outperforms "grievance" (ethnic and religious divisions, political repression and inequality) as an explanation for the source of conflict. Consistent with the work of Humphries (2005) and colleagues, they find that both dependence upon primary commodity exports and a large diaspora substantially increase the risk of conflict. Some individuals or groups may profit from conflict, and some may find enlisting in a militia one of very few employment options, but overwhelmingly, countries suffer greatly. The reasons may seem appallingly obvious, but they are very complex and typically extend well beyond the effects on the combatants themselves and the specific regions in conflict (Messer et al., 2002; Collier et al., 2003). Loss of life, both military and civilian, is just the most brutally newsworthy consequence of conflict. Food production plummets to historic lows, the capacity to educate children is greatly reduced, health care systems collapse, infant mortality rates reach all time highs, and economic output shrinks. The essential requirements for human well-being are thereby erased. Quite simply, you cannot farm a battlefield, work in a burned-out factory, attend a flattened school, or take a sick baby to a bombed-out hospital.

Recent findings on the relationship between conflict and economic growth in Brainard and Chollet (2007) and by Rice et al. (2006), Humphries (2005), Collier and Hoeffer (2004), and Sambanis (2004) provide evidence that GDP per capita correlates with risk of civil conflict outbreak. For example, average GDP per capita of countries that experienced war in the last five years was $1,100, while those that did not was $5,764. Countries with annual GDP per capita above $5,000 are estimated to have a 1 percent risk of experiencing civil conflicts in the next five years while those with less than $250 GDP per capita have 15 percent risk factor for the same period. GDP per capita dropped from almost $1,000 to less than $100 in Liberia during the period of civil conflict. Chauvet et al. (2007) show that on average poor countries involved in civil conflict lose 1.6 percent of GDP growth for every year they are in conflict. Collier et al. (2003) show that a typical civil war decreases national income levels by 15 percent and increases the poverty rate by 30 percent, both with lasting effects—approximately half the loss of disability-adjusted life years occurs after the end of hostilities.

Collier et al. (2004) describe how the consequences of civil wars "ripple out in three rings"; first are internally displaced people, second are impacts on adjacent countries, and third are global effects. Civil wars create territory outside control of any formal government, and 95 percent of production and supply routes of hard drugs, with its attendant global impact, occurs in conflict zones. They further point out that safe haven for international terrorists is most often in ungoverned conflict zones. Few countries are willing to invest in states involved in conflict other than to support one of the antagonists. With the possible exception of the extractive industries that are obliged to operate in places where economic reserves such as oil and diamonds are found, few businesses or states will invest in conflict zones.

The work of official aid agencies, NGOs, and other organizations that normally provide assistance in economic and other development programs become refocused during conflicts on providing relief and containing the scale of the tragedy. Organizations such as the Red Cross, the International Rescue Committee (IRC), and Doctors without Borders (MSF), whose focus is almost exclusively on the immediate crises of the conflict, become the only external parties present in the regions. Internally displaced people (IDP) occupy refugee camps that are often located across the borders in neighboring countries (the second ripple). IDPs who may have developed some level of immunity to local diseases such as malaria often become susceptible and suffer health consequences. In the camps, people's lives are on hold as they mark time until the conflict subsides. Health care can be difficult to provide in camps as is education, and refugees are rarely able to undertake any economically productive activity. International aid agencies can sometimes provide education in refugee camps at a higher level than in the refugee's country that may lead to reluctance of refugees to return after conflict end.

Many IDPs move away from conflict regions to urban centers, where they form massive slum settlements on the outskirts of cities—Luanda during the Angolan conflicts is a good example (Guha-Sapir and Gomez, 2006)—that are the peri-urban equivalent of refugee camps, putting already weak city management capabilities under huge stress. In Africa, a significant component of rapid postcolonial urbanization was fueled by conflicts that drove civilians from conflict areas into relative safety of peri-urban slum settings.

Collier and Hoeffer (2004) and Humphries and Richards (2005) both describe so-called conflict traps. They are analogous to poverty traps that will be discussed later in which the conditions of poverty further weaken economies and generate increased poverty. Trapping agents for conflict include development policies (development failures can lead to conflict but development agenda are often abandoned during periods of conflict), economic structures (countries with weak manufacturing and reliance on natural resources are more prone to conflict but conflict leads to disincentives to investment in manufacturing), human capital (low levels of human capital cause low growth and lead to conflict, but conflicts also reduce human capital by removing educational systems and inflicting major health burdens). The notion of trapping structures is key to understanding the plight of poor countries and has broad applicability. We will suggest below how it might come into play in understanding the disasters outcomes on development opportunities.

POVERTY AND THE BURDEN OF DISASTERS

Only massive natural disasters that cause great destruction and loss of life can vie for media attention with outbreaks of armed conflict.

The vastness of destruction in the most devastating disasters like the Boxing Day 2004 earthquake and tsunami have caused many commentators to invoke comparisons to battlefields and war zones in describing these scenes. The energy from that earthquake equaled the sum of all previous earthquakes in the preceding 40 years (Lay et al., 2005). (CRED [2007] puts the number of dead at around 235,000, but the total will never be known and could be as high as 300,000). Other major disasters this century include the Bhuj earthquake in Gujarat, India in 2001, the Bam earthquake in Iran in 2003, the European heat wave the same year, European flooding in 2002 and 2005, and the 2005 Pakistani earthquake. None captured headlines in the United States as Hurricane Katrina did when it made its deadly landfall in Pass Christian near New Orleans on August 29, 2005. Death tolls from disasters carry uncertainties almost as large as those associated with armed conflicts, especially those in poor countries where census data may be unavailable or out of data and unreliable. In the early years of the twenty-first century, disaster mortality exceeded a half million and may be 800,000, comparable to noncombatant, conflict mortality.

Modern society has added some new disasters. The Chernobyl nuclear reactor failure in Ukraine in 1986 caused a plume of radioactive fallout over parts of the western Soviet Union, Eastern and Western Europe, Scandinavia, the United Kingdom, Ireland, and eastern North America. The immediate death toll was less than 100—mainly those attempting to contain the accident—but more than 300,000 people were permanently displaced and a large area is so contaminated that it may never be re-occupied (Swiss Agency for Development and Cooperation, 2007). Even more tragic was the chemical release in the Bhopal disaster in 1984 in the city of Bhopal, Madhya Pradesh, India. It involved accidental release of 40 metric tons of methyl isocyanate gas from a Union Carbide pesticide plant and caused nearly 3,000 immediate deaths; it may have caused 20,000 deaths from related illnesses with 120,000 continuing to suffer illnesses related to the incident.

Generally we refer to natural (as distinct from man-made) disasters as resulting from *natural hazards*—events that are regular, though extreme processes in the earth. *Hazards* transform into *disasters* through human agency. A commonly accepted meaning of "disaster" involves the essential notion that the impact of a natural extreme is such that affected communities cannot cope without external assistance. This sense of disaster places human agency largely *after* the extreme event has occurred. Natural events may or may not lead to a disaster depending on the coping capacity of effected communities. A number of authors question the appropriateness of the adjective "natural" as a modifier to "disaster" (Hartman and Squires, 2006).

Wars and armed conflicts have always been understood as a continuum from preceding political/social events that create the conditions for conflict to precipitate, the conflict itself, and the re-arrangements that follow in the period of reconstruction. Feedbacks between consequences of conflict and their causes are becoming increasingly clear, with environmental factors deeply implicated (UNEP, 2007). It has been shown that the experience of conflict in poor countries significantly increases the likelihood of further conflicts (Collier and Heoffler, 2004). The same ex ante and ex post conditions of human agency determine the scale and consequences of disasters and the potential for their repetition. Conflict traps may have their equivalent in disaster traps. Replace *conflict* with *natural disaster* in Collier's notion of *negative development* and the concept retains all its potency.

A very great deal is understood about the causes of earth's extreme behavior, and the spatial distribution extreme events (and in many instances the temporal distribution) is systematically mapped. Many important cities like Tokyo, Mexico City, Tehran, and San Francisco are located where risk of very large earthquakes is extremely high. Large earthquakes are mercifully quite infrequent and seldom recur in exactly the same place, and this may contribute to the unwitting location of these major centers of commerce and culture in fairly dangerous places. Individual earthquakes provide no warning. Volcanoes can be almost equally destructive as single events but most give warning by seismic rumbling and puffing out smoke. The size of an eruption is hard to predict, but scientists are usually able to tell that an eruption is imminent and call for evacuation. Volcanic soils are fertile and hence people have developed agricultural settlements quite close to very hazardous volcanoes. Important cities like Seattle lie distinctly within the zone of potentially massive devastation that would occur should Mt. Rainier erupt explosively, which surely it will. Hurricane-generating mechanisms are well understood as are their geographical and seasonal ranges. Once formed, they can be carefully tracked and reasonable predictions made of their growth and projected path. Despite repeated experience, significant populations and commercial assets have taken up in almost all the hurricane-prone regions of the world.

Hurricanes, earthquakes, and volcanoes are referred to as *rapid onset* disasters. They destroy lives and private and public property, including essential infrastructure like roads and bridges requiring major capital inflows for recovery. *Slow onset* disasters include drought and disease outbreaks and focus their damage on humans. Very little infrastructure is lost except through neglect when sick or starving people are unable to provide proper repair and upkeep. Droughts and major infectious diseases causing mortality are largely confined to the tropics and subtropics (North Korea may be the exception, since famine conditions are believed to be prevalent there).

Disasters have provided little deterrent to spread of civilizations and as a result, vast communities worldwide are at risk from forces that cannot be modified. The gravity of the risks now being faced has been brought into focus by two recent studies by UNDP (2004) and the World Bank (Dilley et al., 2005). Both show that disasters in poor countries take more lives in both absolute *and* relative terms—more people killed in total and more people killed as a proportion of population. In a chilling echo of the conclusions regarding conflict, they show that development status is a robust predictor of disaster mortality (figure 2). For instance: Niger and Norway have approximately equal population density but disasters severity is more than an order of magnitude greater for those in Niger. Citizens of New Zealand and of Morocco have roughly equal levels of exposure to flooding events, yet the mortality risk for Moroccans is two orders of magnitude higher than that of New

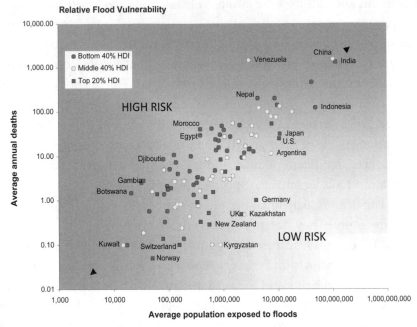

Figure 2. Graph showing the variability of mortality risk to flood disasters. Note that almost all of the most vulnerable are in poorer countries as measured by the Human Development Index. (Source: UNDP).

Zealander: New Zealand ranks 19th in HDI and Morocco ranks 125th. Flood mortality for people in Botswana and in Germany is roughly the same, although German's exposure level is three orders of magnitude greater. Botswana's HDI ranking is 132nd, while Germany is presently 20th. Drought has not been responsible for human fatalities in a developed country since the Dust Bowl in the United States in the 1930s and those deaths were not due to starvation but to health effects, such as so-called dust pneumonia. Major mortality from infectious disease like malaria is also economically restricted to poor countries, having been essentially eradicated from all developed countries.

Within countries, disasters have their greatest impact on the poorest. The very old and very young are at risk and women generally more than men, simply because strength may be required to survive (women comprised 90 percent of the victims of the 1991 cyclone in

Bangladesh; see L. Aguilar [2004]; also Oxfam [2005]; Gender and Disaster Network). Neumayer and Plumper (2007) show that disaster experience lowers life expectancy of women compared to men, that the greater strength of the disaster the greater effect, and that women of higher socioeconomic status experience smaller effects. Their conclusion that it is the *"socially constructed gender-specific vulnerability of females built into everyday socioeconomic patterns that lead to the relatively higher female mortality"* (emphasis added) applies to all socially marginalized groups (emphasis added). The burden of disasters is often greatest still on the urban poor in peri-urban slums surrounding major cities in developing countries—some of the most hazardous places on earth to live; fragile homes on steep hillsides that easily give way to landslides after soaking rains, flood-prone riverbanks, and swamps (Davis, 2006). Many disaster victims worldwide lived and died in these settings.

Nature's force and human agency severely wounded the richest country on earth on August 29, 2005 when Hurricane Katrina made landfall. Immediate mortality may have been around 1,600, but studies suggest that excess mortality continued many months after (Stephens et al., 2007). Much higher death counts result from adding those who died of prior health conditions such as heart disease or respiratory conditions fatally aggravated by the event. Nontraditional deaths such as suicides, and those who were shot for looting, are not usually included in totals. Many died months later after enduring harsh conditions of displacement, moving from one shelter to another to finally giving up hope, and succumbing to illnesses they had previously managed to keep reasonably under control. We are currently completing an extensive study of mortality from hurricane Katrina (www.katrinalist. columbia.edu) that will attempt a complete accounting of all who died of immediate and secondary effects, determine causes, circumstances, and establish vulnerability factors. In an uncomfortable reminder of the inequality in burden faced by disaster victims, Katrina's deceased were poor, elderly, socially isolated people living on their own, lacking means to escape or not trusting those who advised that escape was required.

ECONOMIC GROWTH TRAJECTORIES AND DISASTER OUTCOMES

Determining economic loss involves substantial uncertainties (Benson and Clay, 2004; Chhibber and Laajaj, 2007), in part due to nonuniform reporting (Guha-Sapir, et al., 2004). For rapid onset disasters, reporting focuses on immediate or direct losses of productive infrastructure. In developed countries with high rates of insurance coverage, accurate estimates of insured property losses are made quickly. The relationship to total economic losses is variable, and in poorer countries where very little property is insured and built infrastructure has low monetary value, total losses are hard to estimate and interpret. Low economic losses in poor countries (Pelling et al., 2002) may be very large relative to total economy measured in GDP per capita (Linneroof-Bayer, et al., 2005) and have great impacts on development. Poor people's livelihoods are most disrupted, but because they frequently live outside the formal economy their contributions to economic loss may appear negligible. Paralleling consequences of armed conflict, long-term effects include disincentives to foreign investment and trade agreements if exporters cannot guarantee products, reduced child development due to loss in education facilities, and loss of worker productivity if public health facilities are damaged.

One simplification assesses the development-critical capital stock losses—roads and other means of transport essential to commerce, dams, power systems, schools, and hospitals. Development setback time could be approximately double the time those assets took to acquire—assume time taken to rebuild is the same as taken to acquire the assets and that development time is lost during rebuilding. This might have been the calculation made by President Carlos Roberto Flores of Honduras after Hurricane Mitch in 1998 when he claimed it destroyed 50 years of progress.

Though Hurricane Mitch entirely overwhelmed Honduras, disasters and conflicts seldom overwhelm entire countries. In the 2004 tsunami, fishing vessels and tourist hotels in Sri Lanka were destroyed or badly damaged, but hotels have largely recovered, since their owners had the capacity to rebuild quickly and fishing vessels were replaced with new, more efficient vessels that are producing larger catches. Being confined to a coastal strip the economy was not severely impacted. The US economy easily buffered effects of Hurricane Katrina. The vast size of countries like the Democratic Republic of Congo and Sudan allows conflicts to be relatively isolated from the lives of most people. Khartoum is undergoing a construction boom and Sudan as a whole is experiencing rapid growth, in part due to the country's oil wealth. The Sudanese economy remains healthy because those who live in Darfur contribute so little. Conflicts that overwhelmed the capitals of Somalia and Liberia brought both countries to a halt, then to absolute decline. Natural disasters that seriously impact major cities can have a greater effect on development than those that impact rural settings. Crop losses in economies deeply dependent on agriculture can cause significant short-term losses, but these economies can recover if the disaster does not repeat soon after (Benson and Clay, 2004).

Given the need to assess comparative risks to different societies, development institutions like the World Bank, the UNDP, and regional financial institutions such as the Inter-American Development Bank and Asian Development Bank have constructed indices of disaster risk to prioritize investments in disaster management and reduction. *Vulnerability* to harm from both physical and social forces has emerged as a key concept. *Social vulnerability*, though conceptually very complex, attempts to provide a way to understand how people and societies may be quite differently impacted by physically similar events, beyond the risks posed by the fragility of their dwellings (Cardona, 2005; Comfort et al., 1999; Cutter and Emrich, 2006; Vincent, 2004). The use of indices is an important part of the way in which development banks and international agencies have begun to "mainstream" disaster considerations into development planning (see UNISDR [2007] as one example).

Disasters interact with development in a complex manner (Hallegatte et al., 2006; Toya and Skidmore, 2006). Fundamentally, disasters impart macroeconomic shocks through rapid loss of productive capital stocks, similar to systemic shocks caused by purely finan-

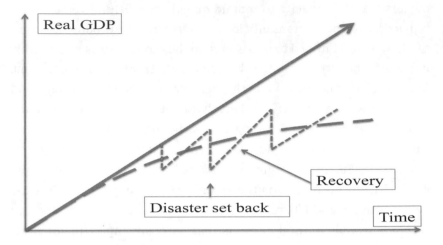

Figure 3. In the figure, the heavy line with an arrowhead is the hypotheti-cal economic growth of a country free of disasters. The jagged line indi-cates the effect of a series of disasters and the dashed line is the average depressed growth trajectory that results from disaster impacted growth.

cial forces (Lustig, 1999). For two countries, identical in every way other than one experiences periodic rapid onset disaster macroeco-nomic shocks, the latter should experience slower growth because national savings are used for reconstruction to prior conditions that could have been used to improve conditions in health care, schooling, and infrastructure for economic growth. (See figure 3, after Freeman [2000]; see Narayan [2003] for a specific example of repeated cyclones negatively impacting private income, consumption, savings, real GDP, and real national welfare in Fiji.) Disaster-effected growth is actually punctuated with periodic set-backs (figure 3) in which the economy falls to a point it occupied some past time. To return to the original growth curve, new growth must occur at a rate considerably *greater* than experienced before the disaster. This is plausible if large amounts of external aid are available quickly and efficiently used. Economic re-growth may be initially fast, fueled by external aid then level off, but another disaster occurs before the economy recuperates. Every new shock causes a further setback. Economies performing weakly prior to disaster will experience weak postdisaster regrowth, leading to absolute decline.

If aging or inefficient productive capital stock are replaced by new, more efficient infrastructure, postdisaster growth could move above the projected pre-disaster growth. Skidmore and Toya (2002) have suggested through empirical analysis of long-run data that higher frequencies of climate disasters correlate with higher rates of human capital accumulation, increases in total factor productivity, and economic growth. They argue that while disasters reduce physical capital, they may increase return to human capital. A form of *Schumpeter's Gale* (Schumpeter, 1942) may be appropriate. After two years New Orleans' economy is thought to be almost 80 percent of its pre-Katrina levels although population is only about 66 percent (Lui and Plyer, 2007), suggesting that output per person has increased! Many of those displaced were not contributing to economic production, and industries critical to New Orleans' economy, such as gambling, recovered quickly. Did Katrina's winds blow in Schumpeter's gale of creative destruction?

The following heuristics place disasters in the context of simple growth scenarios.

DISASTER OUTCOMES FOR LINEAR GROWTH

The logic of setback and recovery applies easily for linear growth in figure 4. The kernel of figure 3 could nominally be simply overlain. Growth occurs for trajectories above the 45° line so the disaster-depressed curve could generate economic decline at least for some period of time. For a strong economy with high total GDP per annum, disaster losses will usually be a small percentage of the total economic capacity. Disaster losses will be much more important in a relative sense for countries nearer the origin of the curve than well away from the origin, even if the value of assets lost in monetized terms is the same or less.

DISASTER OUTCOMES FOR "SOLOW" GROWTH

A more realistic growth curve depicts an economy that converges to a stable condition after initially rapid growth (Jones, 2002; Eurmacro,

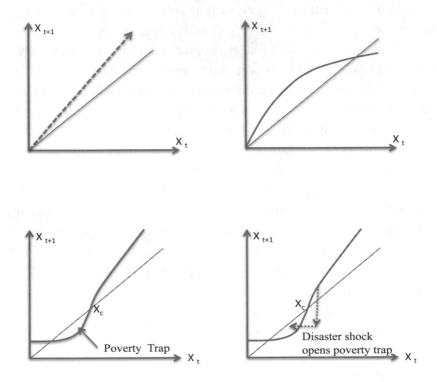

Figure 4. Upper left panel shows a simple linear growth function in which the current welfare on the vertical axis depends in a linear way on the welfare in the previous period on the horizontal axis. The upper right panel shows growth in a neo-classical Solow model in which growth converges.

The lower right panel shows a growth curve for a poverty trap in which the initial condition of growth condemns the economy to stagnation in a very low equilibrium. The lower right suggests that there may be a critical region in the growth function where disasters can cause an economy to fall into a trapping situation.

2007). In Solow-type growth, the economy enters an equilibrium condition after an extended period of growth. Growth may be slow in this region and disaster losses are likely to be a small percentage of the total economic output and hence buffering by the large economy may be effective, but there is very little experience of major disasters impacting economies that are strong but slowly growing. Many countries that have achieved late stages of Solow-type growth are in temperate zones, relatively free from large disasters. Rather than achieving resilience during their strong growth phase, they may in fact be somewhat more susceptible than their overall economic development might imply.

Away from the convergence point, economies are growing well and total GDP is high. Disasters may be much more manageable in this case as capital losses represent a small percentage of total GDP and savings are high; at the same time, intrinsic growth might make recovery possible without external assistance. India refused external aid for 2004 tsunami relief, believing its own economy could buffer the losses.

DISASTER OUTCOMES FOR POOR COUNTRIES—THE IMPORTANCE OF POVERTY TRAPS

Solow growth does not depend on the initial point from which growth occurs and implies that poorer economies should experience rapid growth. That this is not the case is the unhappy reality for most countries that lie in the lower HDI rankings. Poor countries may not simply be stalled at the initial phase of growth on a Solow trajectory, but may be caught in so-called poverty traps: a stable equilibrium in which conditions that create poverty become self-perpetuating (Sachs et al., 2004; Azariadis and Stachurski, 2004 and references therein). Starting conditions of poor countries are a critical determining factor and may cause growth to be negative, and permanently so without exogenous stimuli (figure 4). Trapping mechanisms include low marginal productivity of capital in settings where basic infrastructure is lacking, savings rates that can be very low or negative, and rapid population growth with very low capital-labor ratios.

A key recent insight into poverty traps suggest that in many instances the mechanism may be dominated by a suite of complex codependencies between human well-being and earth's natural systems (Bloom et al., 2003; Gallop et al., 1999; Sachs and Warner, 1997). Access to clean water, along with soil fertility, the state of public health, and forest services are only a few examples of what can bring about traps. Poor health is clearly an outcome of poverty due to living conditions and insufficient health care services, but poor health causes children to miss school and reduces labor productivity, exacerbating poverty. Cause and consequence become interlinked in a feedback trap when the quest for basic human needs causes environmental degradation, depletion of forest resources, fertile soils, and other natural assets that then deepen the conditions that perpetuate poverty. Though resulting *from* poverty these outcomes are equally *determinants* of poverty: the cruel backlash of a desperate struggle to survive or break the bonds of poverty. These codependencies are multi-interactive, nonlinear, and cross many scales, with emergent properties including potential for extremely rapid fluctuations.

Repeated disaster shocks that are systemic across poor economies could in themselves generate traps. Savings are depleted as they are used for recovery, then lack of savings makes the ability to recover from the next shock more problematic; the inability to recover completely from one event causing the impact of the next to be more severe, and so on. An economy in a poverty trap may *not* be severely impacted by a disaster if there is little productive base to lose. Where situations are truly desperate, as in Somalia or Zimbabwe, disasters may make little difference.

Alternately, the effect of a major disaster shock could be to plunge weakly growing economies into poverty traps (Barrientis, 2007; Carter et al., 2007). If this is the case the most telling impact of a disaster may come for economies near the transition between a trapped situation and the beginnings of growth. These points could be highly susceptible to perturbation so that a disaster could send a weakly growing economy into a trap that is triggered by the disaster then maintained in that condition by the multitude of factors that give rise to poverty traps. So, for instance, a disaster could destroy hospitals leading to a health care trap, or a critical industry leading to unemployment, or critical transportation infrastructure so that commerce is significantly impeded. The key suggestion made here is that the disaster itself may not be the determining factor in creating a poverty trap, but disasters may throw countries into poverty traps maintained by other factors. Emerging economies dependent on a few industries with minimal infrastructure in support of education, public health, and commerce as well as immature institutions and weak governance will be particularly susceptible to severe setbacks from disasters. This is also the region of growth where Schumpeter's gale may apply. If old, inefficient capital assets and public infrastructure are destroyed in a disaster but replaced by new more efficient assets, then economies may receive a boost, propelling them further away from the trapping situation so that a following disaster may be withstood more effectively.

THE NEXUS OF POVERTY, ENVIRONMENT, NATURAL, AND CONFLICT DISASTERS

Darfur has a long history of ethnic rivalry coupled with livelihood tensions (Flint and DeWaal, 2006). Conditions are relentlessly harsh. Armed conflicts have historically waged between Arab pastoralists and settled African farmers and between tribal groups, especially during times of scarcities. To these persistently difficult base conditions add persistent drought in the Horn of Africa that is now more than a decade long (Biasutti and Giannini, 2006). Normally harsh conditions become unbearable and food shortages extreme for people and their livestock. Typical of many parts of Africa, Arab pastoralists traditionally moved their herds into farming areas seasonally for forage and are now forced to move progressively deeper into regions farmed by African tribes of the Fur, Massaleet and Zagawa communities. They stay much longer than before and have even created settlements of their own. Groups that were always in tension are now face to face, struggling for scarce resources just to survive. Conflict erupts, rages until exhausted combatants agree to stop fighting, a fragile peace ensues until the next crisis inevitably erupts because scarcity never really ends.

Darfur may portend a dangerous new future. Darfur is characterized by extreme poverty, a growing population, growing water stress and desertification. Homer-Dixon (1991) was one of the first to suggest that causal links may exist between environmental system changes and outbreak of armed conflict through the agency of resource scarcity.

Kaplan (1994) elevated the concern this notion generates and argued that the world is doomed to increasing resource-based conflicts, and that we are already well down that pathway. Though perhaps over-wrought in Kaplan's rendition, the potential for scarcity-driven conflict is alarmingly real and supported by many careful studies (Brainard and Chollet, 2007). Actual situations may involve many interacting social factors that create vulnerability to outbreak of violence (Levy et al., 1995; Fearon and Laitin, 2004), with environmentally-driven scarcity implicated as a triggering mechanism (Sachs, 2007a). The root cause may be less associated with absolute scarcity than with inequity in which, for instance, a dominant group (perhaps an elite minority) controls available resources and deprives, or is perceived to deprive or restrict, another group of those resources. The existence of a demo-graphic bulge of unemployed youth in poor countries is known to be a contributor to outbreaks of conflict (Urdal, 2007). The robust conclu-sion of these studies is succinctly captured by Paul Collier: "economic development is the sine qua non of achieving a major reduction in the global incidence of civil war" (Collier, 2007).

Global climate change threatens economic development (Stern 2007, IPCC 2007). Failures of economic development threaten peace. Hence, climate change threatens peace. Barnett (2001), Reuveny (2007); Raleigh and Urdal (2007), and Nordas and Gleditsh (2007) have all argued that climate change could increase the level of scarcity stress to the extent that broad regional security with global implications becomes concerning. Start with Darfur and spread that crisis through climate change-induced stress. While it is well understood that the largest absolute changes will occur in high latitudes, relatively small changes on harsh basal conditions in the tropics will utterly devastate poor economies and threaten peace. No poor society has developed robust-ness to natural fluctuations in ambient climate, nor do they have any significant adaptation capacity for a base line shift to a harsher ambi-ent state. Many parts of the poor world will become uninhabitable, or uneconomic, and hundreds of millions of people may be compelled to relocate, becoming environmental refugees (Sachs, 2007b).

Poverty stalks natural disasters and conflict equally. Poverty sets the preconditions that ensure natural swings in earth's behavior transform into the tragedy of disasters, just as poverty ensures that natural swings in social dynamics transform into the tragedy of conflict. Disasters and conflicts, never fully recovered, leave a trail of destruction and scarcity that foreshadow and induce the next tragedy. Weakened by one, we are more susceptible to the next; and the two cooperate in bringing tragedy. The aftermath of both natural disasters and conflicts leaves environmental degradation and scarcity that fuels the engine of poverty and amplifies poverty's tragic consequences in further conflict and disaster. As climate change worsens conditions for the poor, so it portends a world where disasters are the norm and conflicts are everyday and everywhere. Conditions in the Lower 9th Ward of New Orleans are not exactly like those in Darfur, but it is not an easy place to live either. Home to the poorest people in New Orleans, and some of the poorest in the nation, it is geographically and socially isolated. The physical and social preconditions of tragedy were there also, though it took Katrina's harsh light to reveal it to the nation.

The eminent ecologist and humanist E. O. Wilson has said that humankind will pass through a harrowing bottleneck this century as population approaches 9 billion and life support systems become desperately strained. As we imperil the earth's carrying capacity ecosystem by lost ecosystem, species by lost species, aquifer by dried up aquifer, river by depleted river, glacier by retreating glacier, desert by encroaching desert, year by hotter year, we may be setting the base conditions for a global Darfur-like tragedy.

NOTES

1. Among many, the following examples are typical of what can be found on the Web today: <http://www.zmag.org/content/showarticle. cfm?ItemID=8694>; <http://www.commondreams.org/views05/0907-24.htm>; <http://www.pbs.org/newshour/essays/july-dec05/rodri-guez_9-06.html>. Perhaps the most compelling is by the CNN Africa correspondent Jeff Koinange, who happened to be in New Orleans at

the time of the hurricane. See <http://www.cnn.com/2006/US/08/30/btsc.koinange/index.html>.

2. An ordinal ranking of countries and an explanation of the calculation of HDI can be found at <http://hdr.undp.org/hdr2006/statistics/> and <http://ucatlas.ucsc.edu/world.html>.

3. This adjustment allows the value of the dollar locally in all countries in terms of its buying power to be directly compared. That is, it removes the factor that goods may appear to cost less in poorer countries and hence the cost of living may seem much cheaper to a nonresident.

4. A commonly used measure is the Gini. Figures are at <http://hdr.undp.org/hdr2006/statistics/indicators/147.html>.

5. Figures are available from the US Census Bureau <http://www.census.gov/hhes/www/income/income06/statemhi2.html>.

6. Human Rights Watch estimates that 250,000 children are engaged in conflicts and many of them are recruited improperly or abducted into the ranks. See <http://hrw.org/campaigns/crp/child_soldiers/>.

REFERENCES

Aguilar, L. "Climate Change and Disaster Mitigation." International Union for Conservation of Nature (IUCN) fact sheet 2004 <http://www.generoyambiente.org>.

Barrientos, A. "Does Vulnerability Create Poverty Traps?" CPRC. Working Paper 76. Institute for Development Studies, Sussex University, May 2007.

Barnett, J. "Security and Climate Change." Canterbury, New Zealand: Macmillan Brown Centre for Pacific Studies and the Tyndall Centre for Climate Change Research at University of Canterbury, New Zealand, October 2001.

Barsky, L., J. Trainor and M. Torres. "Disaster Realities in the Aftermath of Hurricane Katrina: Revisiting the Looting Myth." *Quick Response Research Report* 184. Newark, Del.: Disaster Research Center, University of Delaware, 2006.

Benson, C. and E. J. Clay. "Understanding the Economic and Financial Impacts of Natural Disasters." The World Bank. Disaster Risk

Management. Series 4. Washington, D.C.: World Bank, 2004.

Biasutti, M. and A. Giannini. "Robust Sahel Drying in Response to Late 20th-Century Forcings." *Geophysical Research Letters* 33 (June 2006).

Bloom, D.E., D. Canning and J. Sevilla. "Geography and Poverty Traps." *Journal of Economic Growth* 8 (2003): 355-378.

Brainard, L., and D. Chollet, eds. "Too Poor for Peace?" Washington, D.C.: Brookings Institution Press, 2007.

Brice, S. E., C. Graff and J. Lewis. "Poverty and Civil War: What Policy-makers Need to Know." Brookings Economy and Development. Working Paper. 2006.

Burnham, G., R. Lafta, S. Doocy and L. Roberts. "Mortality after the 2003 Invasion of Iraq: A Cross-sectional Cluster Sample Survey." *The Lancet* 368 (October 2006): 1421-1428.

Burnham, G., Riyadh Lafta, Shannon Doocy and Les Roberts. "Mortality in Iraq—Authors' Reply." *The Lancet* 369 (January 2007):103-104.

Cardona, O. D. "Indicators of Disaster Risk and Risk Management, Program for Latin America: Summary Report." Inter-American Development Bank, Sustainable Development Department, Washington, D.C., 2005.

Carter, M.R., P.D. Little, T. Mogues, and W. Noguta. "Poverty Traps and Natural Disasters in Ethiopia and Honduras." *World Development Report* 35:6 (2007).

Center for Research on the Epidemiology of Disasters (CRED). 2007 <http://www.cred.be/>.

Chauvet, L., A. Hoeffler, and P. Collier. "The Cost of Failing States and the Limits to Sovereignty." United Nations University/World Institute for Development Economics Research <http://www.wider.unu.edu/publications/working-papers/research-papers/2007/en_GB/rp2007-30/>.

Chhibber, A. and R. Laajaj. "Disasters, Climate Change and Economic Development in Sub-Saharan Africa: Lessons and Future Directions." Independent Evaluation Group, World Bank Evaluation Brief 3, Washington, D.C., 2007.

Collier. P., and A. Hoeffler, "Greed and Grievance in Civil War." *Oxford Economic Papers* 54 (2004): 563-593.

Collier, P. *The Bottom Billion: Why the Poorest Countries Are Failing and What Can Be Done about It.* Oxford: Oxford University Press, 2007.

Collier, P., V.L. Elliot, H. Hegre, A. Hoeffler, M. Reynal-Querol and N. Sambanis. "Breaking the Conflict Trap: Civil War and Development Policy." Washington, D.C.: World Bank and Oxford University Press, 2003.

Comfort, L., B. Wisner, S. Cutter, R. Pulwarty, K. Hewitt, A. Oliver-Smith, J. Wiener, M. Fordham, W. Peacock, and F. Krimgold. "Reframing disaster policy: the global evolution of vulnerable communities." *Environmental Hazards* 1 (1999): 39-44.

Cutter, S. L. and C. T. Emrich. "Moral Hazard, Social Catastrophe: The Changing Face of Vulnerability along the Hurricane Costs." *The Annals of the American Academy.* 6 (4) (2006): 102-112.

Davis, M. *Planet of Slums.* London: Verso 2006.

———. "An Inferno with Valet Parking." *Guardian,* October 27 2007.

Dilley M., R. Chen, U. Deichmann, A. Lerner-Lam, and M. Arnold, with J. Agwe, P. Buys, O. Kjekstad, B. Lyon, and G. Yetman. *Natural Disaster Hotspots: A Global Risk Analysis.* Washington, D.C.: World Bank, 2005.

Eckerman, Ingrid. "The Bhopal gas leak: Analyses of causes and consequences by three different models." *Journal of Loss Prevention in the Process Industry* (2005): 213-217. See also <http://en.wikipedia.org/wiki/Bhopal_Disaster>.]

Faye, M.L., J.W. McArthur, J.D. Sachs and T. Snow. "The Challenges Facing Landlocked Developing Countries." *Journal of Human Development* (March 5, 2004).

Fearon, J.D. and D.D. Laitin. "Neotrusteeship and the Problem of Weak States." *International Security* 28.4 (2004): 5-43.

Flint, J. and A. de Waal. "Darfur: A Short History of a Long War." London Zed Books, 2006.

Freeman, P. K. "Infrastructure, Natural Disasters and Poverty." *Managing Disaster Risk in Emerging Economies.* Eds. A. Kreimer and M. Arnold. Washington, D.C.: World Bank, 2000: 23-29.

Gallup, J. L., J. D. Sachs, and A. Mellinger. "Geography and Economic Development." *International Regional Science Review* (August 22, 1999): 179-232.

Guha-Sapir, D. and V. Gomez. "Angola: The Human Impact of War: A Data Review of Field Surveys in Angola between 1999-2005." CRED, Louvain-la-Neuve, Belgium, 2006.

Hartman, C., and G. D. Squires. *There Is No Such Thing as a Natural Disaster: Race, Class, and Hurricane Katrina.* New York: Routledge, 2006.

Helleagard S., J-C. Hourcadec, and P. Dumasc. "Why Economic Dynamics Matter in Assessing Climate Change Damages: Illustration on Extreme Events." *Ecological Economics* 62 (April 2007): 330-340.

Homer-Dixon, T. "On the Threshold: Environmental Changes as Causes of Acute Conflict." *International Security* 16: 2 (Fall 1991).

Humphreys, M. "Natural Resources, Conflict, and Conflict Resolution." *Journal of Conflict Resolution* (August 2005): 508-537.

Humphreys, M., and P. Richards. "Prospects and Opportunities for Achieving the MDGs in Post-conflict Countries: A Case Study of Sierra Leone and Liberia." CGSD Working Paper no. 27. Earth Institute, Columbia University, New York, 2005.

IPCC Fourth Assessment Report. 2007 <http://ipcc-wg1.ucar.edu/wg1/wg1-report.html>.

Kaplan, R. "The Coming Anarchy." *Atlantic Monthly* 273 (February 1994): 44-76.

Kosatsky, T. "The 2003 European Heat Waves." *Euro Surveillance* 10 (2005): 148-149.

Lay, T., et al. "The Great Sumatra-Andaman Earthquake of 26 December 2004." *Science* 308 (May 2005): 1127-1130.

Levy, M. A. "Is the Environment a National Security Issue?" *International Security* 20:2 (Fall 1995).

Linneroof-Bayer, J., R. Mechler, and G. Pflug. "Refocusing Disaster Aid." *Science* 309 (2005): 1044-1046.

Lustig, N. "Crises and the Poor: Socially Responsible Macroeconomics." *Economia* (Fall 2000).

Messer, E., M. J. Cohen and J. D'Costa. "Armed Conflict and Hunger." *Armed Conflict and Public Health: A Report on Knowledge and Knowledge Gaps.* Eds. Debarati Guha-Sapir and Willem G. van Panhuis. Brussels: World Health Organization and CRED, 2002.

Miguel, E. "Global Poverty, Conflict and Insecurity." The Tangled Web: The

Poverty-Insecurity Nexus. The 2006 Brookings Blum Roundtable, Brookings Institution, Washington, D.C., 2006 < http://www.brookings.edu/events/2006/0802sustainable-development.aspx>.

Narayan, P. K. "Macroeconomic Impact of Natural Disasters on a Small Island Economy: Evidence from a CGE Model." *Applied Economics Letters* 10:11 (September 2003): 721-723.

Neumayer, Eric, and T. Plumper. "The Unequal Burden of War: The Effect of Armed Conflict on the Gender Gap in Life Expectancy." *International Organization* 60 (2006): 723-754.

"News Analysis: A Firestorm, a Deluge, and a Sharp Political Dig." *New York Times*, October 27, 2007: A11.

Nordhaus, W. D. "Geography and Macroeconomics: New Data and New Findings." *PNAS* 103 (March 2006): 3510-3517.

Noy, J. "The Macroeconomic Costs of Natural Disasters." Working Paper, University of Hawaii, 2007 <www.www2.hawaii.edu>.

Oxfam. "The Tsunami's Impact on Women." 2005 <http://www.oxfam.org/en/files/bn050326_tsunami_women/>.

Pelling, M., A., Ozerdem, and S. Barakat. "The Macro-economic Impact of Disasters." *Progress in Development Studies* 2 (2002): 283-305.

Raleigh, Clionadh, and Henrik Urdal. "Climate Change, Environmental Degradation and Armed Conflict." *Political Geography* (forthcoming).

Reuveny, R. "Economic Growth, Environmental Scarcity and Conflict." *Global Environmental Politics* 2 (2002).

Rice, Susan E., et al., "Poverty and Civil War: What Policymakers Need to Know." Brookings Institution, Global Economy and Development, Washington, D.C., December 2006.

Roberts, L., R. Lafta, R. Garfield, J. Khudhairi, and G. Burnham. "Mortality Before and After the 2003 Invasion of Iraq: Cluster Sample Survey." *The Lancet* 364 (November 2004): 1857-1864.

Sachs, J. D. "Sustainable Developments: Climate Change Refugees." *Scientific American* (June 2007) V http://www.sciam.com/article.cfm?id=climate-change-refugees-extended>.

———. "Poverty and Environmental Stress Fuel Darfur Crisis." *Nature* (September 2007).

Sachs, J. D. and D. Bloom. "Geography, Demography, and Economic Growth in Africa." *Brookings Papers on Economic Activity* 2 (1998).

Sachs, J. D., A. D. Mellinger, and J. L. Gallup. "The Geography of Poverty and Wealth." *Scientific American* (March 2001).

Sambanis, Nicholas. "Using Case Studies to Expand the Theory of Civil War." Social Development Department, Environmentally and Socially Sustainable Development Network. International Bank for Reconstruction and Development/The World Bank, Washington, D.C, May 2003.

Serageldin, I. "World Poverty and Hunger—the Challenge for Science." *Science* 296 (April 2002): 54-58.

Schumpeter, J. A. "The Process of Creative Destruction." Winchester Mass: Unwin, 1942.

Skidmore, M., and H. Toya. "Do Natural Disasters Promote Long-Run Growth?" *Economic Inquiry* 40 (October 2002): 664-687.

Small Arms Survey. 2007 <http://www.smallarmssurvey.org/>.

Solow, R. M. "The Economics of Resources or the Resources of Economics," *American Economic Review* 64:2 (1974): 1-14.

Stephens Sr., Kevin U., D. Crew, K. Chin, P. G. Greenmough, F. M. Burkle Jr., S. L. Robinson, and E. R. Franklin. "Excess Mortality in the Aftermath of Hurricane Katrina: A Preliminary Report." *Disaster Medicine and Public Health Preparedness* 1 (July 2007): 15-20.

Swiss Agency for Development and Cooperation. 2007 <http://www.chernobyl.info/>.

Tierney, K., C. Bevc and E. Kuligowski. "Metaphors Matter: Myths, Media Frames, and Their Consequences in Hurricane Katrina." *The Annals of the American Academy of Political and Social Sciences* 604 (March 2006): 57-81.

Toya, H. and M. Skidmoreb. "Economic Development and the Impacts of Natural Disasters," *Economics Letters* 94 (January 2007): 20-25.

United Nations Development Programme (UNDP). "Disaster Risk Reduction: A Challenge for Development." New York: United Nations, 2004.

_____. *Human Development Report 2006, Beyond Scarcity: Power, poverty and the global water crisis*. New York: Palgrave Macmillan, 2006.

United Nations Environment Programme (UNEP). *Sudan: Post-Conflict Environmental Assessment*. Nairobi: UNEP, 2007.

UN International Strategy for Disaster Reduction (UNISDR). 2007 <www.unisdr.org/hfa>.

Urdal, Henrik. "The Demographics of Political Violence: Youth Bulges, Insecurity and Conflict." *Too Poor for Peace? Global Poverty, Conflict and Security in the 21st Century*. Eds. Lael Brainard and Derek Chollet. Washington, D.C.: Brookings Institution Press, 2007: 90–100.

Vincent, Katharine. "Creating an Index of Social Vulnerability to Climate Change in Africa." Tyndall Center for Climate Change Research. Working Paper 56 (August 2004): 41.

Part II
Acquiring Vulnerabilities that Potentiate Disasters

Ron Kassimir
Introduction: The Potential for Catastrophe

THE CONTRIBUTIONS IN THIS SECTION MAKE CLEAR THAT WHILE certain forces of nature have the potential to become catastrophic, a disaster can only be fully achieved through the playing out of human choices, political processes, and social structures. The pursuit of wealth and power, the setting of public priorities, the design of political institutions, and tolerance for inequality and discrimination, these authors argue, shape both the extent to which a potential disaster is realized and the highly uneven distribution of vulnerability to nature's destructive capacity.

With Katrina either standing in the foreground or lurking in the background of these essays, it is not surprising they present a dark view and critical tone. The authors reflect on the human forces that put the greatest risk on those already marginalized when disaster strikes, that allow the evasion of accountability, and that prevent lessons from being learned and so produce a sense of déjà vu with each subsequent disaster. From different perspectives, each author provides a social and political autopsy of Katrina and similar events, both recent and in the past.[1]

Yet, they also contend that, if human decisions and public policies greatly influence the extent and differential impact of disasters, some man-made elements can also be deployed to prevent disasters or mitigate their effects. The papers take a historical perspective on the politics of disasters and show how the choices, institutions, and policies that create and distribute vulnerability change over time. At the same time, they reflect on the current moment, especially in the United States, in which the political and economic winds of the past 30 years have blown in the direction of deregulation, privatization of critical infrastructure, and the vulnerability of public service institutions (for example, the Army Corps of Engineers) to both pork barrel politics and ideological preferences. Last, they all argue (some more explicitly than others) for changes in the way the US political system works and on whose behalf it works for. Major reforms are needed if we are to ever shake that déjà vu feeling when the forces of nature next threaten us, and especially the most vulnerable among us.

As a social autopsy of Katrina's devastation of New Orleans and a social history of vulnerability to disasters in the American South, Robert D. Bullard's article explores the multiple ways in which preexisting race and class relations shaped the distribution of risk for individuals and communities. From a political economy of race perspective, Bullard shows that the vastly differential effects of Katrina on New Orleans' African-American population was no random occurrence but the outcome of a long history of discrimination and social marginalization. African-American communities were located in parts of the city both more environmentally dangerous and more vulnerable to flooding. At the same time, poorer households lacked cars that proved to be the only way to escape Katrina's force, and a public transportation system was barely in place to help those who did not own a car.

Bullard argues that it is not surprising that communities underserved in "normal" times in terms of social services were bound to suffer disproportionately in the context of crisis. Bullard's account thus focuses on how inequalities long predating the storm produced differential vulnerability to the power of nature. He also shows how these same inequalities unevenly distributed political clout in ways that made evacuation so difficult for so many (for example, a poor public transport system) and government response so slow and skewed—from support for resettlement to the temporary locating of victims in "toxic trailers." Bullard calls attention to the importance of community groups and self-help activities in a context where the vestiges of a social contract are stripped away, but emphasizes the centrality of more and more just government action in dealing with such emergencies.

Joseph W. Westphal's contribution focuses on one of the key players in the before and after story of Katrina: the Army Corps of Engineers. The paper does not focus primarily on the corps' role in New Orleans, but rather on how its capacity to support the US water infrastructure and to protect populations from the kind destruction wrought by Katrina has changed over time. Westphal traces those changes through an analysis of the corps' capacities, the setting of its priorities, and the role of political institutions, bargaining, and ideologies in this process. Westphal shows that the ability to make tough decisions in investing in water infrastructure in the United States has always been limited by a decentralized, federal political system that can hold public works hostage to local electoral competition and pork barrel politics. At the same time, he provides an account of how, beginning in the 1980s, seemingly small regulatory, legislative, and budgetary changes reduced the corps ability to set priorities and operate most expeditiously and efficiently in those areas where it was mostly needed.

For example, under the Reagan administration, the set of requirements to be met if a proposed project was to be implemented by the corps was loosened, allowing many more projects in a pipeline now less shaped by need than by political bargaining. Cost-sharing by local communities was also introduced, making it less likely that projects needed in poor areas would happen. These changes increased the likelihood that the most vulnerable places and their most vulnerable citizens would be put at risk. In emphasizing these features, Westphal gives us a way to see how the bureaucratic politics of Washington can connect to outcomes like New Orleans. The author concludes by arguing that change at the macropolitical level is possible. In particular, he recommends a mechanism for setting priorities for water infrastructure investment insulated from politicized decision-making. He also suggests that cost-sharing be reformed so as not to punish areas of great need that lack their own resources.

While Westphal sees the decentralization of American government as a problem for mitigating the vulnerability to disaster, Charles Perrow attends to the centralization, or what he calls the concentration, of people, energy, and market power in greatly increasing both the risk of disasters and the magnitude of their effects. The two perspectives complement each other: while government decision making and action is parsed out across states, municipalities, federal agencies, and, more recently, private actors, corporate power is concentrated in ways that not only reduce competition but also protect ostensibly private but very real sources of social power from public accountability.

Perrow's view is particularly broad. His interest encompasses the disaster potential from natural occurrences, industrial accidents, and terrorism. Vulnerability in the United States to the damage these events can cause are exacerbated by the three concentrations, many of which are themselves the effect of public (in)action or the influence of powerful corporate actors. Perrow shows how concentrations of people in risky locations as well as public exposure to hazardous substances both increase the likely negative consequences of a disaster and, since 9/11, have received far less attention than a terrorist threat. The interests of insurance companies (in the case of risky settlement patterns) and of industrial and shipping companies (in the case of the production and transport of hazardous chemicals) are part of this story. But the concentration of corporate power in general, and especially in the areas of electrical and nuclear power and information technology, are Perrow's greatest concern. The deregulation that has been the hallmark of much American policymaking in recent times has produced two somewhat counterintuitive (at least from a neoclassical economic perspective) dynamics. First, deregulation has led not to the dispersion of market power, but to its concentration in the hands of a few firms within each sector. Second, the increase in the size of firms has not led to economies of scale in terms of efficiency and cost, but rather unchecked monopoly power in precisely those sectors that have huge implications for the security of ordinary citizens.

Perrow is not arguing against the need, or at least the inevitability of large and complex systems in a twenty-first-century economy and society. Rather, he argues that the positive effects of large-scale organization can be better achieved through networks of smaller units rather than the command and control model of large integrated firms. But this and other changes require public action, and in particular the re-regulation of the powerful industries mentioned above. Like Westphal, Perrow sees a need to deal with those aspects of a decentralized electoral system that gives much power to small states and allows for many openings for influence and patronage. He also makes the case for campaign finance reform and the strengthening of antitrust and liability laws and judicial processes that might limit the scope and shift the incentive structures of private actors. Ominously, Perrow muses on the future calamities that may be needed to shake us out of our stasis since even Katrina was apparently not strong enough, at least in this respect.

Irwin Redlener's essay adds two crucial lenses to the vulnerability issue. As a doctor, he offers a practitioner's reflections on the public health dimensions, which includes how pre-existing health conditions shape vulnerabilities during disaster. Second, he brings a comparative international perspective, putting Katrina in the context of other events from around the world—from the earthquake in Pakistan to the cyclone in Myanmar. Indeed, most powerful in his contribution, and most frightening for many Americans, is how readily the risks facing disadvantaged communities in the United States resemble those in less developed parts of the world. The effects of preexisting inequalities in distributing vulnerability is not the province of any one place.

Like Westphal and Perrow, Redlener points out the absence of long-term planning that maintain the déjà vu sensation of each disaster. And like Bullard, he emphasizes the "relationships between preconditions and disaster consequences" from the quality of public works and transportation systems to the availability of medical care. Redlener concludes by arguing that it is only through addressing and reducing the inequalities that lead to vulnerability that we can break the déjà vu cycle in which almost every disaster is most disastrous for those people who already face the toughest odds in everyday life.

NOTES

1. On the notion of a "social autopsy," see Klinenberg (2002).

REFERENCES

Klinenberg, Eric. *Heat Wave: A Social Autopsy of Disaster in Chicago*. Chicago: University of Chicago Press, 2002.

Charles Perrow
Disasters Evermore? Reducing Our Vulnerabilities to Natural, Industrial, and Terrorist Disasters

I HAVE A SIMPLE MESSAGE: DISASTERS FROM NATURAL, INDUSTRIAL, and technological sources, and from deliberate sources such as terrorism, are inevitable, and increasing. We may prevent some and mitigate some, but we cannot escape them. At present we focus on protecting the targets, or reducing the damage to them or the people involved. We do not do an adequate job at this; our organizations are not up to it and rarely will be. Meanwhile we neglect the more basic strategy of reducing the size of the targets. This involves reducing three kinds of concentrations. First, there are the concentrations of humans in risky locations. Second, there are the concentrations of energy found in hazardous materials in populated areas. Finally, there are the concentrations of corporate power that sit astride our critical infrastructure.

Some targets are not reducible and mitigation is all we can do. Cities will not be abandoned because they sit on earthquake faults, though we can reverse their growth somewhat and make them much safer. Nor can we do much about meteorites, tsunamis, volcanoes, or tornadoes. The spread of destructive energy from these is so vast, rapid, and often unpredictable that reducing the size of targets will have little effect. And with pandemics and bioterrorism, it is just too easy for their deadly organisms to spread for us to do much more than remediation.

But other than tornadoes, these kinds of disasters are extremely rare. Our frequent disasters are hurricanes, floods, explosions, and fires. We can expect more of these in our near future, and reducing the size of their targets is feasible, though difficult.

DECONCENTRATING POPULATIONS

The US population has steadily been moving to risky locations along the Florida and Gulf coasts, as well as to seismically active locations on the West Coast. Other papers in this volume detail this movement and the increasing property damage sustained, especially from hurricanes. There are also substantial threats from increased settlement densities near our major rivers with their vulnerable levees, especially in the St. Louis area. Substantial settlements in the Sacramento Valley of California are as much as 10 feet below the rivers because of the compacting of the earth, the removal of vegetation, and ever higher levees. Since the levees are poorly maintained, these settlements are vulnerable to both floods and earthquakes. Dikes around the largest lake in Florida are also threatened and thus thousands of homes and fresh water supplies for lower Florida (20).* Dense settlements are creeping closer to Mount Rainer, and an eruption of that mountain could send lava flows all the way to Seattle (16). This is a more remote danger than the others, but the state could consider limiting settlements in the direct path of the expected lava flows.

Hurricane Katrina in 2005 has not proved to be a wake-up call for addressing hurricane vulnerabilities. New building goes on in all the southeastern coastal areas, and despite the recommendations of experts, flooded areas of New Orleans are being resettled (Ripley, 2006). Rather than wait for another Katrina to depopulate vulnerable area, we should forbid further building in vulnerable areas and relocate the most vulnerable populations. New Orleans is an important port and center of oil and gas facilities, but it is estimated that the employment in these industries is only about 10,000 people (28). The city could be one-third its pre-Katrina size, and at that size it could be protected.

But what about Miami, Tampa, or Charleston? First we should eliminate federal subsidies for flood insurance (see the paper by Howard Kunreuther in this volume) since this is a perverse incentive, and remove the power of states to keep risk insurance below the market rate. At present the insurance industry, to keep its business with its profitable lines in these states, has to raise the rates of the profitable lines to subsidize the losses from water and wind damage. This is a substantial market failure. State legislatures should regulate the insurance companies to ensure that premiums are based on real risks, but are not likely to do so. In addition, building standards are both inadequate and often not enforced, as many studies have shown. State legislatures are understandably reluctant to address these problems seriously since a significant number of them receive campaign financing from real estate and building interests, have pro-growth policies, and compete with other states. The federal government could set national standards for buildings and evacuation routes in risky areas and employ inspectors to enforce the standards. The billions that the federal government spends on disaster relief and rebuilding could thereby be drastically reduced, making the expenditures on enforcement a trivial cost.

I would expect that over a 10-year period the population of Miami and the vulnerability of the remaining population would be substantially reduced as a result of such policies. The death toll from the next hurricane that hits it could be reduced by several thousand because of both mitigation measures and a reduced population. Living in a city with such a high probability of disaster should be a luxury, and residents should pay the true market price rather than having the rest of the nation subsidize it. If global warming continues to accelerate, cities such as New York that are presently not at a great deal of risk may have to undergo the same trauma of risk-based market premiums, enforced standards, and expensive evacuation routes in order to survive (Roy, 2007).

DECONCENTRATING HAZARDOUS SUBSTANCES

According to industry-supplied government data, there are 123 locations in our nation that could release a vapor cloud that could endanger over 1 million people, killing many of them outright (Grimaldi and
Gugliotta, 2001). Our nation is littered with weapons of mass destruction and very little is being done to deconcentrate these weapons or
remove them from dense settlements. Indeed, in November 2007 the
Department of Homeland Security issued new regulations on the reporting of stockpiles of hazardous chemicals that substantially reduced the
sizes that must be reported. For example, a facility does not have to
report the storage of less than 2,500 pounds of chlorine or even the
theft of 450 pounds or less. A terrorist with that much chlorine could
cause mass casualties. According to an editorial in the *New York Times,*
"In a recent study, Greenpeace reported that the chemical industry
spent more money in a year lobbying to defeat strong chemical plant
legislation than the Department of Homeland Security spent on chemical plant security" ("Chemical Industry," 2007).

Nor are big organizations safer. The larger the chemical plant
the more frequent the accidents, and the more frequent the unwanted
emissions (Grant, Jones, and Bergesen, 2002; Kleindorfer et al., 2003).
Chemical plants have insisted on voluntary standards, though now,
with an aroused Congress, they are backing off. They did well; those
that institute the low standards the industry advocates were inspected
less often. The result: it turned out that they had higher emission
rates than those that did not institute the voluntary standards and
were inspected more often by the government (King and Lenox, 2000).
Instituting voluntary standards meant you could get by with more emissions because you were not inspected.

Many of these potential weapons move through cities on rail cars,
over half of which do not meet even the already low federal standards
for safety. They could be triggered by nature, accidents, or terrorists.
Railroad tank cars holding 90 tons of deadly chlorine gas, some of them
covered with graffiti, routinely pass through the heart of our cities even
within a few blocks of the White House. States and municipalities are

more worried about this than the federal government, which has frustrated local attempts to require rerouting away from densely settled areas. The federal government, backed by the Supreme Court, declares that the low national standards preempt the attempts by state and local governments to protect their citizens.

Congress was rewriting the act that governs railroad safety in 2007, but the draft legislation ignores the route issue as well as the standards for freight cars. Instead, it seeks to protect passengers from terrorists (Perrow and Clarke, 2007). Placing a suitcase bomb on a freight car filled with poisons or explosives—an act easy enough to carry out as numerous investigative journalists have documented—would kill several thousand people rather than a few passengers. Two issues may account for this myopia: the power of shippers and the railroads over Congress and the political advantage that derives for members of Congress who address the terrorist issue rather than concentrations of hazardous materials in urban areas. Cities need chlorine, but would it cost all that much more to limit the shipments to 30 tons, and to set tough standards for the freight cars and the track safety? Fortunately, the few cases of accidents with chlorine tankers have been in rural areas, but that is not where a terrorist would strike. As the *New York Times* editorial puts it: "Just consider the result of an accidental train derailment in North Dakota in 2002—a cloud of deadly chemicals hundreds of feet high and several miles long—and magnify it by what would happen if terrorists planned and carried out an attack in a highly populated area" ("Chemical Industry," 2007).

Many concentrations are in highly populated areas. An unwelcome deconcentration of stored oil in a New Orleans neighborhood took place when Katrina hit. A tank was ruptured and 1,800 homes became uninhabitable. Katrina caused an even larger oil spill but it did little damage because it was in a rural area outside the city, where we should confine necessary concentrations. We were lucky during the 1993 Mississippi River flood that struck St. Louis. A large collection of propane storage tanks in the city were almost dislodged by the flood (19). A spark, easily produced under such circumstances, even by metals rubbing against each other, could have led to a massive explosion. A huge quantity of diesel fuel, stored in the basement of the World Trade Center came close to ignition and would have made the disaster of September 11 far worse. Large quantities of fuel are stored in "telecommunication hotels" in the downtowns of most of our large cities. Most of us do not know about this, but some of the people living in nearby apartment buildings in New York City have protested the location of such huge buildings. The economic rationale for these concentrations is trivial compared to the risks that they present.

CONCENTRATIONS OF ECONOMIC AND POLITICAL POWER

Roughly 85 percent of our critical infrastructure is controlled by corporations, most of them private, though a few are municipalities, generally water companies and port authorities. Since the deregulation movement began in the 1970s, we have seen increased concentration in areas such as electric power, telecommunications, banking, the chemical industry, transportation in all its forms, and medical care. This concentration has made critical sectors increasingly vulnerable to natural, industrial, and terrorist disasters. What was once regulated could once again be regulated. Deregulation has not dispersed these targets, but concentrated them.

Deregulation of the electric power industry started in earnest in the 1990s and has resulted in higher costs (even controlling for rising fuel costs), more expensive outages—yet higher profits for the industry (229-34). Most important for our purposes is the increasing unreliability of the most important sector of our critical infrastructure. The consolidation of generating plants has freed utilities from local controls and allowed them to send electricity over greater distances in order to realize small savings in the cost of power. They are not required to invest in improving the electric power grid, so outages are more frequent. The outages cost consumers and the nation as a whole around $100 billion a year, while the investment of $10 to $12 billion a year for 10 years would make the grid highly reliable (Amin and Schewe, 2007). The nation as a whole bears the cost of outages, while the cost to the utilities is trivial, which means that the industry resists attempts to make the grid reliable. The target in this case is the grid itself, which can be compromised by the interaction of small failures by a few utilities in conjunction with hot weather and high demand, as was the case in the 2003 Northeast blackout. Prior to deregulation, such failures had limited impact since the electricity traveled much shorter distances. Since it would be very difficult to break up the concentration in ownership of the utilities that generate and distribute electricity, federal legislation is required to force the very profitable industry to modernize the grid (engineers describe it as "third world") and restrict the distances that electricity can be sent in order to realize small savings in the cost per kilowatt.

Electric power is vulnerable to all three of our disaster sources: weather—heat waves and winter storms, for example, both of which are increasing; industrial accidents such as software failures and failed emergency devices, as in the case of the 2003 blackout in the Northeast; and terrorist attacks, some as primitive as blowing up transmission towers (an attack actually carried out by domestic terrorists several years ago), or a more sophisticated disabling of two or three generating stations through Internet attacks upon their computerized controls. In addition to increased federal regulations, we should change the laws so that utilities are liable for the damages incurred in outages. A few successful lawsuits would quickly bring about changes in industrial reliability practices, and even some deconcentration of ownership.

For the 103 nuclear power plants, the risk goes far beyond the outages that can affect every part of our critical infrastructure. These plans constitute the most dangerous concentrations of hazmats (hazard-ous materials) in the nation. A serious accident in these plants would produce deadly radiation that could kill a few hundred thousand people. About one-half of our population lives within 50 miles of a nuclear power plant, and with a large release and the right wind orientation its killing power could extend that far. We have not had such an accident as yet, but we have come close many many times (chap. 6). Considering the entire fuel cycle and the substantial nuclear welfare program of the US government, nuclear power is our most costly source of power. The harm of coal-fired plants can be greatly reduced with known technology; the potential harm of existing nuclear power plants cannot be reduced, nor can the new designs proposed to eliminate the radiological danger. We should retire our present plants as fast as possible.

About half of our plants have spent storage pools outside of the reactor building and thus are vulnerable to a terrorist attack (162 ff). (At least one of these pools was so poorly maintained and overloaded that the Nuclear Regulatory Commission had to intervene in its operation, and one suspects that many more are vulnerable to small accidents, poor maintenance, and overloading.) There is often more radioactive material in spent storage pools than in the reactor itself, and a breach of the pool walls, possible with a drive-by shooting, would cause the spent rods to emit radioactive particles in a few minutes, like sparklers on the Fourth of July. Merely disabling the controls and the emergency water spray with grenades would cause the cooling water to boil away in a few hours. The plants are poorly guarded, safety drills are unrealistic (the corporation that supplies most of the guards receives advanced warning and the details of mock attacks that are supposed to test security), and serious security failures have occurred in the past.

However, I do not think nuclear power plants are attractive targets for terrorists; we would be much safer if current expenditures on security were diverted to intensify the inspections of the Nuclear Regulatory Commission. After a well-publicized near-accident at the Millstone Plant in Connecticut, the NRC increased inspections. The industry objected and Senator Pete Domenici (R., N.M) called NRC officials into his office and told them that unless inspections were reduced the budget of the NRC would be greatly cut by the Senate committee that he headed. The NRC complied (171).

The next most critical node in our critical infrastructure is the Internet, and its reliability and security have always been threatened by the concentrated economic power of the Microsoft Corporation. In brief the problem is as follows. When Microsoft gained a preeminent position over its few competitors with its first operating system, neither reliability nor security was of great concern (An operating system is the software that runs a computer). Few critical infrastructure facilities relied heavily on the small, low-powered computers, and there was no public Internet to connect to. Now all these facilities are heavily dependent on the reliability of operating systems, and most of them make use of the Internet.

As successive versions of its immensely successful Windows operating system came out, the versions were updates of the previous versions. The limited concern with reliability and security meant that old "legacy" codes were still utilized, but they still had their flaws or "bugs" that previously had not been consequential. Indeed, one of these bugs, an inconsequential one, has survived for 13 years through all the versions up to the new Vista version in 2007 (Fiveash, 2007). Even a major rewriting of the code of the operating system following the failure of the Longhorn project to modernize the software did not eliminate it.

I am far less concerned about the reliability of Microsoft's operating systems (open source systems such as Linux and UNIX, and the Macintosh systems are much more reliable) then I am with the security issue. Microsoft's practice has been to *integrate* applications (Excel, PowerPoint, Word, for example) into the operating system rather than having them ride on top of the system as *modules*. This limits competition from competing applications and increases Microsoft's profits and market share. But it also makes it easy for a hacker to exploit the "sloppy" code that Microsoft is accused of using in order to deposit viruses into the operating system itself. More seriously, it allows hackers to insert a "bot" that will allow the hacker to take control of the machine. Hackers have broken into power plants, but the extent to which they have taken control of them is not clear. (The Government Accountability Office is worried and calls for more transparency in this area.) They have also broken into military sites and accessed their files, something that would have strategic consequences, though probably not catastrophic potential. It is estimated that over half of all computers connected to the Internet are infected with these bots, enabling the intruder to get thousands of computers to try to access an Internet address at once, overloading the server (which distributes the messages to their sources) and rendering the server inoperative. Military establishments and the FBI are among the sites that have been shut down for days in denial of service attacks (256-58). As a result of Microsoft's vulnerability to hackers, and of course terrorists, Russian hackers/terrorists, encouraged by their government, shut down much of Estonia's government Internet services and facilities, as well as its newspapers and banking system for several days in 2007 (Perrow, 2007).

This presents a major vulnerability. Clever terrorists could take control of nuclear power plants, the electric power grid, our military facilities, banking services, and even hospitals all because Microsoft's Windows operating systems command 95 percent of the market for computers that access the Internet. The competitive strategy that makes it hard for competitors to supply programs and applications to run on the various versions of Windows, including Vista, has made it easy for hackers and potential terrorists to wreak havoc. But it has insured, at least to date, that Microsoft has no serious competitor in computer operating systems. Had Microsoft been broken up in 1999 in such a way that would promote competition that would be based upon reliability and security we would have more of both. Instead, we have "Windows for warships," wherein all new naval vessels will be Windows based, rather than using Linux or UNIX, as most of them now are. Reportedly, naval engineers are quite upset (Page, 2007).

Microsoft has only about a 10 percent share of software production. Large companies write their own software or buy it from IBM, Cisco, or a German company called SAP, which are the major producers of commercial software. But increasingly the programs they sell to business and industry to manage production, accounting, and other business functions are connected to the Internet through Windows operating systems. Thus, while their own software may be reliable and secure, once it is connected to the insecure Windows software it is hard to prevent intrusion by hackers or terrorists. Microsoft's tiny competitor, the Apple operating system made by Apple, has not made much of a dent in these commercial applications despite its higher reliability and security (it relies on a modular structure much more than Microsoft, which uses an integrated structure). The "first mover" advantages of Microsoft are just too great when customers prefer identical platforms for transactions with others.

It is often said that Microsoft is so vulnerable to viruses and bots because it is the biggest target. That is certainly true, and is consistent with my argument that we reduce the size of the targets. If hackers had to deal with a dozen different operating systems accessing the Internet, successful attacks would be more dispersed, limited, and require more effort from attackers. But in addition, it is Microsoft's decision to keep to an integrated structure for competitive reasons that makes it vulnerable, whereas Apple machines and those running open source software (Linux, UNIX) are much more likely to emphasize modules. There must be some integration, of course, and Apple's operating systems can be attacked, but it is more difficult. In addition, studies show that patches (corrections) are delivered to open source systems much sooner than Microsoft patches.

Finally, there is some reason to be optimistic. One state, Massachusetts, will now require all new computers to use open source programs which will translate into considerable savings in purchasing software. If the federal government, which buys 40 percent of all software, were to do the same it would be a revolution. The domination of Microsoft's Windows would disappear. In addition, all computer users will soon be able to purchase a cheap "thin client" that allows access to the Internet but has no memory or other programs. One then downloads programs from the Internet, either buying them, renting them, or in many cases getting them for free with sidebar advertisements (Of course this will require a bit more computer literacy than buying a machine with Windows loaded on it). With programs operating as modules, the hacker or the terrorist would be unable to take control of your computer or degrade it with viruses. The National Security Agency is now spending millions in a futile attempt to catch malevolent hackers and would-be terrorists. They should support the development of thin clients instead, and require the government to purchase open source software.

NETWORKS AND ECONOMIES OF SCALE

One objection that has been raised to my argument is that industrial and other concentrations generate economies of scale because of their size. While this may be true in a few cases, it does not seem to apply to the ones we are concerned with. The concentrations in the industries that have catastrophic potential are well beyond the size required for *production* efficiencies. The companies are very large and their size gives them market power and political power. New technologies often make downsizing not only possible but profitable, even in the chemical industry (We once thought that steel mills had to be gigantic and integrated, but the most productive ones are now mini mills). Furthermore, economies of scale can be achieved by networks of small firms as well as by one large firm. Just as modularity rather than integration reduces the complexity of large systems and increases reliability, so do networks of firms make complexity manageable and systems more reliable than the integrated firm (for reviews of this important organizational development, see Amin, 2000; Perrow, 1992; Perrow, 2002; Piore and Sable, 1984; Uzzi, 1996). Networks have several characteristics that reduce vulnerabilities. I will consider four examples: the Internet, the power grid before deregulation, networks of small firms as found in many countries, and, alas, terrorist networks.

▸ *Size:* They all can be very large systems. The Internet is the largest "organization" in the world, and the power grid is the largest "machine" in the United States. Networks of small firms can range from 10, as with packaging machines, to 100, as with furniture manufacturers in northern Italy, to several hundred as is the case with biotech networks in the United States. Terrorist networks can range from under 10 to over 100 cells.

▸ *Reliability:* The system reliability of the four ranges from high, as with the Internet and the grid, to moderate with networks of small firms, which are capable of self-adjusting behavior in response to disturbances, and moderate with terrorist groups whose reliability is surprisingly high given that they are always under attack by nations.

▸ *Efficiency:* The efficiency of these large systems is remarkable. It is extremely high with the Internet, given the volume of traffic, and was very high in the case of the grid before deregulation. Networks of small firms are very efficient since they achieve network economies of scale. Terrorist networks are efficient because of low maintenance and operating costs. Efficiency includes the ability to recover from failures. Destroying one terrorist group does not threaten the whole, and similar resilience exists in the other three cases.

▸ *Authority structure:* All four examples have authority structures that are in marked contrast to the vast majority of firms and organizations. Conceptualizing and measuring authority levels in organizations is difficult and controversial, but I would suggest that these examples are unusual in that there are really only four levels of hierarchy rather than ten or fifteen. The top level is concerned with goal setting, coordination, and monitoring rather than command and control. In the case of the Internet and the grid, the top levels are nonprofit, highly professional personnel in tiny groups or committees who function almost as "civil servants." Networks of small firms have only informal coordinating and goal-setting agents, and they have no formal authority. The small-firm examples are diverse, but the top level may include distributors (who in many cases are also producers or suppliers), an informal group, or a nonprofit agency such as a local trade association. Terrorist networks are particularly interesting in this connection since there are multiple groups claiming the goal-setting function, but most of the coordination seems to take place at the middle levels rather than the top.

The second level deals with spatial considerations, such as root or domain addresses in the Internet, major connections in the grid, transportation problems in the networks of small firms, and allocation of resources in terrorists networks. The third level is the support staff that deals with such areas as finances, media relations, and recordkeeping. The importance and the functions of these two intermediate levels varies greatly among the four examples. The lowest level is far and away the largest. This is where the actual operations are carried out. This level has a great deal of autonomy, much more so than in the vast majority of organizations.

Two points are important about these four examples. First, it is possible to have radically decentralized systems that are huge, reliable, and efficient. The individual organizations in them have a great deal of autonomy, and the top is concerned with coordination rather than control. This is vastly different from the conventional model of either organizations or of systems. Second, we are bound to have large *systems* in our highly interconnected nation, but we do not necessarily need the systems to be dominated by large *organizations*. A system made up of many rather than a few organizations has more resiliencies and more redundancies. While we think of our nation and its economy as highly interdependent, most of the relationships are ones of dependency and many lack the safeguards of redundancy. Though these four systems are highly interconnected, the relations between the nodes of these networks are predominantly ones of interdependency—that is, reciprocity—rather than dependencies—that is, authority. More of our critical infrastructure could be configured in this way.

WHAT IS TO BE DONE?

All three sources of disasters have increased in recent decades. At the same time, we have also experienced a large program of deregulation that started in the 1970s. The concentrations of people, hazmats, and corporate power have increased as a consequence. It is time to re-regulate many activities and introduce new regulations. We need to introduce or strengthen regulations regarding settlement patterns, building standards, and evacuation routes in the case of population concentrations. We also need strengthened risk-based insurance, with subsidies only to low-income families. We need to strengthen (and enforce) existing regulations regarding hazmats, and introduce new ones for new hazards. We need to foster more competition in the corporate area, in part by reinstating old antitrust laws and creating new ones to handle the new technologies. In all three cases we need to ensure that organizations, including the government, are subject to liability actions in courts.

Would the public stand for this? I believe so. Public opinion polls consistently show that people are against big government and heavy regulations when asked about these issues in general questions. These general questions assume that all else is equal, and so we all are for having the smallest government possible and the fewest regulations. But when asked about specific areas the public generally calls for more regulation and approves of strong government actions.

If the public would support stronger government action, why are these sentiments not reflected in a large enough number of our elected representatives to make a difference? I can only sketch out my answers to this question here. Most points will be very obvious, but it is well to be reminded of them.

The problem starts with the flawed electoral system. A major problem is the unrepresentative character of the Senate, in which small states are over-represented. For example, in 2004 the powerful Homeland Security Appropriations Subcommittee, responsible for the homeland security budget, was largely made up of senators from small states. They insisted that a large proportion of the funds had to be distributed equally among the states, regardless of the states' exposure to risk.

Another major problem is the lack of either campaign finance limits or restricting candidates to only public funding for federal offices. (We should have either for state offices also.) Before the advent of television, candidates did not need a great deal of money to run for office, and thus were not beholden to large campaign contributors in order to win. Television, being such a powerful persuader, changed that. As television ads became more and more expensive as well as more and more crucial, only big business could make donations large enough to matter. Even incumbents with safe legislative seats need major funds and need to be wary of challenging big business because there could be a challenger from the same party that will be friendlier to business. Our nation has struggled with the issue of limiting or controlling campaign financing for decades, but those who benefit from it are the ones that have to limit it.

Congress periodically attempts to cope with lobbies, but only trivial restrictions have been imposed. The number of lobbyists and the amount of money spent on lobbying by both Congress and federal agencies has soared in the last decade, making regulatory reform almost impossible. Of course, members of Congress benefit from the many ways that big business can contribute to their political and personal welfare, so it will always be difficult to get a sufficient number of them to vote against their personal interests or their political security. There is not much difference between the two parties on this issue.

Ultimately it is the federal courts that control government regulation (though over time it is the electoral system that determines its composition). Our federal courts have been gradually growing more conservative and skeptical of government regulation since the administration of President Ronald Reagan. This shift drastically increased under President George W. Bush's administration. A basic shift has been the expansion of private rights at the expense of community rights—ruling, for example, that wetlands can be settled by private developers. But something more specific appears to be at work in our present Supreme Court and the federal appeals courts. In 2006, individual rights of the homeowners in the city of New London, Connecticut were abrogated and developers successfully persuaded the city to condemn private housing in favor of commercial development. The Supreme Court has also consistently ruled that federal standards preempt state and local standards when the latter were higher in such matters as chemical plant safety and security, rail transport of hazmats through cities, and state and local standards regarding levees and dams. Attempts to rewrite the legislation to prevent such rulings have failed in Congress.

The area of liability is also one that the federal judicial system approaches with great caution and a distinctively conservative philosophy. It has proved to be very difficult for victims of industrial accidents—for example, chemical and rail accidents—to successfully sue the organizations responsible for these accidents. The legislation covering these risky activities and areas often exempts them from liability, and challenges to the laws and rulings have been unsuccessful, though there are exceptions. A change in these laws, if upheld by the Supreme Court, which is unlikely, would do more than anything else to force industry to play safer. It would, for example, bring the insurance industry into the area of safety in industry. Firms would have to take out much more insurance and the insurance industry would penalize those that did not change their risky practices. Firms that are safer would have lower insurance costs.

The conservative cast of the federal courts shows up in cases of preventing anticompetitive behavior. Plaintiffs sued Microsoft for anticompetitive behavior in the late 1990s. A federal judge found the company guilty of anticompetitive behavior and proposed a remedy (unfortunately, not one that would have done much to promote competition in the area of operating systems). But a federal appeals court rejected the remedy, though agreeing that Microsoft was guilty. A small fine and some ineffective restrictions followed (262-263, 273-274). (The European Union has been more successful in a similar suit against Microsoft. Restrictions on industry are generally tighter in Europe.)

WILL FURTHER CALAMITIES HELP?

Sometimes major calamities bring about major changes, as after the great Chicago fire in 1871 and the 1906 San Francisco earthquake. Following the 9/11 attack we had a major organizational disaster, the Department of Homeland Security. In addition to widespread corruption and mismanagement in the handling of the billions spent by the department both before and after Katrina, the vast majority of funds are spent on airline security and bioterrorism rather than the vastly more predictable natural disasters that we face, let alone industrial targets that are capable of killing millions. The Katrina disaster has taught us little. We are resettling the flooded areas, and the new National Response Plan has been severely criticized by several state and local agencies for its vagueness and insensitivity to local environments (Hsu, 2007). The response to Katrina itself was unbelievably inept, but worse yet, we do not seem to have learned from its lessons.

Would future calamities help? Here are some of the events that could alert us. A nuclear power plant accident (near misses are common in this industry); a rail car with hazmats in a city (three freight cars were crushed in the Minnesota bridge collapse in 2007, but fortunately they were empty); a mad cow disease outbreak (the Food and Drug Administration lightened feedlot restrictions in 2007); a few chemical plant explosions (the industry kills approximately 270 employed workers each year and an unknown number of contract workers); contamination of milk silos (though a public warning by Stanford Professor Larry Wien, that the government tried to repress, has brought about some positive changes in practices); yearly massive power outages (we came very close to one in 2005, and perhaps more since they are not disclosed [244]); a massive Internet attack (the National Security Agency is very concerned about this); and, of course, more hurricanes and floods.

None of these are remote possibilities and I think they are more probable than a serious terrorist attack (though not a bomb in the subway or a mall, which is quite possible).

Before we give up in despair we should recall that it has taken us about 100 years to develop a regulatory system. The number of regulatory agencies that concern disasters has increased steadily (FDA, OSHA, NIOSH, FAA, etc.) They have weakened in the last seven years, but can be revived. Moreover, the number of public interest and watchdog organizations has grown enormously. But it bothers me greatly that the environmental movement has not awakened to the need for target reduction, but is more worried about polar bears and wolves. If its ability to inform and arouse people were applied to the dangers I have discussed, we might find enough congressional representatives to get some of the important bills that deal with these issues out of committees and up for votes, where the voice of public interest and environmental groups, by raising public concern, might make a difference. We need to shrink the targets of nature's wrath, the industrial accident, and the terrorists' jihad. We should dismantle the Department of Homeland Security and instead have a Department to Homeland Vulnerabilities, drawing upon the National Academies and other experts to roughly rank our vulnerabilities. Taking its findings, we can create a commission modeled on the Defense Base Closure and Realignment Commission (BRAC), which is not tied to any particular locality or interest, and can broadly publicize its recommendations, informing the public and putting pressure upon the public's representatives in Congress.

I have not mentioned global warming, though I believe that is the most fearsome threat that we face. Since we seem to do little about the more proximate threats that I have been dealing with, which are challenging but eminently manageable, I am discouraged about this possibly unmanageable though distant threat.

NOTES

* This article draws on *The Next Catastrophe: Reducing Our Vulnerabilities to Natural, Industrial, and Terrorist Disasters* (2007). Citations to that book will give only the page number(s) in parenthesis— (41), for example— or chapter number, in the text.

REFERENCES

Amin, Ash. "Industrial Districts." *A Companion to Economic Geography*. Eds. E. Sheppard and T. J. Barnes. Oxford: Blackwell, 2000.

Amin, Massoud, and Phillip F. Schewe. "Preventing Blackouts." *Scientific American* (May 2007): 60-67.

"Chemical Industry 1, Public Safety 0." *New York Times*, November 7, 2007.

Fiveash, Kelly. "Vista Attacked by 13-Year-Old Virus." *The Register*, September 17, 2007 <http://www.theregister.co.uk/2007/09/17/vista_hit_by_stoned_angelina/>.

Grant II, Don Sherman, Andrew W. Jones, and Albert J. Bergesen. "Organizational Size and Pollution: The Case of the U.S. Chemical Industry." *American Sociological Review* 67 (June 2002): 389-407.

Grimaldi, James V., and Guy Gugliotta. "Chemical Plants Feared as Targets." *Washington Post*, December 16, 2001.

Hsu, Spencer S. "Proposed Disaster-Response Plan Faulted." *Washington Post*, September 12, 2007.

King, Andrew A, and Michael J. Lenox. "Industry Self-Regulation without

Sanctions: The Chemical Industry's Responsible Care Program."
Academy of Management Journal 43 (2000): 698-716.

Kleindorfer, Paul R., James C. Belke, Michael R. Elliott, Kiwan Lee, Robert A. Lowe, and Harold I. Feldman. "Accident Epidemiology and the U.S. Chemical Industry: Accident History and Worst-Case Data from RMP*Info." *Risk Analysis* 23:5 (October 2003): 865-881 <http://www.blackwell-synergy.com/links/doi/10.1111/1539-6924.00365/abs>.

Page, Lewis. "Windows for Warships Nears Frontline Service." *The Register*, February 26, 2007 <http://www.theregister.co.uk/2007/02/26/windows_boxes_at_sea/>.

Perrow, Charles. "Small Firm Networks." *Networks and Organizations*. Eds. Nitin Nohria and Robert G. Eccles. Boston: Harvard Business School Press, 1992.

——. *Organizing America: Wealth, Power, and the Origins of Corporate Capitalism*. Princeton: Princeton University Press, 2002.

——. *The Next Catastrophe: Reducing Our Vulnerabilities to Natural, Industrial, and Terrorist Disasters*. Princeton: Princeton University Press, 2007.

——. "Microsoft Attacks Estonia." *The Huffington Post*, May 26, 2007 <http://www.huffingtonpost.com/charles-perrow/microsoft-attacks-estonia_b_49333.html>.

Perrow, C., and Lee Clarke. "The Next Railroad Catastrophe." *The Huffington Post*, June 20, 2007 <http://www.huffingtonpost.com/charles-perrow-and-lee-clarke>.

Piore, Michael, and Charles Sable. *The Second Industrial Divide*. New York: Basic Books, 1984.

Ripley, Amanda. "Why We Don't Prepare for Disasters." *Time* (August 20, 2006).

Roy, Srabani. "Coastal Mega-Cities in for a Bumpy Ride." *Inter Press Service*, March 28, 2007.

Uzzi, Brian. "Social Structure and Competition in Interfirm Networks: The Paradox of Embeddedness." *Administrative Science Quarterly* 42 (March 1997): 35-67.

Robert D. Bullard
Differential Vulnerabilities: Environmental and Economic Inequality and Government Response to Unnatural Disasters

ON AUGUST 29, 2005, HURRICANE KATRINA MADE LANDFALL NEAR New Orleans, leaving death and destruction across the Louisiana, Mississippi, and Alabama Gulf coast counties.* Katrina was the most destructive hurricane in US history, costing over $70 billion in insured damage. Katrina was also one of the deadliest storms in decades, with a death toll of 1,836, and still counting. Katrina's death toll is surpassed only by the 1928 hurricane in Florida (estimates vary from 2,500 to 3,000 deaths) and the 8,000 who perished in the 1900 Galveston hurricane (Kleinberg, 2003; Pastor et al., 2006).

After some two and a half years, reconstruction continues to move at a slow pace in New Orleans and the Louisiana, Mississippi, and Alabama Gulf coast region. The lethargic recovery is now beginning to overshadow the deadly storm itself (Kromm and Sturgis, 2007). Questions linger: What went wrong? Can it happen again? Is government equipped to plan for, mitigate, respond to, and recover from natural and man-made disasters? Can the public trust government response to be fair? Does race matter when it comes to disaster relief?

WHY FOCUS ON THE SOUTH?

This paper uses the events that unfolded in New Orleans, the Gulf coast region, and the southern United States as the sociohistorical backdrop for examining social vulnerability and government response to unnatural disasters. The case studies of disparate treatment date back more than eight decades. The South is unique because of the legacy of slavery, Jim Crow segregation, and entrenched white supremacy. The region has a history of black business ownership, black home ownership, and black land ownership. Most black farmers are located in the South. It is no accident that the South gave birth to the modern civil rights movement and the environmental justice movement. And the vast majority (over 95 percent) of the 105 historically black colleges and universities are located in the South.

The 2000 census showed that African Americans ended the century by returning "home" to the South—the same region they spent most of the century escaping. Since the mid-seventies, reverse migration patterns indicate that more blacks are entering the South than leaving for other regions. Today, over 54 percent of the nation's blacks live in the South (McKinnon, 2000). In the 620 counties that make up the southern "blackbelt," stretching from Delaware to Texas, African Americans comprise a larger percentage of the total population than they do in the country as a whole—about 12 percent. In the 15 southern states (excluding Texas and Florida), blacks make up 22.8 percent of the population, compared with 3.5 percent for Hispanics.

Transportation serves as a key component in addressing poverty, unemployment, and equal opportunity goals, ensuring access to education, health care, and other public services. American society is largely divided between individuals with cars and those without cars (Bullard and Johnson, 1997). The private automobile is still the dominant travel mode of every segment of the American population, including the poor and people of color.

Nationally, only 7 percent of white households do not own a car, compared with 24 percent of African-American households, 17 percent of Latino households, and 13 percent of Asian-American households. Cars are an essential part of emergency evacuation plans. Disaster evacuation plans across the nation assume that people own a car. Nearly 11 million households in the United States lack vehicles, or more than 28 million Americans who would have difficulty evacuating their area in an emergency.

In 1997, to encourage better disaster planning, the Federal Emergency Management Agency (FEMA) launched Project Impact, a pilot program that provided funding for communities to assess their vulnerable populations and make arrangements to get people without transportation to safety (Elliston, 2004). The program reached 250 communities and proved quite effective. However, the Bush administration ended the program in 2001, and funds once earmarked for disaster preparation were shifted away.

For many individuals who do no own a car or drive, public transit is the primary mode of travel. However, transit does not always get you where you need to go. More important, many of the nation's regional transportation systems are "regional" in name only—with a good number of "separate and unequal" urban and suburban transit systems built along race and class lines. Too often race has literally stopped regional transit in its tracks.

New Orleans and Jefferson Parish, Louisiana, for example, run separate bus systems. Passengers on the New Orleans Rapid Transit Authority (NORTA) and Jefferson Transit are forced to switch buses at the parish line. Even Hurricane Katrina floodwaters did not wash away the stubborn cultural divide that separates New Orleans from its suburbs. In November 2006, New Orleans and Jefferson Parish councils met to try to end the longtime regional transportation roadblock and bring the fractured city and suburban bus system in sync (Moran, 2006). The two jurisdictions had a chance to combine forces a year after Katrina, when Jefferson Parish awarded a three-year contract for management of its bus system. NORTA made a bid for the job, but Jefferson Parish chose a private Illinois company that offered a better deal.

On August 28, 2005, Mayor Ray Nagin ordered New Orleans first ever mandatory evacuation since the city was founded in 1718. Hurricane Katrina demonstrated to the world the race and class disparities that mark who can escape a disaster by car. Emergency plans were particularly insufficient with regard to evacuation for the car-less and "special needs" populations—individuals who cannot simply jump into their cars and drive away (Department of Homeland Security, 2006). At least 100,000 New Orleans residents—and more than one-third of New Orleans' African-American residents—did not have cars to evacuate in case of a major storm (City of New Orleans, 2005). Over 15 percent of the city's residents relied on public transportation as their primary mode of travel (State of Louisiana, 2000; Bourne, 2004; City of New Orleans, 2005).

New Orleans had only one-quarter the number of buses that would have been needed to evacuate all car-less residents. Katrina's evacuation plan worked relatively well for people with cars, but failed to serve people who depend on public transit (Litman, 2005).

After more than 80 percent of New Orleans flooded after the levee breach, most of the city's 500 transit and school buses were without drivers. About 190 NORTA buses were lost to flooding. Most of the NORTA employees were dispersed across the country and many were made homeless (Eggler, 2005). Disaster planners failed the weakest and most vulnerable in New Orleans—individuals without cars, nondrivers, children, the disabled, the homeless, the sick, and the elderly (Riccardi, 2005). Katrina exposed a major weakness in mass evacuation plans and for a moment focused the national spotlight on the heightened vulnerability of people without cars—a population that faces transportation challenges in everyday life (Dyson, 2006).

GOVERNMENT RESPONSE TO WEATHER-RELATED DISASTERS

In the real world, all communities are not created equal. Some are more equal than others. If a community happens to be poor, black, or located on the "wrong side of the tracks," it receives less protection than communities inhabited largely by affluent whites in the suburbs. Generally, rich people tend to take the higher ground, leaving the poor and working class more vulnerable to flooding and environmental pestilence. Race maps closely with social vulnerability and the geography of environmental risks (Pastor et al., 2006).

Much of the death and destruction attributed to "natural" disasters is in fact unnatural and man-made. Humans prefer to make Mother Nature or God the villain in catastrophic losses from tsunamis, earthquakes, droughts, floods, and hurricanes, rather than placing responsibility squarely on social and political forces (Steinberg, 2003). What many people often call "natural" disasters are in fact acts of social injustice perpetuated by government and business on the poor, people of color, the disabled, the elderly, the homeless, those who are transit dependent and non-drivers—groups least able to withstand such disasters.

Quite often the scale of a disaster's impact has more to do with the political economy of the country, region, and state than with the hurricane's category strength (Jackson, 2005). Similarly, measures to prevent or contain the effects of disaster vulnerability are not equally provided to all. Typically, flood-control investments provide location-specific benefits—with the greatest benefits going to populations who live or own assets in the protected area.

Weather-related disasters, including hurricanes, floods, droughts, and windstorms, are growing in frequency and intensity. Since 1980, 10,867 weather-related disasters have caused more than 575,000 deaths and have forced millions to flee their homes. Since 1980, the cost of weather-related disasters amount to more than $1 trillion (Worldwatch Institute, 2003). In 2004 alone, weather-related disasters caused $104 billion in economic losses, almost twice the total in 2003.

Each year communities along the Atlantic and Gulf coast are hit with tropical storms and hurricanes, forcing millions to flee to higher ground. Hurricanes Dennis, Katrina, and Rita displaced hundreds of thousands of people, destroyed tens of thousands of homes, and disrupted oil rigs and refineries. Historically, the Atlantic hurricane season produces on average ten storms, of which about six become hurricanes and two to three become major hurricanes.

The 2005 hurricane season produced a record of 27 named storms, topping the previous record of 21 storms set in 1933. It also saw 13 hurricanes—besting the old record of 12 hurricanes set in 1969 (Tanneeru, 2005). Twelve was the most hurricanes in one season since record keeping began in 1851. Three of the hurricanes in the 2005 season reached Category 5 status, meaning they had wind speeds greater than 155 mph at some point during the storm. Katrina's death toll (1,836) made it the third most deadly hurricane in the U.S.—surpassed, as was noted earlier, only by the 1928 hurricane in Florida (2,500 to 3,000) and the 1900 Galveston hurricane (8,000). The past events will show how marginalized populations are at risk to the built and natural environment. It will also show how various levels of government have responded differently to black and white disaster victims.

Mississippi River Flood (1927)

In his 1997 book, *Rising Tides: The Great Mississippi Flood of 1927 and How It Changed America*, John M. Barry details one of the most destructive natural disasters in American history (Barry, 1998). The 1927 flood was the worst flood to strike the country until the flooding caused by Hurricane Katrina in 2005. In the spring of 1927, incessant rains pushed the Mississippi River to over 30 feet in height and began eroding the levees from Cairo, Illinois to Greenville, Mississippi. More than 27,000 square miles were inundated, and thousands of farms and hundreds of towns were wiped away by floodwater. Estimates of the damage ranged from $246 million to $1 billion (roughly $2 billion to $7.8 billion in modern dollars). The official death toll reached 246 with perhaps thousands more African-American deaths uncounted.

Nearly a million people in the Mississippi Delta were made homeless. White racism and Jim Crow added to the disaster. Government response to the flood is a classic case of environmental racism. Whites were evacuated, while 330,000 African Americans were interned in 154 relief "concentration camps." Over 13,000 flood victims near Greenville, Mississippi were taken from area farms and evacuated to the crest of an unbroken levee, and stranded there for days without food or clean water, while boats arrived to evacuate white women and children. Many blacks were detained and forced to work on the levee at gunpoint during flood relief efforts.

Black work gangs and their families were held as virtual prisoners in dreadfully squalid concentration camps set up along miles of the Greenville levee (Barry, 1998). Thousands of displaced residents, black and white, left the land and never returned—accelerating black migration to the North and thus changing the political landscape of the country.

Florida Okeechobee Hurricane (1928)

In September 1928, the Okeechobee hurricane struck Florida with devastating force. It was the first Category 5 hurricane ever officially recorded in the Atlantic. The eye of the storm passed ashore in Palm Beach County with 140 mph winds, then struck a populated area on the southern edge of Lake Okeechobee (Brochu, 2003). The only bulwark between the low-lying communities and the massive lake was a 5-foot mud dike constructed to hold back the Lake Okeechobee during summer rains.

In his book, *Black Cloud: The Deadly Hurricane of 1928*, Eliot Kleinberg provides a graphic account of Florida's deadliest storm (Kleinberg, 2003). When the hurricane had passed, the dike broke and 2,500 to 3,000 people drowned, making it the second-deadliest hurricane in US history, behind the Galveston, Texas hurricane of 1900 that killed 8,000 people.

Nobody really knows how many people died in the storm. For years, the Red Cross set the death toll at 1,836. In the summer of 2003, the National Hurricane Center increased the death toll from 1,836 to 2,500, with an asterisk suggesting the total could be as high as 3,000. Some accounts put the deaths closer to 3,500 (Barnes, 1998). Half of the

6,000 people living in the farming communities between Clewiston and Canal Point perished. More than 75 percent of the recorded deaths were black migrant workers, segregated in life and abandoned in death.

Palm Beach County in the 1920s was, as today, home to one of the world's great wealth enclaves with its glittering ocean drawing tourists from around the world. But just a 30-minute drive to the west takes you into a world of dirt roads, farmfields, poverty, and shantytowns inhabited largely by blacks migrant workers from the Deep South and the impoverished islands of the Caribbean. The 1928 Okeechobee hurricane "killed more people than the 1906 San Francisco earthquake (about 700), more than sinking of the *Titanic* (1,505), and probably more than the estimated 3,000 who died on September 11, 2001" (Kleinberg, 1998: xiv).

Devastation was complete. Although the storm destroyed everything in its path with impartiality, it hit the poor low-lying black areas around the lake the hardest. Belle Glade, Pahokee, and South Bay were virtually wiped off the map (Klinkenberg, 1992). Bodies, livestock, and lumber floated everywhere. Some survivors used bloated cows as rafts and splintered lumber as paddles. The bodies of the dead overwhelmed officials. The few caskets available were used to bury the bodies of whites. Other bodies were either burned or buried in mass graves. Burials were segregated and the only mass gravesite to receive a memorial contained only white bodies.

The savage storm was even immortalized in African-American writer Zora Neal Hurston's classic novel, *Their Eyes Were Watching God* (Hurston, 1998). However, no amount of public relations and government cover-up could hide the horror left by the floodwaters—especially damage the storm inflicted on the black population and the racism by whites that followed.

Hurricane Betsy, New Orleans (1965)
Hurricane Betsy struck the state of Louisiana and the city of New Orleans in 1965. Before Hurricane Katrina, Betsy was the most destruc-

tive hurricane on record to strike the Louisiana coast. The damage and flooding throughout the state covered 4,800 square miles, killed 81 people, caused about 250,000 to be evacuated, and disrupted transportation, communication, and utilities service throughout the eastern coastal area of Louisiana for weeks.

Betsy hit the mostly black and poor New Orleans Lower Ninth Ward especially hard. Betsy accelerated the decline of the neighborhood and out-migration of many of its longtime residents. This is the same neighborhood that was inundated by floodwaters from Katrina. Over 98 percent of the Lower Ninth Ward residents are black and a third live below the poverty level.

Many black New Orleans residents still believe that white officials intentionally broke the levee and flooded the Lower Ninth Ward to save mostly white neighborhoods and white business district. Many older blacks are still bitter about being trapped in attics after rising floodwaters from Hurricane Betsy in 1965. Blacks from diverse socioeconomic backgrounds believe the flooding of the Lower Ninth Ward and other black areas after Betsy was a deliberate act stemming from New Orleans Mayor Victor Schiro, who was not known for his progressive views on race, ordering the levees breached and floodwaters pumped out of his well-to-do white subdivision, Lake Vista, and into the Lower Ninth Ward (Remnick, 2005). Whether a conspiracy rumor or fact, the "Betsy experience" is the primary reason many Lower Ninth Ward residents keep hatchets in their attics. This mistrust of government probably saved thousands of lives after the levee breach four decades later when Katrina struck in 2005.

Debris from Betsy was dumped at the Agricultural Street landfill. Two mostly black New Orleans subdivisions, Gordon Plaza and Press Park, were later built on a portion of land that was used as a municipal landfill. The landfill was classified as a solid waste site but hazardous waste ended up at the site (Lyttle, 2004).

In 1969, the federal government created a home ownership program to encourage lower income families to purchase their first home. Press Park was the first subsidized housing project on this program in New Orleans. The federal program allowed tenants to apply 30 percent of their monthly rental payments toward the purchase of a family home. In 1987, 17 years later, the first sale was completed. In 1977, construction began on a second subdivision, Gordon Plaza. This development was planned, controlled, and constructed by the US Department of Housing and Urban Development (HUD) and the Housing Authority of New Orleans (HANO). Gordon Plaza consists of approximately 67 single-family homes.

In 1983, the Orleans Parish School Board purchased a portion of the Agriculture Street landfill site for a school. That this site had previously been used as a municipal dump prompted concerns about the suitability of the site for a school. The board contracted engineering firms to survey the site and assess it for contamination of hazardous materials. Heavy metals and organics were detected at the site.

Despite the warnings, Moton Elementary School, an $8 million "state of the art" public school opened with 421 students in 1989. In May 1986, the Environmental Protection Agency (EPA) performed a site inspection at the Agriculture Street landfill community. Although lead, zinc, mercury, cadmium, and arsenic were found at the site, based on the Hazard Ranking System (HRS) model used at that time, the score of 3 was not high enough to place them on the National Priorities List (the National Priorities List, or NPL, is the list of hazardous waste sites eligible for long-term remedial action financed under the EPA's federal Superfund program. The EPA regulations outline a formal process for assessing hazardous waste sites and placing them on the NPL).

On December 14, 1990, the EPA published a revised HRS model in response to the Superfund Amendment and Reauthorization Act (SARA) of 1986. On the request of community leaders, in September 1993, an Expanded Site Inspection (ESI) was conducted. On December 16, 1994, the Agriculture Street landfill community was placed on the National Priorities List (NPL) with a new score of 50.

The Agriculture Street landfill community is home to approximately 900 African-American residents. The average family income is $25,000 and the educational level is high school graduate and above. The community pushed for a buyout of their property and to be relocated. However, this was not the EPA's resolution of choice. A cleanup was ordered at a cost of $20 million; the community buyout would have cost only $14 million. The actual cleanup began in 1998 and was completed in 2001 (Lyttle, 2004).

The Concerned Citizens of Agriculture Street landfill filed a class-action suit against the city of New Orleans for damages and cost of relocation (Bullard, 2005). The residents filed the suit in order to force a relocation from the contaminated neighborhood. They were in the end forcibly relocated by Katrina. In January 2006, after 13 years of litigation, Seventh District Court Judge Nadine Ramsey ruled in favor of the residents—describing them as poor minority citizens who were "promised the American dream of first-time homeownership," though the dream "turned out to be a nightmare" (Finch, 2006). Her ruling could end up costing the city, the Housing Authority of New Orleans, and Orleans Parish School Board tens of millions of dollars.

Hurricane Hugo, South Carolina (1989)

In September 1989, Hurricane Hugo made its way to shore in South Carolina. Hugo caused 49 deaths, widespread damages and losses estimated to exceed $9 billion, temporary displacement of hundreds of thousands of people, and disruption of the lives of about 2 million people. Twenty-six of South Carolina's 46 counties, covering two-thirds of the state, were declared federal disaster areas. Following Hugo, African-Americans and less-educated victims received less help than similarly affected victims who were white or more educated (Kaniasty and Norris, 1995).

Bureaucratic blindness and biased relief assistance in South Carolina following Hugo further marginalized an already economically marginalized African American population, leaving behind many blacks who lacked insurance and other support systems. These practices deepened existing economic divide between blacks and whites (Cannon et al., 2004).

Hurricane Andrew, Miami-Dade and South Florida (1992)

Hurricane Andrew struck southern Florida in 1992 and forced an estimated 700,000 residents from their homes (Pittman, 2002). Over 250,000 people were left homeless, 15 were killed, and 1.5 million were left without water, electricity, and telephones. At least 75,000 homes were destroyed and 108 schools were damaged (3 were destroyed).

An estimated 100,000 South Dade residents moved away from the area and this migration changed the area's racial makeup. In studying race and social vulnerability in Hurricane Andrew, disaster researchers at Florida International University found that:

> some neighborhoods are located on the wrong side of the tracks, the bad side of town, or in slums and urban war zones. Others are on the right side of the tracks, uptown, upscale, or on the good side of down. Minorities, particularly black households, are disproportionately located in poor quality housing segregated into low-valued neighborhoods. This segregation creates communities of fate that can take on added salience in a disaster context. Race and ethnicity linked to housing quality—not because of ethnically based cultural variations in housing preferences as is true in some societies—but because race and ethnicity are still important determinants of the economic resources, such as income and credit, critical for obtaining housing (Peacock et al., 1992: 173).

Blacks were more vulnerable to hurricane damage due to residential segregation, location of their neighborhoods, and the conditions of their housing. Andrew marginalized the already marginalized.

Recovery was also problematic for black Miami neighborhoods, where poorer quality building construction and insufficient insurance made these neighborhoods more vulnerable. Post-hurricane relocation was impeded for blacks. For example, "blacks were less likely than Anglos to relocate after the hurricane not only because of possible economic constraints, but because of barriers created by residential segregation" (Peacock et al., 1992: 201).

Tropical Storm Alberto (1994)

In July 1994, Tropical Storm Alberto dumped at least 17 inches of rain on parts of Georgia, flooding the basins of the Flint and Ocmulgee Rivers. The floods were responsible for 30 deaths. Albany got the worst of Alberto. The flood displaced more than 22,000 residents in Albany and damaged 6,500 buildings, having an estimated $1 billion impact in the state overall, including $500 million in damage to uninsured property and $200 million in agricultural losses (Harrison, 1994).

Albany's nearly 80,000 residents make up most of the population of Dougherty County. African Americans compose 65 percent of Albany's population. On average, Albany education level is lower than the state, and poverty is greater than at the national level. Over 27 percent of the city's population is below the poverty level. Medical facilities and transportation are also lacking.

The flood devastation in south-central Albany was so widespread that local leaders feared many residents would not resettle there, thereby weakening black voting strength in a city where blacks make up a majority of the population but only in 1994 had won a majority of the seats on the city commission. Floodwaters from the Flint River consumed nearly two-thirds of the 204-acre campus of historically black Albany State University, founded in 1903. Located on the banks of the Flint River, the 204-acre campus required a $112 million extensive construction and renovation as the result of a devastating flood in 1994. The construction created a new campus for Albany State students and the Albany community.

Seven weeks after floods ravaged southwest Georgia, the hardest hit sections of mostly black Albany had hardly begun (Harrison, 1994). The legacy of racial separation and distrust tore people apart and delayed help from getting to the most needy storm victims. Racial tension, which is generally high, was heightened by the way disaster relief, rebuilding, and recovery were handled.

Black Farmers and USDA Disaster Relief (1997)

Black farmers have suffered severe damage from natural disasters such as floods, droughts, tornados, and hurricanes. They, like other farmers, suffer in the aftermath of the natural disasters with losses of crops, livestock, supplies, equipment, barns, and storage areas. These losses result in reduced family income, delayed production, stunted business growth, and for some, a total loss of their livelihood.

Unlike black farmers, white farmers get results from the United States Department of Agriculture (USDA) when they apply for disaster relief, emergency loans, and operating loans. Black farmers get the runaround. Melvin Bishop, a black farmer testifying at the Eatonton, Georgia stop of the Economic Human Rights Bus Tour along with several other black farmers, summarized the problem: "Even more devastating than the tornado was being denied USDA funds appropriated for emergency disaster and relief purposes. The process involved in waiting and standing in long lines to shuffle paper, completing forms and applications, was physically, mentally, and emotionally draining" (Mittal and Powell, 2000).

Melvin Bishop is among hundreds of black farmers who filed administrative complaints or lawsuits charging that for decades USDA loan officials have discouraged, delayed, or rejected loan applications because of their race. Federal officials have upheld these charges. The farmers say that such discrimination is a major reason that the nation's already tiny corps of black farmers is dwindling at three times the rate of farmers nationwide.

In 1997, African-American farmers brought a lawsuit against the USDA, charging it with discrimination in denying them access to loans and subsidies mandated by law. The lawsuit was filed in August 1997 on behalf of 4,000 of the nation's 17,000 black farmers and former farmers. A consent decree was signed in January 1999. The estimated cost of the settlement ranges from $400 million to more than $2 billion (Estes, 2001).

Hurricane Floyd, Eastern North Carolina (1999)

Hurricane Floyd pounded more than 30 North Carolina counties on September 1999 and dropped an estimated 15 to 20 inches of rain. Floyd left 17,000 homes uninhabitable, 56,000 damaged, and 47,000 people in temporary shelters in eastern North Carolina (Wing et al., 2002). Eastern North Carolina is a poor rural area with large concentration of African Americans.

Hurricane Floyd flooded the banks of the Tar River, drowning Princeville, the nation's first town chartered by blacks in the United States. Princeville is located in Edgecombe County, which was 57.5 percent black according to the 2000 census. Much of the town was lost when flooding from back-to-back hurricanes hit the all-black town. Before the flood struck, Princeville was a town of 2,100 residents, 850 homes, 30 businesses, and 3 churches. The town covers 40 streets spread over 1.3 square miles.

Hurricane Floyd's floodwater exposed the people to contaminants from a variety of sources, including municipal solid waste facilities, sewage treatment facilities, hazardous waste facilities, underground storage tanks containing petroleum products, and thousands of dead hogs. More than six years after Hurricane Floyd, many black families were still suffering from respiratory infections, skin irritations, moldy homes, and unmet home repair needs that leave them vulnerable to future storms (Solow, 2004).

Hurricane Katrina, New Orleans (2005)

On August 29, 2005, Hurricane Katrina laid waste New Orleans, an American city built below sea level in 1718 on the banks of the Mississippi River. New Orleans, like most major urban centers, was in peril long before Katrina floodwaters devastated the city (Pastor et al., 2006). Katrina was complete in its devastation of homes, neighborhoods, institutions, and community. Flooding in the New Orleans metropolitan area largely resulted from breached levees and flood walls (Gabe et al., 2005). The city's coastal wetlands, which normally serve as a natural buffer against storm surges, had been destroyed by offshore drilling, Mississippi River levees, canals for navigation, pipelines, highway projects, agricultural and urban development.

Over the past century more than 2,000 of the original 7,000 square miles of coastal marsh and swamp forests that formed the coastal delta of the Mississippi River have vanished. An average of 34 square miles of south Louisiana land, mostly marsh, has disappeared each year for the past five decades. More than 80 percent of the nation's coastal wetland loss in this time occurred in Louisiana. From 1932 to 2000, the state lost 1,900 square miles of land to the Gulf of Mexico (Tibbetts, 2006). Hurricane Katrina pushed New Orleans closer to the coast because of extensive erosion at the coastal edge. This is a national problem. A range of groups, including researchers, policymakers, and environmentalists, are calling for restoration of wetlands and barrier islands to help protect New Orleans the next time a hurricane strikes.

Emergency planners at FEMA have known for decades which populations are most vulnerable and what types of people are most likely to be left behind in disasters—individuals who are poor, sick, elderly, young, or of color. In 2001, FEMA experts ranked a hurricane striking New Orleans, a terrorist attack on New York City, and a strong earthquake in San Francisco as the top three catastrophic disasters most likely to occur in the country (Berger, 2001).

A 2004 FEMA Hurricane Pam simulation foretold the Katrina disaster (Federal Emergency Management Agency, 2004). The exercise was held at the State Emergency Operations Center in Baton Rouge using realistic weather and damage information developed by the National Weather Service, the US Army Corps of Engineers, the Louisiana State University Hurricane Center, and other state and federal agencies to help develop joint response plans for a catastrophic hurricane in Louisiana.

The disaster response team developed action plans in critical areas such as search and rescue, medical care, sheltering, temporary housing, school restoration, and debris management. Few of Hurricane Pam's simulation action plan preparedness tasks had been implemented prior to Hurricane Katrina. Writer Joel K. Bourne, Jr. (2004) also predicted with eerie accuracy the disaster that would follow if a powerful hurricane would strike New Orleans.

CLEANING UP AFTER KATRINA

Katrina has been described as one of the worst environmental disasters in American history. Some commentators predicted that it would take the "mother of all toxic cleanups" to handle the untold tons of "lethal goop" left by the storm and flooding ("The Mother," 2005). However, the billion-dollar question facing New Orleans is which neighborhoods will get cleaned up, which ones will be left contaminated, and which ones will be targeted as new sites to dump storm debris and waste from flooded homes.

Hurricane Katrina left debris across a 90,000-square-mile disaster area in Louisiana, Mississippi, and Alabama, compared with a 16-acre tract in New York on September 11, 2001 (Luther, 2006). Louisiana parishes had 25 times more debris than was collected after the 9/11 terrorist attack in 2001. More than 110,000 of New Orleans' 180,000 homes were flooded, and half sat for days or weeks in more than six feet of water (Nossiter, 2005). An additional 350,000 automobiles had to be drained of oil and gasoline and then recycled; 60,000 boats were destroyed; and 300,000 underground fuel tanks and 42,000 tons of hazardous waste must be cleaned up and properly disposed at licensed facilities. Government officials peg the numbers of cars lost in New Orleans alone at 145,000 (Dart, 2006).

The Politics of Waste Disposal

What has been cleaned up, what gets left behind, and where the waste is disposed of appears to be linked more to political science and sociology than to toxicology, epidemiology, and hydrology. Weeks after Katrina struck, the Louisiana Department of Environmental Quality (LDEQ) allowed New Orleans to open the 200-acre Old Gentilly landfill to dump construction and demolition waste from the storm (Burdeau, 2005). Federal regulators ordered the unlined landfill closed in the 1980s. In December 2005, more than 2,000 truckloads of debris were entering the landfill in east New Orleans every day (O'Driscoll, 2006).

Just four months after the storm, the Old Gentilly landfill grew about 100 feet high. LDEQ officials insist that the old landfill, which is still operating, meets all standards. But residents and environmentalists disagree. Even some high-ranking elected officials expressed fear that reopening of the Old Gentilly landfill could create an ecological nightmare (Russell, 2005). In November 2005, four days after environmentalists filed a lawsuit to block the dumping, the landfill caught fire.

In April 2006, the Army Corps of Engineers and the Louisiana Department of Environmental Quality issued permits that allowed Waste Management Inc. to open and operate a construction and demolition-related material landfill in New Orleans East. The new landfill is located on Chef Menteur Highway, which runs through much of New Orleans East, where the majority of the population is African American. Waste Management pledged to give the city 22 percent of all revenue derived from the site.

Every week, Waste Management picks up an average of 45 pounds of trash from each home, 20 more pounds per home than pre-Katrina. The new landfill could accept as much as 6.5 million cubic yards of vegetation and other debris generated by Katrina, including roofing materials, wallboard, and demolition debris, which are considered less harmful than other types of waste.

But after Katrina, the state LDEQ expanded its definition of what is considered construction debris to include potentially contaminated material (Luther, 2005). Yet, regulators acknowledge the potential toxic contamination threat from storm-related wastes. Much of the disaster debris from flooded neighborhoods in New Orleans has been mixed to the point that separation is either very difficult or essentially impossible.

Government officials assert that the risk of hazardous materials being dumped at the new Chef Menteur landfill is insignificant and that current sorting practices are adequate to keep hazardous waste out of the landfill. They also insist protective liners are not needed for construction and demolition landfills because demolition debris is cleaner than other rubbish (Eaton, 2006). Construction and demolition landfills are not required under federal law to have the protective liners required for municipal landfills, which are expected to receive a certain amount of hazardous household waste. LDEQ provided a permit for the landfill.

Landfill opponents think otherwise. Many fear the government's willingness to waive regulations will mean motor oil, batteries, electronics, ink toner, chlorine bleach, drain cleaners, and other noxious material will almost certainly wind up at the unlined landfills (Russell, 2006). The Chef Highway landfill is about four miles west of the Old Gentilly landfill and just 0.8 miles from the nearest apartments in a mostly Vietnamese-American community. More than a thousand Vietnamese-American families live less than two miles from the edge of the new landfill. Residents view the landfill as a roadblock to community recovery and rebuilding. After mounting public pressure, the Chef Menteur landfill was shut down by Mayor Nagin in August 2006.

A "Safe" Road Home

Two years after Katrina, one-third of New Orleans' residents had not made it back home (Liu and Plyer, 2007. New Orleans' population stood at 223,388 in July 2007—or about 68 percent of its pre-Katrina July 2005 population. The road home for many Katrina survivors has been a bumpy one, largely due to slow government actions to distribute the $116 billion in federal aid to help residents rebuild. Only about $35 billion has been appropriated for long-term rebuilding. Most of the

Katrina money coming from Washington has not gone to those most in need—and the funding squeeze is stopping much of the Gulf coast from coming back (Kromm and Sturgis, 2007).

As of August 6, 2007, only 22 percent of the applicants to Louisiana's Road Home program had gone to closing. More than 180,424 Road Home applications had been received—far higher than the 123,000 the program was originally designed to handle (the Road Home program was designed to provide compensation to Louisiana homeowners affected by Hurricanes Katrina or Rita for the damage to their homes. The program afforded eligible homeowners up to $150,000 in compensation for their losses to get back into their homes) (LOCD). From January 2007 to August 2007, the average benefit per applicant had fallen by more than $12,000—from a high of $81,000 to $68,734.

In March 2006, seven months after the storm slammed ashore, organizers of "A Safe Way Back Home" initiative, the Deep South Center for Environmental Justice at Dillard University (DSCEJ), and the United Steel Workers (USW), undertook a proactive pilot neighborhood cleanup project—the first of its kind in New Orleans (Wright, 2006). The cleanup project, located in the 8100 block of Aberdeen Road in New Orleans East, removed several inches of tainted soil from front- and backyards, replacing the soil with new sod, and disposing of the contaminated dirt in a safe manner.

Residents who choose to remove the top soil from their yards— which contains sediments left by flooding—find themselves in a Catch-22 situation, with the LDEQ and EPA insisting the soil in their yards is not contaminated and the local landfill operators refusing to dispose of the soil because they suspect it is contaminated. This bottleneck of what to do with the topsoil was unresolved a year and a half after the devastating flood.

Although government officials insist the dirt in residents' yards is safe, Church Hill Downs, Inc., the owners of New Orleans' fairgrounds, felt it was not safe for its million-dollar thoroughbred horses to race on. (The fairgrounds is the nation's third-oldest track; only

Saratoga and Pimlico have been racing longer.) The owners hauled off soil tainted by Hurricane Katrina's floodwaters and rebuilt a grand-stand roof ripped off by the storm's wind (Martell, 2006). The fairgrounds opened on Thanksgiving Day, 2006. Surely, if tainted soil is not safe for horses, it is not safe for people—especially children who play and dig in the dirt.

The Safe Way Back Home demonstration project serves as a catalyst for a series of activities that will attempt to reclaim the New Orleans East community following the devastation caused by Hurricane Katrina. It is the government's responsibility to provide the resources required to address areas of environmental concern and to assure that the workforce is protected. However, residents are not waiting for the government to ride in on a white horse to rescue them and clean up their neighborhoods.

The DSCEJ/USW coalition received dozens of requests and inquiries from New Orleans East homeowners associations to help clean up their neighborhoods block-by-block. State and federal officials labeled the voluntary "A Safe Way Back Home" neighborhood cleanup efforts as "scaremongering" (Simmons, 2006). Despite barriers and red tape, thousands of Katrina evacuees are slowly moving back into New Orleans' damaged homes or setting up travel trailers in their yards. Homeowners are gutting their houses, treating the mold, fixing roofs and siding, and slowly getting their lives back in order. One of the main questions returning residents have: "Is this place safe?"

Residents are getting mixed signals from government agencies. The Louisiana Department of Environmental Quality announced that there is no unacceptable long-term health risk directly attributable to environmental contamination resulting from the storm. Yet, these same officials warn residents to keep children from playing in bare dirt, and advise them to cover bare dirt with grass, bushes, or 4to 6 inches of lead-free wood chips, mulch, soil, or sand. EPA and LDEQ officials tested soil samples from the neighborhood in December 2005 and claim there was no immediate cause for concern. Although lead, arsenic, and other toxic chemicals turned up in samples, state toxicologists describe the soil in New Orleans as consistent with what they saw before Katrina (Williams, 2006).

In sharp contrast, Natural Resources Defense Council (NRDC) scientists arrived at different conclusions (Solomon and Rotkin-Ellman, 2005). NRDC's analyses of soil and air quality after Hurricane Katrina revealed dangerously high levels of diesel fuel, lead, and other contaminants in Gentilly, Bywater, Orleans Parish, and other New Orleans neighborhoods.

In August 2006, nearly a year after Katrina struck, the federal EPA gave New Orleans and surrounding communities a clean bill of health, while pledging to monitor a handful of toxic hot spots (Brown, 2006). EPA and LDEQ officials concluded that Katrina did not cause any appreciable contamination that was not already there. Although EPA tests confirmed widespread lead in the soil—a prestorm problem in 40 percent of New Orleans—the EPA dismissed residents' calls to address this problem as outside the agency's mission.

In June 2007, the US General Accounting Office (GAO) issued a report criticizing EPA's handling of contamination in post-Katrina New Orleans and the Gulf Coast (GAO, 2007). The GAO found inadequate monitoring for asbestos around demolition and renovation sites. Additionally, the GAO investigation uncovered that "key" information released to the public about environmental contamination was neither timely nor adequate, and in some cases, easily misinterpreted to the public's detriment.

The GAO (2007) also found that the EPA did not state until August 2006 that its 2005 report, which said that the great majority of the data showed that adverse health effects would not be expected from exposure to sediments from previously flooded areas—applied to short-term visits, such as to view damage to homes.

In March 2007, a coalition of community and environmental groups collected over 130 soil samples in Orleans Parish. Testing was conducted by Natural Resources Defense Council (Fields et al., 2007).

Sampling was done at 65 sites in residential neighborhoods where post-Katrina EPA testing had previously shown elevated concentrations of arsenic in soils. Sampling was also done at 15 playgrounds and 19 schools. Six school sites had levels of arsenic in excess of the LDEQ's soil screening value for arsenic. The LDEQ soil screening value of 12 milligrams per kilogram (mg/kg) normally requires additional sampling, further investigation, and a site-specific risk assessment. It is clear that the levels of arsenic in the sediment are unacceptably high for residential neighborhoods.

Toxic FEMA Trailers
Shortly after Katrina, FEMA purchased about 102,000 travel trailers for $2.6 billion or roughly $15,000 each (Spake, 2007). Surprisingly, there were reports of residents becoming ill in these trailers due to the release of potentially dangerous levels of formaldehyde. In fact, formaldehyde is the industrial chemical (found in glues, plastics, building materials, composite wood, plywood panels, and particle board) that was used to manufacture the travel trailers.

In Mississippi, FEMA received 46 complaints of individuals who indicated that they had symptoms of formaldehyde exposure, which include eye, nose, and throat irritation, nausea, skin rashes, sinus infections, depression, mucus membranes, asthma attacks, headaches, insomnia, intestinal problems, memory-impairment, and breathing difficulties. The Sierra Club conducted tests of 31 trailers and found that 29 of them had unsafe levels of formaldehyde. According to the Sierra Club, 83 percent of the trailers tested in Alabama, Louisiana, and Mississippi had formaldehyde levels above the EPA limit of 0.10 parts per million.

Even though FEMA received numerous complaints about toxic trailers, the agency only tested one occupied trailer to determine the levels of formaldehyde in it (Committee on Oversight and Government Reform, 2007). The test confirmed that the levels of formaldehyde were extraordinarily high and presented an immediate health risk to the displaced occupants. The monitored levels were 75 times higher than what the National Institute of Occupational Safety and Health recommend for adult exposure in industrial workplaces. Unfortunately, FEMA did not test any more occupied trailers and released a public statement discounting any risk associated with formaldehyde exposure (Babington, 2007).

FEMA deliberately neglected to investigate any reports of high levels of formaldehyde in trailers so as to bolster FEMA's litigation position just in case individuals affected by their negligence decided to sue them. More than 500 hurricane survivors and evacuees in Louisiana are pursuing legal action against the trailer manufacturers for being exposed to the toxic chemical formaldehyde. Two years after Katrina hit, 46,700 families who lost their homes to Hurricane Katrina lived in government-issued trailers—roughly 33,000 of those families were in Louisiana and about 13,000 were in Mississippi.

In July 2007, FEMA stopped buying and selling disaster relief trailers because of the formaldehyde contamination. FEMA administrator R. David Paulison admitted that the trailers used by displaced Katrina residents were toxic and concluded that the agency should have moved faster in addressing the health concerns of residents (Cruz, 2007). In August 2007, FEMA began moving families out of the toxic trailers and finding them new rental housing. On November 2007, a federal judge in New Orleans ordered FEMA and Paulison, its top administrator, to submit a "detailed plan" for testing the trailers for formaldehyde levels. The Centers for Disease Control and Prevention, the lead agency in developing parameters for testing the travel trailers, was scheduled to test 500 randomly selected travel trailers and mobile homes for the toxin, starting December 21, 2007 (Kim, 2007).

Post-Katrina Levee Protection

An Army Corps of Engineers flood risk report published in 2007 shows a disproportionately large swath of Black New Orleans once again is left vulnerable to future flooding (Army Corps of Engineers Interagency Performance Evaluations Task Force, 2007). After three years and $7 billion of levee repairs, the Army Corps of Engineers has estimated that there is a 1 in 100 annual chance that about one-third of the city will be flooded with as much as six feet of water (Schwartz, 2007).

The mainly African-American parts of New Orleans are still likely to be flooded in a major storm. Increased levee protection correlates closely with race of neighborhoods; black neighborhoods such as the Ninth Ward, Gentilly, and New Orleans East receive little if any increased flood protection. These disparities could lead insurers and investors to think twice about supporting the rebuilding efforts in vulnerable black areas.

The Lakeview area resident can expect 5.5 feet of increased levee protection. This translates into 5.5 feet less water than they received from Katrina. Lakeview is mostly white and affluent; New Orleans East is mostly black and middle class. This same scenario holds true for the mostly black Lower Ninth Ward, Upper Ninth Ward, and Gentilly neighborhoods. There is a racial component to the post-Katrina levee protection. Whether you are rich, poor, or middle class, if you are a black resident of New Orleans, you are less protected and you have received less increased flood protection from the federal government than the more white and affluent community of Lakeview.

THE RACIAL DIVIDE IN DISASTER RELIEF

Using case studies dating back some 70 years, this paper uses New Orleans, the Gulf coast region, and the southern United States as a historical backdrop to answer the research questions of emergency response and race. Clearly, there is a racial divide in the way the US government responds to various types of emergencies in black and white communities. Government response to weather-related (natural disasters), epidemics, industrial accidents, toxic contamination, and bioterrorism threats points to clear preferences given to whites over blacks.

Differential response is linked to "white privilege" that provides preferences for whites while at the same time disadvantaging blacks, and making them more vulnerable to disasters and public health threats. Hurricane Katrina exposed the systematic weakness of the nation's emergency preparedness and homeland security. There can be no homeland security if people do not have homes to go to and if they lose trust in government to respond to an emergency in an effective, fair, and just manner.

What gets cleaned up and where the waste is disposed are key environmental justice and equity issues. Pollution from chemical plants located in populated areas poses a health threat to nearby residents. The plants themselves also pose a threat as possible targets for terrorism.

Although both black and white hurricane survivors find themselves in similar circumstances (displacement from their homes), blacks, because of institutional discrimination, may face different experiences and challenges than whites in rebuilding their lives, homes, businesses, institutions, and communities. Thousands of Gulf coast Louisiana, Mississippi, and Alabama residents also lost their homes in the hurricane. The relief and recovery efforts are not adequately meeting the needs of many African-American survivors in the disaster zone. Many of these same individuals and communities were "invisible" before Katrina struck. At every class level, racial discrimination artificially limits opportunities and choices for African Americans. Unfortunately, this sad fact of American life was not washed away by the floodwaters of Katrina.

Clearly, race skews government response to emergencies, whether natural or man-made, such as weather-related disasters, toxic contamination, public health threats, industrial accidents, and terrorism threats, with whites seeing faster action and better results than blacks and other people of color. No Americans, black or white, rich or poor, young or old, sick or healthy, should have to endure needless suffering from unnatural disasters.

NOTES

* Research contained in this paper was supported by a grant from the Ford Foundation. The views expressed are those of the author and do not reflect those of the foundation.

REFERENCES

Army Corps of Engineers Interagency Performance Evaluations Task Force (IPET). *Risk and Reliability Report* (June 20, 2007) <nolarisk. usace.army.mil>.

Babington, Charles. "FEMA Slow to Test Toxicity of Trailers." *USA Today,* July 19, 2007.

Baker, Earl J. *Hurricane Hugo, Puerto Rico, the Virgin Islands, and Charleston, South Carolina, September 17-22, 1989.* Washington, D.C.: National Academies Press, 1994 <www.nap.edu/books/0309044758/ html/166.html>.

Barnes, Jay. *Florida's Hurricane History.* Chapel Hill: University of North Carolina Press, 1998.

Barry, John M. *Rising Tide: The Great Mississippi Flood of 1927 and How It Changed America.* New York: Simon and Schuster, 1998.

Berger, Eric. "Keeping Its Head Above Water." *Houston Chronicle,* December 1, 2001: A29.

Bourne, Joel K. Jr. "Gone with the Water." *National Geographic* (October 2004): 92.

Brochu, Nicole Sterghos. "Florida's Forgotten Storm: The Hurricane of 1928." *The Sun-Sentinel,* September 14, 2003.

Brown, Matthew. "Final EPA Report Deems N.O. Safe." *The Times Picayune,* August 19, 2006.

Bullard, Robert D. *The Quest for Environmental Justice: Human Rights and the Politics of Pollution.* San Francisco: Sierra Club Books, 2005.

Bullard, Robert D., and Glenn S. Johnson. *Just Transportation: Dismantling Race and Class Barriers to Mobility.* Gabriola Island, B.C.: New Society Publishers, 1997.

Burdeau, Cain. "New Orleans Area Becoming a Dumping Ground," *Associated Press,* October 31, 2005. Cannon, Terry, Ian Davis, Piers Blaikie, Ben Wisner, eds. *At Risk: Natural Hazards, People's Vulnerability, and Disasters.* New York: Routledge, 2004.

City of New Orleans. *City of New Orleans Comprehensive Emergency Management Plan.* City of New Orleans, 2005. Available at <www.cityof no.com>.

Cruz, Gilbert. 2007. "Grilling FEMA Over Its Toxic Trailers." Time. com. July 19, 2007 <http://www.time.com/time/nation/article/0,8599,1645312,00.html>.

Dart, Bob. "Junk Cars, Boats Slow Recovery in Big Easy." *The Atlanta Journal-Constitution,* July 5, 2006:A1.

Department of Homeland Security (DHS). *National Plan Review, Phase 2 Report.* Washington, D.C.: DHS, 16 June 2006 <www.emforum.org/news/06061601.htm>.

Dyson, Michael Eric. *Come Hell or High Water: Hurricane Katrina and the Color of Disaster.* New York: Basic Books, 2006.

Eaton, Leslie. "A New Landfill in New Orleans Sets Off a Battle." *The New York Times,* May 8, 2006:A1.

Eggler, Bruce. "RTA Back on Track Slowly, Surely." *The Times Picayune,* October 14, 2005: B1.

Elliston, Jon. "Disaster in the Making." *The Orlando Weekly,* October 21, 2004.

Estes, Carol. "Second Chance for Black Farmers." *Yes! Magazine* (Summer 2001).

Fields, Leslie, Albert Huang, Gina Solomon, Miriam Rotkin-Ellman, and Patirce Simms, *Katrina's Wake: Arsenic-Laced Schools and Playgrounds Put New Orleans Children at Risk.* New York: NRDC, August 2007.

Federal Emergency Management Agency (FEMA). "Hurricane Pam Exercise Concludes." Press Release. July 23, 2004 <www.fema.gov/news/newsrelease.fema?id=13051>.

Finch, Susan. "Ag Street Landfill Case Gets Ruling: City Ordered to Pay Residents of Toxic Site." *The Times-Picayune,* January 27, 2006: A1.

Gabe, Thomas, Gene Falk, Maggie McCarthy, and Virginia W. Mason. *Hurricane Katrina: Social-Demographic Characteristics of Impacted Areas.* Congressional Research Service. Report no. RL33141. Washington, D.C.: Congressional Research Service, November 2005.

General Accounting Office. *Hurricane Katrina: EPA's Current and Future Environmental Protection Efforts Could Be Enhanced by Addressing Issues* and Challenges Faced on the Gulf Coast. Washington, D.C.: GAO Report to Congressional Committees, June 2007.

Harrison, Eric. "Legacy of Racism Dams Up Post-Flood Effort in Georgia." The Los Angeles Times, August 26, 1994.

Hurston, Zora Neal. Their Eyes Were Watching God. New York: Harper Perennial Classics, 1998.

Jackson, Stephen. "Un/natural Disasters, Here and There." Understanding Katrina: Perspectives from the Social Sciences. Social Science Research Council <http://understandingkatrina.ssrc.org/Jackson/>.

Kaniasty, K., and F. H. Norris. "In Search of Altruistic Community: Patterns of Social Support Mobilization Following Hurricane Hugo." American Journal of Community Psychology 4 (August 23, 1995): 447-477.

Kim, Eun Kyung. "Air Testing in FEMA Trailers Begins Next Week." USA Today, December 13, 2007.

Kleinberg, Eliot. Black Cloud: The Deadly Hurricane of 1928. New York: Carroll and Graf Publishers, 2003.

Klinkenberg, Jeff. "A Storm of Memories." The St. Petersburg Times, July 12, 1992: 1F.

Kromm, Chris, and Sue Sturgis. Blueprint for Gulf Renewal: The Katrina Crisis and a Community Agenda for Action. Durham, N.C.: Institute for Southern Studies, August/September 2007.

Liu, Amy, and Allison Plyer. The New Orleans Index: A Review of Key Indicators of Recovery Two Years after Katrina. Washington, D.C.: Brookings Institution and Greater New Orleans Community Data Center, August 2007.

Litman, Todd. Lesson from Katrina and Rita: What Major Disasters Can Teach Transportation Planners. Victoria, B.C.: Victoria Transport Policy Institute, September 30, 2005.

LOCD. Disaster Recover Unit <http://www.doa.louisiana.gov/cdbg/DRhousing.htm>.

Lyttle, Alicia. "Agricultural Street Landfill Environmental Justice Case Study." University of Michigan School of Natural Resource and

Environment <www.umich.edu/~, Desnre492/Jones/agstreet.htm>.

Luther, Linda. *Disaster Debris Removal after Hurricane Katrina: Status and Associated Issues.* Washington, D.C.: Congressional Research Service, June 16, 2006.

Martell, Brett. "Horse Racing Returns to New Orleans." *Associated Press,* November 23, 2006.

McKinnon, Jesse. *The Black Population: Census 2000 Brief.* Washington, D.C.: Department of Commerce, August 2001.

Mittal, Anuradha, and Joan Powell. "The Last Plantation." *Food First* (Winter 2000) <http://www.foodfirst.org/pubs/backgrdrs/2000/w00v6n1.html>.

Moran, Kate. "Public Transit on Agenda at Joint N.O., Jeff Session." *The Times Picayune,* November 6, 2006.

"The Mother of All Toxic Cleanups." *Business Week* (September 26, 2005).

Nossiter, Adam. "Thousands of Demolitions Are Likely in New Orleans." *The New York Times* October 2, 2005.

O'Driscoll, Patrick. "Cleanup Crews Tackle Katrina's Nasty Leftovers." *USA Today,* December 12, 2005.

Pastor, Manuel, Robert D. Bullard, James K. Boyce, Alice Fothergill, Rachel Morello-Frosch, and Beverly Wright. *In the Wake of the Storm: Environment, Disaster, and Race After Katrina.* New York: Russell Sage Foundation, May 2006.

Peacock, Walter Gillis, Betty Hearn Morrow, and Hugh Gladwin. *Hurricane Andrew: Ethnicity, Gender, and the Sociology of Disasters.* Miami: Florida International University, Laboratory for Social and Behavioral Research, 1992.

Pittman, Craig. "Storm's Howl Fills The Ears of Survivors." *St. Petersburg Times* August 18, 2002.

Remnick, David. "High Water: How Presidents and Citizens React to Disaster." *The New Yorker* (October 3, 2005).

Riccardi, Nicholas. "Many of Louisiana Dead Over 60." *The Atlanta Journal-Constitution,* November 6, 2005: A6.

Russell, Gordon. "Landfill Reopening is Raising New Stink," *The Times_Picayune,* November 21, 2005.

————. "Chef Menteur Landfill Testing Called a Farce: Critics Say Debris Proposal 'Would Be a Useless Waste of Time.'" *The Times-Picayune,* May 29, 2006.

Sanchez, Thomas W. Rick Stolz, and Jacinta S. Ma. *Moving to Equity: Addressing Inequitable Effects of Transportation Policies on Minorities.* Cambridge: The Civil Rights Project, Harvard University, June 2003.

Schwartz, John. "Army Corps Details Flood Risks Facing New Orleans." *The New York Times,* June 20, 2007.

Simmons, Ann S. "New Orleans Activists Starting from the Ground Up." *The Los Angeles Times,* March 24, 2006.

Solomon, Gina M., and Miriam Rotkin-Ellman. *Contaminants in New Orleans Sediments: An Analysis of EPA Data.* New York: NRDC, February 2006.

Solow, Barbara. "Cracks in the System." *The Independent Weekly,* September 8, 2004 <indyweek.com/durham/2004-09-08/cover.html>.

Spake, Amanda. "Dying for a Home: Toxic Trailers are Making Katrina Refugees Ill." *The Nation* (February 15, 2007).

State of Louisiana. *Southeast Louisiana Hurricane Evacuation and Sheltering Plan.* Baton Rouge: State of Louisiana, 2000 <www.ohsep.louisiana.gov/plans/EOPSupplementala.pdf>.

Steinberg, Ted. *Acts of God: The Unnatural History of Natural Disasters in America.* New York: Oxford University Press, 2003.

Tanneeru, Manav. "It's Official: 2005 Hurricanes Blew Records Away." CNN.com. December 30, 2005 <www.cnn.com/2005/WEATHER/12/19/hurricane.season.ender/>.

Tibbetts, John. "Louisiana's Wetlands: A Lesson in Nature Appreciation." *Environmental Health Perspective* 114 (January 2006): A40-A43.

U.S. House of Representatives, Committee on Oversight and Government Reform. "Committee Probes FEMA's Response to Reports of Toxic Trailers." July 19, 2007.

Williams, Leslie. "Groups Warn About Arsenic in Soil." *The Times Picayune,* March 24, 2006.

Wing, Steve, Stephanie Freedman, and Lawrence Band. "The Potential of Flooding on Confined Animal Feeding Operations in Eastern North Carolina." *Environmental Health Perspective* 110 (April 2002).

Worldwatch Institute. "Fact Sheet: The Impacts of Weather and Climate Change." September 23, 2003 <www.worldwatch.org/press/news/2003/09/15/>.

Wright, Beverly. "A Safe Way Back Home." Deep South Center for Environmental Justice, Dillard University, March 29, 2007 <www.dscej.org/asafewayhome.htm>.

Irwin Redlener
Population Vulnerabilities, Preconditions, and the Consequences of Disasters

HAVING SPENT MORE THAN THREE DECADES WORKING ON THE FRONT lines of public health, primarily providing direct medical care or developing programs for medically underserved children in rural and urban environments in the United States, I came to the field of disaster preparedness and response sporadically and hesitantly. After leading international disaster response teams and deploying mobile medical units in response to US disasters, my familiarity with respect to these challenges was purely programmatic and technical. What has been surprising and, to a large extent, disconcerting, has been an appreciation developed since 2001 of the complexity and inadequacy of societal preparation for, mitigation of, and recovery from very large-scale disasters.

In a perfect illustration of our nation's proclivity for postevent crisis response and our resistance to longer-term planning and system investment, the nation put a rush order on developing a massive bureaucracy designed to fast track new systems for preventing and responding to terrorism and large scale natural disasters. FEMA and many other agencies were incorporated into the new Department of Homeland Security, billions of dollars were appropriated and, seemingly, a substantial focus on disaster prevention and management was emerging in the aftermath of the attacks on the World Trade Center in New York City.

What actually materialized, however, in the frantic push to create new systems, has, so far, failed to provide credible, cost-effective, evidence-based systems of disaster preparedness and response. Overall, I suspect that the government efforts spurred on by the attacks of 9/11 represent not only an extraordinary level of spending, but also a lack of accountability that is virtually unprecedented in recent US history.

In fact, after watching—and working among—the efforts to respond effectively to the disasters precipitated by Hurricanes Katrina and Rita, and the subsequent flooding of New Orleans, it is clear that much needs to be done in all aspects of this field. But perhaps no challenge is more pressing than coming to grips with the realities facing families whose "disaster risk profile" is exacerbated by vulnerabilities that include long-term income fragility, social marginalization, or chronic illness.

PRECONDITIONS AND PUBLIC HEALTH

Questions around preconditions and disaster consequence vulnerabilities among affected populations may be seen from the broad perspectives of public health. And in a certain sense, "all roads lead to public health implications." Fragile buildings and infrastructure, poor roads, insufficient transportation systems, reduced access to clean water and food, or limited availability of good medical care are among the preconditions that, even prior to a disaster, create ongoing public health consequences. When disaster affects such populations, however, the impact is far greater and the response and recovery more complex than is the case for populations with greater resources. Any number of examples can effectively illustrate this point. Resource-rich communities have the ability and capacity to construct buildings that are relatively earthquake resistant, including advanced materials and construction strategies such as diagonally trussed skeletons. Such buildings may sustain much higher earthquake force levels than less sophisticated construction in developing countries. An example of the latter was the 1976 earthquake that struck Guatemala at a Richter force of 7.6, killing as many as 25,000 people, injuring 80,000 and leaving nearly 1.5 million homeless. Buildings made from simple stone and adobe simply could not withstand a quake that might have shaken—but not destroyed—buildings constructed with earthquake-resistant materials and designs.

Similar demonstrations of the relationships between preconditions and disaster consequences have been consistently seen after the recent earthquakes in Pakistan and China, the cyclone that struck Myanmar (Burma), and numerous other catastrophic events. The formula remains the same: preconditions related to a wide range of vulnerabilities affect morbidity, mortality, and marginalization of populations affected by disasters.

Obviously, the same formula is applicable to disparate conditions in the United States, particularly when looking at resource-rich versus resource-poor communities. Conditions in economically disadvantaged rural communities, for instance, can present an array of precondition-related vulnerabilities highly reminiscent of circumstances seen in developing countries. Working in rural Arkansas some years ago, our medical teams confronted the consequences of inordinately high rates of fires in houses that were poorly constructed wood-frame dwellings, without central heating. Families would use portable wood or kerosene burning stoves to provide warmth. Such heaters were subject to falling over, flying embers, toxic fumes, and other problems that could lead to medical conditions like asthma and bronchitis or actually start fires that, in turn, would lead to high rates of burn and smoke injuries among residents.

Other preconditions that regularly lead to increased disaster vulnerability may be seen in disadvantaged communities. One particularly important factor is the capacity to move people or rescuers in the event of a major disaster. The evacuation of a large population being threatened by an impending hurricane, for instance, presents special challenges when the communities in question have limited resources. Citizens without access to private vehicles would be entirely dependent on public transportation systems. If the latter systems are not available, the possibility of timely, effective evacuations becomes considerably more difficult so that communities are at far greater risk. Similarly, the effective movement of responders in a disaster-affected area is dependent on access via roads and other modalities of rapid movement such as boats and aircraft. Interestingly, national surveys conducted by the Marist Institute for the National Center for Disaster Preparedness at Columbia University's Mailman School of Public Health and the Children's Health Fund show that people generally expect help to arrive promptly, no matter what the conditions. The 2007 survey showed that 33 percent of individuals expect help to arrive within one hour of a call to "911"; approximately two-thirds expected a response within two or three hours.

The impediments to providing routine but essential services to disadvantaged individuals suggest challenges that become greatly magnified in a major disaster scenario. When I worked as a physician in rural Arkansas, making house calls to treat bedridden patients was routine. After clinic hours, aides would accompany physicians to the homes of patients who needed care, but were unable to get to the office in town. When the weather was good and the roads were dry, getting to the patient was not a problem. But during the rainy season, the unpaved, ungraveled country roads would turn to mud. Our pick-up truck or clinic car simply could not make it through; so patients who may have truly needed medical care were unable to get these and other essential services. This is precisely what happens in any poor community—domestically or internationally—and is a situation than can paralyze response efforts following a major catastrophe.

During the 1985 sub-Saharan drought, which led to one of the world's deadliest famines, movement of individuals to relief centers and supplies to affected parts of the region were substantially affected by road and transportation challenges—sometimes in ways that were unanticipated or counterintuitive. For instance, prolonged drought led to extreme drying of riverbeds that, in turn, lost the capacity to absorb water. In the event of a flash rainfall, rivers would quickly and transiently fill, making crossing virtually impossible.

Other times, the terrain and the weather are not the problems; vehicles are. Economically disadvantaged families who own cars are more likely to have older models in various states of disrepair and regularly not working. If there are not alternative forms of transportation, such vehicles may not be available for pre-disaster evacuation or even for getting to needed medical care.

HURRICANE KATRINA AND THE FLOODING OF NEW ORLEANS

In considering the notion of disaster consequences with respect to Hurricane Katrina and the flooding of New Orleans in 2005, it is useful to put the scenario in some perspective. Thirteen years earlier, Hurricane Andrew struck the south Florida communities near Homestead as a true category 5 storm with an impact zone of approximately 300 square miles. The devastation was ferocious (some $27 billion of damage, but less than 100 fatalities). In contrast, Hurricanes Katrina and Rita never reached a category 5 at landfall, but caused well over $100 billion in damages, some 2,000 fatalities, and an impact area of more than 93,000 miles. While the "return to normal" following the 1992 disaster took considerable effort, much of it was focused on structural rebuilding.

In contrast, the gulf areas affected by Katrina were still struggling with recovery three years after the storm. Rebuilding of infrastructure was clearly important, but finding appropriate shelter, permanent housing, and community-based services for displaced populations has become a nearly intractable challenge. Over time, families and individuals with resources found their way to new neighborhoods and rebuilt their connections to schools, health care, and employment. But those who had limited resources prior to the disaster fare far worse, continuing to struggle with uncertainty and growing problems around health, mental health, and identification of employment opportunities.

So, what do we know about the preconditions that affected disaster vulnerability among Katrina survivors? The two states most affected, Louisiana and Mississippi, are routinely cited as having the highest child poverty rates in the United States. Approximately 20 percent of Louisiana's children lived in families with annual incomes below $10,000. Schools in both states are also far below national standards and in New Orleans, most public secondary schools are on state watch lists. Although public transportation systems were highly limited in hard-hit areas prior to the storms, many people in the poorest communities did not own private vehicles. Access to health care in the two states was also problematic with few children having regular access to a primary care medical home.

With destructive, high-powered winds smashing the coastal communities of the gulf states and unprecedented flooding of New Orleans, many health care facilities, including doctors' offices, clinics, and hospitals, were affected. Communities already considered "medically underserved" prior to the disaster became true crisis zones as the demand for medical services soared, while working health care facilities became scarce. An estimated 4,000 physicians left the region from New Orleans alone. Major teaching hospitals, like Tulane Medical Center and Charity Hospital of Louisiana State University, were knocked out of service. This meant that essential medical services, particularly those that focused on subspecialty care, disappeared, leaving patients with unusual or serious conditions in even more precarious states. Medical records were lost, along with the doctors and nurses. The existence of a serious medical or mental health condition prior to the storm made people far more vulnerable to the disaster and its aftermath.

And other conditions and situations also led to increased vulnerability. Some 20 to 25 percent of people in New Orleans either had significant disabilities prior to the storm or were taking care of people with such challenges. Evacuation, sheltering, getting needed caretakers, or assuring a reasonable supply of prescription medications had become exceedingly difficult for people with chronic needs. Similarly, there were great concerns about the frail elderly who were residents of nursing facilities. Impossible to evacuate, these individuals remained in extreme danger throughout.

In another difficult scenario, approximately 60 to 70 children with cancer found themselves without access to their treating oncologists, without their medications, and unable to obtain medical records. Many of these children ended up transported to Tennessee for treatment by specialists who had no idea what medications these patients were on or where they were in the scheduled protocol time line. This was yet another instance of preexisting medical conditions substantially increasing vulnerability for individuals during and after a major disaster.

RECOVERY AS AN AFTERTHOUGHT

The initial response by government to the widespread disaster in the gulf was a demonstration of mass disorganization and incompetence. Images of people waiting for assistance on the rooftops of submerged houses and countless stories of people stranded and poorly treated in mass congregate shelters were seen virtually immediately around the world. There was simply no hiding from the reality of government failure in the initial response to a major natural catastrophe.

The prolonged recovery from the Katrina disaster is another story. While the failures are rampant and profound, the stories are not on the front pages of newspapers. Yet the case could be made that recovery inadequacies are far more grave than the failures of the initial response. Current recovery problems include prolonged stays for displaced persons in inadequate temporary shelters, exposure to formaldehyde in the trailers, poor or no access to health and mental health services, poor access to schools for children, and lack of employment opportunities for their parents. Tangled bureaucracies of state and federal government, nongovernmental organizations, and special commissions have impeded the development of rapidly implementable plans needed to care for nearly 20,000 families still living in temporary shelters. But the public remains generally unaware of what is happening in the gulf. Here again, the fact is that the remaining displaced families and individuals are poor and predominantly nonwhite.

In effect, we saw conditions in the gulf that amounted to the proverbial "perfect storm": a major natural disaster striking a highly vulnerable population when government disaster response capacity was ill-prepared to provide effective, coordinated services.

INVESTMENT IS KEY

It is abundantly clear that the public health impact of large-scale disasters is dependent on the degree to which the population affected is at risk or vulnerable prior to the catastrophic event. When health, nutrition, and economic status are suboptimal and when general community conditions lack a basic level of support, the public health consequences of any major disaster are substantially exacerbated. That is why investing in community support systems, income stability, and access to appropriate services should be part of effective and comprehensive disaster planning.

Joseph W. Westphal
The Politics of Infrastructure

NO RECENT NATURAL DISASTER SINCE PERHAPS THE GREAT MISSISSIPPI floods of 1927 and 1993 has had such an immense impact on our national pride and confidence as did Katrina. The reason was evident from the time the storm began to form in the Gulf of Mexico and even after it hit land: our government at all levels was dazed and confused. The infrastructure and organizational structures operating for decades and costing billions of dollars were overwhelmed. This was a disaster of great proportions, taking place in one of the poorest communities in our country and affecting some of the most important economic structures in the land—our largest port, a huge network of oil and gas pipeline and production facilities, offshore drilling, shipbuilding, and some of our largest fisheries, to just cite a few examples. Much has been written and debated about this event and its effects on both the local area and the nation, and this paper is not intended to replicate that work. The focus here is on the process used to support and invest in the nation's water resources infrastructure. I will describe changes that have come about in recent years and why this process may in fact put people and communities at greater risk.

Our vulnerability to such disasters is seen through many lenses. It is about people and relationships but also about places and nature. It is about how we live and the structures we build to protect us, manage our commerce, enhance sustainability, and give pleasure to our lives. In Louisiana and the Mississippi River watershed, it is about levees, channels, port facilities, housing, and flood plain management. Indeed, a significant part of our nation's infrastructure revolves around water, so the effects of hurricanes and floods are significant and often catastrophic for people and governments alike. This paper examines the politics of water resources infrastructure in order to better understand how decision-making processes may create vulnerabilities that potentiate disasters.

The matter of politics being at the center of decisions and actions regarding a nation's infrastructure is well understood and requires little or no verification. A long-standing and popular definition given to us by Harold Lasswell is that politics is about "who gets what, when and how," and when it comes to deciding about building infrastructure, this concept is at the heart of every decision. Therefore, this paper is not about proving politics is integral to infrastructure development, but rather identifying those factors that enhance the vulnerabilities of the process, allowing for poor priority-setting and unnecessary and sometimes ineffective infrastructure policy and projects. However, there are things that we can be doing to address many of the issues behind the conditions that make us vulnerable to disasters, conditions that for future generations are simply unacceptable.

This paper will focus on three key steps in current water infrastructure project development: planning, funding mechanisms, and decision making. The hypothesis is that all three contribute to infrastructure development that can accentuate risk and vulnerability for communities around the country. For these purposes, "planning" is a study process to determine if a project is necessary, feasible, and a good investment by the nation. "Funding mechanisms" refers to who pays, how much, and when. The nation has infrastructure that requires financial resources for continued operation, maintenance, and modernization. These priorities clash with both the need for new infrastructure and all the political and policy variables that abound. Finally, the synthesis of all this is a decision-making process that is often fragmented and unstable with no clear set of priorities and standards.

The underlying assumption is that these three steps all work to enhance a political rationale at some cost to sound forecasting, better priority setting and good science and engineering. In addition, we must recognize the framework of government within which these activities take place. First, we operate as a federal system, which makes local and state governments the largest lobby in Washington. Second, decentralization of power in Congress gives every community great influence over distribution of resources to fund local projects. Third, special interests can harness that power to gain access and support while presidents have a difficult time controlling this widespread desire for economic development.

To better understand how water resources infrastructure has been developed, we must examine the Civil Works responsibility of the U.S. Army Corps of Engineers (Corps). The Civil Works program is essentially responsible for the nation's water development through such areas as flood control, recreation, navigation, wetlands protection, and environmental restoration. One important factor of this program is that it is housed in the Department of the Army and led by a combination of military and civilian leaders, although its workforce of approximately 35,000 civilian employees has only about 650 military members.

This is important because the Corps is a large agency with a dual mission that should be an asset, but whose role is little understood by the public and government alike. The Corps's mission to provide support during war can be enhanced by the experience it gains in its civil duties in peacetime. Experience, research and development, and personnel training are only some of the factors that can build a trained and ready support group for combat. The Corps should be an even greater asset in peacekeeping. All this is, of course, subject to politics, which on the civil side has to do with the congressional appetite for "projects." On the executive side it has more to do with balancing national priorities and is often caught in ideology and partisan battles.

THE HISTORICAL CONTEXT

The United States does not have a single public works agency. Like most aspects of government action, regulation, and policy, infrastructure development is spread across many departments and agencies. Without getting into the details of government jurisdiction and authority, the Department of Transportation has jurisdiction over highways, mass transit, and bridges; the U.S. Army Corps of Engineers over dams, hydropower, and flood control nationwide (the Department of the Interior has some of the same responsibilities west of the Mississippi River). The Department of Energy oversees nuclear waste disposal, hydropower, and energy plants. These agencies along with the Environmental Protection Agency (EPA) and the Departments of Commerce, Defense, Agriculture, and others share environmental regulatory, clean-up, and enhancement responsibilities, and in many cases have joint or sequential authorities that increase confusion, inaction, and enhance political influence on policy decisions.

The authority of the Army that allowed it to oversee water infrastructure came from Congress during the nineteenth century. As early as 1824, Congress was mandating that Army engineers work on plans to move traffic on canals and rivers. In the mid-1800s, Congress asked the Army and its Corps of Engineers to develop a plan to control flooding on the Mississippi River. In 1899, Congress passed the River and Harbors Act, giving the Corps its first regulatory authority. It required the Corps to be the agency to monitor and regulate dumping of debris and dredged material into waters used for navigation. Many others followed this act during the twentieth century, expanding the Corps's planning, construction, and regulatory authority.

With this expansion came the significant growth of water projects across the nation, all aimed at stimulating growth and economic development. Coming at the heels of this expansion were significant new laws passed in the 1970s that focused on environmental protection. The National Environmental Policy Act of 1969 (NEPA), the Federal Water Pollution Control Act of 1972 (better known as the Clean Water Act), the Endangered Species Act of 1973, and the creation of the Environmental Protection Agency in 1970 all had an immediate impact on the Corps's planning and construction agenda. These laws now required interagency coordination and collaboration, and gave the Corps further regulatory authority.

Another important development affecting the Corps's planning construction work came in the late 1970s and the '80s. Increased concern for environmental protection, along with federal budget constraints during the Carter and Reagan administrations, worked to reduce both the number of new projects and funding. During those two decades some important developments helped shape the current issues surrounding the Corps infrastructure planning and construction agenda. This era was marked by significant change in the planning process as well as in funding mechanisms, although the question persists whether, in the long run, the decision-making system was in fact improved.

THE PLANNING PROCESS

In 1965, Congress passed the Water Resources Planning Act, which created the Water Resources Council as an interagency group made of several cabinet departments. The Department of the Interior was its convener and lead agency; other members of the council were the Departments of Agriculture, Transportation, Energy, Commerce, Housing and Urban Development, and the Army Corps of Engineers. The EPA, which did not exist at that time, was added to the council in 1970.

The idea behind the council was to have a group that would think broadly about national infrastructure and coordinate efforts among the various federal agencies. In 1973, the council issued the Principals and Standards for Planning Water and Related Land Resources (P&S), under which projects had to meet four major objectives. These were national economic development, environmental quality, regional economic development, and other social effects. The P&S required an agency to look at alternatives and evaluate them based on both national economic development and environmental quality (National Research Council. 1999). Simply put, before you build a project you have to look at alternatives to that project, you have to measure the cost-benefits of those different alternatives, and you have to look at environmental impacts.

In 1983, when Ronald Reagan's administration included James Watt as secretary of the interior and chairman of the Water Resources

Council, a new methodology was issued that dramatically changed the existing policy for project planning. The Economic and Environmental Principles and Guidelines for Water and Related Land Resources (P&G) replaced the P&S. The P&G also specified the four objectives of the P&S, but it defined them as ways to account for "significant effects of a plan on the human environment" and stated that NED was the only alternative required:

> The planning process leads to the identification of alternative plans that could be recommended or selected. The culmination of the planning process is the selection of the recommended plan or the decision to take no action. . . . The alternative plan with the greatest net economic benefit consistent with protecting the Nation's environment (NED plan) is to be selected (Water Resources Council, 1983).

A more significant difference between the P&S and the P&G was the fact that the latter were in fact "guidelines" and were not seen as requirements, as in the case of the P&S. Under the P&G the Corps would undertake the following steps in their planning process:

▸ Specify problems and opportunities
▸ Inventory and forecast conditions
▸ Formulate alternative plans
▸ Evaluate effects of alternative plans
▸ Compare alternative plans
▸ Select recommended plan

This process involves two important phases, leading to what is called the "chief's report," a formal request from the Corps for approval by the secretary of the Army and inclusion in the formal authorization and appropriations request to Congress. The first phase is called the reconnaissance level, funded by federal funds, to determine if the proposed project has merit and can be studied and designed. The Corps would produce a Project Study Plan (PSP) and then a Feasibility Cost-Sharing Plan (FCSA). The latter came as a result of a significant policy change during the Reagan administration. Concerned with reducing government spending and what the administration defined as "pork," Reagan and Congress agreed to require cost sharing for all projects. The FCSA report would provide the cost-sharing formula and outline the cost and study process. Much of this would be negotiated with the local sponsor, a city, county, state or non-governmental organization that would have to raise approximately 50 percent of the cost of the project. After this process was completed, the Corps would enter a Feasibility Phase, which requires an examination of alternative plans to meet the national economic development (NED) formula. Once terms are agreed to the project goes to pre-construction engineering and design, culminating in the report of the Chief of Engineers that—with approval of the assistant secretary of the Army for civil works—can be forwarded to Congress for authorization and appropriations.

FINANCING WATER PROJECTS

While the processes have made sense and there are mechanisms for taking projects offline, the sheer number of projects around the country and their increasing costs have produced significant struggles between the president and Congress. From President Jimmy Carter to President George W. Bush, every administration has attempted to reduce spending on civil works by producing "hit lists" and simply refusing to support authorizations and appropriations.

In the 1960s Congress decided to get more sophisticated in how it dealt with constituency matters, Realizing that continuous attention to district and state issues and bringing home more redistributed tax dollars could increase reelection margins and make them virtually unbeatable as incumbents, Congress began to increase significantly its own budget for staffing and analytical support. Besides helping with social security issues, or supporting legislation that positively impact each member's state and region, water resource development became an ever more significant electoral resource. From flood control projects to port development, from locks and dams to hydropower, the Corps became an instrument of the Congress for meeting the needs of the states.

The insatiable appetite for taking credit for infrastructure continued to grow as members of Congress became more sophisticated in elections and politics. As the number of projects grew, the Corps found itself having to spend more time on managing all the projects in the works and less time on planning and looking at how best to foresee the needs of the future. In addition, cost sharing created its own problems. One was the fact that cost sharing resulted in favoring those communities that had an ability to pay, so naturally those communities that could afford to raise funds to match the federal outlay got their projects but poor communities continued to struggle. While exceptions have been made, their ability to develop has been stymied.

A second problem resulting from cost sharing has been the forging of partnerships between the local sponsor and the Corps. If each is paying half the cost and both have a significant say in how the project is designed and built, then it is more a partnership than simply a federal project. Why is this a problem? The Corps refers to those sharing in the projects as "partners" or sometimes as "clients." It is common to treat a partner as an equal, and we all know the old saying, "the customer is always right." This relationship makes it very difficult for the Corps not to support the partnership or to modify a project it sees as wasteful or environmentally unsustainable.

There will never be enough money to fund all of the state's infrastructure needs adequately. What this means is that in the desire to bring new projects online, existing projects get less money and consequent delays make the projects even more expensive. This creates a backlog of projects that may reach upward of $50 billion today. Many of these projects were begun decades ago and may no longer be justified or meet current environmental goals. The backlog of work has strained the planning function and placed emphasis on what the Corps calls "project management." The goal is to complete projects and manage a huge portfolio that equally underfunds modernization as well as operations and maintenance.

DECISION MAKING

The emphasis on managing projects along with changes in the P&G have resulted in a decision process that is decentralized and unable to set national priorities and goals. While there have been many studies decrying the poor state of our nation's infrastructure, there remains no overarching plan to address this as a mater of national priority.

Katrina may be the best example of how little we learn from history as well as how rigid our decision making has become. From the early nineteenth century, when the Corps pursued the policy of building levees as opposed to letting the river run its natural course, we have seen numerous floods and hurricanes devastate communities along the Gulf coast. The overwhelming manipulation of the river and coast have helped to erode natural barriers to hurricanes and resulted in significant impacts on communities and the environment. The Corps is often seen as the architect of projects when in fact projects are often hatched by local entities, industry, and support from members of Congress. The Corps then finds itself in the middle of a very intense balancing act between the administration it serves under and the local communities that want a greater share of the economic pie. As pressures on construction and project management due to an ever-increasing workload have reduced the Corps's planning capability, the Corps finds itself supporting projects with fewer resources and less overall support.

The tools that the Corps operated with prior to the adoption of the Principles and Guidelines of the Reagan administration gave it the ability to question unsupported or simply bad projects and to use planning to modify projects and plans to meet stricter standards. Recent criticism of the Corps, much of it coming from Congress, has focused on what critics believe is a failed study process, poor design alternatives and lack of oversight. All of these had been its strengths, yet in today's political environment and the significantly increased workload, those tools have largely eroded.

Our most significant vulnerability grows out of these issues with planning and their effects on financing and decision making. The process has little ability to correct itself, and therefore the mistakes of past are to be a part of our future. While it would make sense to rebuild New Orleans in ways to avoid a repetition of the destruction caused by Katrina, the exact opposite is happening. Priorities and resources are flowing to new public works in the very places where Katrina showed us our greatest vulnerability.

CONCLUSIONS

Among the most important areas of work for the Corps are flood control and watershed management, which includes environmental restoration and development. The Corps has many other responsibilities but these two are among its most difficult, political, and costly. One could fill a room with reports, articles, studies, and books describing best practices, outlining policy alternatives, suggesting solutions, and providing technical and scientific knowledge. Yet, despite all that we know about the business and engineering of infrastructure and all the lessons learned from the many disasters, Katrina showed significant failures in both technical and operational areas.

As the nation faces an aging infrastructure where resources for maintenance and modernization have been relatively limited, the policy process must be reexamined and discipline must be inserted into financing and decision processes. At the macro level, a comprehensive examination of national priorities and how states may be assisted in strengthening their capacities for improving infrastructure should be undertaken immediately. This could be accomplished by convening a presidential task force that is organized by the executive with the Congress. Setting funding priorities and reforming the process would be the primary goals of the task force.

Such a task force should consider a number of changes to the operational and financial frameworks under which the Corps functions. The Corps is currently completely dependent on project money to sustain its workforce and maintain its expertise and capacity. This means that the cost to projects is high, and with cost sharing the Corps has fewer resources for planning and environmental assessments. This also means projects are delayed and reduced in scope. One solution is to fund the base operational requirements of the Corps through appropriations made directly to the agency. This would ensure that such functions as planning and research are not compromised. Some may argue that this would give Congress greater incentives to initiate more projects. However, by developing a budget that has the federal government funding base operations, the pressure on the federal portion should limit that incentive.

The Corps should also be asked to review the process it had under the Principles and Standards and find the best and most sustainable practices to incorporate into a revision of the Principles and Guidelines. Along with reforms to cost sharing, this endeavor should have as its goal to incorporate more consistent watershed approaches to planning and find ways to accelerate study process to bring more projects to a quicker completion.

The Congress and the president should also consider some agreement on completing or deleting projects that make up the significant backlog of work. This action would allow for new projects to be considered that would face a shorter completion time frame than projects face today.

These are but a few recommendations among many that have been made by such distinguished organizations such as the National Academy of Sciences and the National Research Council. They are aimed at strengthening the ability of the agency to say no to projects that are environmentally unsustainable, not economically feasible and lacking in widespread support. They will not eliminate or necessarily reduce the interest in projects often seen as politically motivated nor will they place great discipline on financing such projects, but they should introduce greater rationality into the process.

REFERENCES

National Research Council. *New Directions in Water Resources.* Washington, D.C.: National Academy Press, 1999.

Water Resources Council. *Economic and Environmental Principles and*

Guidelines for Water and Related Land Resources Implementation Studies. Washington, D.C.: Government Printing Office, 1983.

Part III
Keynote Address

Nicholas Scoppetta
Disaster Planning and Preparedness: A Human Story

IN DECEMBER 2001, MAYOR-ELECT MICHAEL BLOOMBERG ASKED ME
TO become the city's thirty-first fire commissioner. I had already
announced that I would leave the Administration for Children's
Services, where I had been commissioner for six years, and was planning on leaving government. But, like all New Yorkers, I had watched in
horror as events unfolded on September 11, 2001, and I knew that the
New York City Fire Department (FDNY) was the hardest hit of all city
agencies in the attacks. Being asked to help rebuild this storied New
York institution was an honor, and saying yes was my duty.

Disaster preparedness is at the forefront of the FDNY's mission,
as it is for first responders in cities and towns across the country. Even
just a passing awareness of current events makes it clear why disaster
preparedness is so important. At the time this conference was held,
California was still reeling from some of the worst fires in its history.
New Orleans had yet to be rebuilt. And for many people in New York,
the memory of 9-11, our worst disaster, is still painfully fresh.

The New York City Fire Department has been on the ground in
each of those disasters. In addition, in our day to day operations, the
FDNY oversees fire and life safety for our 8 million inhabitants and the
millions more who work and visit the city every day. We respond to all
emergency medical and fire calls in the more than 321 square miles of
the five boroughs. In 2007 our more than 11,000 firefighters put out
over 50,000 fires. Our emergency medical technicians and paramedics
responded to 1.3 million calls.

In the last several years we have responded to a wall collapse and landslide on a busy highway, two building explosions, a single engine plane crashing into a high-rise apartment building, a huge fire at an ExxonMobil oil storage facility and a citywide blackout. All of these critical situations were handled skillfully by our members with minimal loss of life.

In a city this size, literally anything can happen. So how to manage the monumental task of protecting it? Two elements are absolutely vital in this equation: capability and flexibility.

Capability is having the necessary tools at our disposal—including the most reliable and up-to-date equipment—and placing our resources in locations where they will be most accessible and effective. It means having plans at the ready to deal with the events that are likely to occur. And most important, it means having well-trained first responders.

The importance of planning and preparedness cannot be overstated. But of course plans and preparations alone will not come to the rescue in a difficult moment. We must have people who are capable of implementing those plans.

We simply do not know what the next major incident is going to be, and so we must be flexible. We have to be ready for whatever happens. It could be a chemical attack. It could be a Category 5 hurricane. It could be another blackout or brownout. To put it another way, we plan for *an* event; we do not plan for *the* event.

Of course, the biggest event in the FDNY's history came on September 11, 2001. It was an event that changed everything for the department. And it brought the concept of disaster preparedness to the forefront in state and local governments across America as never before.

Before 9/11, our firefighters were mainly trained to respond to unintentional acts. While loss of life and unknown dangers were always part of the job, it was not until the World Trade Center attack in 2001 that the department was faced with the reality of responding to an attack deliberately designed to kill thousands upon thousands of people. That grim realization was compounded by the terrible losses this department suffered that day. The numbers are well known, but are no less astounding for their familiarity. 343 members were killed, with a combined 4,400 years of experience—all in the space of 102 minutes. We lost people of every rank: from firefighters straight out of our training academy to our highest ranking officers, including the chief of the department and the first deputy commissioner. Then came the retirements. In 2002, almost 1,300 uniformed members retired from the department. In 2003, 700 members retired. Before 9-11, about 500 people could be expected to retire in a year. In the last 6 years, 50 percent of the department turned over.

I became commissioner on January 1, 2002, three months after the terrorist attacks. We immediately turned our attention to the monumental task of rebuilding this great institution, which was at that time a department in mourning.

The first step was to get some help in figuring out what went right and what went wrong with our response on 9-11. I asked the renowned consulting firm McKinsey & Company to analyze our response to the attacks, review our operations and procedures, and make recommendations as to how we could increase our preparedness.

McKinsey produced a comprehensive and detailed report, and in response to its findings, we set about implementing the recommendations, including presenting the FDNY's first ever strategic plan.

McKinsey's report and our strategic plan laid out a road map for strengthening the department by setting a clear set of priorities. September 11 showed us that the rules of the game had changed. In response, our priorities had to change as well.

We greatly enhanced the training given to our members of all ranks, both fire and emergency medical services (EMS). When I came to the department, our firefighters spent 13 weeks at our training academy before coming on the job. Now, they study and train for 23 weeks.

We have also stepped up our more specialized training. We trained more than 3,600 fire and EMS members in advanced hazardous materials response, which is nearly five times the number we had before 9-11.

In addition, we devised two advanced-level courses for our officers: one in conjunction with Columbia University that focuses on management, and another with West Point that focuses on combating terrorism. These two programs give our senior members a level of training and education unprecedented in the department's history.

One of the key points made in the McKinsey report was the department's need for a technologically sophisticated operations command center. In 2006 we opened a $17 million state of the art facility located in our headquarters. The New York City Fire Department Operations Center (FDOC) gives us unprecedented situational awareness and the ability to direct operations remotely. There we have access to maps, building records, and information on local infrastructure that helps our commanders make informed tactical decisions. The FDOC has the capability to receive real-time video feeds so commanders in the FDOC can see how the incident is progressing. And it is our critical point of contact with city, state, and federal agencies.

There have been several instances when the FDOC proved critical to our operations. In May 2007 a fire broke out on the roof of the building that housed the leather goods company Coach in Manhattan. From the street it looked as though the top floor and roof were on fire. Our video feed showed that the fire was confined to wooden storage sheds on the roof. This entirely changed our tactics and allowed firefighters to quickly suppress the fire.

We made other crucial improvements in technology. Most important, we deployed new handie-talkie radios to the field. These radios provide significant advantages over the models that were in use on 9-11. Our current radios also support many more channels and use the ultra-high-frequency (UHF) band, which allows for greater penetration in buildings and, crucially, allows for interoperability with other agencies, including the Police Department, which uses UHF. In addition, we developed a system for mobile communication in high-rise buildings that consists of handie-talkies, high-powered post radios, and battalion car repeaters. In effect, we devised a mobile communications system that is similar to the system used by the military that we carry with us.

We have made improvements to the equipment that we give our members to improve their safety. Last year we deployed radiation detectors and new masks that protect from chemical and biological agents. We also began using new and improved personal safety ropes that allow our firefighters a secure way to escape a building should they become trapped.

One issue that became glaringly clear after September 11, 2001 was that better coordination and information sharing was needed between first responder agencies. Until then the FDNY had functioned on its own, with little thought given to seeking outside help. After the devastating attacks, however, we realized, along with most other agencies, that cooperation is absolutely vital.

In 2005, Mayor Bloomberg and the Office of Emergency Management developed a Citywide Incident Management System, known as CIMS, a protocol for managing emergencies that involve multiple agencies. CIMS defines how citywide emergencies or large-scale multiple incidents will be managed, and uses as a template the National Incident Management System known as NIMS.

Another major change was our development of Incident Management Teams. IMTs are made up of emergency professionals to respond to and provide support at large-scale events that are likely to last more than 24 hours—the kind of event where first responders can quickly become overwhelmed.

The FDNY learned how helpful IMTs could be in the immediate aftermath of 9-11, when the massive recovery operation was under way at the World Trade Center. The IMT concept had been developed by the United States Forestry Service primarily to deal with natural disasters. After the attacks, a Forestry Service Incident Management Team came to New York and offered to help the FDNY effort at Ground Zero. It turned out they were of enormous assistance with logistics and planning, keeping our members fed and supplied with everything they needed and effectively putting a management umbrella over the recovery operation.

This was a departure from how things were normally done. As one chief put it at the time "if you had told us six weeks ago that the Forestry Service would be bailing us out, we would've had you committed."

We began training our members in Incident Management protocol in 2003. Then, in 2005, disaster struck the Gulf states in the form of

Hurricane Katrina. And when the call for help came from Louisiana, we were in a position to respond.

Within 24 hours, we had 350 firefighters medically evaluated, inoculated, and on their way to New Orleans, including 24 members of our Incident Management Team. They arrived to find the city in shambles and the New Orleans Fire Department exhausted and drained. Our members were able to help not just put out fires, but also transport supplies and establish a command support structure. In total, 650 of our members were activated for duty in New Orleans—at full strength, the entire New Orleans Fire Department had about 700 members.

In October we sent 7 IMT-trained members to California to help the agencies there deal with the fires that were sweeping across the state. They were put to work dealing with logistics, making sure that the people fighting the fire had all the water, fuel, food, and sanitary supplies they needed. In August 2006, we sent a team to forest fires in Idaho. We will soon have 150 members trained in this management specialty.

Here in New York, the department has partnered with multiple agencies both at drills and tabletop exercises and at real-life events. And it has paid off. For example, in July 2007 a 24-inch steam pipe that lay underneath a busy street in Midtown Manhattan exploded. A geyser of superheated steam and debris burst through the pavement. Our response had to be coordinated among several agencies: the police, Con Edison, the Department of Health, the Department of Environmental Protection, and the Office of Emergency Management. We successfully set up a unified command, under a protocol established by the Citywide Incident Management System.

And, in what was perhaps the most groundbreaking inter-agency project in our history, in September 2007 we partnered with the Department of Homeland Security in an intelligence-sharing project that included fire departments from across the country. It is well known that it is highly unusual for federal government to share intelligence reports with local governments. We now receive these reports—an indication of just how much that paradigm has changed.

A couple of public misperceptions persist about the FDNY's response on 9-11. The most prevalent is that chaos and confusion reigned at the site before the buildings collapsed. While there were flaws in the responses of all the emergency agencies, including the FDNY, video footage and photographs show that firefighters and fire officers acted in a cohesive, disciplined, and professional manner in accordance with their training. Moreover, they had received training specific to the World Trade Center. Firefighters and fire officers knew the buildings well. They even conducted drills in them and tested the radio repeater system.

Firefighters, it is often said, are a special breed. And that is no cliché. They love to fight fires, they crave the action. They are the last man out. They are always anticipating "the big one." But no one in the department could ever have imagined that "the big one" would happen in the way it did.

For the firefighters who responded to the World Trade Center after the planes hit and who faced the job of rescuing trapped civilians, the awesome severity of the situation was immediately and terribly clear. Put simply, no one had seen anything like this before. Not even the most senior men with 30 or 40 years on the job. Not even the two highest-ranking officers, Chief of Operations Daniel Nigro and Chief of Department Pete Ganci.

As they drove across the Brooklyn Bridge together to get to the burning Trade Center, Chief Nigro said to Chief Ganci: "This is going to be the worst day of our lives." Chief Ganci was killed in the collapse of the Trade Center towers.

Despite this grim reality, firefighters and fire officers like Captain Terry Hatton did their job. Terry was a well-respected officer in command of one of our elite units, Rescue 1. A fellow firefighter and friend recounts that he saw Terry in the command post set up in the North Tower that morning. Terry said: "I love you, brother. This might be the last time I see you." They hugged, anticipating the worst, then Terry went up into the building. He never made it out.

Another remarkable story is that of Battalion Chief Orio Palmer. Chief Palmer—an accomplished athlete and marathon runner—took an elevator to the fortieth floor of the South Tower and from there proceeded to the upper floors, on foot, carrying 75 pounds of equipment, looking for trapped survivors. As he made his way toward the massive fire, he methodically radioed crucial information and warnings about breached walls and nonworking elevators. He climbed all the way to the seventy-eighth floor, just below the impact zone.

There he found numerous bodies and fire. On the tape of his radio transmissions, he is heard gasping, shocked at what he sees. He called for two hose lines. He realized the fire is too big to put out, but hoped to soak down the stairways and get above the firestorm raging on the eight floors above him to rescue people trapped there. He radioed one of his officers, who is a few floors below him, calling for the hose lines. The response came back immediately: "we're on our way."

Minutes later the radio falls silent. There is a deafening roar as 91 floors of steel and concrete collapse, crushing Chief Palmer, his team, and hundreds of others.

The poet Emerson wrote "There is properly no history; only biography." I think that, in times of life-threatening crisis, in times of disaster, the most important protagonists are often ordinary men and women who, in the course of their everyday tasks, perform extraordinary deeds.

Responding to a disaster requires logistical and tactical planning and scientific calculation. But disaster response is also a human story, a contest between personal will and adversity, and of the human spirit challenging terrible odds.

It is the story of people like Chief Ganci, Captain Hatton, Chief Palmer, and the chiefs who currently direct operations at the Department, Chief of Department Sal Cassano, Chief of Operations Pat McNally, First Deputy Commissioner Frank Cruthers, and the thousands of others who responded to the Trade Center attack, overcame the staggering losses, and went on to build a stronger, even more dedicated and better prepared department.

Our safety, our future, perhaps our very existence may well depend on such people.

Part IV
What "Really" Happens When Disasters Happen: Preparations and Responses

Joel Towers
Introduction: What "Really" Happens When Disasters Happen: Preparations and Responses

THIS SECTION EXPLORES HOW COMMUNITIES AND INDIVIDUALS PREPARE for, and respond to, disasters and the extent to which they do that directly, indirectly or subconsciously. By asking, or perhaps stating "What 'Really' Happens When Disasters Happen," Erwann Michel-Kerjan, Elliot Aronson, Enrico L. Quarantelli, and Howard Kunreuther unpack the personal and political calculus of disaster preparation and response.

To begin, however, it may be of some use to attempt to clarify what may have been meant by the presence of those postmodern quotation marks surrounding "Really" in the session title. What is it about reality in the context of disasters that promises a socially constructed encounter? A shifting and provisional reality in relation to disasters is especially destabilizing given that the brute force of most disasters is, presumably, powerful enough to push aside preoccupations with positivist narratives. Some other force must clearly be at play.

I would argue, and the essays that follow make clear, that the temporal and social geography of risk is shifting. Risk, and the human capacity to manage it, conditions reality to a significant enough degree as to raise critical questions about what is "really" happening—even amid the destruction left in the wake of disaster. Risk defines both the limits of preparation and the character of response to disaster. And yet risk itself is a shifting commodity whose boundaries are constantly rewritten as a result of the dynamic relationship among markets, society, and the natural environment. This relationship is perhaps best exemplified by the phenomena know as the "hundred-year storm." The hundred-year storm is a benchmark not only in the mapping of risk and therefore the positioning of all sorts of infrastructure and buildings but a psychological milestone that sets human consideration of risk in a temporal landscape well beyond average human life expectancy. It is the perceived outsized improbability of hundred-year storm events—the perceived stability of climate within the "known" temporal dimensions of human life that allows for large-scale infrastructure investments and human settlements in territories of risk. When disaster strikes these territories of risk communities, politicians, and individuals can be comforted by the random and awesome brutality of nature.

Many interesting questions arise, however, when the hundred-year storm begins to occur with greater frequency as a result of the combined effects of climate change and increased sea levels. In other words, global warming has the ability to shift the temporal framework on which many personal and political decisions are predicated by altering the landscape of risk. The Metropolitan East Coast Assessment, a regional component of the U.S. National Assessment of the Potential Consequences of Climate Variability and Change (2000), indicates that by the end of this century "storm surges equivalent to one hundred year floods would recur every thirty-three years on average." The question then shifts to what happens when risk horizons are foreshortened? What is altered when society can no longer blame nature alone for disasters? How will preparations for disasters and responses to them change? The following papers make significant headway in addressing these and other questions while considering "What 'Really' Happens When Disasters Happen.'

Erwann O. Michel-Kerjan
Toward a New Risk Architecture: The Question of Catastrophe Risk Calculus

A CAUSE FOR CONCERN
From Catastrophes to Mega-Disasters: A New Era Calls for a New Model

THE CONFERENCE ORGANIZED BY THE NEW SCHOOL ON "DISASTERS: Recipes and Remedies" in New York in fall 2007 combined the contributions of many complementary fields pertaining to catastrophe management.* In this paper, I will discuss the challenge of the *calculus of risk*, but I would like to begin with a broader proposition—the need for a new risk architecture.

In many ways, the catastrophe risk management field is at a crossroads today as we are faced with disasters of a totally new nature and scale. And while a tremendous amount of research has been done to better understand disasters in past decade, there have been recent important events that have seriously challenged the established paradigm. The year 2008 is the most recent illustration of more extreme events to come.

In the new era we have entered, good risk calculus is more about finding the right balance between art and science.[1] Not very long ago, disasters were considered to be low probability events because they did not occur often. In a sense, that assumption was reassuring for the economist: the expected losses of these disasters (understood here as the potential loss associated with a disaster multiplied by the probability of that event occurring) was often relatively low. But in the first few years of the twenty-first century, the world has faced a string of catastrophes of a totally new dimension: the September 11, 2001 terrorist attacks; a major blackout in August 2003 that deprived electricity to over 50 million North Americans in just a few seconds; and seven hurricanes that hit the United States within a 15-month period—to name a few just in the United States. And catastrophes are often even more destructive when they occur in poor or even developing countries: for instance, the Indian Ocean tsunami in December 2004, or the major earthquake in the Sichuan province in China in May 2008 that killed nearly 50,000, only a few weeks after a major cyclone killed over 100,000 in Myanmar (Burma).

In fact, there has not been a 6-month period in the past few years without a major crisis that simultaneously affected several countries or industry sectors. In the terrorist attacks of 9/11, a superpower was challenged on its own soil in an unprecedented way. After 9/11, the reality of international terrorism became clear, and national security took first priority on the US agenda. The event has had an enduring impact on the rest of the world as well. Hurricane Katrina, a violent but long-anticipated hurricane, overwhelmed a vulnerable coastline, met an unprepared government, and inflicted lasting damage on a population. A superpower failed to meet the most basic needs of its citizens in crisis (White House, 2006). In the case of the US-Canada blackout, a massive failure of the electric power-distribution system demonstrated how human error and short-term competitive pressure resulting in poor risk management can jeopardize our critical infrastructures: a 10-second event. The December 2004 tsunami was responsible for the deaths of nearly 300,000 people in just a few hours because an alert system was not in place (although in this case, the economic impact was mostly local).

While the aforementioned extreme events all seem quite different—different types of catastrophes, different countries, and different impacts on the rest of the world—they share some common features:

the speed at which they occurred and their large-scale destabilization or destruction.[2] We know from experience that these two characteristics deeply affect decision-making and reaction capacity. The sudden can paralyze. The large-scale disorients. In a few hours it is not clear anymore who has the power, resources, and even legitimacy to act.

Are these events somehow related in the sense that they define a new pattern? If so, is it not clear that there is a need for a new risk management architecture?

A New Risk Architecture Is Still to Be Defined

The severity of these events demonstrates that the world is changing, and that we have entered a new era (Lagadec and Michel-Kerjan, 2005; Lagadec, 2007). On many critical points relating to extreme event preparedness, the conventional thinking is wrong. Conventional thinking holds that risks are mainly local and routine; that it is possible to list all unforeseen events that could take place, determine their probability based on past experience, measure the costs and benefits of specific risk protection measures, and implement these measures for each risk. Many organizations and governments are making decisions using risk and crisis management tools based on these outdated assumptions. As a result, these organizations do not have the agility needed to move quickly to respond to unplanned events and global risks that have occurred at an increasing rate in the recent past. Their failure to adequately prepare impacts not only them, but also a number of other interconnected organizations.

This state of affairs is no longer sustainable. It is clear that the hallmarks of this new era include more and more unthinkable events, previously unseen contexts, and pressure for private companies and government authorities to react extremely quickly, even when they cannot predict the impact their actions will have. Bottom line: if a company, a city, or a country still applies the old paradigm to this new era, it is allocating its resources in the wrong direction. I would like to offer a view of six defining features of this new risk architecture.

Growing interdependencies—globalization: As a result of a growing globalization, social and economic activities are more dependent on each other. While this is not totally new, we have reached a degree of interdependence that no other society has experienced before us: what happens on one continent today can affect those on another continent tomorrow. In other words, we see the emergence of "*security externalities*" (Auerwald, Brancomb, Laporte, and Michel-Kerjan, 2006; see also Kunreuther and Heal, 2003 on "interdependent security"). Conventional thinking holds that individual countries and individual organizations have the capacity and expertise to manage catastrophic risks. In an increasingly globally interdependent world, this is not true.

Change in scale—from local to global risks: Hyperconcentration of value at risk will lead to more devastating consequences when catastrophe strikes. Dealing with large-scale disasters is much more challenging than dealing with a series of local small accidents. Many do not appreciate the radical difference. Resources and collaborative effort needed simultaneously are not simply cumulative, but exponential. Furthermore, global response and global reaction capacity are needed. Multinational coordination becomes critical.

Extreme costs, extreme benefits—a new loss dimension: The new risk architecture is also characterized by a much greater variance in possible losses and gains. With increasing urbanization and concentration of social and economic activities in high risks areas (over 50 percent of the United States population is now living in coastal areas), costs of catastrophes are increasing because of the concentration of assets and first- and second-order ripple effects.

The recent events in the United States have translated into unprecedented economic consequences. Hurricane Katrina killed 1,300 people and forced 1.5 million people to evacuate the affected area—a historic record for the nation. Economic damages are estimated in the range of $150 to $200 billion, a third of which was covered by either private insurance (wind damage; about $45 billion) or public insurance (flood damage; $20 billion by the Federal National Flood Insurance

Table 1. The 20 Most Costly Insured Catastrophes in the World, 1970-2007[3]

	Event	Victims (Dead or Missing)	Year	Area of Primary Damage
$46.3*	Hurricane Katrina	1,836	2005	USA, Gulf of Mexico, et al.
35.5	9/11 Attacks	3,025	2001	USA
23.7	Hurricane Andrew	43	1992	USA, Bahamas
19.6	Northridge Earthquake	61	1994	USA
14.1	Hurricane Ivan	124	2004	USA, Caribbean, et al.
13.3	Hurricane Wilma	35	2005	USA, Gulf of Mexico, et al.
10.7	Hurricane Rita	34	2005	USA, Gulf of Mexico, et al.
8.8	Hurricane Charley	24	2004	USA, Caribbean, et al.
8.6	Typhoon Mireille	51	1991	Japan
7.6	Hurricane Hugo	71	1989	Puerto Rico, USA, et al.
7.4	Winterstorm Daria	95	1990	France, UK, et al.
7.2	Winterstorm Lothar	110	1999	France, Switzerland, et al.
6.1	Winterstorm Kyrill	54	2007	Germany, UK, NL, France
5.7	Storms and floods	22	1987	France, UK, et al.
5.6	Hurricane Frances	38	2004	USA, Bahamas
5.0	Winterstorm Vivian	64	1990	Western/Central Europe
5.0	Typhoon Bart	26	1999	Japan
4.5	Hurricane Georges	600	1998	USA, Caribbean
4.2	Tropical Storm Alison	41	2001	USA
4.2	Hurricane Jeanne	3,034	2004	USA, Caribbean, et al.

*In billions of US dollars. (indexed to 2007.)
Sources: Data from Swiss Re and Insurance Information Institute

Program—another historic record). Federal relief to the victims and for local reconstruction is estimated to be over $125 billion—yet another historic record.

On the financial side, the figures are telling: twenty of the most costly catastrophes to the insurance industry in the world over the past 38 years (1970-2007) occurred after 1987 (in 2007 prices corrected for inflation). Furthermore, of these 20 catastrophes, half of them (10) occurred since 2001 (see table 1), 9 of them in the United States.

Figure 1. Disaster Presidential Declarations Per Year (Peak-Values Correspond to Some Presidential Election Years)

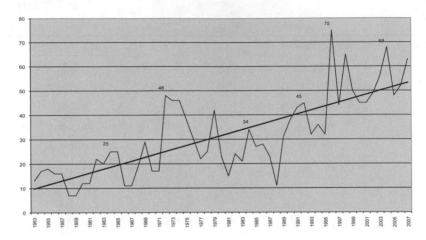

Sources: Author's calculation with data from the U.S. Department of Homeland Security

Hurricanes Ike, which hit the United States in September 2008, will undoubtedly be in this top 20 ranking.

On a positive side, this wider variance in the level of risk also creates new business opportunities. For instance, catastrophe bonds (cat bonds), which are financial instruments transferring catastrophe exposure to investors on the financial markets, have quickly developed in the aftermath of the 2005 hurricane season in the United States (Lewis, 2007). In 2006, 20 cat bonds were issued ($4.7 billion issued and $8.7 billion capital outstanding), compared with 11 in 2005 ($2.1 billion issued and $2.9 outstanding), the previous record. In 2007, the total value of cat bonds issued for natural disasters alone was $7.1 billion; 27 transactions were completed, a new record compared with the 10 transactions closed in 2005 (Michel-Kerjan and Morlaye, 2008).

Another measure of the recent change in disaster occurrence in the United States is the increase of the number of US presidential disaster declarations over the past 53 years, which shows clearly an upward trend (as depicted in figure 1). Overall, the number of presidential disaster declarations has dramatically increased over the past 50 years: there had been 162 over the period 1955-1965, 282 over 1966-1975, 319 over the period 1986-1995, and 545 for 1996-2005 (Michel-Kerjan, 2008). On average, the average annual number of declarations has increased by 10 every decade since the 1950s.

Under the current US system of disaster assistance, the governor of the state(s) can request that the president declare a "major disaster" and offer special assistance if the damage is severe enough. Although the president does not determine the amount of aid (the House and Senate do), he or she is responsible for a crucial step in the process. This obviously raises the questions of what are the key drivers of such a decision, whether some states are more likely to benefit from such situation than others, and if so, when does this occur.

As figure 1 also shows, many (although not all) of the peak years correspond to presidential election years. This is consistent with recent research that has shown that election years are a very active time for disaster assistance (all other things being equal). Four salient examples are the Alaska earthquake in 1964 (a presidential election year), Tropical Storm Agnes in June 1972, Hurricane Andrew in September 1992 and the four hurricanes in 2004. More recently, it has also been shown that a battleground state with 20 electoral votes has received more than twice as many presidential disaster declarations as a state with only three electoral votes (Reeves, 2004, 2005). In that sense, it is almost impossible to dissociate the economics of catastrophe management from politics (Gross, 2008). Research also shows that a driving force with respect to the actual provision of government relief is the occurrence of disasters where the losses are large (Moss, 2002). All things being equal, a victim of natural disasters might get access to more disaster relief if the disaster affects a large number of people.

In the case of Hurricane Katrina, Governor Kathleen Blanco declared a state of emergency on August 26, 2005 and requested disaster relief funds from the federal government on August 28. President George W. Bush declared a state of emergency on August 28, an action that frees federal government funds and puts emergency response activities, debris removal, and individual assistance and housing programs under federal control (Congressional Research Service, 2005). Under an emergency declaration, federal funds are capped at $5 million. On August 29 in response to Governor Blanco's request, the president declared a "major disaster," allotting more federal funds to aid in rescue and recovery. By September 8, Congress had approved $52 billion in aid to victims of Hurricane Katrina. As of October 2007, the total federal relief allocated by Congress for the reconstruction of the areas devastated by the 2005 hurricane season was nearly $125 billion.

Confusing distribution of the role and responsibilities—preparedness: If one asks people on the street, "Who do you think is in charge of preparing the country against future crises?" the most cited response will certainly be state and federal governments (whether as regulators or first responders). However, although government entities certainly play a crucial role, a large portion of critical services that allow our countries to operate is owned or operated by the private sector (85 percent in the United States, for example). We must look at how private actions affect public vulnerability so that we are better prepared.

Celerity—toward a just-in-time society: The development of rapid transportation and cheap communication has created a "just-in-time" society. People and products are moving faster and faster from one part of the globe to the other. While this provides a wide range of positive return, there is also a flip side: risks are more likely to spread across very rapidly. Thanks to jet travel, for instance, viruses now fly business class, too, so a pandemic starting in Asia today might very well spread extremely rapidly.

Uncertainty, if not ignorance: We were trained to solve problems with clear questions and clear scientific knowledge. Knowing the risk profile, we made investment decisions. Unfortunately, historical data does not shape the future anymore, given how rapidly the world is changing.

While this is a simplified framework, these six complementary features fit a large number of recent crises we all have witnessed in different parts of the world and across industries. The rest of the paper focuses on the last element of this framework—the challenge of quantifying risks under uncertainty, if not ignorance. We will use large-scale natural disasters and terrorism threats as two illustrative cases. Calculating risks associated with natural hazards has typically been easier than calculating risks associated with terrorism. In their similarities and differences, these two risks highlight the fact that, in a quickly evolving environment, the calculus of risk might become as much a matter of art as science.

THE CALCULUS OF RISK I: THE CASE OF NATURAL DISASTERS

Our discussion in the previous section raises the question as to what the future will look like. Using the United States as an example, we would like to focus on three drivers of the radical evolution of the cost due to natural disasters. These three drivers—*increasing urbanization in hazard-prone areas, increasing value at risk, and global warming*—are likely to continue to influence the social and economic cost of future disasters.

Increasing Development and Value at Risk in Hazard-Prone Areas

In 1950, about 30 percent of the world's population—then 2.5 billion people—lived in urban areas. By 2000, the number of people living in urban areas had increased to 50 percent, and the United Nations estimates that this will increase to 60 percent of the world population, projected to be 8.3 billion by 2025. A direct consequence of this trend is the increasing number of so-called megacities, with populations above 10 million located in hazard-prone areas. In 1950, New York City was the only such a megacity. By 2015, there are estimated to be 26, including New York (17.6 million) and Los Angeles (14.2 million). This urbanization and increase in population translates into an increased concentration of exposure to natural disasters.

The development of Florida for tourism and retirement is an illustrative example. The population of the state has increased significantly over the past 50 years: 2.8 million inhabitants in 1950, 6.8 million in 1970, 13 million in 1990, and a projected 19.3 million residents in 2010

Table 2. Top 20 Hurricane Scenarios (1900–2005) Ranked Using 2005 Inflation, Population, and Wealth Normalization

Rank	Hurricane	Year	Category	Cost range ($ billion) in 2005
1	Miami (SE FL/MS/AL)	1926	4	140-157
2	Katrina (LA/MS)	2005	3	81
3	North Texas (Galveston)	1900	4	72-78
4	North Texas (Galveston)	1915	4	57-62
5	Andrew (SE FL and LA)	1992	5-3	54-60
6	New England (CT/MA/NY/RI)	1938	3	37-39
7	SW Florida	1944	3	35-39
8	Lake Okeechobee (SE FL)	1928	4	32-34
9	Donna (FL-NC, NY)	1960	4-3	29-32
10	Camille (MS/SE LA/VA)	1969	5	21-24
11	Betsy (SE FL and LA)	1965	3	21-23
12	Wilma	2005	3	21
13	Agnes (FL/CT/NY)	1972	1	17-18
14	Diane (NC)	1955	1	17
15	4 (SE FL/LA/AL/MS)	1947	4-3	15-17
16	Hazel (SC/NC)	1954	4	16-23
17	Charley (SW FL)	2004	4	16
18	Carol (CT/NY/RI)	1954	3	15-16
19	Hugo (SC)	1989	4	15-16
20	Ivan (NW FL/AL)	2004	3	15

Source: Data from Pielke et al. (2008)

(a nearly 600 percent increase since 1950). With more individuals living in these areas, coupled with an increase in property values of their homes, there is a much higher probability of large-scale losses from hurricanes and flooding than 15 years ago. If Hurricane Andrew had occurred in 2007 rather than 1992, it would have inflicted more than double the economic losses than at the time of the disaster. In the same vein, the large 1926 Miami hurricane that hit the state when Florida was far less populated would inflict more than $140 billion of direct economic damage if it were to happen again today (Pielke et al., 2008).

These figures do not come as a surprise if one looks at the concentration of assets in Florida. Today, nearly 80 percent of insured assets in Florida are located near the coast, the area most subject to hurricane damage. As of December 2007, this represented over $2.3 trillion of insured exposure ($1.4 trillion for commercial exposure and $900 billion of residential exposure), according to the modeling firm AIR Worldwide.

Likewise, New York has over $2 trillion of insured value located directly on the coast (which is about 60 percent of the total insured value in the state). The coastal insured value for the top 10 states (ranked in terms of insured value on their coast) combined accounts for more than $8.3 trillion. Such huge concentrations of insured value in highly exposed areas almost guarantees that any major storm that hits these regions will inflict billions if not hundreds of billions of dollars in economic losses unless the residential construction and infrastructures are properly protected by effective risk reduction measures.[4]

To better understand our new vulnerability, table 2 shows the cost of major hurricanes that occurred in the United States in the past century, adjusted for inflation, population, and wealth normalization (that is, an estimate of what each of these hurricanes would have cost had they hit in 2005 in total direct cost).[5] This exercise has been done in several studies, the most recent of which, by Pielke et al. (2008), normalizes mainland US hurricane damage from 1900–2005 to 2005. Table 2 provides estimates for the top 20 most costly hurricanes, assuming they had occurred in 2005. The authors propose two ways to normalize these losses, each of which gives a cost estimate. The table provides the range of costs between these two estimates, along with the year when the hurricane originally occurred, as well as the hurricane category on the Saffir-Simpson scale.

Risk Calculus: Application to Hurricane Risks in Florida[6]

As part of a multiyear research effort currently undertaken by the Wharton Risk Center in conjunction with Georgia State University and

Table 3. Exceedance Probability of Insured Residential Losses in Florida (in billions of dollars)

$1	$2	$5	$10	$15	$20	$25	$30	$40
42.5%	35.9%	24.5%	15.0%	10.1%	6.9%	5.0%	3.9%	2.5%

$50	$60	$75	$100	$125	$150	$200	$250	$350
1.7%	1.3%	0.81%	0.41%	0.22%	0.11%	0.028%	0.005%	0.00012%

Sources: Wharton Risk Center - FHCF Data 2005; simulation by RMS.

the Insurance Information Institute, we have worked with one of the leading catastrophe modeling firms, Risk Management Solutions (RMS), to help us better quantify the risk of hurricane in several states. RMS has provided us with an analysis of the data from the Florida Hurricane Catastrophe Fund (FHCF) book of business as of 2005. Because the FHCF is a mandatory state reinsurance program, it has every residential insurance policy written in the state by private insurers and the state-run insurer, called Citizens. Data collected for this simulation include all lines of coverage of the FHCF. Total insured value (TIV) by the fund at the end of 2005 was estimated to be $1.7 trillion for the entire state of Florida. We focus on wind coverage only.[7]

Table 3 provides estimates of the annual probability that insured wind losses from hurricanes will equal or exceed different magnitudes for 18 thresholds ranging from $1 billion to $350 billion. For example, there is a 42.5 percent chance that there will be at least $1 billion of insured residential losses in Florida next year. The probability that hurricanes will inflict at least $10 billion of insured residential losses in Florida next year is 15 percent, and there is a 1.7 percent chance that insured losses will be at least $50 billion.

As we can see from this table, the probability decreases significantly as the threshold level of losses increases. For very high levels of insured losses ($100 billion and greater), the exceedance probability is less than 0.5 percent. This translates into a hurricane that occurs less than once every 200 years. Of course, such an unlikely catastrophic event could occur during the next hurricane season. By undertaking this analysis for all possible levels of insured hurricane losses, one can

Figure 2. Loss Exceedance Probability Curve for FHCF Portfolio

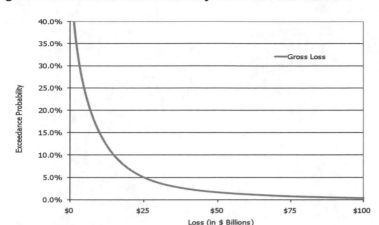

Source : 2005 Florida Hurricane Catastrophe Fund Portfolio and RMS.

generate the entire exceedance probability curve for the FHCF.[8] Figure 2 provides this curve for losses up to $100 billion.

To measure the uncertainty surrounding these estimates, one needs to utilize data on the average annual expected losses and the standard deviation for each postal zone in the state. For all Florida postal zones combined, the average annual expected loss for Florida residential insurance is $5.4 billion and the standard deviation is $13.9 billion (a 2.55 coefficient of variation).

Even if the average expected loss is identical in two regions, their standard deviations can differ significantly. To illustrate this point, we compared the insured losses from hurricanes in the postal zones within Miami-Dade County with 46 counties in the northern part of Florida, depicted in figure 3.

The 46 counties taken together had the same expected annual insured losses as Miami-Dade County. Figure 4 depicts the two EP curves for these two regions. Although the EP curves between the two regions look similar, their standard deviations are quite different. For both Miami-Dade County and the 46 northern counties in Florida, the average annual expected loss is approximately $900 million. The standard deviation of losses for Miami-Dade is $4.2 billion (a coefficient of

Figure 3. 46 Counties Whose Combined Annual Expected Loss Equals Miami-Dade's Alone

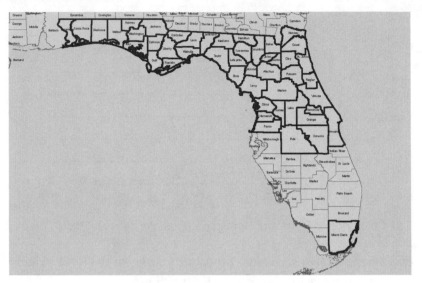

variation of nearly 5) and for the 46 northern counties it is $2.8 billion (a coefficient of variation of nearly 3).[9] This uncertainty in losses poses serious problems for preparedness and resource allocation.

Possible Impact of Climate Change on Risk Estimate: Likelihood versus Intensity[10]

There have been numerous discussions and scientific debates as to whether the series of major hurricanes that occurred in 2004 and 2005 might be partially attributable to the impact of a change in climate.[11] Without passing judgment on these issues, we summarize below the key questions and the scientific evidence presented to address them.

Is a change in climate likely to affect the number and severity of weather-related catastrophes? One of the expected effects of global warming will be an increase in hurricane intensity. This has been predicted by theory and modeling and substantiated by empirical data on climate change. Higher ocean temperatures lead to an exponentially higher evaporation rate in the atmosphere which increases the intensity of cyclones and precipitation.

Figure 4: Loss Exceedance Probability Curve comparing Miami-Dade County to 46 counties in Northern Florida

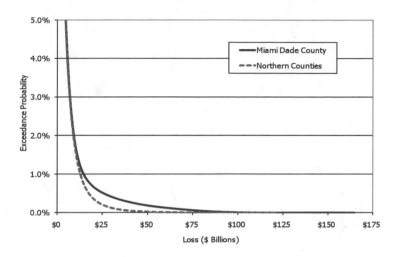

Source: 2005 Florida Hurricane Catastrophe Fund Portfolio and RMS.

Emanuel (2005) introduces an index of potential destructiveness of hurricanes based on the total dissipation power over the lifetime of the storm. He shows a large increase in power dissipation over the past 30 years and concludes that this increase may be due to the fact that storms have become more intense, on the average, and/or have survived longer at high intensity. His study also shows that the annual average storm peak wind speed over the North Atlantic and eastern and western North Pacific have increased by 50 percent over the past 30 years.

A paper by Webster et al. (2005), published a few weeks later, indicates that the number of Category 4 and 5 hurricanes worldwide has nearly doubled over the past 35 years.[12] In the 1970s, there was an average of about ten Category 4 and 5 hurricanes per year globally. Since 1990, the number of Category 4 and 5 hurricanes has averaged 18 per year. Focusing only on the North Atlantic (Atlantic/Caribbean/Gulf of Mexico), Category 4 and 5 hurricanes have increased from 16 in the period of 1975-1989 to 25 in the period of 1990-2004 (a 56 percent increase).

Figure 5. Global Warming and Its Impact on Variability in the Extremes

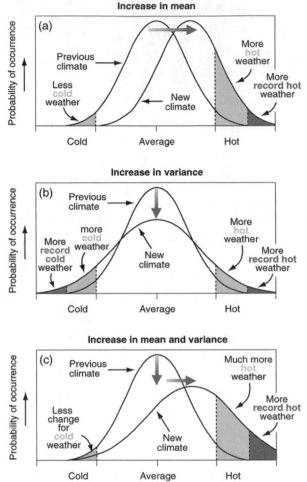

Note: The graph shows the effect on extreme temperatures when (a) the mean temperature increases; (b) the variance increases; and (c) when both the mean and variance increase for a normal distribution of temperature.

Source: Intergovernmental Panel on Climate Change.

The Webster et al. (2005) study concludes that "global data indicate a 30-year trend toward more frequent and intense hurricanes." This significant increase in observed tropical cyclone intensities, linked to warming sea surface temperatures that may be associated with global warming, has been shown in another study (Hoyos et al., 2006). One consequence of global warming is that we are likely to see more variability in the extremes, as depicted in figure 5.

But this is not to say that there is consensus by scientists on the relationship between hurricane activity and global warming.14 In a perspective article published in *Science*, Landsea et al. (2006) point out that subjective measurements and variable procedures make existing tropical cyclone databases insufficiently reliable to detect trends in the frequency of extreme cyclones. This conclusion is reinforced in a summary of articles on global climate change by Patrick Michaels, past president of the American Association of State Climatologists, who notes that all studies of hurricane activity that claim a link between human causation and the recent spate of hurricanes must also account for the equally active period around the middle of the twentieth century. Studies using data from 1970 forward begin at a cool point in the hemisphere's temperature history, and hence may draw erroneous conclusions regarding global climate change and hurricane activity (Michaels, 2006).

In 2007, a reanalysis of global tropical cyclone data since 1980 that addressed inaccuracies related to the interpretation of satellite recordings was published (Kossin et al., 2007). The reanalyzed data shows a lack of global trend in the number and percentage of Category 4 and 5 hurricanes and power dissipation index (PDI) globally, thus contradicting the results of Webster et al. (2005). An increase in PDI and in number and proportion of Category 4 and 5 hurricanes was still found for the Atlantic. While this supports the results of Emanuel (2005) for the Atlantic, the lack of a global increase in tropical cyclones activity, despite the increase in tropical sea-surface temperatures in all basins, "poses a challenge to hypotheses that directly relate globally increasing tropical sea surface temperature to increase in long-term mean global hurricane intensity" (Kossin et al., 2007). The Atlantic also appears to be characterized by large natural variability on the multidecadal scale with a shift to a more active phase around 1995 (World Meteorological Organization, 2006; Goldenberg et al., 2001).

The current debate in the scientific community regarding changes in the frequency and intensity of hurricanes and their relationship to global climate change is expected to be with us for a long time to come. The results to date do raise issues for the insurance industry to the extent that an increase in the number of major hurricanes over a shorter period of time may translate into a greater number hitting the coasts, likely causing damage to many more residences and commercial buildings today than they would have in the 1940s.

Another important aspect of the emerging consensus that anthropogenic climate change is occurring is that other stakeholders will likely become much more vocal than they have been up to now. Indeed, discussions and proposals to address potential consequences of global warming have not only emerged in more countries, they have also emerged in sectors that had not traditionally paid a lot of attention to it. For instance, while the debate on climate change had mainly been driven by NGOs, government and international bodies, and research institutions, now the private sector in general, and the financial institutions in particular, are increasingly involved and are sometimes the true drivers.

For instance, in April 2004, a group of 13 public pension funds managing over $800 billion in assets wrote a letter to US Securities and Exchange Commission (SEC) Chairman William Donaldson asking him to clarify that climate change is indeed a material risk requiring disclosure on SEC filings and to strengthen current disclosure requirements, for example, by providing interpretive guidance on the materiality of climate change risks. More recently, in June 2006, this now-enlarged group of investors—50 members of the Investor Network on Climate Risk (INCR), representing nearly $3 trillion in assets—reiterated this demand to the new SEC chairman (Ceres, 2006). The way these new stakeholders in the climate change field perceive the risk of future disasters and how they prepare—or expect companies they invest in to prepare—is likely to have important consequences.

THE CALCULUS OF RISK II: THE CASE OF TERRORISM THREAT

We now turn to another source of extreme events, the threat of terrorism. The discussion will focus on the main features of terrorism that makes this risk more difficult, if not impossible, to quantify, examine how terrorism risk financial coverage has been priced before and after the September 11, 2001 terrorist attacks, and try to infer some proxies for an implicit probability of attack.

Calculating Risk of Extreme Events: Why Is Terrorism Different?

The nature of international terrorism has changed drastically in the past two decades. Twenty years ago, terrorism consisted primarily of local political activities. But recent years have seen the emergence of a new kind of threat: extremist, religious-based terrorism (Hoffman, 2006; Enders and Sandler, 2006). Most of these terrorist groups, including Al Qaeda, have demonstrated a willingness to inflict mass casualties and to view civilians as a legitimate target. That change has led to fewer but larger attacks with a considerably larger number of casualties. The world's 15 worst terrorist attacks, as indicated by the number of casualties and fatalities, have all occurred since 1982, with two-thirds of them occurring between 1993 and 2006. In that sense, here we have also entered an era of potential catastrophes of a totally new scale. Moreover, there have been many near misses in the last few years. Among the most recent attempts were the attempted bombings of commuter trains in Germany on July 31, 2006 and the thwarting of a plot to bomb as many as 10 passenger planes bound for the United States from the UK in August 2006. Large terrorist attacks have the potential to destabilize entire nations, with numerous ripple effects and long-term impacts. While mega-terrorism risk shares several of the features of other extreme events, it also presents a set of distinctive characteristics:

▸ There are many plausible scenarios of attacks that would lead to overwhelming losses; the possible methods of a mega-terrorist attack are limited only by terrorist ingenuity. Consider the following illustration: the direct property losses, business interruption costs, and workers' compensation payments resulting from a five-ton truck bomb in one of the tallest high-rises in a major US city could go as high as $15 billion for a single building, depending on the location and the timing of the attack. Simultaneous attacks could inflict losses in the $100 billion range.[16] The use of weapons of mass destruction (WMD) is even more threatening. A 10-kiloton nuclear bomb planted in a shipping container that explodes in the port of Long Beach, California could have an even more devastating impact, with total *direct* costs estimated to exceed $1 trillion (not to mention ripple effects on trade and global supply chains; the ports of Los Angeles and Long Beach handle 30 percent of US shipping imports by value and are the largest ports of entry in the US) (Meade and Molander, 2006).

▸ The origin of the attack and its effects do not require proximity; for example, the destruction of the World Trade Center's towers in New York City could be attributed in part to the failure of security at Logan Airport in Boston, which shows that one company's operation can be disrupted by the failure of others to take sufficient protection measures (Kunreuther and Michel-Kerjan, 2005).

▸ Although terrorism risk models have been developed in the past two years, they are primarily designed to specify insurer's *potential exposure* to losses from a wide range of scenarios characterizing the attack (Kunreuther, Michel-Kerjan, and Porter, 2005). The models are not well suited to estimating the likelihood of any of these scenarios *occurring*. In contrast to natural disasters, for which large historical databases and scientific studies are publicly available, data on current terrorism threats are either not available at all or partly concealed by federal agencies for national security reasons.

▸ In addition to the lack of historical data relevant to the nature of today's threats, estimating the likelihood of a terrorist attack means aiming at a moving target, resulting in *dynamic uncertainty*, which is a key feature of terrorism risk. The risk of future terrorist attacks depends on the terrorists' will to attack and their chosen modes, as well as on the protective measures undertaken by those at risk and on actions taken by the government to enhance general security and commercial entities to protect their employees and assets. This point was underscored by the 9/11 National Commission (2004) report on terrorist attacks. Thus, terrorism risk depends on actions by both the private and public sectors and is continuously evolving, which makes the risk of future terrorist events extremely difficult to estimate.

▸ There is uncertainty about the *timing of an attack*. From the eight years that separated the first World Trade Center bombing in 1993 and the 2001 attacks, one could infer that terrorist groups program their attacks far in advance and strike when the public's attention and concern about terrorism have receded.

▸ When it comes to sharing the watch and responsibilities, a government's actions here and abroad directly affect the level of risk imposed on businesses and citizens (security measures, intelligence, foreign policy). Moreover, foreign policy decisions made by a government can affect the desire of terrorist groups to attack a certain country or its interests abroad (Lapan and Sandler, 1988; Lee, 1988; Pillar, 2001).

As a result, one faces a serious problem in quantifying terrorism risk and evaluating the best strategy to protect citizens and physical assets. It is worth noting here that due to the difficulty in estimating the likelihood of a terrorist attack, insurance companies that cover commercial firms against the risk of terrorism use scenarios to determine their maximum exposure to a range of possible attacks that vary by location and mode of attack.[17] However, few insurers consider the likelihood of these scenarios occurring in determining their exposure;[18] most use the "what if" approach.

Table 4. Natural Hazards Versus Terrorism Risks

	Natural Hazards Potential catastrophic losses	Terrorism Risks Potential catastrophic losses
Historical Data	Some historical data	Very limited historical data 9/11 event was the first mega-terrorist attack.
Risk of Occurrence	Risk reasonably well specified	Considerable ambiguity of risk Terrorists can intentionally adapt their strategy depending on their information on vulnerabilities.
Geographic Risk	Specific areas at risk	All areas at risk Some cities may be considered riskier than others, but terrorists may attack anywhere, at any time.
Information	Information sharing New scientific knowl-edge on natural haz-ards can be shared with all stakeholders.	Asymmetry of information Governments keep secret new information on terrorism for obvi-ous national security reasons.
Event Type: Interdependent Security	Natural event To date, no one can influence the occur-rence of an extreme natural event (e.g., earthquake).	Resulting event Governments can influence terror-ism (e.g., foreign policy; interna-tional cooperation; national secu-rity measures).

Table 4 summarizes some of the differences between natural hazards and terrorism threat that affect the quantification of these two categories of risks.

Inferring Implicit Probability of Terrorist Attacks from Terrorism Insurance Prices

Before September 2001—and despite terrorist attacks that occurred in the 1990s in several European countries, including Spain, France, and the UK, and the first attack on the World Trade Center in New York City in 1993—terrorism risk was, in practice, covered as an unnamed peril by standard risk commercial policies in the United States. Hence, on the morning of 9/11, many companies that suffered

Table 5. Change in Implicit Probability of Terrorist Attack: Illustration with Chicago's O'Hare Airport

Before 9/11 (in $ million)			After 9/11 (in $ million)			Change
Limit	Premium	Implicit probability	Limit	Premium	Implicit probability	200-fold
$750	$0.175	1 in 4300	$150	$6.9	1 in 22	

the attacks may have been surprised to discover that they were actually covered against such events. And many insurers and their reinsurers were brought to the realization that they were financially responsible for the insured portion of the losses: $35 billion, one-third of which was for business interruption. At that time, this was the most costly catastrophe ever in the history of insurance (now the second, after Hurricane Katrina).

As a response to 9/11, public-private partnerships were established in several developed countries (for example, the United States, Germany, France) in order to provide commercial enterprises with financial coverage. More than six years have passed since this tragedy, and terrorism insurance markets that developed after 2001 have had time to mature. With regard to risk calculus, a look at the evolution of terrorism insurance prices will offer some indications of the market's (buyers and suppliers) judgment of the likelihood of future attacks.

Consider the case of the terrorism insurance policy of the Chicago's O'Hare Airport. Before 9/11, the airport was covered against the consequences of a terrorist attack up to $750 million; it paid an annual premium of $175,000 for this coverage. That is an implicit probability of one in 4,300 years (assuming, for sake of simplicity here, no insurance administrative cost included in the premium). After the attacks, the best deal the airport could find was at one-fifth the earlier coverage, to $150 million for a m multiplied by nearly 40; now an implicit probability of 1 in 22. Table 5 shows the comparison between the two policies.

Was the new implicit probability for an attack against O'Hare airport right or wrong? Of course, it is hard to tell, but the airport bought that coverage.

Table 6-A. Terrorism Insurance Price Comparison between the United States And Germany (Mean, Excluding Standalone—Overall Book)

Overall Book	U.S.	Germany	Difference Germany/ U.S.
Aggregate			
Premium/Quantity of insurance purchased	0.0270% (1 in 3,700)	0.0685% (1 in 1,460)	~2.5
Small accounts	< $200 million	< Ð150 million	
Premium/Quantity of insurance purchased	0.0185% (1 in 5,400)	0.0240% (1 in 4,170)	~1.3
Large accounts	> $200 million	> Ð150 million	
Premium/Quantity of insurance purchased	0.0317% (1 in 3,150)	0.1299% (1 in 760)	~4.1

Note: Implicit probability in parentheses.

Table 6-B. Terrorism Insurance Price Comparison between the United States And Germany (Mean, Excluding Standalone—Financial Institutions Only)

Financial Institutions	U.S.	Germany	Difference Germany/ U.S.
Aggregate			
Premium/Quantity of insurance purchased	0.0697% (1 in 1,430)	0.0688% (1 in 1,450)	~1.0
Small accounts	< $200 million	< Ð150 million	
Premium/Quantity of insurance purchased	0.0782% (1 in 1,280)	0.0259% (1 in 3.860)	~0.3
Large accounts	> $200 million	> Ð150 million	
Premium/Quantity of insurance purchased	0.0796% (1 in 1,250)	0.1400% (1 in 715)	~1.8

In order to provide more substantial evidence on terrorism insurance pricing (in effect, a proxy for implicit likelihood of an attack), it is possible to undertake a series of analyses of insurance pricing in the United States and several Europeans countries (France, Germany, and the UK) over the past five years.

Below, we provide a snapshot of a much broader analysis of US and German terrorism insurance markets by focusing on the following two sets of data: 1) a sample of 1,623 large firms in the US market (insured value higher than $200 million); and 2) the 1,153 large firms in Germany. For each of these companies, we collected data on premiums paid for terrorism insurance along with quantity of insurance purchased by the company. Using the means of these distributions, it is possible to run the data for all companies (as summarized in table 6-a), which provides a macro-perspective on implicit probability for different sizes of company at an aggregate country level. One can also focus on a specific industry sector to compare similar companies (table 6-b for instance provides the results for financial institutions). The last column on the right reports the multiple of German prices in relation to those in the United States. Figures in parentheses provide a proxy for the implicit probability of loss given these prices (in the case where the price would perfectly represent the expected loss and would not include any other elements such that administrative cost or the cost of capital—a simplifying assumption)

As shown in these summary tables, five years after 9/11 a huge disparity exists in the price of coverage in the United States and Germany. After taking into account differences in the size of the firms, the price of comparable coverage in Germany appears to be at least 30 percent—and, by some estimates, as much as four times—higher than in the United States. On the other hand, if we confine our analysis to financial institutions only and consider the aggregate samples, the price of coverage appears roughly equivalent. For smaller firms, the price is as much as two or three times lower in Germany than it is in the United States, but 50 percent to 80 percent higher for large accounts (depending on what measure of price one selects). This result can be explained

Figure 6. Difference between Terrorism Risk and Risk Perception Over Time

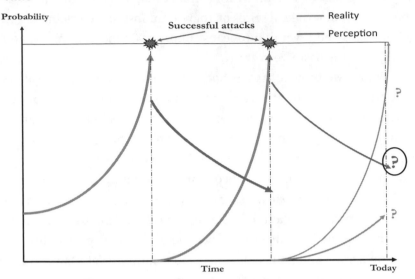

in part by the fact that, in the case of small accounts, Extremus does not charge different premiums to different industry sectors, while premiums in the United States are highest for financial institutions.

This analysis illustrates how the price for terrorism coverage varies from one country to another. While one might expect that terrorism is a greater threat to the United States than it is to Germany, on average, the perceived likelihood—as translated into the price of financial coverage against that risk—goes in the opposite direction. There may be other reasons for this price difference that are independent of the perception of the risk (federal reinsurance provided for free to US insurers, adverse selection in the German market, difference in the nature of coverage, etc.).[20]

The main takeaway here is that it is hard to quantify with certainty the probability of future terrorist attacks. Today, the market perception of the probability of an attack against financial institutions (most of them located in large cities, often considered a prime target) is nearly 1 in 1,400. That seems to be a very low probability if one considers that terrorism is one of the top issues on the US political agenda today.

Seven years without any (publicized) terrorist attacks on US soil might have lowered the perception of that risk considerably. An attack on US soil next month will certainly lead to a major increase in prices, reflecting a reevaluation of the risk, despite the fact that the risk itself has not necessarily changed (some might actually argue that the risk of a new attack the year after one has taken place is low because of increased attention and reinforced level of security established as a reaction to the first attack) (see figure 6 for an illustration).

ART OR SCIENCE? HOW RISK ESTIMATES CHANGE AFTER DISASTERS

I would like to conclude on a last note: the uncertainty related to the estimate of future disaster is even more challenging because it is dynamic. Indeed, as illustrated by large-scale natural disasters and continuously evolving terrorism threat, a series of major disasters tomorrow is likely to influence many stakeholders to change their view about future events. The series of seven hurricanes that made US landfall in 2004 and 2005 offers a perfect illustration of that dynamic aspect of risk estimate. Let's focus here two important groups of stakeholders in that regard: rating agencies and modeling firms.

Rating agencies provide independent evaluations of economic strength of commercial enterprises, including the financial stability of insurers/reinsurers and their ability to meet their obligations to policyholders in the case of a disaster. During the past few years, rating agencies have paid increasing attention to the impact that catastrophic risks will have on their assessment of the financial stability of insurers and reinsurers. The rating given to a company will affect its ability to attract business, and hence its pricing and coverage decisions. For example, the rating agency A. M. Best undertakes a quantitative analysis of an insurer's balance sheet strength, operating performance, and business profile. Evaluation of catastrophe exposure plays a significant role in determining ratings since these are events that could threaten the solvency of a company. Projected losses from disasters occurring at specified return periods (a 100-year windstorm/hurricane or a 250-year earthquake) and the associated reinsurance programs to cover them are two important components of the rating questionnaires that insurers are required to complete.

A. M. Best's approach has been an important step forward in the incorporation of catastrophic risk into an insurer's capital adequacy requirements. Until recently, the rating agency has been including probable maximum loss (PML) for only *one* of these severe events (100-year windstorm/250-year earthquake, depending on the nature of the risk the insurer was mainly exposed to) in its calculation of a company's risk-adjusted capitalization. In 2006, as a result of the 2004 and 2005 hurricane seasons, A. M. Best introduced a second event as an additional stress test. If the main exposure facing the insurer is an earthquake, the second event is increased from a 1-in-250-year event to a 1-in-100-year event (A. M. Best, 2006). These new requirements have increased the amount of risk capital that insurers have been forced to allocate to underwrite this risk and have made them more reluctant to provide this coverage unless they are able to raise premiums sufficiently to reflect these additional costs.

The changes in risk estimates and the new requirements by rating agencies have significantly affected the way insurers are managing their exposure. Indeed, the exact same portfolio of risks that an insurer was covering in July 2004 was much more "risky" in July 2006, due to the changes in the way these ratings have been redefined.

Modeling firms. As illustrated by the analysis of hurricane risk in Florida presented earlier in this paper, many organizations in the public and private sectors have turned to firms that specialize in the business of modeling catastrophe risks to assist them in determining catastrophe risk exposure.[21] Over the past 10 years, these companies have become important players in the field of catastrophe insurance and reinsurance. These firms were subject to some criticism for failing to increase their risk assessment in advance of the 2004-2005 storm seasons. It should be noted that catastrophe modeling and risk assessment face a number of informational challenges, as well as market and regulatory acceptance. For instance, the Florida Commission on Hurricane Loss

Projection Methodology refused to certify Risk Management Solution's medium-term view of hurricane activity filed in 2006 that reflected the recent increase in hurricane frequency and intensity being experienced in the Atlantic basin. RMS had to modify its model so its estimates of hurricane activity rates for the next five years are now based on a straight historical average of the number of hurricanes recorded since 1900 (RMS, 2007).

Ultimately, it may have been necessary for the United States to experience the recent increase in the occurrence of natural disasters in order for modeling firms to adjust their models. Due to parameter uncertainty, it is never possible to know whether a given model has accurately estimated the true underlying risk of loss and associated probability distributions. Indeed, it is a challenge to estimate the risk of catastrophes in an inconstant and rapidly evolving environment.

While the old risk management paradigm focused mainly on expected loss as the key measure to consider in making decisions, recent catastrophes make it clear that the uncertainty associated with this estimate has become an element of considerable importance. A high variance means that some periods will be very quiet while others will be particularly devastating. A good preparedness plan is one that takes a long view on these issues. In this regard, one needs to be mindful that it might be extremely difficult to maintain the long view if our country has *not* experienced any major disasters during several years. There is a tendency for all of us, whether in the role of homeowner, decision maker in a private or public sector organization, or as a political representative at the state, local, or federal level, to pay attention only to short-run crises. In the new era of global risks and interdependencies we have entered, how people make long-term decision under uncertainty will be an important element to consider in developing the new risk architecture.

NOTES

*   I would like to thank Howard Kunreuther for ongoing interaction on these issues over the years, as well as Elliot Aronson, Lee Clarke,

Arien Mack, Charles Perrow, and Enrico Quarantelli for more recent interaction on some of the elements discussed in this paper. Financial support for this research was provided by the Wharton Risk Management and Decision Processes Center and the Chair on Sustainable Development at the Ecole Polytechnique in Paris.

1. The word "architecture" is chosen here on purpose. The word comes from the Greek "*architeckton*," which can be broken in two. The beginning of the word, "arch," is the part that means "the first," the responsibility that comes with priority. The second part of the word "tekton" is closely related to "tekniki," the word that the Greeks used for a technique. But this word, in turn, is very close to "techni," the word Greeks also used for "art."

2. The two crises that are unfolding as this paper is written, the subprime crisis and the food price crisis, certainly share these attributes as well.

3. This table excludes payments for flood by the National Flood Insurance Program in the US—for example, $17.3 billion in 2005 as a result of Hurricanes Katrina and Rita.

4. In Kunreuther and Michel-Kerjan (forthcoming), we show that proper mitigation measures in place can reduce the level of loss associated with a 100-year-return period hurricane in Florida by nearly 50 percent.

5. These estimates might vary, depending on underlying assumptions over such a long period of time, such as inflation, population growth, and wealth normalization in the studied area; moreover, mitigation and building codes will have an important impact on total losses.

6. I thank Jack Nicholson of the Florida Hurricane Catastrophe Fund (FHCF) for providing us with the FHCF data base and Patricia Grossi and Robert Muir-Wood of Risk Management Solutions (RMS) for their analyses of the FHCF data. They provided us with the relevant exceedance probability curves and tables presented in this section.

7. I use here the new generation of models developed by RMS in 2006; see my discussion about the changes that occurred in cat risk modeling as a result of the 2004/2005 hurricane seasons earlier in this paper.

8. An exceedance probability (EP) curve specifies the probabilities that a certain level of losses will be exceeded in a specific location (or its entire portfolio) over a specific period of time (e.g., one year, five years, etc.). These losses can be measured in terms of dollars of damage, fatalities, illness or some other unit of analysis.

9. The coefficient of variation is the ratio of the standard deviation of a given variable to its mean.

10. This subsection is based on Kunreuther and Michel-Kerjan (2007).

11. For more details on the scientific evidence regarding climate change and its impact see the Stern Report (2006).

12. Category 4 hurricanes have sustained winds from 131 to 155 miles per hour; Category 5 systems, such as Hurricane Katrina at its peak over the Gulf of Mexico, have sustained winds of 156 mph or more.

13. See Weitzman (2007, 2008) for an insightful discussion about the importance of considering the possibility of truly catastrophe output related to climate change. The author argues that the Stern Report underestimates this risk of catastrophe change in climate.

14. See for instance the exchange between Pielke, Landsea, and Emanuel (2005) and Chan (2006).

15. For more discussion on this issue see Mills (2005).

16. See chapter 6 in Wharton Risk Center (2005).

17. When asked the question "Does your company consider scenarios in its catastrophe/exposure management process?" 92 percent of the insurers who responded to a 2005 Wharton questionnaire answered "Yes." One company responded to the above question by noting: "Our company uses deterministic terrorist attack scenarios, and the associated Probable Maximum Loss (PML) estimates of these scenarios, to establish and manage exposure concentrations within major metropolitan areas and/or surrounding landmark properties." See Wharton Risk Center (2005).

18. As illustrated by the following responses to the question: "Do you take estimates of the likelihood of the various known scenarios into account when making underwriting decisions?"

"Not really. There is little historical data to predict future events."

"Likelihood is very unpredictable for terrorist acts."

"Our company does not believe that estimates of the frequency of terrorist attacks are credible at a country, regional or specific property level."

See Wharton Risk Center (2005)

19. These two datasets were provided by Marsh, a leading insurance broker, for the US market and by Extremus, the German insurance company established in 2002 to cover against terrorism for the German market. I am grateful to Marsh's John Rand and Jill Dalton and Extremus's Bruno Gas for providing special runs of their datasets. The complete set of results, which constitutes the first international comparison of terrorism insurance prices, was published in Michel-Kerjan and Pedell (2006).

20. For a discussion of these other elements, see Michel-Kerjan and Pedell (2006).

21. For a comprehensive presentation of the evolution of catastrophe modeling, see Grossi and Kunreuther (eds.) (2005).

REFERENCES

A. M. Best. *Methodology: Catastrophe Analysis in A.M. Best Ratings*. April 2006.

Auerswald, Brancomb, Laporte, and Michel-Kerjan, eds. *Seeds of Disaster, Roots of Response: How Private Action Can Reduce Public Vulnerability*. Cambridge: Cambridge University Press, 2006.

Ceres. "Investor Network on Climate Risk Letter." June 14, 2006.

Chan, J, "Comment on "Changes in Tropical Cyclone Number, Duration, and Intensity in a Warming Environment." *Science* 311 (March 24, 2006): 1713-1724.

Congressional Research Service. "Federal Stafford Act Disaster Assistance: Presidential Declarations, Eligible Activities, and Funding." Washington, D.C.: Congressional Research Service, Library of Congress, 2005.

Emanuel, K. "Increasing Destructiveness of Tropical Cyclones over the Past 30 Years." *Nature* 436 (August 2005): 686-688.

Enders, W., and T. Sandler. *The Political Economy of Terrorism*. Cambridge: Cambridge University Press, 2006.

Fleckenstein, M. "Rating Agency Recalibrations." *The Review: Cedant's Guide to Renewals 2006* (2006): 40-43.

Goldenberg, S. B., C. W. Landsea, A. M. Mestas-Nunez, and W. M. Gray. "The Recent Increase in Atlantic Hurricane Activity: Causes and Implications." *Science* 293 (2001): 474.

Gross, D. "Winning by a Landslide Why More Disasters Are Declared During an Election Year." *Newsweek* (February 29, 2008).

Grossi, P. and H. Kunreuther, eds. *Catastrophe Modeling: A New Approach to Managing Risk*. New York: Springer, 2005.

Hoffman, B. *Inside Terrorism*. New York: Columbia University Press, 2006.

Höppe, P., and R. Pielke, eds. *Report of the Workshop on Climate Change and Disaster Losses*, May 25-26, Hohenkammer, Germany, October 2006.

Hoyos, C., P. Agudelo, P. Webster, and J. A. Curry. "Deconvolution of the Factors Contributing to the Increase in Global Hurricane Intensity." *Science* 312 (April 7, 2006): 94-97.

Insurance Journal. "S&P to Implement New Way to Assess Insurer Cat Risk." March 31, 2006.

Intergovernmental Panel on Climate Change. *Climate Change 2007*. January 2007.

Journal of Contingencies and Crisis Management. Special Issue 4 (2003).

Kossin, J. P., J. R. Knapp, D. J. Vimont, R. J. Murnane, and B. A. Harper. "A Globally Consistent Reanalysis of Hurricane Variability and Trends." *GRL* 34 (2007).

Kunreuther, H., and G. M. Heal. "Interdependent Security." *Journal of Risk and Uncertainty* 26:2-3 (2003): 231-249.

Kunreuther, H., and E. Michel-Kerjan. "Terrorism Insurance 2005: Where Do We Go from Here?" *Regulation. The Cato Review for Business and Government* (Spring 2005): 44-51.

———. "Climate Change, Insurability of Large-Scale Risks and the Emerging Liability Challenge." *Penn Law Review* 155:6 (June 2007): 1795-1842.

————. *At War with the Weather: Managing Large-Scale Risks in a New Era of Catastrophes*. Cambridge: MIT Press, forthcoming.

Kunreuther, H., E. Michel-Kerjan, and B. Porter. "Extending Catastrophe Modeling to Terrorism and Other Extreme Events." *Catastrophe Modeling: A New Approach to Managing Risk*. Eds. P. Grossi and H. Kunreuther, with C. Patel. Boston: Kluwer, 2005.

Lagadec, P. "Over the Edge of the World." *Crisis Response Journal* 3:4 (2007): 48-49.

Lagadec, P., and E. Michel-Kerjan. "A New Era Calls for A New Model." *International Herald Tribune,* November 1, 2005.

Lagadec, P., E. Michel-Kerjan, and R. Ellis. "Disaster via Airmail. The Launching of a Global Reaction Capacity After the 2001 Anthrax Attacks." *Innovations* 1:2 (2006): 99-117.

Landsea, C. W., B. A. Harper, K. Hoarau, J. A. Knaff. "Can We Detect Trends in Extreme Tropical Cyclones?" *Science* 313 (28 July 2006): 452-454.

Lapan, H., and T. Sandler. "To Bargain or Not to Bargain: That Is the Question." *American Economic Review* 78:2 (1988): 16–20.

Lee, D. "Free Riding and Paid Riding in the Fight Against Terrorism." *American Economic Review*. 78:2 (1988): 22–26.

Lewis, M. "In Nature's Casino." *The New York Times Magazine* (August 26, 2007.

Meade, C., and R. Molander. *Considering the Effects of a Catastrophic Terrorist Attack*. Santa Monica: Rand, August 2006.

Michaels, P. "Is the Sky Really Falling? A Review of Recent Global Warming Scare Stories." *Policy Analysis* 576 (August 23, 2006).

Michel-Kerjan, E. "Disasters and Public Policy: Can Market Lessons Help Address Government Failures." *National Tax Journal*. Proceedings of the 99th Annual Conference of the National Tax Association (2008) (in press, 2008).

Michel-Kerjan, E., and F. Morlaye. "Extreme Events, Global Warming, and Insurance-Linked Securities: How to Trigger the 'Tipping Point.'" *Geneva Papers on Risk and Insurance* 33:1 (2008): 153-176.

Michel-Kerjan, E., and B. Pedell. "How Does the Corporate World Cope with Mega-Terrorism? Puzzling Evidence from Terrorism Insurance

Markets." *Journal of Applied Corporate Finance*, 18:4 (2006): 61-75.

Mills, E. "Insurance in a Climate of Change." *Science* 308 (August 12, 2005): 1040-44.

Moss, D. *When All Else Fails: Government as the Ultimate Risk Manager.* Cambridge: Harvard University Press, 2002.

National Commission on Terrorist Attacks Upon the United States. *The 9/11 Commission Report.* Washington, D.C., July 2004.

Perrow, C. *The Next Catastrophe: Reducing Our Vulnerabilities to Natural, Industrial, and Terrorist Disasters.* Princeton: Princeton University Press, 2007.

Pielke, R., Jr., J. Gratz, C. Landsea, D. Collins, M. Saunders, and R. Musulin. "Normalized Hurricane Damage in the United States: 1900–2005." *Natural Hazard Review* (February 2008).

Pielke, Jr., R., C. W. Landsea, and K. Emanuel. *Nature* 438 (2005): 22/29

Pillar, P. *Terrorism and US Foreign Policy.* Washington, D.C.: Brookings Institution Press, 2001.

Reeves, A. "Plucking Votes from Disasters." *Los Angeles Times,* May 12, 2004.

———. "Political Disaster? Electoral Politics and Presidential Disaster Declarations." Working paper, Kennedy School of Government, Harvard University, 2005.

Risk Management Solutions (RMS). "Hurricane Model Re-Certified by Florida Commission." Press release. June 25, 2007.

Stern Review. *The Economics of Climate Change.* London: H. M. Treasury, December 2006.

Webster, P. J., J. A. Curry, J. Liu, G. J. Holland. Response to Comment on "Changes in Tropical Cyclone Number, Duration, and Intensity in a Warming Environment." *Science* 311 (March 24, 2006): 1713c.

Webster, P., G. Holland, J. Curry, and H. R. Chang. "Changes in Tropical Cyclone Number, Duration, and Intensity in a Warming Environment." *Science* 309 (September 16, 2005): 1844-1846.

Weitzman, M. "The Stern Review of the Economics of Climate Change." Book review. *Journal of Economic Literature* 45:3 (2007): 703: 724.

———. "On Modeling and Interpreting the Economics of Catastrophic

Climate Change." Working paper, Department of Economics, Harvard University, 2008.

Wharton Risk Center. *TRIA and Beyond. The Future of Terrorism Risk Financing in the US.* Philadelphia: University of Pennsylvania, Wharton School, Philadelphia (2005): 230.

White House. *The Federal Response to Hurricane Katrina: Lessons Learned.* Report under the direction of Frances Fragos Townsend, Washington, D.C., February 2006.

World Meteorological Organization (WMO). Statement on Tropical Cyclones and Climate Change. WMO 6th International Workshop on Tropical Cyclones, San Jose, November 2006.

Elliot Aronson
Fear, Denial, and Sensible Action in the Face of Disasters

I MUST BEGIN THIS ESSAY WITH A CONFESSION: I AM NOT AN EXPERT on disasters. I have not studied disasters directly, nor do I know much about the major differences among various kinds of disasters. What I do know something about is how the human mind works; how people think, feel, and behave in a wide variety of complex situations (Aronson, 1999, 2008; Tavris and Aronson, 2007). To the extent that this knowledge may apply to disasters, I suspect that it will be useful in helping people respond rationally to avoid falling victim to a disaster (for example, by immunizing themselves from infection during a pandemic), or to prepare themselves for an inevitable disaster (like a hurricane), or to respond sensibly to a disaster (like an act of terrorism) once it occurs.

After spending the past 50 years doing experiments on human behavior, I am convinced that people do not often behave in a rational manner. That is, our behavior frequently fails to conform to that of the "rational actor" in economic forecasts—much to the consternation of most economists and policymakers (see Kahneman and Tversky, 1984, 1996). Human behavior is not always rational, but it is fathomable. And, to the extent that we can understand the variables that produce rational and irrational behavior, we can find ways to help people make more sensible decisions. In the arena of "how people respond to disasters," such an understanding will save lives.

Specifically, the question I want to raise is this: How can we use our knowledge of how the mind works to help people act in ways that can prevent the disaster, prepare for it or, at the very least, help them respond to a disaster in ways that will reduce its impact?

To answer this question, I begin with the emotion of fear. How do people respond when they are frightened? If there is a disaster in the offing (say, a terrorist attack, a hurricane, or a pandemic) and a policymaker wants people to follow a particular course of action to save their lives, should he or she scare them? If so, would it be more effective to induce a great deal of fear? Or might a great deal of fear be overwhelming? Would inducing a low or moderate amount of fear be more effective? These are vital questions that any official at the national, state, and local level interested in curtailing the damage inflicted by disasters should know about. Fortunately, data are available on this issue.

Let me begin with two stories. In 1741, the distinguished American theologian Jonathan Edwards delivered a series of lectures throughout New England in which he vividly described the torments of hell that awaited all sinners who were unredeemed. He told his audiences that, in order to escape the ravages of hell, they must give over their lives to Jesus. Eyewitness accounts indicate that the sermons left the congregations swooning and "breathing of distress and weeping." The records show that, wherever Edwards preached, thousands gave over their lives to Christ as part of the Great Awakening of eighteenth-century America. Some of today's skeptics might not regard hellfire as a realistic disaster, but for a believer in eighteenth-century New England, the threat of hell was very real, and what could be a greater catastrophe than to spend all of eternity having your flesh melted by its unbearable fires? Jonathan Edwards demonstrated that scaring the hell out of people is an effective way to induce people to act in what they perceive as being in their own best interests.

Some 245 years later, two social psychologists informed UCLA college freshmen, during their orientation week, that most experts were convinced that there was a high probability of an earthquake in the Los Angeles area during the next several years (Lehman and Taylor, 1987). The information was accurate. Half the students had been randomly assigned to recently constructed dorms that, because they were new and therefore built to conform to the most recent California building codes, were relatively safe seismically. The other half of the students had been assigned to older dorms that were far more vulnerable to collapse or suffer significant damage in the event of an earthquake. A few months later, all the students were tested on their knowledge of earthquakes. Which group did better?

Generalizing from the Jonathan Edwards example, it would be easy to conclude that the students living in seismically unsafe dormitories would be most frightened and therefore would be more highly motivated to take action—in this case, at the very least, to inform themselves about the nature of earthquakes and what they might do in case an earthquake struck. In contrast, the students in the safe dorms, because they felt less vulnerable to any impending earthquake, would be less motivated to inform themselves.

The results did not support these conjectures. Those living in the unsafe dorms were obviously more frightened at the time they were first informed. But a few months later, they remained woefully uninformed about what to do in case of an earthquake. Why?

The answer lies in a major difference between the UCLA experiment and the Jonathan Edwards phenomenon. Of course there were many differences. Given what we know about Edwards's reputation, it is highly likely that he was a more exciting speaker than the UCLA researchers. He also may have made his audience feel greater levels of fear. Yet we know that the students in the unsafe dorms were plenty scared. Why didn't they take action? I suggest that Jonathan Edwards did something that the UCLA researchers failed to do. Not only did he scare his audiences, but he also provided them with a concrete, doable, and (for them) effective strategy: all they had to do was come forward and accept Christ as their savior. For the students in the older dorms, there was little they could do to avert disaster—short of moving out of the dormitory, which would not have been easy to do. Let's face it: if there is an earthquake in the middle of the night and your dormitory starts shaking, there is little you can do to protect yourself. If you wake up in time, you can dive under a heavy table, but it would be silly to try to leave the building.[1] Accordingly, immediately after their session with the researchers, the students in the vulnerable dorms were stuck with the fear of an impending earthquake coupled with a feeling of helplessness.

They were also experiencing cognitive dissonance, the discomfort people feel when faced with an inconsistency between two beliefs, or between a belief and an action: for example, the dissonance between "I'm a smart person who knows better than to take chances" and "Here I am, continuing to live in an unsafe building." To reduce that dissonance, most people will either move out or change their perceptions of how dangerous their environment really is (See Festinger, 1957; Festinger and Aronson, 1960; Aronson, 2007).

How did the UCLA students reduce their fear, their helplessness and their dissonance? When the researchers returned after three months, they asked the students to estimate the probability of an earthquake occurring in the Los Angeles area. Those living in the safe dorms gave an accurate estimate, one very close to the probability statement that the researchers had initially informed them about. But the students in the unsafe dorms grossly underestimated the probability of an earthquake. In only three months, they succeeded in reducing both their fear and their cognitive dissonance by convincing themselves that an earthquake was unlikely to occur. In the absence of specific recommendations, the students in the unsafe dorms went into denial.

During the past 40 years, a great many experiments in social psychology have demonstrated that the best way to persuade people to behave in a reasonable, responsible manner when their health and safety are at stake is to induce a high degree of fear while providing them with recommendations for action that are *concrete, effective, and doable* (Leventhal, 1970; Leventhal, Singer, and Jones, 1965; Pratkanis and Aronson, 1992; de Hoog et al., 2007). For example, suppose you are a physician and you believe that it is imperative for women to do monthly breast self-examinations and have annual mammograms, because early detection of breast cancer will save lives. Research has shown that you will be more effective at getting your patients to comply if you induce high fear rather than a low or mild degree of fear (Ruiter et al., 2001).

It is a very simple formula, and it works in a wide variety of situations that range from increasing regular tooth brushing to decreasing drunk driving to checking for the existence of radon in one's home. The higher the fear and the more concrete, effective, and doable the recommendation, the more likely it is that people will comply. But research has also shown that if you scare the hell out of people and fail to provide them with all three of those factors, then fear will *not* produce reasonable responses to danger. Instead, it will produce denial. People will convince themselves that the disaster is unlikely to occur, thus assuaging both their fear and their cognitive dissonance (see Pratkanis and Aronson, 2002; Leventhal, 1970; Maddux and Rogers, 1983). In this context, it should be clear that, psychologically, denial in the face of fear and helplessness is not crazy. Although it does not protect us from the imminent danger, it does help us sleep at night and go about our business during the day without being in a constant state of fear and discomfort.

There are more than 100 experiments in social psychology demonstrating the relationship between fear, information, sensible action, and denial. The research on this issue is so vast and well documented that any college sophomore who has taken a course in introductory social psychology knows it backward and forward. With this in mind, what are we to make of it when a high-ranking public servant like Michael Chertoff, the director of Homeland Security, says (as he did on July 10, 2007) that he had a "gut feeling" that there would be a terrorist attack on American soil sometime in the summer? He didn't say what it might be, where it might take place, or what people might do either to escape or respond to the attack. He thus induced fear without offering any information—much less any specific, effective, doable recommendations for action. Some observers suggested that Chertoff's "gut feelings" might have been politically motivated—to remind us that we are in danger of terrorism, capitalizing on the general belief that the Republicans are tougher on terror than the Democrats. In fairness to Chertoff, he might have been honestly attempting to alert the public to a possible threat. But it is disconcerting to think that the director of Homeland Security is less well informed than the average college sophomore; that he is oblivious of the fact that inducing fear, in and of itself, is by no means benign; and that by making a vague fear-arousing statement, he is doing harm by inducing citizens to go into denial—and, therefore, to become complacent. Furthermore, if the government continues to issue vague warnings about bogus threats, those warnings will be greeted by a huge national yawn, which would be a highly dangerous outcome.

Unfortunately, Chertoff was not the first director of Homeland Security to induce fear without a proposal for action. That honor goes to Tom Ridge, just months after the destruction of the World Trade Center on 9/11. He put the country on red alert, and then he advised us to simply go about our business but to be vigilant. Vigilant for what? Where? What should we do? Keep our eyes peeled for young swarthy men with mustaches? Ridge did not say.

Then, of course, there was the great anthrax scare of 2003. That fiasco can be summarized in five words: duct tape and plastic sheeting. The Department of Homeland Security issued a directive advising the public that, in the event of a general anthrax attack, people could protect themselves by creating a "safe room" in their homes through the judicious use of duct tape and plastic sheeting. This directive produced a temporary shortage of duct tape before it was ridiculed in the press and on television. In terms of our formula, the directive was concrete, specific, and doable. There was only one problem: most experts agreed that creating a "safe room" in this manner would be totally ineffective against anthrax spores. Indeed, many of these experts believed that the application of duct tape and plastic sheeting might cut off the supply of oxygen and therefore could actually harm anyone in the "safe room."

When fear mongering without concrete recommendations for action is further complicated by the incompetence of the agency that is supposed to be protecting the public from harm, the average citizen will feel even more powerless and angry. Government incompetence seems to have begun even in the weeks following 9/11, when, it now appears, the Environmental Protection Agency seriously underestimated the danger to the lungs of first responders and clean-up workers from their exposure to the toxicity of the dust and debris at ground zero. But of course the greatest example of incompetence followed the devastation caused by Hurricane Katrina in 2005, when FEMA's slow and inadequate response alarmed the entire nation. FEMA's director, Michael D. Brown, ignored the ample warnings from the National Hurricane Service that one of the country's biggest hurricanes was on its way and to evacuate the populace immediately. After the hurricane struck, citizens were urged to take shelter in the Superdome, but the Superdome was undersupplied with food and water; at the same time, toilet facilities were woefully inadequate and police protection was virtually nonexistent. (Whatever Brown might have been up to, he was definitely not doing "a heck of a job," as President George W. Bush was to remark on finally visiting the city.

The research of experimental social psychologists shows that these incredible blunders—the ineptness of the government's response to the threat of disaster and to disaster itself—is not only dysfunctional in its immediate effect but also in the long-term psychological consequences for the public. People will be willing to sacrifice a few conveniences for an increased feeling of safety and security; for example, they will put up with the annoyance of airport security lines if they think the tedious inspections of their shoes and shampoos are making them safer. But learning that incognito government inspectors have been able to smuggle bomb parts through the screening devices makes airline passengers feel both vulnerable and increasingly resentful. If the screeners can't find the real dangers, what's the point of taking off my shoes, removing my belt, and putting my shampoo in a Ziploc bag? Discovering that we are in the hands of incompetent agencies and their staff produces feelings of helplessness that, in turn, intensify the denial mechanism: "There's nothing we can do, and even if we can do something, it won't work anyway." Indeed, I would suggest that of all the disasters that have befallen our nation in the twenty-first century—hurricanes, tornadoes, floods, wildfires, the terrorist attacks on 9/11—perhaps the greatest disaster has been the ineptitude of the Bush administration in dealing with them.

TAKING A CLOSER LOOK AT WHAT IS DOABLE

Thus far, we have seen that a communication that produces high fear can lead to sensible action but only if the communication also contains recommendations for action that are concrete, effective, and doable. If the communication lacks a concrete recommendation for action (as in Chertoff's gut feeling) or if the concrete recommendation is ineffective (as was the case with the duct tape directive), people will strive to minimize the danger. Now, let us look at the third factor: whether the action is doable. The main point I want to make here is that what seems doable from the outside looking in might not be doable from the inside. To illustrate this point, let us look at condom use and the AIDS pandemic, which for many years has been a serious and tragic international public health disaster.

AIDS is a scary disease, but it is preventable because it is primarily the result of voluntary sexual activity. According to our formula, the solution would appear to be simple: scare the hell out of sexually active people and strongly recommend that they either abstain or use condoms. Many abstinence-only until marriage sex "education" programs do try to scare young people—having sex before marriage, the teenagers are told, will give you terrible diseases, ruin your reputation and your self-esteem, and may even cost you your life. But the solution they offer, "just wait until marriage," has proved difficult for most teenagers and young adults to follow, and these programs have been almost unanimously ineffective in delaying age of first intercourse (Hauser, 2004).[2] Worse, they seem to *reduce* young people's likelihood of using contraception of any kind.

So how about scaring the hell out of teenagers about sexually transmitted diseases and then providing the specific advice to use condoms to protect themselves? At first glance, condom use would appear to be nonproblematic. What could be more doable than slipping on a condom? And yet, in this country alone, in 2004, there were 9 million cases of sexually transmitted diseases in the age group 15-24, and most of those cases were the human papilloma virus, which can lead to serious reproductive problems. Most STDs are treatable, but the medical and psychological costs are high, and, most important, the huge numbers reveal in the most concrete manner that a staggeringly high number of sexually active young people are having unprotected sex. If condoms are so easily doable, why are so many young people not "doing" them?

I became involved in this problem about 20 years ago, when the chief medical officer on my campus expressed alarm at the high incidence of STDs among our students. He felt that, if nothing were done, it was only a matter of time before AIDS would strike the campus, and if it did, given the high degree of sexual activity, it might spread rapidly.

Our students had been informed by lectures and pamphlets of the dangers of unprotected sexual activity. This information campaign was designed to produce high levels of fear. And yet, a high percentage of students acted as if they were oblivious to the problem; they continued to engage in unprotected sex. They weren't oblivious to the dangers; they simply chose not to think about them. My colleagues and I conducted interviews and surveys on campus. We found that students knew all about AIDS, were plenty scared of it, and knew that condom use would protect them. Yet only 21 percent of the sexually active students were using condoms regularly, a percentage not significantly different from the percentage on most college campuses across the nation.

Why weren't students using condoms? Our interviews revealed that most students considered condoms to be unromantic, an interference with the spontaneous flow of lovemaking; they thought condoms were antiseptic, better associated with the bathroom than the bedroom. Moreover, the information campaign had done its job all too well. Condoms had become so thoroughly associated with AIDS that when the students thought of condoms they started thinking about the possibility of dying a horrible death. These were not the kinds of thoughts they wanted to have in their minds while they were getting ready to make love; such thoughts have a way of reducing passion. So they went into denial. They told us, "Surely none of *my* friends will get AIDS" or "I am certain that I could spot someone with AIDS a mile away." Fear of AIDS drove them deeper into denial.

What could we do? Interesting problem. The students didn't need additional information because they already knew all about AIDS, and they already knew that condoms offer reliable protection. They just weren't using them. Their denial led them to the conclusion that "condoms are great for other people, but I don't really need them."

My first idea was that because our students thought of condoms as a cumbersome, antisexual device, perhaps if we made condoms more romantic—less like a medical thing and more like a part of foreplay—students would begin using them. Accordingly, I produced and directed a 5-minute erotic video showing an attractive young couple making love. (The IRB informed me that as long as I didn't actually show anyone's genitalia and explicit activity, they approved.) The video was more suggestive than explicit, more "R-rated" than "X-rated." The key aspect of the video made it clear that, under the sheets, just barely hidden from view, the woman was putting the condom on her partner. There was a great deal of sighing and oohing and aahing so that it was reasonably clear that putting on the condom was a mutual act and a mutually exciting one. We showed the video to a few hundred sexually active students. They loved it. They rated it highly, and, most important, most of them began to use condoms—but only for two or three weeks. Then almost all of them stopped using them. When we interviewed the students later, we found that after a few trials they realized that they were not having nearly as much fun as the gorgeous couple on the video seemed to be having, so they gave up using the condoms.

So I decided to try an end run around the issue. Instead of trying to use direct persuasion on our sexually active students, I tried to invoke feelings of cognitive dissonance by challenging their self-concept as individuals of integrity. My earlier research inspired by the theory of cognitive dissonance showed that most people believe that they have integrity and that they will do almost anything to avoid feeling like a hypocrite. So my strategy, in a nutshell, was to induce students to try to convince younger, sexually active people to use condoms and then to confront these students with their own hypocrisy—with the fact that they were not practicing what they were preaching. Theoretically, this would produce enormous dissonance and the best way for them to reduce this dissonance would be to begin to practice what they were preaching; that is, to use condoms.

The idea can be clarified by a hypothetical example. Suppose you are a sexually active college student and you do not use condoms regularly. On going home for Christmas vacation, you learn that Charlie, your 17-year-old brother, has just discovered sex, and is boasting to you about his varied sexual encounters. Chances are, as a caring, responsible older sibling, you would warn him about the dangers of AIDS and other STDs and urge him to use condoms. Suppose I overheard this exchange and said to you, "That was good advice you gave Charlie; by the way, how frequently do *you* use condoms?" This statement forces you to become mindful of the dissonance between your self-concept as a person of integrity (one with the intelligence to want to avoid getting an STD) and the fact that you are behaving hypocritically. How might you reduce dissonance? By starting to practice what you have just finished preaching; in short, by starting to use condoms yourself or requiring your partner to use them.

In a series of experiments, my graduate students and I constructed a procedure that was similar to this scenario (Aronson, 1991; Aronson, Fried, and Stone, 1991; Stone, Aronson et. al., 1994). We recruited sexually active college students and asked them to deliver a speech about the dangers of AIDS and the importance of using condoms. We videotaped each speech, and informed the speakers that their video would be shown to high-school students as part of a sex-education class. In the crucial condition, after they made the videotape, we got them to talk about the situations where they had found it impossible to use condoms, making them mindful of their own hypocrisy.

The results were impressive. Students in the "hypocrisy" condition purchased and used condoms significantly and substantially more regularly than students in the control condition, who made the same videotaped speech but were not made mindful of the fact that their own behavior was hypocritical. Moreover, the effects of the hypocrisy induction were still apparent some several months later, when, in a telephone survey, the overwhelming majority of students in the hypocrisy condition told an interviewer (who was not connected to the original experiment) that they were still using condoms regularly.

This approach is, of course, highly individualistic. If the erotic film had been effective, it would have been far more economic and practical; we could have shown it to a huge number of people all at once. Unfortunately, it didn't work (which, by the way, is, in and of itself, an important finding, given how many "public service" announcements attempting to change people's sexual behavior are on film or print ads). The "hypocrisy" technique, while far from economical, is not impractical, however. For example, we have had some success building the process into high school sex education classes. In these classes, students present arguments to their fellow students about the importance of using condoms. They are then asked to examine their own sexual behavior (if any) and compare and contrast it with the advice they were giving others.

We have used the hypocrisy paradigm in other domains as well. One additional example will suffice: energy and water conservation. California has a chronic water shortage, and on my campus in Santa Cruz, the administration has constantly tried to find ways to induce students to conserve water and the energy used to heat that water. Our students are generally ecology minded, forever demonstrating to save the whales and the redwoods. However, the campus administration found it very difficult to persuade them to limit their consumption of water and energy by taking shorter showers. Pamphlets were distributed, flyers were posted urging students to take short showers, all to little avail.

My research assistants and I saw this as an ideal situation in which to apply the hypocrisy paradigm. In this experiment (Dickerson, Thibodeau, Aronson, and Miller, 1992), we stationed a graduate student in the locker room of the campus field house. Her job was to intercept college women on their way from the heavily chlorinated swimming pool to the shower room. In a manner that was precisely parallel to the condom experiment, we varied whether or not students were asked to suggest that other students take short showers and whether or not they were forced to become mindful of their hypocrisy. In the commitment conditions, each student was asked if she would be willing to sign a poster encouraging people to conserve water at the field house and in the dormitories. The students were told that the posters (large and colorful, with the signers' names in large letters) would be placed all over campus. The poster read: "Take shorter showers. Turn off water while soaping up. If I can do it, so can you!" After the student signed the poster, our assistant thanked her for her time. In the mindful conditions we asked the students to respond to a water conservation survey, which consisted of items designed to make them aware of their pro-conservation attitudes and the fact that their showering behavior is sometimes wasteful. In the "non-mindful" condition, the survey consisted of items about the frequency with which she uses the facilities at the field house and about approximately how many showers she usually took per week.

Each of the students then proceeded to the shower room, where another of our undergraduate research assistants (blind to condition) was unobtrusively waiting (with a hidden waterproof stopwatch) to time the student's shower. The results were consistent with those in the condom experiment: we found dissonance effects only in the cell where the subjects were preaching what they were not always practicing—that is, in the condition where the students were induced to advocate short showers and were made mindful of their own past "water-wasteful" behavior. In that condition, they took very short showers. The length of the average shower (which, because of the chlorine in the swimming pool, included a shampoo and cream rinse) averaged just over three and a half minutes (that's short!) and was dramatically shorter than in the unmindful/uncommitted condition.

Taken together, these experiments show that in important situations, sensible behavior that appears doable, at least from the outside looking in, is not often so doable from the insider's perspective. But with some thought and the application of existing knowledge, we can develop strategies to make people more likely to do what is appropriate and sensible for themselves and their communities.

THE DOABLE

I have tried to highlight the importance of understanding how ordinary people respond to disasters and the threat of disaster—not how policymakers think people *should* behave or *wish* they would behave, but how we humans *actually* behave. We are not always rational animals but we are almost always rationalizing animals. To convince people to prepare for disasters and change behavior they are happy with, therefore, we must puncture their rationalizations. We must make them feel vulnerable to the disaster *and* competent in preparing for it or coping with it. Inducing fear is an excellent way to induce people to behave in a rational manner in the face of disaster, but if and only if that fear is accompanied by recommendations for action that are concrete, effective and, doable. Fear without all three of these qualities is counterproductive because it produces denial which, in the face of disaster, can be extremely dangerous. The concept of "doable," however, is tricky. Some recommendations that appear easy to do when viewed from the outside, turn out to be difficult, as when sexually active young adults are urged to use condoms.

Experimental social psychologists have had this knowledge for a long time, and have applied it to a wide array of health and safety issues, from preparing for a disaster (such as earthquakes) to averting a disaster (such as AIDS). It is of vital importance for this knowledge to find its way into the general wisdom of policy makers.

NOTES

1. If a person is a homeowner or even a renter, gaining knowledge pertinent to earthquake preparedness can be much more useful. One can learn to anchor tall bookcases to the wall. One can learn about disconnecting natural gas lines leading into the dwelling to prevent fires, and so on. But when a person is living or working in a public building, there is little one can learn that goes beyond common sense. I have first-hand experience on that score. I was in my office at the University of California at Santa Cruz on October 17, 1989, when the Loma Prieta earthquake struck. My office was about 10 miles from the epicenter. When the building began to shake, I got scared, stood up, and took three steps toward the door. But the room was shaking so violently that I quickly realized that I wasn't going to be able to get out of the building, so I did the natural, common sense thing: I dived under my desk—a few seconds later, the floor-to-ceiling bookshelf came down. If I had been sitting in my chair I would have been buried by books. The point is, I didn't require a knowledge of earthquakes,

their cause, their effects, or what to do in case one hit; what to do was obvious.

2. According to Debra Hauser's (2004) review of 11 abstinence-only programs across the nation, "Evaluation of these 11 programs showed few short-term benefits and no lasting, positive impact. A few programs showed mild success at improving attitudes and intentions to abstain. No program was able to demonstrate a positive impact on sexual behavior over time. . . . Worse, [these programs] show some negative impacts on youth's willingness to use contraception, including condoms, to prevent negative sexual health outcomes related to sexual intercourse. Importantly, only in one state did any program demonstrate short-term success in delaying the initiation of sex; none of these programs demonstrates evidence of long-term success in delaying sexual initiation among youth exposed to the programs or any evidence of success in reducing other sexual risk-taking behaviors among participants."

REFERENCES

Aronson, E. "How to Change Behavior." *How People Change: Inside and Outside Therapy*. Eds. R. Curtis and G. Stricker. New York: Plenum Press, 1991.

———. "The Power of Self-Persuasion." *American Psychologist* 54 (1999): 873-884.

———. "The Evolution of Cognitive Dissonance Theory: A Personal Appraisal." *The Science of Social Influence*. Ed. A. Pratkanis. New York: Psychology Press, 2007.

———. *The Social Animal*. 10th ed. New York: Worth, 2008.

Aronson, E., C. Fried, and J. Stone. "Overcoming Denial and Increasing the Intention to Use Condoms through the Induction of Hypocrisy." *American Journal of Public Health* 81 (1991): 1636-1638.

De Hoog, N., W. Stroebe, and J.B.F. de Wit. "The Impact of Vulnerability to and Severity of a Health Risk on Processing and Acceptance of Fear-Arousing Communications: A Meta-Analysis." *Review of General Psychology* 11 (2007): 258-285.

Dickerson, C. A., R. Thibodeau, E. Aronson, and D. Miller. "Using Cognitive Dissonance to Encourage Water Conservation." *Journal of Applied Social Psychology* 22 (1992): 841-854.

Festimger, L. *A Theory of Cognitive Dissonance.* New York: Row Peterson, 1957.

Festinger, L., and E. Aronson. "The Arousal and Reduction of Dissonance in Social Contexts." *Group Dynamics.* Eds. D. Cartwright and A. Zander. 3rd Ed. New York: Harper and Row, 1960.

Hauser, D. *Five Years of Abstinence-Only-Until-Marriage Education: Assessing the Impact.* Washington, D.C.: Advocates for Youth, 2004.

Kahneman, D., and A. Tversky. "Choices, Values, and Frames." *American Psychologist* 39 (1984): 341-350.

Kahneman, D., and A. Tversky. "On the Reality of Cognitive Illusions." *Psychological Review* 103 (1996): 582-591.

Kohn, P. M., M. S. Goodstadt, G. M. Cook, M. Sheppard, and G. Chan. "Ineffectiveness of Threat Appeals about Drinking and Driving." *Accident Analysis and Prevention* 14 (1982): 457–464.

Lehman, D., and S. Taylor. "Date with an Earthquake: Coping with a Probable, Unpredictable Disaster." *Personality and Social Psychology Bulletin* 13 (1987): 546-555.

Leventhal, H. "Findings and Theory in the Study of Fear Communications." *Advances in Experimental Social Psychology.* Ed. L. Berkowitz. Vol. 5. San Diego: Academic Press, 1970.

Leventhal, H., R. P. Singer, and S. Jones. "Effects of Fear and Specificity of Recommendation upon Attitudes and Behavior." *Journal of Personality and Social Psychology* 2 (1965): 20–29.

Maddux, J. E., and R. W. Rogers. "Protection Motivation and Self-Efficacy: A Revised Theory of Fear Appeals and Attitude Change." *Journal of Experimental Social Psychology* 19 (1983): 469-479.

Pratkanis, A. R., and E. Aronson, E. *Age of Propaganda: The Everyday Use and Abuse of Persuasion.* 2nd ed. New York: W. H. Freeman/Times Books, 2002.

Ruiter, R. A. C., G. Kok, B. Verplanken, and J. Brug. "Evoked Fear and Effects of Appeals on Attitudes to Performing Breast Self-Examination: An

Information-Processing Perspective." *Health Education Research* 16 (2001): 307–319.

Stone, J., E. Aronson, A. L. Crain, M. P. Winslow, and C. B. Fried. "Inducing Hypocrisy as a Means of Encouraging Young Adults to Use Condoms." *Personality and Social Psychology Bulletin* 20 (1994): 116-128.

Tavris, C., and E. Aronson. *Mistakes Were Made (But Not by Me): Why We Justify Foolish Beliefs, Bad Decisions, and Hurtful Acts*. New York: Harcourt, 2007.

Enrico L. Quarantelli
Conventional Beliefs and Counterintuitive Realities

THIS PAPER DISCUSSES MAJOR MYTHS AND WIDELY HELD INCORRECT beliefs about individual and group behaviors in disaster contexts. Why can we categorize such views as invalid? Because now there has been more than half a century of systematic social science studies (and an earlier half century of less well known scattered works) that have established the actual parameters of the behavior of individuals and groups in natural and technological disaster situations (for recent summaries of the extensive research literature, see Lindell, Perry, and Prater, 2006; National Research Council, 2006; and Rodriguez, Quarantelli, and Dynes, 2006). All is not known, and serious gaps remain in knowledge about important topics, but we are at this time far beyond just educated guesses on many dimensions of the relevant behaviors.

Our focus is on six different behavioral aspects of disasters, primarily occurring around the impact time period of such crises. Stated in just a few words, we look at panic flight and at antisocial looting behavior, supposed passivity in emergencies, role conflict and abandonment, severe mental health consequences, and the locus of whatever problems surface. We present what is often assumed, believed, or stated on these matters—at least in popular discourse and to a varying extent in policy, planning, and operational circles—as over against what study and research has found.

The concept of "myths" was coined in the early 1950s by researchers who were studying the natural and technological "disasters" that were taking place in American society at that time. These research-ers were never under any illusion that these were the only kinds of collective crises that societies could suffer. This idea was reinforced in the early 1960s when there were many urban and university riots that "disaster" researchers studied even as they recognized they were along some lines qualitatively different from the earlier natural and technological disasters looked at in the field. To some researchers these became known as "conflict crises." In the decades that followed, addi-tional notions about mega-disasters/catastrophes, as well as even newer kinds of crises, also qualitatively different, crept into the literature.

Without going into the uneven historical evolution of the think-ing about different kinds or types, we need here to identify distinc-tive aspects of the four kinds of collective crises just noted. This is because the idea of the myths is not equally applicable across the board. Particularly important is that the idea makes sense for disasters but needs qualification for catastrophes.

A few researchers have argued for decades that there are disasters and there are catastrophes. This is not simply substituting or replacing one word with another to try to maintain the idea of disaster myths, as has been incorrectly implied (Handmer, 2007, for example). Rather, it involves an attempt to differentiate major differences between one kind of social crisis and another as the result of the impact of a destruc-tive natural or technological agent (see Quarantelli, 2005a). The charac-teristics of a catastrophe in ideal-type terms are the following.

In a space-time framework, a catastrophe occurs when 1) within a relatively short time period, 2) a large but not necessarily fully contiguous area with multiple land uses and diverse communities, is 3) perceived as being subjected to very major threats to life and property, thus 4) requir-ing immediate responses to start restoring a routine social order.

This kind of social occasion results in:

▸ most everyday community functions and social institutions being sharply and concurrently interrupted (in contrast to this not happening in a disaster);

- many organizations, including those that are emergency oriented, either cease operating or do so in a markedly reduced manner (in contrast to a disaster where few organizations in a community deteriorate to such a degree);
- many local community officials and others are unable to undertake their usual work roles (in contrast to this happening only on a small and selective scale in the typical disaster);
- most help or aid has to come from more distant areas (in contrast to massive convergence in a disaster from the community itself and/or from nearby areas);
- the immediate and ongoing crisis is socially constructed by nonlocal mass media supplemented by cable television and Internet bloggers (in contrast to a disaster, where the greatest attention is by the local media with only incidental and brief reporting carried out by cable and national mass communication outlets); and
- high-ranking government and political officials and organizations from the national (and sometime international) level become involved (in contrast to a disaster, where there is at most limited and primarily symbolic attention given by other than local persons and community/state agencies).

Then there is the question on whether our observations and findings about myths in disasters and catastrophes are applicable to conflict-type crises (such as civil disturbances, riots, acts of terrorism, and what the National Science Foundation increasingly labels "willful" disasters) as well as newer or emerging kinds of disasters (such as the spread of SARS and massive computer system disruptions). The answer is that the extrapolation that can be made is limited. There are features of such crises that are not seen or are more important in what has been established about impact-time behaviors in natural and technological disasters and catastrophes (see Quarantelli, Lagadec, and Boin, 2006). So while we make passing observations in what follows on these different behavioral reactions, we do not systematically discuss some distinctive or unique features in conflict crises and the newer kinds of disasters.

THE SIX MYTHS

1. Panic

Perhaps the most frequently used term in connection with disasters and crises is the word "panic." However, the referent of the word is widely diverse both in popular culture and the scientific literature. There are multiple denotations and connotations for the word.

Although written four decades ago, an observation by Jordan unfortunately still is true today. As he noted: "The literature on panic research is strewn with wrecked hulks of attempts to define 'panic.' When these definitions are placed side by side, one is confronted by chaos. . . . There doesn't seem to be a common behavior accepted by all concerned; even flight behavior is excluded" (1963).

Recent extensive discussions using the word (see Orr, 2006; Mawson, 2007) continue to present diverse and heterogeneous references of the term as was done more than half a century ago (see, e.g., Strauss, 1944). In 1954 we wrote: "Almost every kind of socially disorganizing or personally disruptive type of activity has been characterized as panic. The range includes everything from psychiatric phenomena to economic phenomena (e.g., the 'panics' involved in bank runs, stock-market crashes, depressions, etc.)" (Quarantelli, 1954: 268).

In the same article we note that a paper on panic a few years earlier (Meerloo, 1950) cited as examples of panic: lynch mobs, suicidal epidemics, individual and collective anxieties, plundering troops, spy hysterias, military retreats and surrenders, social unrest, war, psychotic behavior, mass hysteria, animal stampedes, confused voting behavior, orgiastic feasts, the activities of war refugees, and group tensions.

From that it could be argued that the only common dimension is that whatever it is, panic is something that is bad or unfortunate from the viewpoint of human beings and their groups.

Collective panic in its various conceptualizations has been more empirically studied, especially in the earliest days of disaster research, than most realize. A keyword search using the word "panic" of the Disaster Research Center (DRC) Resource Collection produced 295 items that included very few non-English sources. In the professional natural and technological disaster literature there are at least five major sources of empirical data, mostly on collective flight behavior.

It was an explicit partial focus of the famous National Opinion Research Center (NORC) field studies, recognized not only as the pioneer work in disaster research but also as a classic piece of research (see Quarantelli, 1988). As such, the almost complete absence of panic flight that was found provided part of the initial formulation about the existence of "disaster myths."

It was a major topic addressed by the National Academy of Sciences (NAS). Our recent perusal of the archives of all National Science Foundation disaster-related committees and groups now in the possession of the DRC found that the topic of panic was intensively pursued for several decades, and a number of informal essays and memos were written on the topic both from re-analysis of previously gathered data as well as newly gathered data.

It was consistently looked for by DRC in its early field work. Field researchers irrespective of the particular focus of the field work involved were supposed to be sensitive to hearing about any possible panic phenomena. In reality, extremely few such instances were ever reported, but that in itself supported the notion that panic flight was very rare.

It was a long focus of empirical research by fire researchers and the National Bureau of Standards (as well as related work done in England; see, e.g., Canter, 1980). Totally independent of traditional disaster research, these researchers were specifically interested in movement of people away from home and other fires. Panic flight was so rarely found that eventually the very concept of "panic behavior" was deemed useless for fire research purposes (Bryan, 1980).

More recently there have been studies of occupant behavior in buildings at times of earthquakes that imply some cases of panic flight (Alexander, 1995). Unfortunately, these studies are innocent of exposure to social science studies of panic that have long distinguished between rational and meaningful evacuation of buildings, and wild and uncontrolled flight. Our own personal first three field studies were of an earthquake, a series of separate house explosions, and a plane crash in a very dense urban neighborhood, where the difference between organized and uncontrolled flight was obvious.

The usage definition more commonly used by students of the problem equates panic with inappropriate flight behavior away from a response to threat or danger. Although used in popular discourse for centuries, the term panic as applicable to collective flight behavior was only conceptually developed in the early 1950s by disaster researchers (Quarantelli, 1954, 1960).

Does panic emerge at times of disasters? It is important to note that it is clear that at times that some reports of panic are just social constructions by mass media outlets. There is a famous study of a 1938 radio broadcast of a supposed "invasion from Mars" (Cantril, 1940), which has been both incorrectly reported and or highlighted by others and that itself conveys an incorrect picture. For example, if carefully read, the huge majority of radio listeners in the 85 percent and higher range simply heard it as a radio show. More important, anecdotal material used in the book taken from newspaper clippings, conveys an impression of widespread panic flight, but that conclusion was not drawn from the purposive sample used. In short, the text nowhere supports the notion of widespread panic flight.

In 1973 another fictitious broadcast reported the following:

> According to reports in the mass media, a fictitious radio broadcast about a disaster at a nuclear power station in southern Sweden caused widespread panic flight among the population in the area. A telephone survey of a representative sample (n = 1,089) in combination with unstructured interviews with police and other authorities indicates that no panic flight at all did occur (Rosengren, Arvidson, and Sturesson, 1975: 303).

In the sense of wild collective flight behavior, our conclusion is that it very seldom occurs since it requires the presence of rarely present concurrent social conditions. The necessary affective/cognitive factors can be categorized in different ways but include at least the following:

▸ Perception of an immediate great threat to self and/or significant others. It is extreme fear rather than anxiety that predominates since the risk to physical survival seems clear. Fear, no matter the magnitude, in itself is not enough to generate panic despite what some users of the term mistakenly assert.
▸ Belief that escape from the threat is possible (a perception that one is trapped does not lead to panic flight; this can be seen in entombed coal miners or sailors in sunken submarines). It is hope, not hopelessness, that drives panic flight.
▸ A feeling of helplessness in otherwise dealing with the threat and particular others are not seen as being able to help. If there is a perception that movement away from the risk is possible, an orderly or organized movement or evacuation from the location usually occurs. Such flight behavior is not panic behavior—as was overwhelmingly the case among the survivors who left the towers in the 9/11 disaster.

These necessary, collective panic-generating conditions can be reinforced by the presence of two other conditions. Flight is more likely to occur among an aggregation of strangers rather than where there are many prior social ties among those present. Also, flight is more likely in social settings where there are prior cultural norms that can make such locations panic inducing (closed and confined physical spaces such as theaters and night clubs).

The concurrent presence of all these conditions can lead to nonsocial behavior that in its most extreme form can lead to the dissolution of the most important social ties (such as mothers abandoning their small children) and violation of normal social norms (such as those fleeing trampling upon one another). In the most extreme case, collective panic flight is the very opposite of organized behavior, although the flight that is directional tends to be short lived in both time and distance, and is not automatically contagious. Nevertheless, panic flights show human beings at their worst.

Fortunately, the phenomenon is rare. We have found clear-cut cases of collective panic flight in less than 100 disasters in a half century of professionally looking for the phenomena, and even in those cases usually only a small minority of those present in the situation engaged in anything resembling panic flight. Even those atypical researchers who still are quibbling over the nature of panic (e.g., Alexander, 1995, who mixes solo and collective "panic") grant that in terms of sheer frequency it is a rare occurrence.

To conclude, collective panic flight in disasters is such a rarity that it is not a major problem and has very little overall negative consequences compared with other bad effects. Also, while some current researchers continue to use the word "panic" in imaginative ways (Clarke, 2002, 2006), we personally think the term should be dropped as a social science concept. The behaviors involved can all be described and explained by other more powerful social science concepts (as Johnson, 1985 used social role). A major move in such a direction would free social scientists from the ambiguities and imprecisions of continuing to use a word drawn from popular discourse.

2. Antisocial Behavior

Is there antisocial behavior, especially looting, during and after disasters? Does Mr. Hyde take over from Dr. Jekyll? Disaster films and popular beliefs (as manifested in reluctance to evacuate because of a concern that one's possessions might be looted) assume such behavior is common.

Popular accounts of some earlier American disasters such as the Johnstown flood or the Galveston hurricane frequently allude to rapes and murders on these occasions. Such violent behaviors were almost always attributed to members of lower-class ethnic or racial groups in the community. However, since such behaviors are seldom mentioned by anyone in recent and current disasters in American communities (except for some very dubious cases that supposedly occurred after Hurricane Katrina in New Orleans), we limit our discussion of antisocial behavior to looting phenomena (although since such attributions still are sometime made especially in catastrophes in developing societies, study of violent antisocial behaviors ought to remain on the research agenda).

The word "looting"—derived via the Hindu *lut* from the Sanskrit *lunt* meaning "to rob"—came into Western European languages to refer to the plundering undertaken by invading armies. Of interest is that since the "to the victors belong the spoils" notion prevailed, the term looting applied to the military was not uniformly viewed as indicating criminal or deviant behavior. There were even applied rules on what buildings could be entered, what could be looted, and the time frame within which the takings could occur (Green, 2006: 9). Only with the advent of international law and especially the Hague Convention of 1907 was looting in a military context universally condemned and prohibited (Green, 2006: 10).

As far as civilian disasters were concerned, negative views about looting developed much earlier. Condemnation of taking goods for one's own use is negatively viewed in Hebrew religious writings and was explicitly prohibited under Roman law (Green, 2006: 10). However, the word "looting" itself was almost never used in both popular and contemporary historical descriptions of disasters. Our examination of a number of such books on disasters in American society in the nineteenth nineteenth century found not a single use of the word "looting" although the illicit taking of goods is often mentioned.

The first systematic and continuing professional use of the word appears to have occurred in the NORC field studies of disasters from 1949 to 1954. However, although personally a member of the field teams, we have no recollection of how and why the word explicitly came to be used. Perhaps it came out of the fact that Charles Fritz, the day-to-day operational manager of the project, had a military background and minor involvement with the US Strategic Bombing Survey (USSBS), which did look at whether antisocial and looting behaviors occurred during World War II in German and Japanese cities. The survey, reinforced by British studies of their own civilian population, concluded that looting was not a serious problem in and after massive air bombings.

There is a substantial but not massive body of empirical and theoretical literature on looting. More is available on looting behavior in civil disturbances than disasters, primarily because of scholarly interest in the disturbances of the 1960s and 1970s in American cities. However, except for an occasional study, little scholarly attention has been paid to the topic in civilian disasters and crises outside of the United States.

Probably the most sophisticated analysis of looting is a very recent article by Green (2006). He describes how looting has been viewed over the centuries, the complicated legal issues in defining the behavior and related activity, and how it tends to be dealt by the US court system and other authorities.

It appears that from a quantitative viewpoint, the DRC over a 43-year period has done the majority of empirical studies of looting. Major attention to looting phenomena has been paid by the center in terms of focused attention in particular studies where specific questions on the topic were part of field study questionnaires. Large-scale survey studies such as on the Xenia tornado and the Wilkes-Barre flood disasters generated considerable quantitative data. Looting in civil disturbances has been done over a number of years (see Dynes and Quarantelli, 1968; Tierney, 1994). Field studies by the DRC of looting in catastrophes such as Hurricane Katrina continue (Barsky, 2007).

The overall conclusions from all the empirical research can be summarized as follows. As we wrote recently (Quarantelli, 2007), looting of any kind is unusual in the typical natural and technological disasters that afflict modern, Western-type societies. But the picture is rather mixed in other kinds of social systems, with looting seemingly occurring more often than not in developing systems (in 2007 there was massive looting in catastrophes in Peru and Columbia). There is also a distinctive pattern to the rare looting that occurs in disasters that is different from what emerges in civil disturbances. There are atypical instances of mass looting that only emerge if a complex set of prior social conditions exist, namely what is seen in a catastrophe rather than just a usual kind of disaster (to the necessary conditions other sufficient conditions are also needed).

Given what many people think they know about Hurricane Katrina and New Orleans, it may not be amiss to discuss that occasion from a research perspective. To some it appeared that the apparent "looting"' behavior that emerged contradicted the notion that looting in disasters was a myth. Actually, anyone who had ever systematically looked at the research literature knew that it never said that looting never happened. The basic proposition advanced from the earliest studies half a century ago was that it was very rare and in many cases almost nonexistent in American-type communities except for some souvenir hunting. That researchers had from the start believed that looting could happen is supported by the well-documented fact that scholars more than three decades ago identified and discussed the four characteristic patterns of looting in natural and technological disasters. We said that when looting did occur, it was socially and overtly condemned by others experiencing the disaster; it was covertly done, undertaken mostly by isolated individuals or pairs, with the objects looted being a matter of chance or opportunity. In contrast, the same researchers noted that in the often massive looting in civil disturbances was socially supported, undertaken overtly by small groups (including family units), socially approved, with the looting taking place at targeted sites. These two distinctive patterns were set forth in numerous publications, but apparently they were never read or if read were badly misread by some who challenge the looting myth.

Hurricane Katrina created a catastrophe in the New Orleans area but a much better case of mass looting occurred in St. Croix in the US Virgin Islands after Hurricane Hugo, which made the former situation look like a picnic (we have earlier reported the following in Quarantelli, 2007). We undertook three extensive field studies including a systematic quantitative survey of all businesses in the four shopping centers or malls on the island. The looting was by any criteria massive. Not only were all consumer goods in sight stolen, but electrical and wall fixtures as well as carpets were also stripped. The biggest malls with over 150 shops as well as two others were swept clean with less than 10 percent of the businesses reporting they were not totally looted.

The looting was initiated by preexisting juvenile gangs of delinquent youths (as was the case in the 1977 New York City blackout) who targeted stores with large amounts of consumer goods such as television stores (but not food supermarkets). The second stage was when initial nonparticipants who did not have everyday criminal lifestyles began taking goods also from other locations such as hardware stores. Finally, a much larger number of people joined in targeting stores with basic necessities (groceries, for example) who generally did not loot items taken by the first two sets of looters. Overall, the looting pattern was that which earlier researchers had found in civil disturbances as discussed previously. (This is a puzzling finding, for which no explanation has been offered by anyone to this date.)

However, widespread rumors to the contrary, we were not able to find a single authenticated case of looting of private residences, schools, hotels, the four banks on the island, the one industrial complex with valuable equipment, or any of the resort hotels. The looters used no physical force, and, at worst, made only unfulfilled verbal threats.

Our explanation of this very atypical occasion of mass looting is that the necessary condition present was simply that it was a catastrophe rather than just a disaster. However, not all catastrophes lead to looting. A recent book using historical data on the 1886 Charleston,

South Carolina earthquake documents that it was clearly a catastrophe, with two-thirds of the population becoming homeless but "no reports of looting and only scattered accounts of thievery" (Cote, 2006: 201).

We would argue that in addition to the necessary conditions there were additional sufficient conditions that tipped the balance toward a major outbreak of looting. As in St. Croix as well as New Orleans, we have identified three such factors. They are a pre-impact concentration of disadvantaged people subject to everyday perceptions of vast differences in lifestyle; a subculture tolerant of minor stealing along with everyday organized youth gangs involved in serious crime such as drug dealing; and a local police force that was inefficient and corrupt (both in New Orleans and St. Croix police officers openly engaged in the looting, something incidentally not found in civil disturbances).

Whatever the extent of the looting, it always pales in significance to the widespread altruism that leads to free and massive giving and sharing of goods and services. Even in St. Croix and New Orleans, the pro-social help given to others swamped the antisocial behavior that did occur. There was no comparison.

Finally, we should note that after the immediate emergency time period, in the days that follow, American police statistics usually indicate that there is an actual decrease in reported criminal behavior such as murder and theft. Traffic and related violations also tend to be below pre-impact levels, although much of that can be attributed to suspension or the ignoring by the police of such legal norms. Eventually, however, all standard criminal behavior rates return to what they were at the time of the impact of the disaster/catastrophe, with future increases following whatever pre-impact trend lines existed.

Yet it has become increasing clear to researchers that there is considerable illegal behavior in the recovery and mitigation phases of American disasters. There is a large amount of "white collar" crime by middle-class participants who turn in false insurance claims or otherwise obtain postdisaster relief aid which they know they are not entitled to receive. Then there are major criminal acts during mitigation activities involving some from the private sector and local government officials. The violations of building codes and zoning regulations are often carried out by network linkages involving, among others, construction and building companies, elements of the real estate sector, and government inspectors. This kind of criminal behavior almost ensures that disasters and catastrophes will be worse than they would otherwise be by way of physical destruction and human casualties. Overall, the frequency and significance of disaster/catastrophe-related white collar and business crimes dwarfs by almost any criteria even the worst of those rare mass looting occasions in catastrophes.

3. Passivity in Emergencies

Clearly, panic and looting are active responses. But the third myth concerns almost the opposite response: that is, the notion that survivors of disasters are stunned into inaction or passivity. The initial shock of undergoing the impact of a disaster supposedly makes individuals dazed and unable to function or react to the situation.

While media accounts often allude to survivors being in a state of shock, the notion of passivity as part of a disaster response comes out of a theoretical essay half a century ago by an anthropologist, Wallace (1954). In fact, he used the term "disaster syndrome" to designate the phenomena he said was often present in the early stage of impact. The term "disaster syndrome" was used to characterize the supposedly dazed, disoriented, shocked, and apathetic characteristics that disaster victims showed. It is worthy of note that another description and analysis of the same disaster studied by Wallace, the Worcester tornado (Rosow, 1977) conveys as we read it a rather different account of the responses of impacted individuals and groups.

The term offered (also favored by Wolfenstein, 1957) failed to be accepted by the other earliest disaster researchers since they saw just the opposite of what Wallace projected (see Aauf der Heide, 2004). Instead of passivity and inaction, they documented over and over again that survivors usually quickly moved to do what could be done in the situation. A good example of this is that by far the bulk of search and rescue activities, digging into the debris, and heading the injured toward medical treatment is overwhelmingly carried out by survivors looking for their family members, neighbors, coworkers, or those known to have been around the pre-impact physical location of survivors (see Denver, Perez, and Aguirre, 2007). These are truly the first responders in disasters, both in terms of time and the numbers of bodies found. Even the very earliest disaster studies found that in the first half hour after impact, usually about a third of survivors searched for missing persons, with about 10 percent taking an active role in rescue (Fritz, 1961: 7). But such activities are seldom reported by the mass media, which understandably instead focuses on the formal search and rescue efforts of emergency organizations (which are only significant if specialized knowledge or equipment are needed—as may be the case if massive piles of debris need to be searched, although, as the World Trade Center site showed after 9/11, the search usually becomes one of finding bodies rather than living injured).

What students of disasters have consistently discovered now for decades is what the earliest researchers reported, namely, a great deal of emergent behavior by survivors. So the research observations and findings have focused on that emergence rather than about the lack of passivity or inaction (or the disaster syndrome). Thus, unlike in the case of panic or looting, where studies have specifically focused on those phenomena, in the case here the myth of passivity is so accepted that, except for the earliest days of study, scientific work has centered on the emergent behavior in disasters.

Two aspects of that emergence should be noted. It is of a collective nature, not in the sense of any overall organization or coordination but in the sense of myriad small informal groupings and networks that are unaware of what others are doing. The behavior is adaptive in that it is functional for the situation, arising because there are immediate problems that need "solving."

This can be further documented in what happened in the New Orleans area during Hurricane Katrina. What we earlier characterized as what is seen in a catastrophe clearly was present in the multiple communities in and around New Orleans. The overall response to that was not the disorganization, social chaos, and dysfunctionality that was the staple reporting by the national mass media. To be sure, certain government agencies for all practical purposes ceased functioning. However, what emerged on a massive scale were smaller, informal entities and network linkages, sometime but not always anchored in pre-impact known groups. Researchers were able to find and study this emergent phenomenon. For example, using field gathered data, DRC field teams were able to research what emerged in neighborhoods, among both informal and rescue teams, in hospitals, and in hotels (see Rodriguez, Trainor, and Quarantelli, 2006). There were literally hundreds of such new groupings in the New Orleans area, including many studied by others (especially in the religious sector), both from within and outside the large impacted area. Written popular accounts of participants in other places such as the city hall and a major jail provide further indications of how widespread pro-social emergent behaviors were in the area (see Forman, 2007, and Inglese, 2007).

Their pro-social and very functional behavior dwarfed on a very large scale the antisocial behavior that also emerged. Improvisation and innovation took place because the everyday traditional routines could not be used or were ineffective in dealing with the problems that had to be addressed. Of course, not all that was created was perfect; there was at times a degree of inefficiency in what was done. However, what came into being not only prevented the New Orleans area from a collapse into total social disorganization, but little by little provided at least semi-solutions for many immediate and intermediate problems that required attention. A decentralized response, as was true of the emergent groups we have discussed, is almost a necessary consequence of a catastrophe.

4. Role Conflict and Role Abandonment

Are participants in a disaster likely to favor familial responsibilities over those that are work related? This question is sometimes posed by emergency managers and crisis planners (as well as by some ideologically driven political activists, such as in anti-nuclear groups). In general, the view of such people is that family will be favored over other responsibilities. A recent online article by medical personnel with the title: "Will the Healthcare Workers Go to Work During Disasters?" suggests that, especially in a crisis such as an avian flu epidemic, perhaps a majority of personnel might not go to work and would instead stay at home with immediate family members (see www.medicalnewstoday.com/printer-friendlynews.php?newsid=70828).

Overwhelmingly, disaster researchers consider the point of view just expressed as a "disaster myth." As a recent review of this topic stated: "Belief in this myth by the public and even government officials continues and has been reinforced through popular culture and erroneous reporting by the mass media" (Kushma, 2007: 4). However, while we agree with this statement, there sometime has been a failure to note an important distinction between role conflict and role abandonment. The quoted author, to her credit, does differentiate between the two and stresses that conflict does not generate abandonment.

The topic has been researched since the earliest days of disaster studies, more than a half century ago (Killian, 1952), with empirical work (such as Marks and Fritz, 1954; White, 1962; Mileti, 1985) predominating over more theoretical analyses (such as Barton, 1963; Quarantelli, 1978; Friedman, 1986). While the body of relevant systematic literature available is not large (we estimate several dozen empirical studies at most), much of it is of a quantitative nature. This probably results from the fact that role abandonment is a behavior that can easily be observed and measured compared to most other disaster phenomena.

The basic themes in the literature are fairly clear cut. Many personnel from emergency and response organizations such as the police and hospitals are subject to considerable role conflict that generates psychological strain and stress. They consciously feel a concern about ensuring the safety of their family and significant others, and yet also feel they have professional responsibilities to carry out their work. Various adaptive and coping mechanisms come into play (such as asking others to check on family members). On the other hand, despite intense role conflict at times, it has been difficult for researchers to find clear-cut authentic cases of role abandonment. In a review of several dozen disasters where more than 500 organizational officials were interviewed, DRC found only a handful of marginal instances of possible role abandonment. Other studies by the National Academy of Sciences (Fritz, 1987, in a major unpublished but excellent review that only surfaced this year), and Meda White, (1962) as well as Mileti (1985) and Rogers (1986) have all supported the findings of the DRC work.

So our concluding proposition is that role conflict is common but role abandonment from that is rare. However, two additional comments need to be made on the topic.

First, the observations and findings made are applicable at present only to American society. There are occasional anecdotal examples described in the literature on disasters elsewhere, but as far as we know, there has not been a single systematic study on the topic in that body of work. Our guess is that a role conflict/role abandonment linkage is so rare elsewhere that it simply has not caught the attention of non-American researchers even though some are extremely conversant with the American literature.

Second, recently some have mentioned that during Hurricane Katrina, 240 of 1,450 officers on the New Orleans police force apparently never reported for work, and later 51 officers were fired for "abandoning their posts" (Kushma, 2007). There is no documented case in all American disasters and catastrophes of any similar kind and scale of role abandonment (however, the behavior of the St. Croix police force during Hurricane Hugo came close to what happened in New Orleans). Clearly, such mass abandonment should be studied and explained, but it may have little to do with being a consequence of role conflict. There is considerable evidence that the New Orleans department was highly dysfunctional long before Katrina, and could not be depended on to carry out its responsibilities in any professional way. In other words, the linkage in Katrina is not between role conflict and role abandonment, but instead between pre-impact major structural flaws and mass work abandonment around impact times. (This might be a research route to follow in the case of developing societies where there have been at least persuasive anecdotal stories of mass role abandonment by government officials of all kinds, especially in catastrophes).

5. Sudden and Widespread Mental Health Breakdowns

Are major mental health problems likely to result from the extreme stress individuals can be subjected to in disasters? Our view is that this is not the case, at least in the sense of being a frequent and significant problem. We should quickly add that this is not the viewpoint of most of those who have professionally addressed the topic in some way or other. So we will be discussing something extremely controversial (see Tierney, 2000), with two widely held but two rather different scientific views about the topic (which is not true of the previous four topics, where there is generally only one major professional social science position).

It would take us too far out of the way to try here a systematic evaluation of the two approaches. Instead, we will note three general points. First, there haves been two points of view for at least a century. Second, the differences stem as we have previously discussed from a variety of factors that seem irreconcilable (Quarantelli, 1985). Third, it makes a practical difference as to which position is the more valid. We elaborate on these points in the following.

Interest in the topic is hardly new. Attention even predates the systematic development of social science disaster studies after World

War II. For example, the Messina, Italy, 1908 earthquake, which killed over 100,000 people, making it one of the largest catastrophes ever, provoked a series of studies on the psychological consequences for victims or, in contemporary terminology, their mental health status. Since we discovered that research only a couple of years ago and there had been no references in the cited literature up to then, we searched and found what had been published, especially in Italian professional journals.

There were a series of articles in a 1911 issue of the *Italian Rreview of Applied Psychology*. Other papers appeared in the *Italian Review of Neuropathology, Psychiatry and Electrotherapy* in 1909 as well in the same year in the *Archives of Criminal Anthropology, Psychiatry, Legal Medicine and Related Sciences*. Almost exclusively, the journal papers focused on what would today be called the negative mental health consequences of the disaster, although there is an interesting footnote in one article that said many individuals reacted well, but that would not be addressed in the article. As far as we can see, this outbreak of studies was never built upon and they seemed to have completely disappeared from the awareness of later scholars until we found them recently.

It should be noted that a focus on mental health effects of disasters (to use present-day terminology) was not peculiar to Italy. An American physician (Robertson in 1907) produced a paper entitled "earthquake shock considered as an etiological factor in the production of mental and nervous diseases." The findings reported are fascinating and relevant to this day. Although somewhat archaic language is used (for example, "insane asylums") the overall conclusion was that the 1906 San Francisco earthquake did not lead, to use today's words, to any increase in mental illness. The data used were interviews with medical personnel and the statistics obtained from what we would currently call mental health centers and hospitals. This study remained uncited in the disaster literature for nearly 100 years, and to this day is still unfamiliar even to those scholars interested in the mental health consequences of disasters.

Thus, the view that disasters create severe and widespread mental health problems as is generally the view set forth in the Messina studies, and the empirically based observation that the San Francisco earthquake did not lead to any significant increase in mental health problems, reflects the current division of professional opinion about the topic. Although finer distinctions have been made (including by this researcher and others—for example, Warheit, 1988; Tierney, 2000), generally speaking there are two camps. One argues that disasters result in widespread and severe mental health problems, that the negative effects are long lasting, dysfunctional for everyday behavior, and in some instances endure for a lifetime. For purposes of labeling, we will call this camp the "trauma of victims" approach. The other position is that mental health problems are comparatively rare and mild as well as being transient. lasting only weeks or maybe a month or two beyond the time of the disaster. This view we will call the problems of living approach.

Second, few challenge that undergoing a disaster or catastrophe will in varying degrees be stressful. The disagreement is on what are the psychosocial consequences of such an experience. In worst case scenarios advanced by the trauma of victims approach, where current emphasis is on post-traumatic stress disorder (PTSD)—in the old days it was called "going insane"—everyone, including people who just read or see in the mass media pictures of catastrophic disasters, is thought of as being potentially negatively affected. The "victims" (note the connotations of that very word) require psychological counseling and briefings.

The problems of living approach argues that while there are immediate widespread effects, much of the reaction is surface, non-persistent, not behaviorally dysfunctional, and that there can be significant positive psychological effects among survivors of disasters. Also the psychosocial difficulties that emerge for survivors are primarily the result of incompetent and ineffective organizations that require structural changes.

This paper is not the place to try and settle the differences between the two approaches. But we can discuss what might account for the differences in them. We have addressed this matter two decades ago (Quarantelli, 1985), discussing nine different factors that may account for the positions. Obviously we believe that overall the nine factors are more supportive of the problem of living approach. They are:

1. Given little overlap in studying the same disasters, it is possible that different researchers and analysts are observing *actual* differences in the mental well-being of those involved in various disasters.
2. What is taken as acceptable data and appropriate data gathering design varies considerably.
3. Data varies in interpretation on the basis of larger theoretical frameworks.
4. Different professional objectives and ideologies are involved leading to vested interests.
5. Differences exist in conceptions of what constitutes disasters.
6. There are differences in the basic models used to approach disaster phenomena.
7. There often is a difference in the length of the time frame used.
8. Overt behavior is considered more important than subjective feeling states in one of the approaches. And,
9. Dysfunctionality of behavior is given different weights in evaluation.

Third, a statement that we wrote 20 years ago still rings true to us:

> If the individual trauma approach is essentially the correct one, we should be extending crisis intervention programs, preparing outreach services for victims, and generally gearing up to handle the psychic trauma of those who have to adjust to the impact of a disaster agent.

On the other hand, if the problem in living perspective is a more valid one, a different strategy and use of resources should be institutionalized. We should be reorganizing the federal, state, and local disaster bureaucracies, giving in-service training to providers and deliverers of services, and generally gearing up to handle a social problem which is mainly the result of organizational inefficiency and ineffectiveness relatively independent of disaster agents" (Quarantelli, 1985: 206).

Finally, it is not amiss to note that few researchers have looked for positive mental health resulting from the experiencing of disasters. Only in the last few years, apart from a few lonely disaster research-ers who suggested it as a viable hypothesis long ago, has consideration been given to the possibility that the experience of a disaster could be positive for mental health.

This is not peculiar to the mental health area. There is a strong assumption that since disasters by usual definitions are something that is bad, the notion that there can be positive or good aspects of such occa-sions tends to be ignored. An unusual exception is Scanlon (1988), who in an excellent article describes and analyzes a variety of ways in which disas-ters can be positive or functional for individuals, groups, communities, and societies. More such outside-of- the-box scholarship is badly needed. The negative aspects of disasters should be empirically determined and must not be simply a priori matters of definition or assumption.

6. The locus of problems

Our sixth point is somewhat different from the previous five. For one, the point here cuts across the previous five topics discussed. It has to do with the implicit or stated major locus of the problems that we have examined. In short, where is the major source of the problematical aspects of crises? Overstated and to be qualified later, the general belief is that in disasters and especially in catastrophe, the major source of problems and difficulties are the individuals involved whose dysfunctional behaviors can be dealt with only by highly centralized, top-down organizations that can impose command and control procedures. It is believed that such kinds of organizations are the only ones able to rise to the occasion of a crisis that usually involves nonfunctioning civilians and individuals.

The research evidence indicates just the opposite. It is the human beings and their informal groupings and linkages that typically rise to the daunting challenges that disasters pose. Formal, highly hierarchical, structured and bureaucratic organizations, whether pre-impact planned or post-impact imposed, are both the source and locus of most problems in community crises.

The basic theme we express here—that human beings do well and crisis relevant organizations do poorly—was noted long ago by the earliest disaster researchers. It is not a new idea. In fact, the strong tendency of much social science research to give priority to studying organizations (as is true of much DRC research), stems from the point made. However, for various reasons, the basic observation was not explicitly named as one of the traditional disaster myths, although the label of myth for the phenomena has recently begun to be used (see Tierney, 2003).

Both in popular discourse and the position of funding agencies, the answer is usually fairly clear. It is the individuals or people in the situation. The US military's support of the pioneering studies of disasters stemmed from a belief that the American civilian population might collapse in the face of atomic attack. This can be seen in the questions posed by the funding agency (OCD) that provided the initial support that led to the establishment of the DRC (see Quarantelli, 2005):

Which elements in a disaster are most frightening or disrupting to people and how can these threats be met?

What techniques are effective in reducing or controlling fear?

What types of people are susceptible to panic and what types can be counted on for leadership in an emergency? What aggressions and resentments are likely to emerge among victims of a disaster and how can these be prevented from disrupting the work of disaster control?

What types of organized efforts work effectively and which do not (that is, in terms of individual leadership, not organizational entities).

The overall theme is one that there would be a need for the "reduction of panic reactions" and the need for social control would be achieved by "securing of conformity to emergency regulations." As a veteran disaster researcher has noted, the assumption is that a crisis will have a disorganizing effect upon individuals: "they panic; they freeze; they become anti-social; they become traumatized; they become self centered: and thus they cannot be counted on for selfless action" (Dynes, 1994: 146). That was the past but it is also the present. As other veteran disaster researchers have observed, many present-day approaches to terrorism and epidemics are similar in their assumptions about how individuals react in crises (Tierney, 2000).

The command and control model, dominant in American society, has been heavily criticized by almost all disaster researchers for half a century as an inappropriate system for dealing with disasters and catastrophes (see, for example, reflecting the consensus of critics, Clarke, 2002; Dynes, 2007; Tierney, 2003). For our purposes, we want to narrowly focus only on the assumptions that the model makes about the behavior of individuals. It is almost taken for granted that disaster victims will react in highly individualistic fashion, will be competitive with others, will be self-centered, make irrational decisions, will be a danger to one another; all this indicating a total collapse of the civil order. Thus, this model assumes that authorities from above need to step in to ensure order. However, as we have indicated, the assumptions made are fundamentally incorrect.

Another unfortunate consequence of making wrong assumptions is that it draws attention away from the fact that responding organizations are usually the major source and locus of most of the problems that surface in disasters and certainly catastrophes. That is what research shows. The myth is that it is the victims, the individuals caught in such crises, who are the source and locus of the problems.

Let us now add some qualifications to our general theme here. Generally speaking, individuals and smaller groupings are unresponsive and uninterested in disasters during normal times. Survey after survey has documented that few Americans (except some living in disaster subcultures) prepare for their possible involvement in a disaster and are not much interested in doing so (Heath, 2007). However, the situation changes drastically at the time of the impact of a disaster, where almost exclusive focus is on what is happening and myriad options on what to do are consciously considered especially in intense interactions with others.

Not all organizations use command and control structures. Religiously oriented groups, for example, in terms of their belief systems, usually have flat structures with little by the way of command roles. Such groupings and networks were prominent in Hurricane Katrina, where the governmental control and command organizations were frequently ineffective and sometimes close to paralysis in the catastrophe.

OTHER POSSIBLE MYTHS

Our essay does not address all possible disaster/catastrophe mythologies. Is mitigation the best way of preparing societies and communities for disasters? A case can and has been made that creating better resilience would be a much better and far less costly path to develop (Douglas and Wildavsky, 1982). Who should be "in charge" at times of crises? As critics have noted, the very question itself makes a highly dubious assumption that some official or organization should and particularly could be in charge in the diffused and decentralized social setting that is typical at the height of a disaster or mega-disaster. Do catastrophes really create the opportunity for major organizational, community, and societal changes? There is some evidence suggesting that at best and only under certain supportive conditions can there be some incremental changes in line with pre-impact trends. Are individuals and groups likely to engage in preparing for disasters if they are aware of disaster-inducing related threats and risks? This is often assumed in disaster educational or information campaigns and in public policies, the notion being that knowledge and information will lead to relevant actions.

Finally, there is a tendency to overstate the collapse of any social system. There are concrete and studied historical occasions that by any criteria were extreme catastrophes. There are documented data on the human and group reactions in Hiroshima after the atomic bombing. Out of a population of 245,000, at least 75,000 were immediately killed and another 75,000 were injured. Around the point where the bomb actually hit, there was total physical devastation for miles around. Yet, within minutes, survivors engaged in search and rescue, helped one another in whatever ways they could, and withdrew in controlled flight from burning areas. Within a day, apart from the planning undertaken by the government and military organizations that partly survived, other groups partially restored electric power to some areas, a steel company with 20 percent of workers attending began operations again, employees of the 12 banks in Hiroshima assembled in the Hiroshima branch in the city and began making payments, and trolley lines leading into the city were completely cleared with partial traffic restored the following day. Given the current status of a modern and vibrant city of Hiroshima, does this overall picture suggest another myth?

REFERENCES

Alexander, David. "Panic During Earthquakes and Its Urban and Cultural Contexts." *Built Environment* 21 (1995): 71-82.

Auf der Heide, Erik. "Common Misconceptions about Disasters: Panic, the '"Disaster Syndrome,'" and Looting." *The First 72 Hours: A Community*

Approach to Disaster Preparedness. Ed. Margaret O'Leary. New York: iUniverse Inc, 2004.

Barsky, Lauren. "Disaster Realities Following Katrina: Revisiting the Looting Myth." *Learning From Catastrophe: Quick Response Research in the Wake of Hurricane Katrina.* Boulder: Institute of Behavioral Science, University of Colorado, 2006.

Barton, Allen. *Communities in Disasters.* New York: Doubleday, 1969.

Bryan, John. "Panic or Non-adaptive Behavior in the Fire Incident: An Empirical Concept." *Second International Seminar on Human Behavior in Emergencies.* Eds. S. M. Levin and R. L. Paulsen. Washington, D.C.: National Bureau of Standards, 1980.

Canter, D. *Fire and Fire Behavior.* Chichester, England: Wiley, 1980.

Cantril, Hadley. *The Invasion from Mars: A Study in the Psychology of Panic.* Princeton: Princeton University Press, 1949.

Clarke, Lee. "Panic: Myth or Reality?" *Contexts* 1:3 (2002): 21-26.

———. *Worst Cases: Terror and Catastrophe in the Popular Imagination.* Chicago: University of Chicago Press, 2006.

Cote, Richard. *City of Heroes: The Great Charleston Earthquake of 1886.* Mt. Pleasant, S.C.: Corinthian Books, 2006.

Denver, Megan, James Perez, and Ben Aguirre. "Local Search and Rescue Teams in the United States." *Disaster Prevention and Management* 16:4 (2007): 503-512.

Douglas, Mary, and Arron Wildavsky. *Risk and Culture.* Berkeley: University of California Press, 1982.

Dynes, Russell. "Community Emergency Planning: False Assumptions and Inappropriate Analogies." *International Journal of Mass Emergencies and Disasters* 12 (1994): 141-158.

———. "Panic and the Vision of Collective Incompetence." *Natural Hazards Observer* 31:2 (2007): 5-6.

Dynes, Russell, and E. L. Quarantelli. "What Looting in Civil Disturbances Really Means." *Trans-action* 5 (1968): 9-14.

———. "The Family and Community Context of Individual Reactions to Disaster." *Emergency and Disaster Management: A Mental Health Sourcebook.* Eds. H. Parad, H. L. P. Resnick and L. G. Parad. Bowie,

Md.: Charles Press Publisher. 1976.

Forman, Sally. *Eye of the Storm: Inside City Hall During Katrina.* Bloomington, Ind.: Author House, 2007.

Friedman, Barbara. "Role Conflict and Role Abandonment in Disasters." *Preliminary Paper 109.* Newark: Disaster Research Center, University of Delaware, 1986.

Fritz, Charles. "Mass Psychology in Times of Disaster." Unpublished ms. Available in the DRC Special Collections.

———. "Emergency Worker Role Conflicts: Potential Significance for Policy and Theory." 1987. Unpublished ms. Available in the DRC Special Collections.

Green, Stuart. Stuart Green, "Looting, Law, and Lawlessness." Working Paper 1511. (August 8, 2006). Bepress Legal Series <http://law.bepress.com/expresso/eps/1511>.

Inglese, Demaree. *No Ordinary Heroes: 8 Doctors, 30 Nurses, 7,000 Prisoners, and a Category 5 Hurricane.* New York: Citadel Press, 2007.

Handmer, John. "Have Disaster Myths Become Legends?" *Natural Hazards Observer* 31:6 (2007): 4-5.

Heath, Brad. "Many Unprepared for a Disaster, but Americans Say the Federal Government Is Even Less Ready" <www.jems/com/print.asp?act=print&vid=286003>.

Johnson, Norris. "Panic and the Breakdown of Social Order: Popular Myth, Social Theory and Empirical Evidence." *Sociological Focus* 20 (1985): 171-183.

Jordan, Nehemian. "What is Panic?" *Discussion Paper HI-189-DP.* Washington, D.C.: Hudson Institute, 1963.

Killian, Lewis. "The Significance of Multiple-Group Membership in Disaster." *American Journal of Sociology* 57 (1952): 309-314.

Kushma, Jane. "Role Abandonment in Disaster: Should We Leave This Myth Behind?" *Natural Hazards Observer* 31:5 (2007): 4-5.

Lindell, M., R., Perry and C. Prater. *Introduction to Emergency Management.* New York: Wiley, 2006.

Marks, Eli, and Charles Fritz. *Human Reactions in Disaster Situations.* Chicago: National Opinion Research Center, University of Chicago, 1954.

Mawson, Anthony. *Panic and Social Attachment: The Dynamics of Human Behavior.* Burlington, Vt.: Ashgate Publishing Company, 2007.

Meerloo, Joost. *Patterns of Panic.* New York: International Universities Press, 1950.

Mileti, Dennis. "Role Conflict and Abandonment in Emergency Workers." *Emergency Management Review* 2 (1985): 20-22.

National Research Council. *Facing Hazards and Disasters: Understanding Human Dimensions.* Washington, D.C.: The National Academies Press, 2006.

Orr, Jackie. *Panic Diaries: A Genealogy of Panic Disorder.* Durham: Duke University Press, 2006.

Quarantelli, E. L. "The Nature and Conditions of Panic." *American Journal of Sociology* 60 (1954): 265-275.

———. "Images of Withdrawal Behavior in Disasters: Some Basic Misconceptions." *Social Problems* 8 (1960): 68-79.

———. "Structural Factors in the Minimization of Role Conflict." *Preliminary Paper* 49. Newark: Disaster Research Center, University of Delaware, 1978.

———. "An Assessment of Conflicting Views on Mental Health: The Consequences of Traumatic Events." *Trauma and Its Wake.* Ed. Charles Figley. New York: Brunner and Mazel, 1985.

———. "The NORC Research on the Arkansas Tornado: A Fountainhead Study." *International Journal of Mass Emergencies and Disasters* 6 (1988): 283-310.

———. "Catastrophes Are Different from Disasters." Understanding Katrina: Perspectives from the Social Sciences. Social Science Research Council, 2005a <http://understandingkatrina.ssrc.org/Quarantelli/>.

———. "The Earliest Interest in Disasters and the Earliest Social Science Studies of Disasters: Sociology of Knowledge Approach." *Preliminary Paper* 349. Newark: Disaster Research Center, University of Delaware, 2005b.

———. "The Myth and the Realities: Keeping the 'Looting' Myth in Perspective." *Natural Hazards Observer* 31:4 (2007): 2-3.

Quarantelli, E.L., Patrick Lagadec, and Arjen Boin. "A Heuristic Approach to Future Disasters and Crises: New, Old and In-between Types." *Handbook of Disaster Research*. Eds. Havidan Rodriguez, E.L. Quarantelli and Russell Dynes. New York: Springer, 2006.

Robertson, J. "Earthquake Shock Considered as an Etiological Factor in the Production of Mental and Nervous Diseases." *California State Journal of Medicine* 5 (1907): 132-134.

Rodriguez. Havidan, E. L. Quarantelli, and Russell Dynes. *Handbook of Disaster Research*. New York: Springer, 2006.

Rodriguez, Havidan, Joseph Trainor, and E. L. Quarantelli. "Rising to the Challenges of a Catastrophe: The Emergent and Pro-Social Behavior Following Hurricane Katrina." *Annals of the American Academy of Political and Social Science* 604 (2006); 82-101.

Rogers, George. *Role Conflict in Crises of Limited Forewarning*. Pittsburgh: Center for Social and Urban Research, University of Pittsburgh, 1986.

Rosengren, Karl Erik, Peter Arvidson, and Dahn Sturesson. "The Barseback 'Panic': A Radio Programme as a Negative Summary Event." *Acta Sociologica* 18 (1975): 303-321.

Rosow, Irving. *Authority in Emergencies: Four Tornado Communities in 1953*. Newark, DE. Disaster Research Center, University of Delaware, 1977.

Scanlon, Joseph. "Winners and Losers: Some Thoughts about the Political Economy of Disaster." *International Journal of Mass Emergencies and Disasters* 6 (1988): 47-63.

Strauss, Anselm. "The Literature on Panic." *Journal of Abnormal and Social Psychology* 39 (1944): 317-328.

Tierney, Kathleen. "Property Damage and Violence: A Collective Behavior Analysis." *The Los Angeles Riots: Lessons for the Urban Future*. Ed. Mark Baldassare. Boulder, Colo.: Westview Press, 1994.

———. "Controversy and Consensus in Mental Health Research." *Prehospital and Disaster Medicine* 15 (2000): 181-187.

———. "Disaster Beliefs and Institutional Interests: Recycling Disaster Myths in the Aftermath of 9-11." *Research in Social Problems and Public*

Policy 11 (2003): 3351.

Wallace, Anthony. *The Worcester Tornado.* Washington, D.C.: Committee on Disaster Studies, National Academy of Sciences, 1956.

White, Meda. *Role Conflict in Disasters: Not Family, But Familiarity First.* Washington, D.C.: National Academy of Sciences, 1962.

Wolfenstein, Martha. *Disasters: A Psychological Essay.* New York: Free Press, 1957.

Howard Kunreuther
Reducing Losses from Catastrophic Risks through Long-Term Insurance and Mitigation

RECENT CHANGES IN THE IMPACTS OF EXTREME EVENTS
Increases in Economic and Insured Losses

The economic and insured losses from natural disasters have increased significantly in recent years, as shown in figure 1 (each vertical bar represents the total economic losses, the darker zone represents the insured portion of it). A comparison of these economic losses over time reveals a huge increase: $53.6 billion (1950-59), $93.3 billion (1960-69), $161.7 billion (1970-79), $262.9 billion (1980-89), and $778.3 billion (1990-99). The current decade has already seen $420.6 billion in losses, principally due to the 2004 and 2005 hurricane seasons, which produced historic records.

Catastrophes have had a more devastating impact on insurers over the past 15 years than in the entire history of insurance. Between 1970 and the mid-1980s, annual insured losses from natural disasters (including forest fires) were in the $3 billion to $4 billion range. The insured losses from Hurricane Hugo that made landfall in Charleston, South Carolina on September 22, 1989 exceeded $4 billion (in 1989 prices). It was the first natural disaster to inflict more than $1 billion of insured losses in the United States. There was a radical increase in insured losses in the early 1990s with Hurricane Andrew (1992) in

Figure 1. Evolution of "Great Natural Catastrophes" Worldwide, 1950-2007: Economic Versus Insured Impact

Great natural disasters 1950 ± 2007
Overall and insured losses

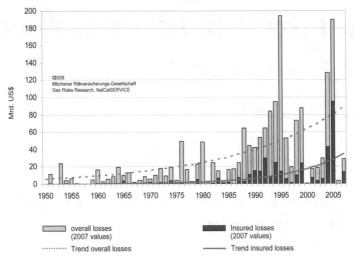

overall losses
(2007 values)

Insured losses
(2007 values)

Trend overall losses

Trend insured losses

Sources: Data from Munich Re; 2008 Geo Risks Research. In billions of US dollars, indexed to 2007.

Florida ($23.7 billion in 2007 dollars) and the Northridge earthquake (1994) in California ($19.6 billion in 2007 dollars). The four hurricanes in Florida in 2004 (Charley, Frances, Ivan, and Jeanne) taken together cost insurers almost $33 billion. Insured and reinsured losses from Hurricane Katrina, which made landfall in the United States in August 2005, are now estimated at $46 billion; total losses paid by private insurers due to major natural catastrophes were $87 billion in 2005. Figure 2 depicts the upward trend in worldwide insured losses from catastrophes between 1970 and 2007 (in 2007 indexed prices; corrected for inflation).

Table 1 reveals the 20 most costly catastrophes for the insurance sector since 1970 (in 2007 dollars). Several observations are relevant here. First, 18 of the 20 most costly events have occurred since 1990. Hurricane Andrew and the Northridge earthquake were the first two

Figure 2. Worldwide Evolution of Catastrophe Insured Losses, 1970–2007

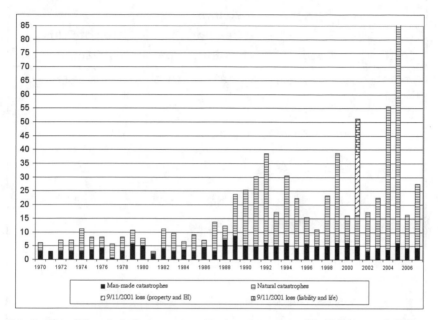

Note: For 9/11, all lines, including property and business interruption (BI). All figures are in billions of US dollars, indexed to 2007.

Source: Wharton Risk Center, with data from Swiss Re and Insurance Information Institute.

disasters that the industry experienced where losses were greater than $10 billion (designated as "super-cats") and caused insurers to reflect on whether risks from natural disasters were insurable. To assist them in making this determination, many firms began using catastrophe models to estimate the likelihood and consequences to their insured portfolios from specific disasters in hazard-prone areas (Grossi and Kunreuther, 2005). With the exception of the terrorist attacks on September 11, 2001, all of the events in the top 20 were natural disasters. More than 80 percent of these were weather-related events: hurricanes and typhoons, storms, and floods, with nearly three-quarters of the claims in the United States.

Losses due to natural catastrophes and man-made disasters were far below the long-term trend in 2006. Of the $48 billion in catastro-

Table 1. The 20 Most Costly Insured Catastrophes in the World, 1970–2007[1]

Cost*	Event	Victims (Dead or Missing)	Year	Area of Primary Damage
$46.3	Hurricane Katrina	1,836	2005	USA, Gulf of Mexico
35.5	9/11 Attacks	3,025	2001	USA
23.7	Hurricane Andrew	43	1992	USA, Bahamas
19.6	Northridge Earthquake	61	1994	USA
14.1	Hurricane Ivan	124	2004	USA, Caribbean
13.3	Hurricane Wilma	35	2005	USA, Gulf of Mexico
10.7	Hurricane Rita	34	2005	USA, Gulf of Mexico
8.8	Hurricane Charley	24	2004	USA, Caribbean
8.6	Typhoon Mireille	51	1991	Japan
7.6	Hurricane Hugo	71	1989	Puerto Rico, USA
7.4	Winterstorm Daria	95	1990	France, UK
7.2	Winterstorm Lothar	110	1999	France, Switzerland
6.1	Winterstorm Kyrill	54	2007	Germany, UK, NL, France
5.7	Storms and Floods	22	1987	France, UK
5.6	Hurricane Frances	38	2004	USA, Bahamas
5.0	Winterstorm Vivian	64	1990	Western/Central Europe
5.0	Typhoon Bart	26	1999	Japan
4.5	Hurricane Georges	600	1998	USA, Caribbean
4.2	Tropical Storm Alison	41	2001	USA
4.2	Hurricane Jeanne	3,034	2004	USA, Caribbean

*In billions of dollars. Indexed to 2007.

Sources: Wharton Risk Center with data from Swiss Re and Insurance Information Institute.

phe-related economic losses, $16 billion was covered by insurance ($11 billion for natural disasters; $5 billion for man-made). Over the past 20 years, only two had insured losses lower than in 2006 (1988 and 1997) (Swiss Re, 2007). According to Munich Re, 950 natural catastrophes occurred in 2007, the most since 1974. They inflicted nearly $27 billion in insured losses.

Increased Development in Hazard-Prone Areas[2]

During the period between 1970 and 2004, storms and floods have been responsible for over 90 percent of the total economic costs of extreme weather-related events worldwide. Storms (hurricanes in North America, typhoons in Asia, and windstorms in Europe) contribute to over 75 percent of insured losses. In constant prices (2004), insured losses from weather-related events averaged $3 billion annually between 1970 and 1990 and then increased significantly to $16 billion annually between 1990 and 2004 (Association of British Insurers, 2005). In 2005, 99.7 percent of all catastrophic losses worldwide were due to weather-related events (Mills and Lecomte, 2006).

There are at least two principal socioeconomic factors that directly influence the level of economic losses due to catastrophe events: degree of urbanization and value at risk. In 1950, approximately 30 percent of the world's population lived in cities. In 2000, about 50 percent of the world's population (6 billion) resided in urban areas. Projections by the United Nations show that by 2025, that figure will have increased to 60 percent based on a world population estimate of 8.3 billion people.

In hazard-prone areas, this urbanization and increase of population also translates into increased concentration of exposure. The development of Florida as a home for retirees is an example. According to the US Bureau of the Census, the population of Florida has increased significantly over the past 50 years: 2.8 million inhabitants in 1950, 6.8 million in 1970, 13 million in 1990, and a projected 19.3 million population in 2010 (almost a 700 percent increase since 1950), increasing the likelihood of severe economic and insured losses unless cost-effective mitigation measures are implemented.

Figure 3. Insured Coastal Exposure as a Percentage of Statewide Insured Exposure (Residential and Commercial Properties) (December 2004).

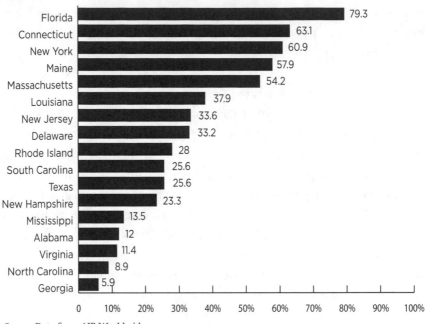

Source: Data from AIR Worldwide.

Florida also has a high density of insurance coverage, with most houses covered against windstorm losses and about one-third insured against floods under the US National Flood Insurance Program (NFIP),[3] according to a study undertaken by Munich Re (2000). The modeling firm AIR Worldwide estimates that nearly 80 percent of insured assets in Florida today are located near the coasts, the high-risk area in the state (see figure 3). This represents $1.9 trillion of insured exposure located in coastal areas (see figure 4). Insurance density is thus another critical socioeconomic factor to consider when evaluating the evolution of insured loss due to weather-related catastrophes.[4]

These factors will continue to have a major impact on the level of insured losses from natural catastrophes. Given the growing concentration of exposure on the Gulf coast, if another hurricane like Katrina

Figure 4. Total Value of Insured Coastal Exposure as of December 2004, Residential and Commercial Properties (in billions of dollars)

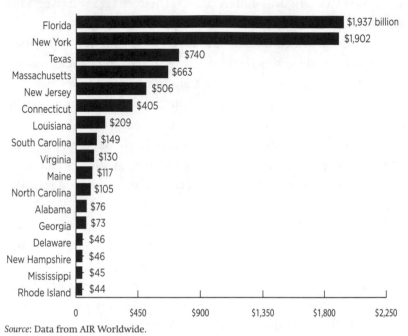

Florida	$1,937 billion
New York	$1,902
Texas	$740
Massachusetts	$663
New Jersey	$506
Connecticut	$405
Louisiana	$209
South Carolina	$149
Virginia	$130
Maine	$117
North Carolina	$105
Alabama	$76
Georgia	$73
Delaware	$46
New Hampshire	$46
Mississippi	$45
Rhode Island	$44

Source: Data from AIR Worldwide.

were to hit the Gulf coast, it would likely inflict significant direct losses (property damage) and indirect losses (business interruption) unless strong mitigation measures are put in place beforehand.

CHALLENGES IN USING MITIGATION TO REDUCE FUTURE LOSSES

We undertook an analysis of four states (Florida, New York, South Carolina, and Texas) to determine the impact of mitigation on reducing losses from hurricanes of different intensities to residential homes. Data on each state's residential-only exposure to hurricane risk was provided by Risk Management Solutions (RMS). Losses are comprised of damage caused by the wind to buildings, contents, as well as victims' additional living expenses (ALE). Our analyses in New York, South Carolina, and Texas were performed looking at both the wind and storm surge peril using the RMS hurricane industry exposure database. The RMS analyses in Florida did not include storm surge damage from hurricanes due to wind, so the Florida figures underestimate the damages relative to the other three states.

RMS also provided data on the losses assuming full mitigation of the structures without determining whether each of the measures was cost effective. In New York, South Carolina, and Texas, we assumed that all houses and buildings were built to the latest standard. In Florida, we assumed that the relevant homes met the building codes for the Fortified . . . for Safer Living program.[5] These building codes are directed only at wood-frame or masonry dwellings, which comprise 80 percent of the residential structures in the state, and include mitigation measures such as roof anchors.

Table 2 details the differences in losses for hurricanes with return periods of 100, 250, and 500 years for each of the four states we are studying if these loss-reduction measures were in place. The analyses reveal that mitigation has the potential for very significant cost savings in all four states, ranging from 61 percent in Florida for a 100-year hurricane to 31 percent in New York for a 500-year event.

The Natural Disaster Syndrome

Recent extreme events have highlighted the challenges associated with reducing losses from hurricanes and other natural hazards due to what I have termed the natural disaster syndrome (Kunreuther, 1996). Many homeowners, private businesses, and the public sector do not voluntarily adopt cost-effective loss-reduction measures. Hence, the area is highly vulnerable and unprepared should a severe hurricane or other natural disaster occur. The magnitude of the destruction following a catastrophe often leads government agencies to provide disaster relief to victims even if prior to the event the government claimed that it had no intention of doing so. This combination of underinvestment in protection prior to the catastrophic event, together with the general taxpayer financing some of the recovery, can be critiqued on both efficiency and equity grounds.

Table 2. Money Saved from Full Mitigation for Different Return Periods

100-Year Event			
State	Unmitigated Losses	Savings from Mitigation	Savings from Mitigation (%)
FL	$84 bn	$51 bn	61%
NY	$6 bn	$2 bn	39%
SC	$4 bn	$2 bn	44%
TX	$17 bn	$6 bn	34%

250-Year Event			
State	Unmitigated Losses	Savings from Mitigation	Savings from Mitigation (%)
FL	$126 bn	$69 bn	55%
NY	$13 bn	$5 bn	37%
SC	$7 bn	$3 bn	41%
TX	$27 bn	$9 bn	32%

500-Year Event			
State	Unmitigated Losses	Savings from Mitigation ($)	Savings from Mitigation (%)
FL	$160 bn	$83 bn	52%
NY	$19 bn	$7 bn	35%
SC	$9 bn	$4 bn	39%
TX	$37 bn	$12 bn	31%

One of the reasons for the natural disaster syndrome is due to the decision-making processes of individuals with respect to events such as a Category 3 or 4 hurricane or a major earthquake. Prior to a disaster, many individuals perceive its likelihood as sufficiently low that they argue, "It will not happen to me." As a result, they do not feel the need to invest voluntarily in protective measures, such as strengthening their house or buying insurance. It is only after the disaster occurs that these same individuals express remorse that they didn't undertake protective measures.

Another reason that individuals do not invest in protective measures is that they are extremely myopic and tend to focus on the returns only over the next couple of years. In addition, there is extensive experimental evidence showing that human temporal discounting tends to be hyperbolic, where temporally distant events are disproportionately discounted relative to immediate ones. As an example, people are willing to pay more to have the timing of the receipt of a cash prize accelerated from tomorrow to today, than from two days from now to tomorrow (Loewenstein and Prelec, 1991). The implication of hyperbolic discounting for mitigation decisions is that we are asking residents to invest a tangible fixed sum now to achieve a benefit later that we instinctively undervalue—and one that we, paradoxically, hope never to see at all. The effect of placing too much weight on immediate considerations is that the upfront costs of mitigation will loom disproportionately large relative to the delayed expected benefits in losses over time.

There is extensive evidence that residents in hazard-prone areas do not undertake loss-prevention measures voluntarily. A 1974 survey of more than 1,000 California homeowners in earthquake-prone areas revealed that only 12 percent of the respondents had adopted any protective measures (Kunreuther et al., 1978). Fifteen years later, there was little change despite the increased public awareness of the earthquake hazard. In a 1989 survey of 3,500 homeowners in four California counties at risk from earthquakes, only 5 to 9 percent of the respondents in these areas reported adopting any loss reduction measures. Palm et al. (1990), Burby et al. (1988), and Laska (1991) have found a similar reluctance by residents in flood-prone areas to invest in mitigation measures.

In the case of flood damage, Burby (2006) provides compelling evidence that actions taken by the federal government, such as building levees, make residents feel safe when, in fact, they are still targets for catastrophes should the levee be breached or overtopped. This problem is reinforced by local public officials who do not enforce building codes or impose land-use regulations to restrict development in high hazard areas. If developers do not design homes to be resistant to disasters and individuals do not voluntarily adopt mitigation measures, one can expect large-scale losses following a catastrophic event, as evidenced by the property damage to New Orleans caused by Hurricane Katrina.

Even after the devastating 2004 and 2005 hurricane seasons, a large number of residents had still not invested in relatively inexpensive loss-reduction measures with respect to their property, nor had they undertaken emergency preparedness measures.

A survey of 1,100 adults living along the Atlantic and Gulf coasts undertaken in May 2006 revealed that 83 percent of the responders had not taken steps to fortify their home, 68 percent did not have a hurricane survival kit, and 60 percent did not have a family disaster plan (Goodnough, 2006).

THE ROLE OF INSURANCE IN ENCOURAGING MITIGATION

Given the significant increase in damage from hurricanes and other natural disasters during the past 15 years because of the growing population and assets in high-risk areas, we need a new approach so property owners undertake effective mitigation measures. In addition to well-enforced building codes there is a role that insurance can play to encourage the adoption of these measures and overcome the "it will not happen to me" and hyberbolic discount rate biases discussed in the previous section. Two principles should guide the development of insurance programs for reducing future losses and allocating the costs of disasters in an efficient and equitable manner.

Principle 1—Premiums Reflecting Risk: Insurance premiums should be based on risk to provide signals to individuals as to the hazards they face and to encourage them to engage in cost-effective mitigation measures to reduce their vulnerability to catastrophes.

Principle 2—Dealing with Equity and Affordability Issues: Any special treatment given to residents in hazard-prone areas (for example, low-income homeowners) should come from general public funding and not through insurance premium subsidies.

Principle 1 is important because its application would provide a clear signal of relative damage to those currently residing in areas subject to natural disasters and those who are considering moving into these regions. Risk-based premiums also enable insurers to provide discounts to homeowners and businesses who invest in cost-effective loss-reduction mitigation measures. If insurers are required to charge artificially low premiums, they have no economic incentive to offer these discounts. In fact, they prefer not to offer coverage to these property owners because it is a losing proposition in the long-run.

Principle 2 reflects a concern for some residents in hazard-prone areas who will be faced with large premium increases if insurers are permitted to adhere to Principle 1. Today, regulations imposed by state insurance commissioners keep premiums artificially lower than the risk-based level in many regions subject to hurricane damage. If insurers charge risk-based premiums, homeowners residing in hurricane-prone areas would pay considerably more for coverage than they currently do.

Risk-Based Rates

The first step in developing an insurance program that would adhere to Principle 1 is to estimate the risk-based rates that would apply to different regions of the country. Catastrophe models have been developed that evaluate the expected losses from hurricanes, earthquakes, and floods, using data from experts to estimate the likelihood of damages resulting from disasters of different magnitudes and intensities. Although there is uncertainty surrounding the estimates from these catastrophe models, they have been widely used by insurers and reinsurers to price the risk.

To enable insurers to charge risk-based premiums, regulators should stay out of the rate-setting business. If one allows a truly competitive market to operate, then insurers would not engage in price-gouging since they would be undercut by another company that profitably markets policies at a lower price. Regulators would still have an important role to play in other aspects of the insurance operation by making certain that insurers have sufficient surplus to protect unsuspecting consumers against the possibility of their becoming insolvent following the next severe disaster.

Affordability of Coverage

The second step in the process relates to the affordability and equity issues indicated in Principle 2. To begin with, it would be critical to measure where and for whom affordability is truly a challenge and whether other individuals residing in these areas (for example, those providing valuable goods and services to other parts of the country) deserve a subsidy.

To assist these individuals, we recommend that some type of insurance voucher be provided by the state or federal government. This type of in-kind assistance (rather than an unrestricted grant) assures that the recipients use the funds for obtaining insurance. If this system were applied to a family in a hazard-prone area, it would pay an insurance premium that reflects risk, and then be reimbursed by the state for a portion of the increased cost of insurance over the prior year's policy. The amount of reimbursement could be determined by their income and the risk-based insurance premium that they are charged.

Several existing programs could serve as models for developing such a voucher system.

Food Stamp Program. Under the food stamp program, a family is given vouchers to purchase food based on its annual income and size of the family. The idea for the program was born in the late 1930s, revived as a pilot program in 1961, and extended nationwide in 1974. The current program structure was implemented in 1977 with a goal of alleviating hunger and malnutrition by permitting low-income house-holds to obtain a more nutritious diet through normal purchasing of food from grocery stores. Food stamps are available to most low-income households with limited resources regardless of age, disability status, or family structure.[6] The program is funded entirely by the federal government. Federal and state governments share administrative costs (with the federal government contributing nearly 50 percent). In 2003, total federal food stamp costs were nearly $24 billion. As of June 2007, more than 26 million individuals benefit from this program (Food Research and Action Center, 2007).

Low Income Home Energy Assistance Program (LIHEAP). The mission of this program is to assist low-income households that pay a high propor-tion of their income for home energy in meeting their immediate energy needs. The funding is provided by the federal government but is admin-istered by the states and federally recognized tribes or insular areas (Guam, Puerto Rico, Virgin Islands, for example) to help eligible low-income homeowners and renters meet their heating or cooling needs (eligibility based on similar criteria than the food stamp program).[7] The federal government became involved in awarding energy assistance funds to low-income households program as a result of the increase in oil prices resulting from the Organization of Petroleum Exporting Countries (OPEC) oil embargo in 1973. Over the past few years, the annual appropriation of this program has averaged $2 billion.[8]

Universal Service Fund (USF).[9] The USF was created by the Federal Communications Commission in 1997 to ensure that consumers in all regions of the country have access to telecommunications services that are reasonably priced relative to those in urban areas. To achieve this goal, the USF provides discounts to low-income individuals in high-cost rural areas, and to other special groups, such as rural health care providers, schools, and libraries in those areas. All telecommunication carriers that provide service internationally and between states pay contributions into the USF. The carriers may build this factor into their billing systems if they choose to recoup this amount from their customers. The USF provides discounts that make basic, local telephone service affordable to more than 7 million low-income consumers. From 1998 to 2006, over $50 billion has been disbursed by this fund.

Who Should Subsidize Insurance?

The above programs use different methods to subsidize low-income families for specific goods and services. With respect to homeowners insurance, there are several different ways that vouchers could be provided that mirror these programs.

General Taxpayer. If one takes the position that everyone in society is responsible for assisting those who reside in hazard-prone areas, then one could utilize general taxpayer revenue from the federal government to cover the costs of insurance vouchers. This is what is currently done by the food stamp program and the low-income home energy assistance program.

State Government. An alternative (or complementary) source of funding would come from taxes on residents and/or commercial enterprises in the state exposed to natural disaster. One argument that could be made for this type of funding arrangement is that states obtain significant financial benefits from economic development in their jurisdictions through the collection of property taxes or other state revenue such as gasoline taxes, state income taxes, and sales taxes. If residents in coastal areas receive greater benefits from the economic development in these regions than others in the state, they should be taxed proportionately more than those residing inland.

Insurance Policyholders. A special tax could be levied on all insurance policyholders for covering the costs of these vouchers. The rationale for this type of tax would be that all homeowners (as opposed to all taxpayers) should be responsible for helping to protect those who cannot afford protection or should be subsidized for other reasons. The justification for such a program would be similar to the rationale for establishing the USF for telecommunication service: providing affordable telephone service to all residents in the country.

LONG-TERM HOMEOWNERS INSURANCE[10]

Need for Long-Term Insurance

Based on the principle of risk-based rates, insurers should consider marketing long-term insurance contracts on residential property as a way of providing stability to homeowners and encouraging adoption of cost-effective mitigation measures. There is precedent for long-term contracts in insurance—Benjamin Franklin created the Philadelphia Contributionship for the Insuring of Houses from Fire in 1752. It eventually became the Green Tree Mutual Assurance Company, which closed its doors in 2004.[11]

Short-term insurance policies create significant social costs. Evidence from recent disasters reveals that many consumers fail to adequately protect their homes or even insure at all, creating a welfare cost to themselves and a possible cost to all taxpayers in the form of government disaster assistance. To illustrate, the Department of Housing and Urban Development (HUD) reported that 41 percent of damaged homes from the 2005 hurricanes were uninsured or underinsured. Of the 60,196 owner-occupied homes with severe wind damage from these hurricanes, 23,000 (38 percent) did not have insurance against wind loss (U.S. Government Accountability Office, 2007).

The absence of long-term insurance (LTI) also results in direct private costs to both the insurer and the insured. The private value of the LTI over a period of N years is higher than the sum of N one-year insurance contracts if the risk remains constant over time for two reasons: 1) LTI reduces the transaction costs to consumers should their annual homeowners policy not be renewed and to insurers should homeowners cancel their policy, and 2) an LTI reduces the uncertainty to homeowners as to whether their premiums will be significantly increased following a severe disaster.

For a long-term insurance policy to be feasible (say, 10 or 25 years), insurers would have to be able to charge a rate that reflects their best estimate of the risk over that time period (Principle 1). The uncertainty surrounding these estimates could be reflected in the premium as a function of the length of the insurance contract, in much the same way that the interest rate on fixed-rate mortgages varies between 15-, 25-, and 30-year loans. Insurance vouchers could be provided to homeowners who cannot afford coverage at risk-based rates (Principle 2).

The obvious advantage of a long-term insurance contract from the point of view of policyholders is that it provides them with stability and an assurance that their property is protected for as long as they own it. This has been a major concern in hazard-prone areas where insurers have cancelled policies following severe disasters such as those that occurred during the 2005 hurricane season.

Encouraging Adoption of Mitigation Measures

Long-term insurance also provides economic incentives for investing in mitigation where current annual insurance policies (even if they are risk-based) are unlikely to do the trick due to the behavioral considerations discussed in the previous section. To highlight this point, consider the following simple example. Suppose a family could invest $1,500 to strengthen the roof of its house so as to reduce the damage by $30,000 from a future hurricane with an annual probability of 1/100. An insurer charging a risk-based premium would be willing to reduce the annual charge by $300 (that is, 1/100 x $30,000) to reflect the lower expected losses that would occur if a hurricane hit the area in which the policyholder was residing. If the house was expected to last for 10 or more years, the net present value of the expected benefit of investing in this measure would exceed the upfront cost at an annual discount rate as high as 15 percent.

Under current annual insurance contracts, many property owners would be reluctant to incur the $1,500 because they would get only $300 back next year. If they underweight the future, the expected discounted benefits would likely be less than their $1,500 upfront costs. In addition, budget constraints could discourage them from investing in the mitigation measure. Other considerations would also play a role in a family's decision not to invest in these measures: the family may be uncertain as to how long they will reside in the area or whether their insurer would reward them again when their policy is renewed.

A 20-year required insurance policy ties the contract to the property rather than to the individual. In fact, the homeowner could obtain a $1,500 home improvement loan tied to the mortgage at an annual interest rate of 10 percent, resulting in payments of $145 per year. If the insurance premium was reduced by $300, the savings to the homeowner each year would be $155. Alternatively, this loan could be incorporated as part of the mortgage at a lower interest rate.

A bank would have a financial incentive to provide this type of loan. By linking the mitigation expenditures to the structure rather than to the current property owner, the annual payments would be lower and this would be a selling point to mortgagees. The bank would be more fully protected against a catastrophic loss to the property, and the insurer's potential loss from a major disaster would be reduced. These mitigation loans would constitute a new financial product. Moreover, the general public will now be less likely to have large amounts of their tax dollars going for disaster relief. A win-win-win situation for all! (Kunreuther, 2006)

There is an additional benefit to insurers in having banks encourage individuals to invest in cost-effective mitigation measures. The costs of reinsurance, which protects insurers against catastrophic losses, should now decrease. If reinsurers know that they are less likely to make large payments to insurers because each piece of property in a region now has a lower chance of experiencing a large loss, then they will reduce their premiums to the insurer for the same reason that the insurer is reducing its premium to the property owner.

Suppose that an insurer had 1,000 identical insurance policies in the area in which the above family lived, and each one would have a claims payment of $40,000 following a hurricane if homes had not strengthened their roofs. The insurer's loss from such a disaster would be $40 million. Suppose that the insurer wants to have $25 million in coverage from a reinsurer to protect its surplus. If the hypothetical hurricane has a 1 in 100 chance of hitting the region where these families reside, the expected loss to a reinsurer would be $250,000 and the premium charged to the insurer would reflect this. If the bank required that all 1,000 homes have their roofs fortified to meet the local building code and each homeowner's loss were reduced to $10,000, then insurer's total loss would be $10 million should all 1,000 homes be affected, and it would *not* require reinsurance. This savings would be passed on by the insurer in the form of a lower premium.

Open Questions for Designing Long-Term Insurance Contracts

A number of issues and questions associated with the development of a long-term insurance policy have a direct impact on insurers and homeowners, and indirect effects on other stakeholders, that require further research and analysis. Some of the issues that need to be resolved include:

Nature of the Contract: Long-term insurance could be offered by insurers in the form of a fixed-price contract (FPC) for the full term of the policy (for example, 20 years) or an adjustable premium contract (APC) at a variable premium with guaranteed renewal for the term of the policy. The annual premium would be reset based on an index that would have to be simple and transparent. Policyholders will want the option to terminate the contract; mortgage markets provide examples of both good and bad practices. On FPCs, formal arrangements may be necessary to make the insurer whole through provisions such as yield maintenance and defeasance (the two most common methods for dealing with prepayment costs on commercial mortgages). On APCs, the borrower would want the right to terminate the contract within a certain time period of a premium increase notification, such as 3 months.

Protection Against Catastrophic Losses: One would also need to know how the rating agencies will view long-term FPC commitments, since the insurer is now locked into the premium even if the expected losses rise. To protect itself against possible increases in the probability of catastrophic losses over time, insurers marketing FPCs would have to be able to invest in cat bonds or other forms of securitized risks. Some type of government guarantee might be necessary to deal with both insurers' and policyholders' concerns with respect to the ability to pay claims in the future following a catastrophic loss. As for the pricing of the product, FPC premiums would likely be somewhat higher than APC premiums to protect insurers against an increase in the risk during the contract period. This behavior would be similar to the pricing of fixed-rate mortgages relative to adjustable rate mortgages.

One of the central issues will be how high the price of a long-term contract will be, given the ambiguities associated with the risk and the capital costs for covering catastrophic losses. Without some type of protection against large losses either through long-term risk transfer instruments (which currently do not exist) or a government reinsurance program at the state or federal level, the premiums for FPCs are likely to be extremely high so that there would be little demand for this type of coverage.

Understanding the Contract: Those who purchase insurance policies often have a difficult time understanding every aspect of the terms of the contract—what risks are covered, what risks are not, and the basis for being charged a specific rate. The problem is likely to be compounded for a long-term insurance contract. There is an opportunity for insurers to educate consumers as to the basis for the premiums they charge by providing more detail on the types of risks that are covered and the amount charged for different levels of protection. More specifically, insurers could break down the premium into coverage against fire, theft, wind damage, and other losses included in a homeowners policy, and how the premium varied with the length of the long-term contract.

It would be beneficial for insurers to reveal this information so that homeowners will be able to make better decisions by understanding the nature of the contract and what alternative options cost them. They will then be able to make trade-offs between costs and expected benefits, which is impossible for them to do today. Thaler and Sunstein (2008) argue for this type of information disclosure by proposing a form of government regulation termed RECAP (Record, Evaluate, and Compare Alternative Prices). They recommend that the government not regulate prices but require disclosure practices—not in a long, unintelligible document, but in a spreadsheet-like format that includes all relevant formulas.

Requiring Insurance Coverage: One needs to consider whether insurance should be required on all residential property. This would not be a radical change from the current situation—homeowners who have a mortgage are normally required by the bank that finances the loan to purchase coverage against wind damage for the length of the mortgage. Similarly, those in flood-prone areas are required to purchase flood insurance under the National Flood Insurance Program if they have a federally insured mortgage. Insurance coverage is required today for other consumer purchases. Today in all states motorists must show proof of financial responsibility on their automobile insurance policy for bodily injury and property damage liability in order to register their car.

If all homes were required to purchase a homeowners policy it would enable insurers to more easily diversify their risks and hence reduce the likelihood of suffering catastrophic losses over the length of the long-term contract. Another advantage of requiring homeowners insurance is that it will reduce the likelihood of liberal disaster assistance following the next large-scale disaster since victims will have financial protection.

Whether long-term insurance will be attractive to insurers, homeowners, regulators, and other relevant stakeholders will certainly depend on the market conditions that come with it. What is clear today, however, is that we need innovative programs for reducing future losses from disasters that involve combined strengths of the public and private sectors. For insurance to play an important role in this regard, one needs to understand what a policy can and cannot do as a function of the nature of the risk, the type of coverage provided by the insurer and the premium structure.

THE BENEFITS OF MITIGATION

We can summarize the conclusions that emerge from this paper with the following points:

▸ The losses from natural disasters have increased significantly in the past 15 years, and we as a society are more vulnerable to catastrophic losses in future years than we have been in the past.

▸ A principal reason for these increased losses is the continuing economic development in hazard-prone areas. The development of Florida highlights this point: the projected population in Florida in 2010 will be 19.3 million—a 700 percent increase over the 2.8 million inhabitants residing in the state in 1950.

▸ By mitigating existing and new homes with structural measures (for example, better designed roofs) one could reduce future disaster losses significantly. If all residential homes in Florida were fully mitigated, the damage from a 100-year hurricane would be reduced from $84 billion to $33 billion, a decrease of 61 percent.

▸ Individuals are reluctant to invest in cost-effective mitigation for many reasons, including an underestimation of the risk, a focus on short-term returns, and budget constraints.

▸ Insurance provides an opportunity to reward individuals who undertake mitigation measures by offering discounts on insurance premiums. For insurers to want to provide these premium reductions they need to be able to charge risk-based rates. If one wants to subsidize some homeowners in hazard-prone areas (low-income residents), vouchers should come from sources outside of insurance using models such as the food stamp program.

▸ Long-term insurance tied to the property rather than to the individual provides financial stability to individuals residing in hazard-prone areas and should lead to the adoption of cost-effective mitigation measures that would normally not be adopted under annual insurance policies. Such a program raises a number of questions for future research.

NOTES

* This paper incorporates material from a study on Managing Large-Scale Risks in a New Era of Catastrophes (Wharton Risk Management and Decision Processes Center in conjunction with Georgia State University and the Insurance Information Institute, March 2008) and Kunreuther (2008). It reflects many helpful discussions with my colleagues on the project: Neil Doherty, Martin Grace, Robert Klein, Paul Kleindorfer, Erwann Michel-Kerjan, Mark Pauly, and Paul Raschky. Funding for the Wharton Risk Management and Decision Processes Center's "Managing and Financing Extreme Events" project is gratefully acknowledged.

1. This table excludes payments for flood by the National Flood Insurance Program in the United States (for example, $17.3 billion in 2005 as a result of Hurricanes Katrina and Rita).

2. This subsection is based on Kunreuther and Michel-Kerjan (2007).

3. The NFIP is a public insurance program created in 1968. Under the program, insurers play the role of intermediaries between the policyholders and the federal government. Following Hurricane Katrina, the program had to borrow $20 billion from the federal government in 2006 to meet its claims. Congress is considering modifying the program substantially.

4. For additional data on the economic impact of future catastrophic hurricanes see the Financial Services Roundtable (2007).

5. Information on this program is available on the website of the Institute for Business and Home Safety at <http://www.ibhs.org/property_protection/default.asp?id=8>.

6. More details on this program are available at <http://www.frac.org/html/federal_food_programs/programs/fsp.html>.

7. For instance, at the end of August 2007, Secretary of Health and

Human Services (HHS) Mike Leavitt announced that $50 million in emergency energy assistance would be given to 12 states that experienced much hotter than normal conditions during the summer.

8. For more details on this program, see US Department of Health and Human Services at <http://www.acf.hhs.gov/programs/liheap/>.

9. For more details on this program, see <http://www.usac.org/about/universal-service>.

10. The material in this section is based on Jaffee, Kunreuther, and Michel-Kerjan (2008).

11. The Philadelphia Contributionship and other perpetual insurance companies require a large fixed payment at the time that one purchases insurance. The interest earned on this "insurance investment" covers the annual premiums on the property. We thank Felix Kloman for calling attention to this type of long-term insurance relationship. Kloman has favored long-term commitments and partnerships between the insurer and insured for many years, having written columns on the topic in his publication, *Risk Management Reports,* in September 1994 and October 1995.

REFERENCES

Association of British Insurers (ABI). "Financial Risks of Climate Change." June 2005.

Burby, R. "Hurricane Katrina and the Paradoxes of Government Disaster Policy: Bringing About Wise Governmental Decisions for Hazardous Areas." *The Annals of the American Academy of Political and Social Science* 604 (2006): 171-191.

Burby, R., S. Bollens, E. Kaiser, D. Mullan and J. Sheaffer. *Cities Under Water: A Comparative Evaluation of Ten Cities' Efforts to Manage Floodplain Land Use.* Boulder: Institute of Behavioral Science, University of Colorado, 1988.

Financial Services Roundtable. *Blue Ribbon Commission on Mega-Catastrophes Comprehensive Report* (2007).

Food Research and Action Center <http://www.frac.org/data/FSPparticipation/2007_06.pdf>.

Goodnough, A. "As Hurricane Season Looms, State Aims to Scare." *The New York Times,* May 31, 2006.

Grossi, P., and H. Kunreuther, eds. *Catastrophe Modeling: A New Approach to Managing Risk.* New York: Springer, 2005.

Jaffee, D., H. Kunreuther, and E. Michel-Kerjan. "Long Term Insurance (LTI) for Addressing Catastrophic Market Failure." Wharton Risk Management and Decision Processes Center. Working Paper # 2008-06-05.

Kunreuther, H, "Mitigating Disaster Losses through Insurance." *Journal of Risk and Uncertainty* 12 (1996): 171-187.

——. "Disaster Mitigation and Insurance: Learning from Katrina." *The Annals of the American Academy of Political and Social Science* 604 (2006): 208-227.

——. "Catastrophe Insurance: Challenges for the US and Asia" *Asian Catastrophe Insurance.* Eds. C. Scawthorn and K. Kobayashi. London: Risk Books, 2008.

Kunreuther, H., and E. Michel-Kerjan. "Climate Change, Insurability of Large-scale Risks and the Emerging Liability Challenge." *Penn Law Review* 155:6 (June 2007): 1795-1842.

Kunreuther, H., et al. *Disaster Insurance Protection: Public Policy Lessons.* New York: John Wiley and Sons, 1978.

Laska, S. B. *Floodproof Retrofitting: Homeowner Self-Protective Behavior.* Boulder: Institute of Behavioral Science, University of Colorado, 1991.

Loewenstein, G., and D. Prelec (1991), "Negative Time Preference." *American Economic Review* 81:2 (May 1991): 347-52.

Mills, E., and E. Lecomte. "From Risk To Opportunity: How Insurers Can Proactively and Profitably Manage Climate Change." *Ceres.* August 2006.

Munich Re. "Topics 2000. Natural Catastrophes—The Current Position." Special millennium issue. 2000.

Palm, R., M. Hodgson, R.D. Blanchard and D. Lyons. *Earthquake Insurance in California: Environmental Policy and Individual Decision Making.* Boulder: Westview Press, 1990.

Swiss Re. "Natural Catastrophes and Man-made Disasters in 2006." *Sigma* 2 (2007).

Thaler, R., and C. Sunstein. *Nudge: The Gentle Power of Choice Architecture.* New Haven: Yale University Press, 2008.

U.S. Government Accountability Office (GAO). *Natural Disasters: Public Policy Options for Changing the Federal Role in Natural Catastrophe Insurance.* Washington, D.C.: GAO, November 2007.

Wharton Risk Management and Decision Processes Center. *Managing Large-Scale Risks in a New Era of Catastrophes.* Philadelphia: University of Pennsylvnia, Wharton School, 2008.

Part V
The Impact of Disasters on Human Development

Lee Clarke
Introduction: Thinking Possibilistically in a Probabilistic World

DISASTERS SERVE AS FOCUSING EVENTS—FOR PUBLICS, THE MEDIA, politicians, and academics. As the papers in this special issue show, there has been an increase in the number of disasters over the past 30 years or so. There has also been an increase in the severity of disasters—more deaths and greater loss of property. That frequency and consequence are both on upward trends should lead us to expect that attention will be focused ever more sharply on disaster. Indeed, after Hurricane Katrina, scholars throughout the social sciences, even those without any background whatsoever in environmental studies, disaster research, or risk studies, set out to do research on New Orleans or the Gulf Coast. A wide array of reasons can be given for this, but the essential point is that Katrina focused academic attention too. So will the next worst case. When those new researchers prepare to go into the field to do interviews, or prepare to field a questionnaire, or whatever their particular planned foray, they would do well to review the papers in this volume.

The papers in this section demonstrate several interesting points about disasters, and about academic interest in them. One is a remarkable convergence of perspective about what is important. All agree obviously that the extent and dimensions of people's suffering as a result of disaster is important to study. This ranges from the psychological phenomenon of post-traumatic stress disorder to the destruction of community. The damages from disaster can be persistent and deep, these authors conclude. Their conclusion contrasts sharply with one of the common pieces of received wisdom from the mainstream disaster research community: that individuals and communities bounce back and even thrive relatively quickly after disaster. (An overwhelming amount of research on so-called technological disasters contradicts the mainstream disaster conclusion, although none of that work is referenced here.)

Another notable aspect of these readings is that there is broad agreement that conventional approaches to thinking about disaster are insufficient, although again no attempt is made to engage the extant literatures in social science that also quarrel with convention. In any case, one of the slow but significant developments in social science, and in some of the work here, is the realization that the idea of "natural" disaster is more than wrong: it misleadingly draws attention away from the pre-existing conditions that make people vulnerable to hazards in the first place. This has been a commonplace in writings about hazards and disasters since Hewitt (1983) and long before that Sorokin (1942) noted it, obliquely. Katrina and the 2004 tsunami in Indonesia made quite clear that poverty, lack of political power, race, and economic development massively compounded the damage that waves and winds can bring. As Basher says about the effects of disasters, in rich countries people lose their property but in poor countries people lose their lives.

All agree, too, that at least two of the three of the big troika of inequality—race, class, and gender—are crucial. We must understand more fully than we have the dynamics of inequalities to understand both the consequences of disasters and the institutional conditions that either protect people or make them vulnerable. Notably absent at the conference from which these papers came was any deep discussion of gender; indeed, notably absent from the program were women. Their absence was not because of lack of effort on the part of the conference organizers to invite female scholars. Female scholars were invited, but could not attend. Their absence is evidence of a paucity of female scholars in the field.

While we learn new and interesting things about inequalities and disasters from the papers presented in this section, the broader intellectual issue is not generalized and developed: there are patterns in the way society is organized that lead to patterns in how people are made vulnerable to and suffer from disaster. This is a point I developed at length in Clarke (2006), and at the risk of immodesty I take the opportunity to say a few words about it. Scholars and nonscholars are so taken with the extraordinary correlation between being a member of the big troika and suffering that the general point is obscured. Consider for instance the Concorde accident or even September 11. On July 25, 2000 the Concorde, a supersonic jet owned by Air France, caught fire on take-off and crashed soon thereafter into a local hotel. There were no survivors. I do not have details on the passengers, but the tickets to fly on the Concorde at the time cost nearly $11,000. It is a reasonable speculation that all the passengers on the Concorde that day were rich; certainly, we can say that they were privileged. There is a pattern, although it is not likely that any social scientist will ever write a paper about it. In any disaster in which most or all of the victims are poor, we sensibly conclude that some form of discrimination is at play. Not so for rich people. In the case of the collapse of the World Trade Center, too, relatively rich white men were vastly over-represented among those who lost their lives on that worst case day (NIST, 2005). I doubt, however, that we will ever see a social scientist call that an instance of institutional discrimination. The larger point is not that social scientists are more likely to issue positive moral judgments when the group under analysis is among the dispossessed or the powerless, true though that may be. The larger point is that by ruling out of consideration such cases we miss the generalizations that would permit tying the specific findings and concepts from "disaster research" to larger theories and questions of social theory.

REFERENCES

Clarke, Lee. *Worst Cases: Terror and Catastrophe in the Popular Imagination.* Chicago: University of Chicago Press, 2006.

Hewitt, Kenneth. *Interpretations of Calamity*. Boston: Allen and Unwin, 1983.

NIST. "Occupant Behavior, Egress, and Emergency Communications." Washington, D.C.: National Institute of Standards and Technology, 2005.

Sorokin, Pitirim. *Man and Society in Calamity: The Effects of War, Revolution, Famine, Pestilence upon Human Mind, Behavior, Social Organization, and Cultural Life*. New York: Greenwood Press. 1942.

Reid Basher
Disaster Impacts: Implications and Policy Responses

DISASTERS ARISE WHEN A COMMUNITY IS UNABLE TO COPE WITH THE natural hazard it faces. A hazard by itself does not necessarily lead to a disaster. If a community is prepared for storms, for example, with strong buildings built in relatively safe locations, well-protected and healthy ecosystems, an effective warning and evacuation system, and an informed populace, the losses may be modest. Nations and communities can do much to avoid the stresses of extreme hazard events. The term "disaster risk reduction" can be defined as "action taken to reduce the risk of disasters and the adverse impacts of natural hazards, through systematic efforts to analyze and manage the causes of disasters, including through avoidance of hazards, reduced social and economic vulnerability to hazards, and improved preparedness for adverse events" (UNISDR, 2008). From this perspective, the widely used term *natural disaster* is a misnomer, as it reflects and reinforces the unfortunately widespread belief that disasters are acts of God, something that little can be done about, and perhaps even a punishment for the past sins of those affected.

A key characteristic of severe hazards is their relative uncommonness and uncertainty for most places or people, which often leads to lack of awareness and understanding and to complacency or denial of risks by individuals and policymakers alike. The absence of an immediate guaranteed payoff for a risk reduction investment tends to discourage the assignment of political and financial priority to the problem. Moreover, greater rewards are accorded to those leaders who visibly assign attention and resources to respond to disasters than to those who labor unseen to reduce their root causes. The core concept of *risk* arising from natural hazards is not a fundamental mode of thinking or discourse for policymaking, and in addition is greatly overshadowed nowadays by the issue of terrorism, in spite of the decades of evidence of greater losses in lives and economic assets from risks of natural origin.

A second important characteristic is the nature of disasters as complex interactions of the natural and human worlds and hence involving a diverse range of knowledge, spanning the physical, ecological, social, and cultural disciplines as well as engineering, financial, and political perspectives. A major challenge is to link these different types of knowledge to provide answers to disaster-specific questions. Similarly, there is a need to link the equally diverse range of methods and tools of disaster risk reduction, which are largely based on tried-and-tested approaches used in endeavors such as civil engineering, weather prediction, water management, forest protection, urban planning, architecture, insurance, public health, public education, and community action. In the same way that we have seen the environmental science field forged from disparate areas of expertise over the last 40 years, so too can we expect to see the field of disaster studies structured and integrated through multidisciplinary approaches in the coming years.

The third characteristic of note is the multisectoral and multilevel nature of the task to actually implement disaster reduction. All sectors are affected by disaster risk, and all can contribute to the reduction of risks—or, unwittingly, to the inadvertent increase of risks. This means that the responsibility for disaster risk reduction cannot be assigned to one sector or one ministry alone, but must be systematically implemented in all sectors, and particularly in land-use planning, environmental management, infrastructure development, construction, agriculture, water resources, public health and social policy. Equally, it requires efforts at all levels of both governmental and nongovernmental society—from national action to establish public institutions, policies and programs, through city and local government planning and implementation, and civil society and community activity to raise awareness and to identify and manage local risks. These principles are well recognized in the internationally endorsed road map for disaster risk reduction, the Hyogo Framework for Action (UNISDR, 2005).

Finally, the issue of climate change is bringing a new dimension to the field of disaster risk reduction. Among the most immediate concerns associated with climate change is the expected increase in extreme weather and climatic conditions, signs of which are already evident (IPCC, 2007). The burden of past greenhouse gas emissions, coupled with ongoing emissions, means that climate change is inevitable and that adaptation to the changes is essential. In particular, the increases in certain hydrometeorological hazards will require the strengthening of capacities for reducing the impacts of such hazards, including disasters. Fortunately, the methods and tools of disaster risk reduction are readily available, and these, guided by the Hyogo Framework, will need to become a major component of adaptation policies and programs. In the Bali Action Plan, the parties to the United Nations Framework Convention on Climate Change have identified disaster risk reduction strategies as a tool for adaptation (UNFCCC, 2007). At the same time, it should not be forgotten that extreme events and disasters occur irrespective of climate change, and that disasters, particularly in developing countries, represent an existing, major unsolved problem for sustainable development. Climate change, little by little, will simply make this problem worse.

DISASTER CHARACTERISTICS AND TRENDS

The scale of the problem of disasters may be seen from the statistics of the recent 15-year period between 1991 and 2005, derived from the EM-DAT disasters database (CRED, 2008). During this period 3,470 million people were affected, 960,000 people died, and economic losses were $1,193 billion. Most disasters are weather or climate related, mainly from tropical cyclones, windstorms, floods (including flash floods and related land-slides), and droughts. Damaging earthquakes are less common but can cause considerable loss of life and economic damage, such as the 73,338 reported dead in the Pakistan earthquake in 2005 and the $120 billion in economic losses from the Kobe earthquake in 1995. The Indian Ocean tsunami in 2004 was precipitated by an unusually strong undersea earthquake and killed about 226,000 people.

When plotted over time, the EM-DAT data show very noticeable rising trends, particularly for hydrometeorological events; the reported annual numbers have approximately doubled over the last 20 years. The trends in death tolls show a dual effect—first, a significant decline in the occurrence of the exceptionally high death-toll events, which is consistent with advances in the management of floods, storms and famines; and second, a more recent in the baseline average annual death tolls, which is likely associated with population growth and unsustainable development practices. The rise in reported economic losses has been higher than the increases in numbers of disasters or numbers of people affected. Up to 1989, only in one year, 1980, were the losses over $30 billion, while after 1989 the losses every year exceeded this sum and in two years exceeded $150 billion. The data series is strongly affected by a few large events, such as the Kobe earthquake noted above; and Hurricanes Katrina, Rita, and Wilma in 2005, which together contributed losses of $166 billion.

The processes driving the trends in disaster data remain to be properly researched. One factor is that disasters are not intrinsically well-defined phenomena, and are interpreted and recorded in different ways by different actors. Another factor of particular importance is the improvement in the recording of events. Over recent decades, the Brussels-based Center for the Research of Epidemiology of Disasters, which hosts the EM-DAT database, has progressively upgraded its processes for collecting globally comprehensive and consistent information, which comes primarily from media reports and relief agency sources. Improvements in global communications, the rise of the Internet, the globalization of media reporting, and more widespread public awareness and interest have also contributed to better reporting. For these reasons, great caution should be used when analyzing and interpreting trends in the data, particularly in reference to climate change. Simple association of trends does not establish causality. If the American 1930s dust bowl years were to reoccur today, would this be evidence of climate change?

The impacts of disaster events are strongly differentiated by the status of economic development. Poor countries are disproportionately affected by natural hazards, especially in terms of death rates, owing to their intrinsic vulnerabilities and comparatively low capabilities for risk reduction measures, while richer countries tend to sustain the largest economic costs. For example, over the period 1991 to 2005, developing and least developed countries suffered 884,845 deaths and $401 billion in economic losses, while Organization for Economic Cooperation and Development (OECD) countries suffered 61,918 deaths and $715 billion in economic losses. During this same period, seven countries—all either small island states or developing countries—experienced losses in a single year that exceeded their gross domestic product (GDP). Grenada, for example, suffered losses of $919 million as a result of Hurricane Ivan in 2004, which was equal to 2.5 times its 2003 GDP. In such circumstances, disasters will clearly impede a country's development progress by decimating production and diverting scarce national resources to rebuilding activities. At the same time secondary effects such as inflows of relief from donors and the country's foreign diaspora, and the gains from modernizing productive assets, may contribute some economic advantages. A better understanding of the role of disasters on sustainable economic development has been recognized as critical for promoting and guiding investment in disaster risk reduction (UNISDR, 2007a, 2007b).

Increases in economic losses are at least partly due to rapid increases in the value of exposed assets in most countries and to population growth. However, re-insurance data (Munich Re, 2007) show that the insured fraction of these losses is relatively small, varying between about 10 percent and 50 percent for major catastrophes over the last 15 years. Insurance is relatively rare in the developing world, which means that householders and enterprises cannot transfer or share their risks beyond their extended family and local credit sources.

UNDERLYING CONCEPTS OF VULNERABILITY AND RISK

Before humans developed a scientific view of the world, the causes of hazards were unknown and the occurrence and behavior of hazards were largely unpredictable. Earthquakes, tsunami, storms, floods, and drought had an immense effect on human society, and could only be interpreted in terms such as punishments for errant behavior, or acts of gods or spirits, to whom prayers, offerings, or sacrifices might need to be given. The fatalism arising from the sense of powerlessness of societies in face of such forces still remains widespread today, especially among the less educated, and the expression "act of God" is still in active use.

However, over the last 100 to 200 years, a sound and comprehensive scientific knowledge of natural hazards has developed, drawing on geological evidence, historical records, scientific measurement series, and analytical and modeling studies. This has been accompanied by great advances in relevant engineering practice, particularly in structural design, water management systems, and hazard-risk assessment and warning systems. For example, pylons carrying electrical lines can be designed to withstand storm winds, based on knowledge of the stresses that winds exert on pylons, and on estimates or measurements of the wind speeds likely to be experienced by the pylon. Structural designs seek an optimum that balances the costs of construction and the likely costs of failure. The pylon might be designed to just survive the most extreme wind speed expected at the location on average once every 100 years. Equally, an apartment building may be designed not to collapse on its occupants in an earthquake up to a magnitude 8 event. Modern systems for flood control, evacuation, and food aid are likewise based on such foundations of analysis and measurement. As a result, the massive losses of lives recorded in the past (CRED, 2008), such as the 2,000,000 reported deaths from flooding in China in July 1959 and the 300,000 reported deaths from drought in Ethiopia in May 1983, are largely a thing of the past. China still experiences huge floods affecting millions of people, but the loss of life is now measured in hundreds of people. It could be argued that scientific and engineering approaches have saved millions of lives over the past few decades.

Nevertheless, despite these advances in technical expertise, disaster numbers and impacts have not decreased globally, and specific disaster events continue to show significant shortcomings in how societies handle disaster risk. Events like the flooding of New Orleans during Hurricane Katrina show that other, nontechnical perspectives are critically necessary. The reasons for the inadequate state of the levees protecting New Orleans and for the reportedly disorganized response of the authorities to the technically accurate and timely warnings and to the crisis generally are essentially social and political in nature. This is a common problem worldwide. The Hyogo Framework (UNISDR, 2005) identifies social and political factors, particularly lack of both political commitment and public awareness, as major challenges to disaster risk reduction globally.

The impacts of disasters are strongly differentiated at the community and individual level. This is well illustrated by a study of the gender- and age-differentiated death rates in selected Indian coastal villages during the Indian Ocean tsunami of December 24, 2004 (Guha-Sapir, 2007). Most remarkable was the higher death rate for females than for males across most age groups. In the age groups between 30–54 years, the death rates for females were as much as 2–3 times higher than those for men. On the basis of existing knowledge of social roles and capacities we should not be surprised by these data. Gender is often a hidden dimension in disasters, in terms of both impacts and capacities to reduce vulnerability. Gender-blindness and gender-based norms prevent the formation of accurate understanding of risk processes and impede the development of effective policy responses to address and reduce disaster risks. Similarly, age is also a strong and often neglected determinant of risk. In the aforementioned tsunami study, the highest death rates, reaching 10-20 percent of the particular age class, were among children aged 0–8 and people aged 50 and above, while the lowest rates, of less than 4 percent, were for those aged 15–34 years. Within the developed countries, intrinsically vulnerable groups also tend to be the most affected, as was the case in Europe during the heat wave in 2003, which killed approximately 20,000 people and during Hurricane Katrina, when 1,322 people died; in both cases the elderly were disproportionately represented.

A wide range of factors contribute to societal vulnerability to natural hazards, and in many cases these factors are of our own making, through faults of commission and omission, in how we exploit the land and how we build our houses and our cities. Clearly we must understand the processes—technical and socioeconomic—through which vulnerability is created and sustained. Disaster risk accumulates as a result of ignorance and neglect, only to be revealed through the devastation of a major event.

Although uncertainties can be found in the disasters data, there appears to be a growing consensus among researchers and practitioners that disaster risk has been increasing (UNISDR, 2007a). Put simply, populations are growing and more people inhabit risky places and risky dwellings, and exploit and damage the environment upon which they depend. On the rollercoaster ride of development, our societies are undertaking large-scale activities that significantly raise risk, such as settling on flood plains, storm-exposed beaches, and landslide-prone hillsides, and building schools and apartments that will collapse in earthquakes. We clear mangroves for shrimp farms, fill in wetlands for industrial zones, strip forests from steep hillsides, and confine rivers along narrow concrete channels. Extreme rainfalls that previously were absorbed in forests and wetlands now rush down more quickly in pulses that flood towns and cities downstream. At the coast, storm surge and wind-driven waves more easily penetrate cleared land to reach newly exposed settlements. In this light, we can look at growing disasters as largely a sign of unsustainable development.

CLIMATE CHANGE AND DISASTER RISK

Global climate change—itself an iconic sign of unsustainable development—is now already apparent, in line with the general predictions made since the first studies emerged about 1970. The core factor is the warming effect of the added greenhouse gases in the atmosphere, in much that same way that throwing a blanket over the bed at night will increase the sleeper's temperature. With the historical accumulation of atmospheric carbon dioxide and other greenhouse gases from decades of industrial development and land clearances, global warming and other changes are now locked into place, irrespective of the emissions controls and reductions that may be achieved in the coming years. As a result, we can expect more heat waves, rising sea levels, and changes in weather patterns. Areas that used to receive reasonable rainfall may soon find that this is no longer the case and that when droughts occur, they are longer and more intense. At the same time, with more moisture in the warmer atmosphere, we can expect more intense rainfalls when it rains, and this will lead to more flooding. The most vulnerable areas are the classic areas of vulnerability, most notably Africa, on account of its rain-fed subsistence agriculture and its generally low capacities, the low lying and heavily populated deltas of Asia and Africa, and the small and low-lying islands (IPCC, 2007). The poor, nearly everywhere, are at risk because they are intrinsically vulnerable to natural hazards.

Over 2007, a record number of humanitarian "flash appeals" were launched by the United Nations on behalf of disaster-affected countries (ECOSOC, 2008). These are appeals for funds that are raised very quickly after a major event to help countries better handle an event. Most of the appeals were for climate-related events. The reasons for such a large increase are not clear, and while it is consistent with the general projections of climate change, it would be wrong to presume the increase is due to climate change without proper scientific study. Nevertheless, the number is a matter of record and it gives an ominous warning of what the future may hold.

To date, the two issues of disaster risk and climate change have been dealt with in largely separate policy processes and by different government departments. Climate change is usually handled by ministries of science, environment, agriculture, or energy, while disasters are managed by operational ministries concerned with civil protection and responding to emergencies. Disaster risk and disaster risk reduction are relatively new concepts and often have no clear ministerial home. Nevertheless, some countries are becoming aware that disasters are more that just a matter of responding and are starting to establish responsible offices to better understand the root causes and to act to reduce those risks.

Public concern and awareness about climate change offers a new opportunity to address disaster risks, while equally, disaster risk reduction offers ready-made concepts and tools to adapt to climate change. One of the easiest ways to adapt to the effects of climate change is to establish sound policies for managing natural hazards. Adaptation measures can include improved zoning of land, enforcement of suitable building codes, more secure hospitals and other critical facilities, better insurance mechanisms, more effective early warning systems, and encouraging communities to assess their own risks and work together as a community to reduce those risks. The Hyogo Framework specifically identifies the need to "promote the integration of risk reduction associated with existing climate variability and future climate change into strategies for the reduction of disaster risk and adaptation to climate change" (UNISDR, 2005), and the Bali Action Plan's directions for adaptation call for the consideration of: "risk management and risk reduction strategies, including risk sharing and transfer mechanisms such as insurance; . . . disaster reduction strategies and means to address loss and damage associated with climate change impacts in developing countries that are particularly vulnerable to the adverse effects of climate change" (UNFCCC, 2007). Many of the general principles and requirements for adaptation that are listed in the Bali Action Plan are especially relevant to reducing disaster risk, particularly vulnerability assessments, capacity-building, and response strategies, as well as integration of actions into sectoral and national planning.

The need to systematically integrate disaster risk reduction and adaptation into national development strategies has also emerged as a key conclusion from a number of recent international policy forums. In particular, the "Stockholm Plan of Action for Integrating Disaster Risk and Climate Change Impacts in Poverty Reduction" (World Bank, 2007) and the recent Oslo Policy Forum on "Changing the Way We Develop: Dealing with Disasters and Climate Change" (MFA-Norway, 2008) both reiterate this view.

PRACTICAL ACTION TO REDUCE DISASTER RISKS

The city that the author comes from—Wellington, New Zealand— provides an interesting example of natural risk and practical risk reduction measures. It sits astride a set of geological fault lines, one of which slipped in 1855 in a great earthquake that caused one side of the harbor to rise by two meters. This created a strip of new land above sea level that today hosts many central city office buildings and provides a conduit for the main highway and railway lines that connect the city to the rest of the country.

Aware of the risks, the city authorities in the 1980s instituted regulations that required all commercial building owners to either strengthen their buildings to a specific seismic standard or demolish them. Also, following the Japanese experience of highway collapse in Kobe in 1995, the national transportation authorities substantially reinforced the pillars of the suspended highway that runs beside the harbor. In the middle of the city, also beside the harbor, the modern National Museum of New Zealand sits on a special foundation of large rubber and lead blocks, which is designed to absorb the energy of earth-quakes and thus increase the survival prospects of the building and its precious contents. The author's house in the city is about 100 meters from the principal fault line. Like most of Wellington's houses, it is built of wood, so that while it will (and does, in the experience of the author!) shake in earthquakes, it is unlikely to fully collapse. This fault is active and a major earthquake can be expected at any time. National programs established by the civil defense authorities encourage practical preparation for earthquakes and other disasters, providing advice to householders on securing heavy furniture to walls, establishing reserves of water and food, and having a family plan for communication and action in the event of a crisis. These programs include a radio series "When the Siren Goes" and a program aimed at children called "What's the Plan Stan" (MCDEM, 2008).

As a result of decades of development and decision making, the magnitude of the accumulated "risk burden" in some countries is very high, posing a difficult problem for public authorities to address. For example, in many cities in earthquake zones, a sizeable fraction of the buildings may be older-style masonry structures or more modern but inadequately reinforced multilevel structures that are at risk of collapse in a major event, with potentially great loss of life. The destruction of Bam, Iran, which was leveled in 2003 with the loss of about 26,000 lives, is a notable example. The problem facing a government is that the total cost of strengthening or rebuilding extensive areas of housing is enormous and beyond its budgetary capacity. An alternative strategy is to take the following three-prong approach. First, investments are made to selectively strengthen or rebuild those buildings that are either especially at risk or are critical to the operation and safety of the city, such as hospitals and transport and communications facilities. Second, seismic safety standards tailored to the particular risks at different localities are developed and rigorously enforced for all new construction in order to avoid future accumulations of risk. Third, following any particular disaster event, explicit efforts are made to "build back better" in order to avoid the factors that led to or worsened the event and to prevent the resumption of the previous risk.

Another broad area that is challenging but amenable to systematic action is the implementation of policies and measures for improved land-use management and the protection of environmental buffers. These both require the combination of sound scientific knowledge of the risk factors, well-drafted laws and regulations, and strong involvement of well-informed public groups. The challenges mainly arise from the competition of different actors for access to natural resources and the weaknesses in governance that so often result in lack of transparency of decision making and the exclusion of the poor and other disadvantaged groups. In many instances the necessary basis of scientific information, risk assessments, and law are inadequate and need to be specifically developed.

Numerous examples of practical action and experience in disaster risk reduction are available (UNISDR, 2004). In the context of the economics of adaptation, Stern (2006) reports a number of cost-effective disaster risk-reduction initiatives. For example China averted estimated losses of about $12 billion through an investment of $3.15 billion on flood control between 1960 and 2000, while a Brazilian Rio de Janeiro flood reconstruction and prevention project yielded an internal rate of return exceeding 50 percent. High benefit-cost ratios also were reported for a disaster mitigation and preparedness program in Andhra Pradesh, India and a mangrove-planting project in Vietnam to protect coastal populations from typhoons and storms. A study in the US Gulf states showed that the application of hurricane protection methods to properties in 500 locations, at a total cost of $2.5 million, resulted in eight times less damage from Hurricane Katrina than occurred for comparable unprotected properties and avoided property losses of $500 million (Mills and Lecomte, 2006).

INTERNATIONAL ADVOCACY AND GUIDANCE

The Hyogo Framework recognizes the need for a comprehensive global approach to disaster risk reduction that is part of a sustainable development approach and integrated across all sectors and disciplines. Subtitled "building the resilience of nations and communities," it was agreed upon in January 2005 in Kobe, Japan, by 168 governments, amid the heightened awareness and concern following the December 26, 2004 Indian Ocean tsunami. It lays out a foundation of concepts and priorities for the implementation of disaster risk reduction and the roles and expectations of governments and relevant organizations, and sets the intended outcome for the decade 2005-2015 as "the substantial reduction of losses, in lives and in the social, economic and environmental assets of communities and countries." The Hyogo Framework represents a significant reorientation of attention toward the root causes of disaster risks and risk reduction, and away from the traditional preoccupation with disaster response.

Based on a review of past successes and failures in reducing disaster risks, the Hyogo Framework set out five priorities for action, each elaborated into a number of specific areas of attention. These offer a strong basis for developing concrete measures for not only disaster risk reduction but also adaptation to climate change.

1. *Ensure that disaster risk reduction is a national and local priority, with a strong institutional basis for implementation.* This includes such issues as identifying a core ministry with a broad mandate that includes finance, economics, or planning to oversee and guide the development and mainstreaming of disaster risk policies and activities; assigning budgets for risk reduction in relevant sectors and levels of government; developing the basis of laws and regulations needed; organizing national high-level policy dialogues to prepare national strategies; formalizing collaboration and coordination through a multisector mechanism such as a national platform for disaster risk reduction; and developing mechanisms to actively engage women, communities and local governments in the assessment of vulnerability and the formulation of local risk reduction activities.

2. *Identify, assess, and monitor disaster risks and enhance early warning.* Important steps under this priority include developing and disseminating high-quality databases and information about natural hazards and their likely future changes; conducting assessments of vulnerability and especially vulnerable groups; preparing national risk assessments; preparing briefings for policymakers and sector leaders; reviewing the effectiveness of early warning systems; implementing procedures to ensure warnings reach vulnerable groups; and undertaking public information programs to help people understand the risks they face and how to respond to warnings.

3. *Use knowledge, innovation, and education to build a culture of safety and resilience at all levels.* Specific elements include strengthening research programs on disaster risk and resilience; supporting the development of methods and tools; collating and disseminating good practices; undertaking public information programs and publicizing community successes; training the media on disaster risk-related issues; developing education curricula on disaster risk and its reduction; establishing training programs and university studies; and improving mechanisms for knowledge transfer from science to application for risk management in hazard-sensitive sectors.

4. *Reduce the underlying risk factors.* This covers the many environmental and societal factors that create or exacerbate the risks from natural hazards. Measures can include incorporating risk-related considerations in development planning processes and macroeconomic projections; requiring the use of risk-related information in city planning, land-use planning, water management, and environmental and natural resource management; strengthening and maintaining protective works such as coastal wave barriers, river levees, flood ways and flood ponds; requiring routine assessment and reporting of climate risks in infrastructure projects, building designs and other engineering practices; enforcement of building codes; developing risk transfer mechanisms and social safety nets; supporting programs for diversification of livelihoods; and instituting risk reduction activities in plans for recovery from specific disasters.

5. *Strengthen disaster preparedness for effective response at all levels.* Resilience building and early warning systems contribute toward this priority. Other specific actions include the incorporation of disaster risk reduction as an element of humanitarian strategies; developing or revising preparedness plans and contingency plans to account for high-risk settings and the results of risk assessments; preparing assessments and plans to manage projected changes in existing hazards and new hazards not experienced before; and

building or improving evacuation mechanisms, escape routes and shelter facilities.

The Hyogo Framework is increasingly being used by individual organizations and intergovernmental mechanisms to structure and guide their own strategies and programs on disaster risk. These include, for example, the Asian Ministerial Conference on Disaster Risk Reduction and the World Bank's Global Facility for Disaster Risk Reduction and Recovery (GFDRR, 2008). Additionally, the five priorities provide a useful basis for postevent analysis of disaster events in order to identify factors that led to or exacerbated the disaster. Experience in events like Hurricane Katrina suggest that the first priority for action identified by the Hyogo Framework, which calls for strong political commitment and strong institutions, continues to be a major area of weakness.

CONCLUSION

Although the problem of disaster risk is continuing to grow, the prospects for properly addressing it are now brighter than ever before. Public awareness and political interest are increasing, partly as a result of concerns about climate change. Risk reduction strategies have been identified as element of adaptation within the UNFCCC agenda. The necessary methods and tools are available, including the Hyogo Framework as an overall guide for action. Over 100 countries have appointed Hyogo Framework focal points, and many countries, regional bodies, and organizations are beginning to establish strategies and institutions to support disaster risk reduction.

Nevertheless, there remains a continuing mismatch between the magnitude of the problem and magnitude of the response to the problem (UNISDR, 2007b). Disaster risk is generally not adequately assessed and monitored. Disaster risk reduction is not often identified as a requirement of development strategies and programs or funding profiles, and the levels of investment in disaster risk reduction are small. The task of deepening the awareness and engagement of different sectors has barely begun in many countries, and the battle to accord as much prominence to disaster risk reduction as to disaster response is far from over. Significant awareness raising and technical development in the climate change policy community is urgently needed to ensure that disaster risk reduction is a well-formulated component of future international climate change agreements.

Overall, there is a pressing need to scale up the whole risk reduction agenda. The many impressive existing initiatives in strategies, policies, field projects and capacity building need to be expanded and widely replicated, supported strongly by international and regional commitments and funds, with high-level political leadership in countries and automatic inclusion in the major development policy and programs. Disaster risk reduction needs to be recognized by all those who are investing in the development of the country. Without these much larger-scale efforts, we will continue to condemn millions of people to an unnecessarily risky and dangerous future.

REFERENCES

CRED. Custodian of the EM-DAT Disasters Database. Université catholique de Louvain, Centre for Research on the Epidemiology of Disaster, Brussels, Belgium. 2008.

ECOSOC. "Demand for Humanitarian Assistance Will Continue to Rise Worldwide, with Existing Crises Exacerbated by Climate-related Disasters and Food Insecurity." Information release, ECOSOC/6362. New York: Department of Public Information, Economic and Social Council, United Nations. July 15, 2008. See <http://www.un.org/News/Press/docs/2008/ecosoc6362.doc.htm>.

GFDRR. Global Facility for Disaster Risk Reduction and Recovery. Washington, D.C.: World Bank, 2008 <http://gfdrr.org/index.cfm?Page=home&ItemID=200>.

Guha-Sapir, Deborati. Université catholique de Louvain, Brussels, Belgium. Personal communication, 2007.

IPCC. *Fourth Assessment Report: Climate Change.* Intergovernmental Panel on Climate Change. 2007 <http://195.70.10.65/ipccreports/assessments-reports.htm>.

MCDEM. Ministry of Civil Defence and Emergency Management. Wellington, New Zealand, 2008 <http://www.civil defence.govt.nz/memwebsite.nsf/wpg_URL/Being-Prepared-Index?OpenDocument> and <http://www.whatstheplanstan.govt. nz/mcdem/index.html>; <http://www.getthru.govt.nz/>.

MFA-Norway. *Report on the Findings of the Conference: Changing the Way We Develop: Dealing with Disasters and Climate Change.* Oslo: Norwegian Ministry of Foreign Affairs, 2008 http://tsforum.event123.no/UD/ OPF08/pop.cfm?FuseAction=Doc&pAction=View&pDocument Id=15358>.

Mills, E., and E. Lecomte. *From Risk to Opportunity: How Insurers Can Proactively and Profitably Manage Climate Change. 2006* <http://eetd.lbl.gov/EMills/ PUBS/PDF/Ceres_Insurance_Climate_Report_090106.pdf>.

Munich Re. *Natural Catastrophes 2007: Analyses, Assessments, Positions. Topics Geo.* Germany: Munich Re Group, 2008.

Stern Review. *Report on the Economics of Climate Change.* London: Government of the United Kingdom. 2006 <http://www.hm-treasury.gov.uk/ independent_reviews/stern_review_economics_climate_change/ stern_review_report.cfm>.

UNFCCC. United Nations Framework Convention on Climate Change, Bali Action Plan, agreed at the 13th Conference of the Parties (COP). Bali, December 2008 <http://unfccc.int/resource/docs/2007/ cop13/eng/06a01.pdf#page=3>.

UN/ISDR. *Living with Risk: A Global Review of Disaster Reduction Initiatives.* Geneva: Inter-Agency Secretariat of the International Strategy for Disaster Reduction, 2004 <http://www.unisdr.org/eng/about_isdr/ bd-lwr-2004-eng.htm>.

_____. "Hyogo Framework for Action 2005-2015: Building the Resilience of Nations and Communities to Disasters." 2005. <http:// www.unisdr.org/eng/hfa/hfa.htm>.

_____. *Disaster Risk Reduction, Global Review, 2007.* ISDR/GP/2007/3. First Session of the Global Platform for Disaster Risk Reduction, Geneva, June 5-7, 2007a. ISDR/GP/2007/6.

Dean Yang
Risk, Migration, and Rural Financial Markets: Evidence from Earthquakes in El Salvador

TWO FACTS MOTIVATE THIS STUDY.[1] FIRST, LIFE IN RURAL AREAS IN developing countries is prone to many kinds of risk, such as illness or the mortality of household members, crop or other income loss due to natural disasters (weather, insect infestations, or fire, for example), and civil conflict. Second, international migration is substantial and growing: between 1975 and 2000, the number of people worldwide living outside their countries of birth more than doubled to 175 million, or 2.9 percent of world population (United Nations 2002).[2] For example, migration from El Salvador to the United States has grown rapidly: between 1990 and 2001, the number of Salvadoran-born individuals in the United States grew 69 percent, from 469,000 to 790,000.[3] These large migrant inflows in recent decades have become major public policy issues in migrants' destination countries.

This paper concerns the intersection of two subject areas in economics: research on the causes of international migration and research on the ways households in developing countries cope with different types of risk. What connections, if any, are there between the pervasiveness of rural risk in developing countries and these substantial outmigration flows? I shed light on this question by examining how migration from El Salvador responds to economic shocks. The key finding of the paper is that the impact of shocks on outmigration is actually quite nuanced, and perhaps unexpected: the impact of a shock on migration by family members depends on whether the shock is *idiosyncratic* (specific to the household) or *aggregate* (shared with other households in the local area).

Salvadoran households become differentially more likely to have close relatives who are migrants in the year following an idiosyncratic shock (a death in the family), compared to households not experiencing such shocks. By contrast, aggregate shocks (proximity to the massive 2001 earthquakes) lead to differential *declines* in whether a household has migrant relatives.

Migration typically requires that a substantial fixed cost be paid up front. If credit or assistance from others are important methods of financing migration's fixed cost, in theory the impact of economic shocks on migration will depend on whether such shocks also affect access to these financing mechanisms. When shocks are *idiosyncratic* or uncorrelated with shocks experienced by others, shocks are likely to raise migration: they should make families more willing to send members away for higher-wage work, and there should be no effect on mechanisms of migration finance. But *aggregate* shocks may actually lead to *less* migration, if such shared shocks make it more difficult or costly to access credit or interhousehold assistance networks that normally facilitate migration. (A simple model that formalizes this idea is available from the author on request.)

Declines in migration are associated mainly with being located in a quake-affected *area* (rather than the extent of the individual household's earthquake damage), suggesting that the explanation for the differential decline in migration lies in changes in general local conditions. The evidence is strongly suggestive that the decline in migration in the areas closest to the quakes is due to increased difficulty in obtaining financing for migration, via formal and informal credit in particular. Differential declines in migration in quake-affected areas are accompanied by substantial declines in households' granted credit (both informal and formal).

I also present empirical evidence against alternative explanations for the differential decline in migration in the areas closest to the quakes. It is not likely to be because of an increase in the demand for family unity when negative shocks occur, as deaths in the family (which presumably would also raise the desire for family unity) *do* lead to differentially more migration. External disaster assistance to quake-affected areas would not explain the differential migration response, as receipt of outside assistance depends on households experiencing household *damage*, rather than merely being in a quake-affected area. Increased demand for family labor to rebuild damaged households cannot explain the quake-related migration patterns either, as the differential migration changes are more strongly associated with *location* in quake-affected areas than with household damage. Finally, the differential decline in migration in quake-affected areas is not likely to be due to increases in income opportunities in the most quake-affected areas: per worker income and total household income both decline differentially in quake-affected areas.

Numerous studies have examined the mechanisms with which households cope with risk in developing countries. Among others, Townsend (1994), Udry (1994), Ligon, Thomas, and Worall (2002), and Fafchamps and Lund (2003) have documented risk-pooling arrangements among rural households in developing countries intended to smooth consumption in response to shocks. Households may also autonomously build up savings or other assets in good times and draw down these assets in hard times (Paxson, 1992; Rosenzweig and Wolpin, 1993; Udry, 1995), increase their labor supply when shocks occur (Kochar, 1999), or take steps (such as crop and plot diversification) to reduce the variation in their incomes (Morduch, 1993).

A contribution of this paper is to examine a mechanism for coping with shocks ex post on which previous studies have not focused: migration by family members (to both international and domestic destinations). In addition, I shed light on the circumstances under which migration succeeds and fails in this ex post risk-coping function. I emphasize the difficulties in using risk-coping mechanisms when shocks are shared by many households in a locality, so this paper is reminiscent of difficulties in smoothing consumption through asset sales when shocks are aggregate, because other households simultaneously seek to sell their assets, driving down asset prices (Rosenzweig and Wolpin, 1993; Fafchamps, Udry, and Czukas, 1998; and Lim and Townsend, 1998).

Rich countries with large migrant inflows from developing countries have a direct interest in understanding the impact of sending-country economic shocks on international migration. One approach has been to examine the relationship between economic conditions and outmigration using aggregate (country-level) data—for example, Hanson and Spilimbergo (1999), Hatton and Williamson (2003), and Mayda (2003)—generally finding that higher sending-country incomes or wages (relative to those in rich countries) are associated with less outmigration. While suggestive, these findings cannot be interpreted as the impact of sending-country incomes or wages per se, since many other economic conditions tend to change alongside income or wages. For example, macroeconomic reform in sending countries may raise sending-country incomes and also lead to increased credit access. If higher incomes reduce migration, but access to credit facilitates migration, the estimated impact of income on migration will be biased upward. Moreover, none of these studies have highlighted the possibility that shocks in sending countries could actually *reduce* migration.

In contrast to existing research on economic conditions and migration, this paper studies the impact of economic shocks on migration using household-level data.[4] An advantage of this approach is that it is possible to separate the impact of household-level economic shocks from the impact of aggregate economic conditions. More fundamentally, with household-level data it is possible to explore in detail the channels (such as the credit market) through which shocks have their effects.

Halliday (2006) also examines the impact of the 2001 earthquakes on migration from El Salvador, and highlights the negative relationship between a household's quake damage and increases in migration. He argues that the earthquake causes the marginal returns to a potential migrant's labor at home to rise (migrants are needed to help in household reconstruction). In the empirical analysis below I rule out this explanation: the decline in migration is more strongly related with a household's *location* with respect to the two quakes rather than the actual damage a household experiences.

This paper differs from the few household-level migration studies by emphasizing credible identification of the effect of economic conditions on migration. Existing household-level studies are cross-sectional, and do not have plausibly exogenous variation in the causal economic conditions of interest.[5] For example, negative shocks or persistent poverty may induce migration, leading to a negative relationship between household income and migration. But productive investments funded by migrant remittances can raise household income. Therefore, the estimated impact of household income and migration is likely to be severely biased in cross-sectional data, and in a direction that is not obvious *a priori*. Even if reverse causation from migration to income in source households was not a problem, it would be difficult to separate the cross-sectional relationship between income and migration from the influence of unobserved third factors affecting both income and migration (an example of an omitted variable might be the entrepreneurial spirit of household members).

Two aspects of the empirical strategy are key in resolving these identification problems. First, I examine shocks—earthquakes and deaths in the family—that are credibly exogenous, so that bias due to reverse causation is not a concern.[6] But the estimated impact of economic shocks in *cross-sectional* data is still likely to be biased, because the *likelihood* of experiencing a shock may be correlated with time-invariant household characteristics (in other words, omitted variables are still a concern). For example, if shocks occur more frequently in poorer areas, and there is in general more migration from poor areas, estimates of the impact of shocks on migration will be biased upward.

So the second crucial aspect of this paper is its use of panel data, so that estimates of the impact of shocks can be purged of the influence of unobserved time-invariant household characteristics that are jointly related with migration and the likelihood of experiencing a shock. Estimation of the impact of shocks focuses on how shocks are related to *changes* in migration rather than the *level* of migration. To minimize initial differences between shocked and unshocked households, identification of the impact of the quakes relies on assessing how changes in migration are associated with exposure to the quakes among households within the same geographic region (within El Salvador's 14 administrative departments).

EVIDENCE FROM RURAL EL SALVADOR

This section documents that migration from rural areas in El Salvador rises in response to idiosyncratic shocks (death in the family), and declines in response to aggregate shocks.

The evidence is strongly suggestive that the differential decline in migration in areas closest to the quake has to do with increased difficulty in obtaining informal and formal credit. Differential declines in migration in quake-affected areas are accompanied by substantial declines in households' formal and informal granted credit. I find evidence against alternative hypotheses for the differential decline in migration, such as increases in income opportunities or external aid, or an increase in the demand for family unity in the areas closest to quakes.

The size of the ongoing migration flow and the importance of remittances in the economy make the Salvadoran case an important one for research on migration. Few countries surpass El Salvador in terms of recent migrant outflows as a share of the national population. Substantial outflows from El Salvador began with the start of the country's civil war in 1980, and the vast majority of migrants have been destined for the United States and Canada. In 2001, there were roughly 790,000 Salvadoran-born individuals in the United States,[7] a striking figure compared with the total population of El Salvador itself, 6.3 million. By most accounts, the bulk of migration to the United States is illegal, involving a land crossing through Guatemala, across the length of Mexico, and over the US-Mexican border.[8]

Salvadoran migration is also pervasive from the point of view of households remaining in El Salvador.[9] In the year 2000, 16 percent of rural households and 14 percent of urban households reported having one or more household members living overseas.[10]

DATA AND SUMMARY STATISTICS

As discussed in the introduction, panel data is useful for evaluating the impact of shocks on migration so that estimates can be purged of bias due to unobserved time-invariant heterogeneity through the inclusion of household fixed effects.[11] This study primarily uses a high-quality panel dataset of rural households distributed across El Salvador, the FUSADES/BASIS El Salvador Rural Household Survey. This dataset tracks nearly 700 households in four biennial rounds: 1996, 1998, 2000, and 2002. The empirical work of this paper focuses on the latter two rounds of the survey, 2000 and 2002.[12] In a detailed section on migration, the survey collects information on any close relatives who are either internal or overseas migrants.

An indicator for whether a household reports having any migrant relatives will be the main outcome of interest in the empirical analysis. As such, I examine the extent to which shocks affect the propensity for *extended family groups* to send migrants away, as opposed to more narrowly defined households.[13]

In addition, the survey collected information on various unusual events in the past year. The idiosyncratic shock I focus on is an indicator for whether the household reports that any close relative (not exclusively those who live in the same household) died in the past year (the variable "death in family"). Because such shocks may have lagged effects on family groups, I examine how changes in migration between 2000 and 2002 are affected by deaths in the family in 2001 and 1999 (reported at the beginning of 2002 and 2000, respectively). The survey also contains rich detail on savings, credit, and transfers to other households that will be useful in examining the impact of the earthquakes on formal and informal financial instruments in these areas.

Figure 1. Salvadoran Municipal Halls and Epicenters of 2001 Earthquakes

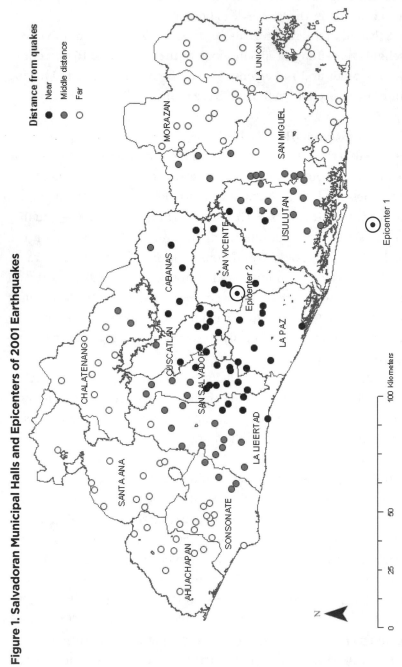

Note: Municipal halls "near" quakes are those within 100 kilometers of first (Jan. 13, 2001) epicenter and 50 kilometers of second (Feb. 13, 2001) epicenter. Those in "middle distance" to quakes are those within 125 kilometers of first epicenter and 75 kilometers of second epicenter (but not in "near" area). All other municipal halls are defined as "far" from quakes.

The measure of the aggregate shock is a household's proximity to the area most highly affected by two massive earthquakes. In January and February 2001, two large earthquakes (measuring 7.8 and 6.6 on the Richter scale, respectively) struck El Salvador, leaving over 1,000 dead and tens of thousands homeless, and causing an estimated $1.6 billion in direct and indirect damage (CEPAL, 2001).

The two epicenters were only about 75 kilometers from one another, so the households most highly affected by the earthquakes were in areas close to *both* epicenters. As measures of how affected a household was by the earthquakes, I construct simple indicator variables of whether a household was initially located (prior to the quakes, in year 2000) in the most highly affected area, and in an area of intermediate distance from both quakes. The household's location is known at the level of the municipality, and geographic coordinates of municipal halls and earthquake epicenters are available from the Salvadoran government's Servicio Nacional de Estudios Territoriales (SNET).

I calculate distances to epicenters as great circle distances from a household's municipal city hall. I then define an indicator variable ("Near quakes") for a household being within 100 kilometers of the first (January 13, 2001) epicenter and within 50 kilometers of the second (February 13, 2001) epicenter.[14] A second variable ("Middle distance to quakes") indicates the household was less than 125 kilometers from the first epicenter and less than 75 kilometers of the second epicenter, but not in the "Near quakes" area. These distance thresholds for defining the earthquake shock indicators are somewhat arbitrary, but were chosen to classify roughly one-quarter of the sample households into each of the two closest quake distance categories, leaving the remaining one-half of sample households outside these two categories.

Figure 1 displays the municipal halls of households included in the sample. Black circles indicate municipal halls in the "Near quakes" area, grey circles those in the "Middle distance," and white circles those outside these two areas. Table 1 presents summary statistics for the 671 sample households.

Table 1. Household Summary Statistics (Values are for year 2000 unless otherwise indicated)

	Mean	Std. dev.	Median
Shocks			
Near quakes	0.27		
Middle distance to quakes	0.25		
Death in family (2001)	0.07		
Death in family (1999)	0.07		
Any earthquake damage (2001)	0.61		
Cost of earthquake damage (2001)	4,254	11,908	500
Household variables used as controls in empirical analysis			
Head has some primary schooling	0.40		
Head has completed primary or more schooling	0.23		
In 2nd quartile of per capita household income	0.24		
In 3rd quartile of per capita household income	0.25		
In 4th quartile of per capita household income	0.25		
Owns a vehicle	0.08		
Owns a refrigerator	0.33		
Owns a television	0.60		
Owns a cooking stove	0.34		
Has indoor plumbing	0.29		
Has electric lighting	0.69		
Number of household members	5.98	2.62	6
Has a migrant relative	0.40		
Has any savings	0.25		
Has informal credit	0.13		
Has formal credit	0.13		
Made interhousehold transfer(s)	0.04		
Member of organization	0.33		
Addenda:			
Distance from 1st (Jan. 13, 2001) epicenter (kms.)	103.7	35.0	100.5
Distance from 2nd (Feb. 13, 2001) epicenter (kms.)	63.6	31.8	65.1
Has an overseas migrant relative	0.32		
Has an internal (domestic) migrant relative	0.12		

continued

Table 1, continued

Income per capita	705	812	461
Income per worker	941	1,113	617
Amount of savings	1,008	4,559	0
Amount of informal credit	349	2,279	0
Amount of formal credit	1,291	7,841	0
Amount of interhousehold transfers	56	429	0
Has a migrant relative (2002)	0.38		
Has an overseas migrant relative (2002)	0.31		
Has an internal (domestic) migrant relative (2002)	0.10		
Has any savings (2002)	0.25		
Has informal credit (2002)	0.23		
Has formal credit (2002)	0.20		
Made interhousehold transfer(s) (2002)	0.06		
Received any aid	0.38		
Amount of aid received	850	2,652	0

Notes: Household characteristics data are from FUSADES/BASIS El Salvador Rural Household Survey (2000 data unless otherwise indicated). Geographic coordinates of municipal city halls and earthquake epicenters are from Servicio Nacional de Estudios Territoriales (SNET), government of El Salvador. The 671 sample households are those observed in both 2000 and 2002 of BASIS survey (24 households dropped out between the two years, and are not included in analysis).

Summary statistics are values for 2000 (prior to shocks). Variables without reported standard errors in table are indicators (0 or 1). Distances to epicenters are great circle distances from household's municipal hall. "Near quakes" means household was within 100 kilometers of first (January 13, 2001) epicenter and within 50 kilometers of second (February 13, 2001) epicenter. "Middle distance to quakes" means household was within 125 kilometers of first epicenter and 75 kilometers of second epicenter, but not in the "Near quakes" area. "Death in family" means a relative (not necessarily living in same household) died in given year.

"Has any savings" means household currently has nonzero savings in a formal savings institution (missing savings assumed to be zero in 36 households). "Has informal credit" means household currently has credit from informal source such as a local lender, friend, relative, store, etc. "Has formal credit" means household currently has credit from a commercial bank, development institution, or other commercial source. "Made interhousehold transfer(s)" means household made nonzero transfers (in cash or kind) to other household(s). "Member of organization" means household was a member of some community group. "Received any aid" means household received assistance from any source outside the household due to the earthquakes or some other event. Levels of income, savings, credit, transfers, and aid are in current US dollars.

EMPIRICAL STRATEGY

Examining the impact of year 2001 shocks on changes between 2000 and 2002 makes it natural to specify the outcome variables in first differences.[15] The most-inclusive regression equation I estimate is the following (for a household i in municipality k in department j):

$$\Delta Y_{ikj} = \alpha + \beta_1 NEAR_k + \beta_2 MID_k + \gamma_1 DEATH01_{ikj} + \gamma_2 DEATH99_{ikj} + \zeta_1 DAMQ1_{ikj}$$
$$+ \zeta_2 DAMQ2_{ikj} + \zeta_3 DAMQ3_{ikj} + \zeta_4 DAMQ4_{ikj} + \theta_j + \varphi'X_{ikj} + \varepsilon_{ikj}$$

The dependent variable is the change in an outcome variable (the migration indicator in most of the analysis) between 2000 and 2002 surveys. The constant term α captures the mean change across all households. The earthquake indicators are essentially in first differences already, because no quakes occurred in 1999 or 2000. $NEAR_k$ is the "Near quakes" indicator, and MID_k is the "Middle distance to quakes" indicator.[16]

I do not specify the death indicator in first differences. Instead, I enter deaths in 2001 and 1999 separately into the regression $DEATH01_{ikj}$ and $DEATH99_{ikj}$ respectively. Using the *change* in the death indicator as the idiosyncratic shock variable instead would impose the restrictions that the impact of death in 1999 and the impact of death in 2001 on the dependent variable are of equal and opposite signs, and that experiencing deaths in *both* years has no effect on the dependent variable (because then the change would be zero). Entering deaths in 1999 and 2001 into the regression separately relaxes these restrictions. In any case, only three households had a death in the family in both 2001 and 1999.

The regression also includes indicators for whether a household's reported damage fell into each of four quartiles of the distribution of damage in the dataset (in US dollars): $DAMQ1_{ikj}$ through $DAMQ4_{ikj}$. (Quartiles are defined excluding the zero values, and all four damage indicators are zero for households reporting zero damage.) The variables related to earthquake damage suffered in 2001 are useful to separate the *direct* impact of the earthquake on migration (via the household's property damage) from the *indirect* impact (for example, via changes in the local credit market). If the earthquake's impacts on migration are primarily indirect, controlling for a household's own earthquake damage should have little effect on the coefficients on the quake distance indicators.

A potential concern is that even though the *timing* of the shocks might have been unexpected, households with certain characteristics might have been more prone to shocks in general. If households with these characteristics also have different ongoing migration trends, such differences could bias the estimated impact of the earthquake shock on migration. For example, if earthquakes typically occur in places with relatively low education levels, and less-educated households have higher ongoing migration growth, then the estimated impact of the earthquake on migration will be biased upwards.

θ_j is a fixed effect for a household's administrative department (of which there are 14 in El Salvador). Including department fixed effects in a first-differenced equation controls for department-specific time trends (this is equivalent to a two-period panel regression in levels, and including department fixed effects interacted with an indicator for the second period.) When department fixed effects are included in the equation, the impact of the shock variables should therefore be interpreted as the impact of shocks on a household's *deviation from the mean change within its department*. The coefficients on the quake indicators will then only derive from the eight departments with internal variation in the quake indicators (see Figure 1).[17]

It is possible that differential time trends may be occurring within departments as well. But it is not possible to control for time trends at the next lower administrative level, the municipality, because the variation in the earthquake shock variables occurs at that level. If any differential time trends occurring within departments are correlated with initial household characteristics *and* with a household's shock variables, the inclusion of a vector of control variables for initial household characteristics in the equation can further help purge estimates of bias. X_{ikj} is a vector of initial (year 2000) characteristics of the household (listed in the middle panel of table 1).

Figure 2: Impact of Earthquake on Migration (Overseas and Internal)
Percentage of households with close relatives who are migrants

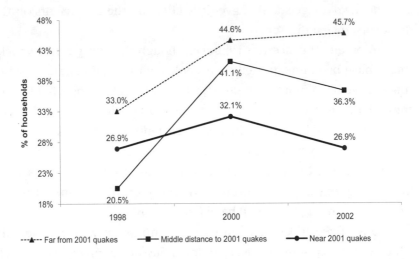

Notes: Data source is FUSADES/BASIS El Salvador Rural Household Survey (1998, 2000 and 2002 rounds). Sample includes 572 households that appear in all three rounds. Both overseas and internal (domestic) migrants are counted. See Table 1 for definitions of quake distance variables.

ε_{ikj} is a mean-zero error term. Standard errors are clustered to account for spatial correlation within municipality.

The coefficients of interest are, first, the coefficients β_1 and β_2 on the indicator variables for proximity to the earthquakes. The identification assumption is that if the earthquakes had not occurred, then changes in the outcome variables would not have varied for households located in the earthquake-affected area, compared with households further away (after controlling for department fixed effects and initial household characteristics). An advantage of focusing on earthquake shocks is that reverse causation is not a worry. First-differencing controls for any time-invariant (levels) differences between households that are shocked and not shocked.

The coefficients γ_1 and γ_2 on deaths in the family will also be of interest in order to compare the impact of these idiosyncratic shocks with the aggregate earthquake shocks. The department fixed effects θ_j and the vector of household characteristics X_{ikj} help account for heterogeneity in migration trends potentially correlated with the shock.

THE IMPACT OF SHOCKS ON MIGRATION

As a first step, I confirm that proximity to the 2001 earthquakes was indeed strongly related to whether a household experienced earthquake damage in the past year. Then I show that households closer to the 2001 earthquakes became differentially less likely to have close relatives who are migrants. By contrast, households experiencing deaths of family members in 2001 become more likely to have migrant relatives.

Regression estimates with department fixed effects (available from the author on request) confirm that closeness to the quakes was associated with higher quake damage for households. Being in the earthquake-affected areas makes a household more likely to experience earthquake damage, and raises the reported cost of earthquake damage: the coefficients on the "Near quakes" and "Middle distance to quakes" indicators are both positive and statistically significant. As one might expect, the households closest to the quakes suffer the most damage (the coefficients on the "Near quakes" indicator are always larger in magnitude than those on the "Middle distance" indicator). The likelihood of earthquake damage among households in the area closest to the quakes was on average 35 percentage points higher than for households in the same department but in areas further away.

The negative impact of the earthquake shock on migration is readily apparent in raw data. Figure 2 tracks the percentage of households in the FUSADES/BASIS dataset reporting they have close relatives who are migrants (both overseas and internal), for households of the three different distances from the quakes, in 1998, 2000, and 2002. The percentage of households with migrant relatives rises in all areas from 1998 to 2000, prior to the quakes. Between 2000 and 2002, the more affected and less affected areas diverge: the percentage of households with migrant relatives falls in the two areas nearer to the quakes, but actually rises slightly in the area furthest from the quakes.

These patterns are confirmed (and in fact magnified) in a regression analysis. Table 2 presents results from regressing the change (between 2000 and 2002) in an indicator for whether a household has any close relatives who are migrants on the shock variables and

Table 2. Impact of Shocks on Migration from Rural Areas, 2000-2002. Ordinary Least-Squares First-Differenced Estimates

Dependent variable: Change in household migration indicator, 2000-2002

Type of migration indicated in dep.variable:	(1) Internal and overseas	(2) Internal and overseas	(3) Internal and overseas	(4) Internal and overseas	(5) Internal and overseas	(6) Overseas	(7) Internal
Near quakes	-0.056 (0.054)	-0.153 (0.051)***	-0.147 (0.054)***	-0.343 (0.074)***	-0.376 (0.073)***	-0.224 (0.069)***	-0.193 (0.101)*
Middle distance to quakes	-0.065 (0.054)	-0.091 (0.047)*	-0.097 (0.049)**	-0.201 (0.049)***	-0.205 (0.052)***	-0.120 (0.048)**	-0.130 (0.081)
Death in family (2001)	-0.025 (0.085)	0.096 (0.065)	0.097 (0.064)	0.107 (0.063)*	0.136 (0.061)**	0.226 (0.085)***	-0.073 (0.056)
Death in family (1999)	0.018 (0.079)	0.017 (0.068)	0.006 (0.069)	-0.002 (0.065)	-0.011 (0.073)	-0.003 (0.064)	0.037 (0.056)
Has migrant relative in 2000		-0.645 (0.040)***	-0.653 (0.041)***	-0.689 (0.040)***	-0.691 (0.039)***	-0.456 (0.042)***	-0.277 (0.041)***
Earthquake damage: Bottom quartile			0.064 (0.057)	0.047 (0.055)	0.051 (0.055)	0.070 (0.050)	0.018 (0.045)
Earthquake damage: 2nd quartile			-0.112 (0.055)**	-0.102 (0.055)*	-0.104 (0.056)*	-0.071 (0.049)	-0.025 (0.057)

	(1)	(2)	(3)	(4)	(5)	(6)
Earthquake damage: 3rd quartile	0.013 (0.033)	-0.050 (0.053)	-0.043 (0.052)	-0.026 (0.053)	0.006 (0.051)	0.010 (0.040)
Earthquake damage: Top quartile	--	0.032 (0.058)	0.027 (0.056)	0.008 (0.059)	-0.026 (0.057)	0.059 (0.050)
Constant	0.297 (0.038)***	0.311 (0.041)***	0.405 (0.045)***	0.345 (0.082)***	0.254 (0.076)***	0.083 (0.084)
Department fixed effects	--	--	Y	Y	Y	Y
Controls for initial household characteristics	--	--	--	Y	Y	Y
Observations	671	671	671	671	671	671
R-squared	0.00	0.33	0.39	0.39	0.43	0.28

* significant at 10%; ** significant at 5%; *** significant at 1%

Note: Standard errors in parentheses, clustered by 166 municipalities. Unit of observation is a household. Dependent variable is change between 2000-2002 in an indicator for whether household has given type of migrant relative at time of survey (takes on values of -1, 0, and 1). See Table 1 for variable definitions. Fixed effects are for 14 administrative departments. Regression coefficients on initial household-level characteristics reported in Table 3b. Household characteristics variables are values in year 2000. Initial household characteristics controls are: indicators for head's level of completed schooling (primary, secondary); indicators for household per capita income quartile; indicators for ownership of vehicle, refrigerator, television, stove, indoor plumbing, and electric lighting; number of household members; indicators for having any savings, any informal credit, and informal credit; indicator for having made any interhousehold transfers; indicator for being member of an organization.

an increasingly inclusive set of control variables and department fixed effects. Column 1 simply regresses the change in the migration indicator on the earthquake shock indicators and the death in family indicators, with no other right-hand-side variables. The coefficients on the quake distance indicators are both negative, but not statistically significantly different from zero. The coefficients on the death in family indicators are both close to zero and statistically insignificant.

The migration changes turn out to be very different for households with and without migrants in the initial year (2000). When an indicator for having a migrant relative in 2000 is added to the regression (column 2), it enters negatively and is highly statistically significantly different from zero. The quake distance variables have now become larger in absolute value (more negative), and are now statistically significantly different from zero (indicating that households closer to the quakes were less likely to have migrant relatives initially). The 2001 death in family indicator has become positive and is approaching conventional levels of statistical significance.

In column 3, the earthquake damage indicators are added to the regression. The coefficient on the indicator for the second quartile of earthquake damage is negative and statistically significantly different from zero, while the coefficients on the other damage indicators variables are smaller in magnitude and are not statistically significantly different from zero. A possible explanation is as follows. Small amounts of quake damage (specifically, the first quartile of reported losses) have little effect on individuals' migration decisions. Intermediate amounts of quake damage (the second quartile of reported losses) lead potential migrants to forestall migration to help in reconstruction (via supplying their own labor).[18] However, when households experience large amounts of quake damage (the third and fourth quartile of reported losses), households have a greater need for migrant *remittances* to help pay for reconstruction (and potentially replace lost income, if productive assets were damaged). This increased incentive for migration on average offsets the desire to have migrants stay home to provide reconstruction labor, so that the highest amounts of quake damage are not correlated with migration changes.

The inclusion of the quake damage indicators has little effect on the coefficients on the quake distance indicators in column 3. This suggests that the impact of the earthquakes on migration has a large *indirect* component (due to living in an earthquake-affected *area*), in addition to any *direct* impact (due to sustaining earthquake damage).

When department fixed effects are included as right-hand-side regressors (column 4), the estimated impact of quake distance on migration derives primarily from differences in the quake distance indicators among different households *within the same department*. As discussed above, this helps control for possible ongoing department-level trends that may be correlated with departmental exposure to the quakes.

Figure 1 depicts the municipal halls of surveyed households (whose locations are used to determine household distances to epicenters), and indicates to which quake distance category they are assigned. In Ahuachapan, Santa Ana, Morazan, and La Union, there are no surveyed households in the two areas closest to the quakes. In La Paz and San Vicente departments, all surveyed households are in the "Near quakes" area. These departments where all households are in the same distance categories do not contribute directly to the estimation of the effects of the "Near quakes" and "Middle distance to quakes" variables (except through their contributions to estimating the other regression coefficients).[19]

With the inclusion of department fixed effects, the differential changes in migration between households nearer and farther from the quakes are magnified: the coefficients on the quake distance indicators become considerably more negative (larger in absolute value) and remain highly statistically significantly different from zero.

What is likely to be happening here? *Without* the inclusion of department fixed effects, the comparison between the departments in the central part of the country (La Paz and San Vicente, where all households are in the "Near quakes" area) with the extreme eastern and western departments (Ahuachapan, Santa Ana, Morazan, and La

Union, where all households are outside the most quake-affected areas) apparently *attenuates* the estimated impact of the quakes on migration. One possible explanation might be that earthquake assistance was disproportionately allocated to La Paz and San Vicente departments, allowing credit markets to continue to function well in the wake of the disaster, so that potential migrants could continue to obtain financing for migration's fixed cost. Including department fixed effects in the analysis keeps households in La Paz and San Vicente from contributing directly to the estimation of the quakes' effect on migration.

Column 5 includes the quake damage variables and all the initial household characteristics controls. These make little difference for the coefficients on the quake distance variables, indicating that the department fixed effects and the indicator for whether a household initially has a migrant relative are effective at controlling for underlying trends in migration across households of different distances from the quakes.

The death in family (2001) indicator becomes larger in absolute value in column 5 when initial household characteristics are included in the regression (compared with column 4), and is now statistically significantly different from zero at the 5 percent level. Deaths in the family may in fact be predictable by family members (as discussed above), and so controlling for year 2000 household observables helps eliminate some of the downward bias induced by (pre-2000) migration *in anticipation* of a family member's death (including year 2000 household characteristics in the regression helps isolate the *unpredictable* portion of a year 2001 death in the family.)

The death in family (1999) indicator is small in magnitude and not statistically significantly different from zero in any regression, providing no evidence of a lagged migration responses to deaths in the family.

Are these migration responses to shocks reflecting overseas or internal migration? The last two columns of the table report coefficient estimates from regressions similar to column 5, but where the household migration indicator is defined for overseas and internal migrants separately. In column 6, the dependent variable is the change in whether a household has any overseas migrant relatives, and in column 7 it is the change in whether a household has any internal migrant relatives.

Columns 6 and 7 indicate that proximity to the quakes has a negative and statistically significant impact on overseas and domestic migration separately. The coefficient on the 2001 death in family indicator is substantially larger in column 6 than in column 5 and is highly statistically significant. In column 7, the coefficient is actually negative and is not statistically significantly different from zero. It seems that when deaths occur, relatives substitute towards overseas migration and away from domestic migration.

In all regressions where the two quake distance indicators are statistically significantly different from zero (columns 2-7), the coefficient on the "Near quakes" indicator is larger in absolute value than the coefficient on the "Middle distance to quakes" indicator.[20] This is sensible: the negative impact of the quake should be largest for households in the most-affected area.

The coefficient estimates in column 5 indicate that being in the area nearest the 2001 quakes reduced the likelihood that a household had a migrant relative (either internal or overseas) differentially by 38 percentage points, with respect to households outside the two most-affected areas. For households in the middle distance to the quakes, the corresponding differential decline is 21 percentage points.

The coefficient on the 2001 death in family indicator indicates that a 2001 death in the family differentially raises the likelihood of having a migrant relative by 14 percentage points, compared with households where no relative died in the past year. This is the net effect of an increase in overseas migration and a reduction in internal migration: the coefficient estimate in column 6 (where the dependent variable refers to only overseas migration) indicates that a 2001 death in the family differentially increased the likelihood that a household had an overseas migrant relative by 23 percentage points, compared with households not experiencing such deaths.

Checking for Pre-existing Trends among Shocked Households ("A False Experiment")

The crucial identification assumption in the empirical analysis is that, in the absence of the earthquake shocks, changes between 2000 and 2002 in whether a household had migrant relatives would have been identical across households of different distances from the quake (as defined by the quake distance indicators). Because data on FUSADES/BASIS households was also collected in 1998, it is possible to conduct a partial test of this identification assumption. I conduct a "false experiment," and ask whether the 2001 shocks can predict the change in the indicator for having a migrant relative between 1998 and 2000 (*prior* to the shocks' occurrence). (Results are not reported here, but are available from the author on request.) There is no evidence that the parallel-trend identification assumption is violated for the earthquake shocks when department fixed effects are included in the regression. Causal inference is therefore likely to be most secure in the regression specification with department fixed effects.

POTENTIAL EXPLANATIONS FOR NEGATIVE IMPACT OF EARTHQUAKES ON MIGRATION

In this section I present empirical evidence for various explanations for the observed negative impact of the 2001 earthquakes on changes in migration between 2000 and 2002. I consider five hypotheses. The hypotheses are that the differential decline in migration occurred because the most quake-affected areas experienced:

1. increased difficulty accessing financial instruments to finance migration;
2. increased demand for family unity;
3. increased aid
4. increased need for family labor in reconstruction;
5. increased income opportunities.

The evidence is strongest for the first hypothesis: that the differential decline in migration was caused by increased difficulty in accessing methods of migration finance in areas closest to the quakes (in particular informal and formal credit).

By contrast, there is empirical evidence against alternative explanations for the differential decline in migration in the areas closest to the quakes. It is not likely to be because of an increase in the demand for family unity when negative shocks occur, as deaths in the family (which presumably would also raise the desire for family unity) *do* lead to differentially more migration. External disaster assistance to quake-affected areas would not explain the differential migration response, as receipt of outside assistance is dependent on households experiencing household *damage*, rather than merely being in a quake-affected area. Increased demand for family labor to rebuild damaged households cannot explain the quake-related migration patterns either, as the differential migration changes are more strongly associated with *location* in quake-affected areas than with household damage. Finally, the differential decline in migration in quake-affected areas is not likely to be due to increases in income opportunities in the most quake-affected areas: per-worker income and total household income both decline differentially in quake-affected areas.

Hypothesis 1: Increased difficulty accessing financial instruments

Two findings so far suggest that general equilibrium phenomena (the effect of aggregate shocks on aspects of a locality as a whole) may better explain the differential decline in migration from the most quake-affected areas. First, idiosyncratic shocks (deaths in the family) increase migration, but aggregate shocks (closeness to the quakes) reduce migration. Second, the impact of the quake on migration depends primarily on being in an earthquake-affected *area*, more than on actual damage from the quake.

I document here that changes in households' use of the instruments that finance migration, and the dependence of the quake's impact on households' *initial* use of these instruments (particularly informal credit) provide strongly suggestive evidence that breakdowns in these financial instruments are behind the decline in migration from areas closest to the quakes.

The dataset contains information on the manner in which house-holds' migrant relatives who left between 1995 and 2000 obtained the funds to pay for migration, as reported in the year 2000 (prior to the shocks), for overseas migrants, internal migrants, and all migrants together.[21] The most common financing source for overseas migration is money sent by other relatives, at 46.4 percent. Savings (19.3 percent) and loans (17.5 percent) make up the next most common financing sources. Households report that internal migration is financed quite differently, with 59.5 percent of migrants relying on savings and none on loans.

There is evidence that some of these financing methods break down when aggregate shocks occur. Table 3 presents regression esti-mates of the main regression equation, but where the outcome variables are changes in a household's participation in four types of financial transactions: savings, informal credit, formal credit, and transfers to other households (which may reflect participation in mutual help or insurance arrangements). There are two regressions for each type of financial transaction. The credit variables (separately for informal and formal credit) are indicators for whether the household was granted any credit in the past year, and the log amount of credit granted. (Informal credit is from a local lender, friend, relative, store, etc. Formal credit is from a commercial bank, development institution, or other commer-cial source.) The savings variables are an indicator for the household's having a savings account in a formal financial institution, and the log amount of savings. The transfer variables are an indicator for making any transfers, and the log amount of transfers in the past year.[22]

For all the financial transactions considered, proximity to the earthquakes is associated with declines in use: the coefficients on the quake distance indicators are nearly all negative in sign in table 3. In all four regressions for formal and informal credit (columns 1-4), the "Near quake" indicators are negative and statistically significantly different from zero, and in the informal credit regressions the coefficients on the middle distance indicator are negative and statistically significantly different from zero as well. Households in the area closest to the quakes experienced differential declines in their likelihood of having credit of 24 percentage points (for informal credit) and 17 percentage points (for formal credit).

In addition, households in the areas closer to the quake saw differential declines in their likelihood of having savings greater than $500 (column 5); households may have needed to draw down their savings to smooth consumption in the face of lower incomes. The decline in savings may also help explain the decline in migration from the quake-affected areas. (Surprisingly, experiencing the top quartile of earthquake damage is associated with an *increased* likelihood of having savings greater than $500 and with *increased* log savings (columns 5 and 6). This may reflect the impact of aid flows to quake-affected areas, which could have overshot households' actual needs in some cases.)

Deaths in the family in 2001 do not have statistically significant relationships with changes in financial transactions generally, except (very tentatively) an increase in the likelihood of making an interhousehold transfer. A death in the family in 1999 is associated with a statistically significant decline in the interhousehold transfers indicator and in log transfers between 2000-2002 (columns 7 and 8). Because the deaths in question are of relatives who are not necessarily *coresident*, these results may arise because households make transfers to the households of dying or deceased relatives.[23]

The fact that use of financial instruments (particularly credit, but also savings) declines in areas closest to the quakes is suggestive that increased difficulty in accessing these instruments may be behind the concurrent decline in migration. This reasoning would receive further support if the impact of the quakes on migration was more negative for households that *initially* (in 2000, prior to the shocks) were using the said instruments. Initial use of an instrument is a proxy measure of a household's general access to an instrument. Increased difficulty in using a particular instrument should not have much effect if a household had no access to the instrument in the first place.

Table 4 presents regression results for estimation of the main regression equation, but now including interaction terms between the

Table 3. Impact of Shocks on Credit, Savings, and Interhousehold Transfers, 2000-2002
Ordinary least-squares first-differenced estimates

Dependent variable:	(1) Change in informal credit indicator	(2) Change in log (amount of informal credit)	(3) Change in formal credit indicator	(4) Change in log (amount of formal credit)	(5) Change in indicator for savings >$500	(6) Change in log (amount of savings)	(7) Change in interhousehold transfers indicator	(8) Change in log (amount of interhousehold transfers)
Near quakes	-0.244 (0.109)**	-1.461 (0.704)**	-0.170 (0.075)**	-1.243 (0.621)**	-0.148 (0.076)*	-0.599 (0.593)	-0.019 (0.042)	-0.170 (0.277)
Middle distance to quakes	-0.182 (0.084)**	-1.204 (0.563)**	-0.027 (0.055)	-0.121 (0.410)	-0.095 (0.047)**	-0.294 (0.349)	-0.022 (0.028)	-0.257 (0.180)
Death in family (2001)	-0.012 (0.069)	0.154 (0.509)	-0.034 (0.058)	-0.291 (0.445)	-0.051 (0.083)	-0.043 (0.616)	0.063 (0.049)	0.331 (0.310)
Death in family (1999)	0.045 (0.076)	0.014 (0.477)	0.039 (0.068)	0.267 (0.514)	0.059 (0.065)	0.179 (0.539)	-0.066 (0.014)***	-0.417 (0.089)***
Earthquake damage: Bottom quartile	0.073 (0.052)	0.405 (0.336)	-0.031 (0.051)	-0.432 (0.379)	0.010 (0.057)	-0.013 (0.438)	0.005 (0.028)	-0.046 (0.176)
Earthquake damage: 2nd quartile	-0.009 (0.040)	-0.082 (0.262)	0.032 (0.035)	0.292 (0.265)	0.000 (0.036)	-0.045 (0.276)	-0.015 (0.018)	-0.100 (0.122)
Earthquake damage: 3rd quartile	0.043 (0.055)	0.171 (0.358)	0.019 (0.041)	0.229 (0.323)	0.068 (0.050)	0.568 (0.382)	0.017 (0.024)	0.123 (0.164)

Earthquake damage: Top quartile	0.009 (0.056)	0.075 (0.357)	-0.026 (0.036)	-0.211 (0.282)	0.059 (0.031)*	0.442 (0.255)*	-0.002 (0.025)	-0.031 (0.166)
Department fixed effects	Y	Y	Y	Y	Y	Y	Y	Y
Controls for initial household characteristics	Y	Y	Y	Y	Y	Y	Y	Y
Observations	671	671	671	671	671	671	671	671
R-squared	0.39	0.41	0.32	0.33	0.22	0.23	0.45	0.45

* significant at 10%; ** significant at 5%; *** significant at 1%

Note: Standard errors in parentheses, clustered by 166 municipalities. Unit of observation is a household. Dependent variables are changes between 2000 and 2002. See table 1 for variable definitions. Fixed effects are for 14 administrative departments. Household characteristics variables are values in year 2000 (coefficients not shown). Variables in logs taken to be zero if variable was zero before taking logs.

Table 4. Interactions between Shock Indicators and Initial Credit, Savings, and Interhousehold Transfers, 2000-2002
Ordinary least-squares first-differenced estimates

	(1)	(2)	(3)
Type of migration indicated in dependent variable:	Internal/ Overseas	Overseas	Internal
Near quakes	-0.329 (0.078)***	-0.178 (0.072)**	-0.196 (0.101)*
Near quakes * Had informal credit (2000)	-0.188 (0.108)*	-0.192 (0.103)*	-0.046 (0.116)
Near quakes * Had formal credit (2000)	0.058 (0.102)	0.094 (0.129)	-0.080 (0.107)
Near quakes * Had savings (2000)	-0.146 (0.092)	-0.167 (0.104)	0.040 (0.076)
Near quakes * Made interhousehold transfers (2000)	0.018 (0.176)	0.049 (0.247)	0.060 (0.191)
Middle distance to quakes	-0.199 (0.061)***	-0.117 (0.057)**	-0.139 (0.081)*
Middle distance to quakes * Had informal credit (2000)	0.012 (0.116)	-0.039 (0.135)	0.103 (0.079)
Middle distance to quakes * Had formal credit (2000)	0.259 (0.132)**	0.123 (0.121)	0.101 (0.126)
Middle distance to quakes * Had savings (2000)	-0.139 (0.110)	-0.072 (0.106)	-0.039 (0.082)
Middle distance to quakes * Made inter-household transfers (2000)	-0.107 (0.201)	0.004 (0.370)	-0.107 (0.217)
Death in family (2001)	0.274 (0.078)***	0.410 (0.103)***	-0.072 (0.073)

continued

Table 4, continued

Death in family (2001) * Had informal credit (2000)	-0.052 (0.130)	-0.032 (0.194)	-0.175 (0.149)
Death in family (2001) * Had formal credit (2000)	-0.554 (0.112)***	-0.481 (0.186)***	-0.075 (0.183)
Death in family (2001) * Had savings (2000)	-0.208 (0.134)	-0.469 (0.149)***	0.203 (0.121)*
Death in family (2001) * Made interhousehold transfers (2000)	0.178 (0.203)	0.440 (0.456)	-0.161 (0.320)
Death in family (1999)	-0.015 (0.075)	-0.006 (0.067)	0.028 (0.057)
Department fixed effects	Y	Y	Y
Controls for initial household characteristics	Y	Y	Y
Observations	671	671	671
R-squared	0.45	0.30	0.18

* significant at 10%; ** significant at 5%; *** significant at 1%
Notes: Dependent variable is the change in household migration indicator, 2000-2002. Standard errors in parentheses, clustered by 166 municipalities. Unit of observation is a household. Dependent variables are changes between 2000 and 2002. See Table 1 for variable definitions. Fixed effects are for 14 administrative departments. Household characteristics variables are values in year 2000 (coefficients not shown). Controls for quake damage quartile also included in regressions (coefficients not shown).

shocks (quake distance indicators and the 2001 death indicator) and indicators for having initially had informal credit, had formal credit, had savings, and made interhousehold transfers. In column 1 (where the dependent variable includes both overseas and internal migration), the interaction term between "Near quakes" and the "Had informal credit" indicator is negative and statistically significantly different from zero. The coefficient on the ("Near quakes" * "Had savings") indicator is also negative and marginally statistically significantly different from zero. Both these results also hold in column 2, when the dependent variable refers to overseas migration alone. The impact of being in the area closest to the earthquakes on the likelihood of having migrant relatives is more negative for households that initially had informal credit (by 19 percentage points in column 1) and that initially had savings (by 15 percentage points in column 1).[24]

Table 4 also indicates that the positive impact of a 2001 death in the family on the change in migration appears primarily in households that do not have formal credit or savings in the year 2000. In columns 1 and 2, the ("Death in family (2001)" * "Had formal credit (2000)") and ("Death in family (2001)" * "Had savings (2000)") interaction terms are negative and roughly equal in size to the coefficient on the "Death in family (2001)" main effect, so that the effect of 2001 deaths on the change in migration is close to zero for households that had either formal credit or savings in 2000. This is also to be expected: if consumption smoothing motivations are behind the responsiveness of migration to deaths, then households with savings and access to credit have less need for migration when deaths occur.

Taken together, the additional results in tables 3 and 4 provide strongly suggestive evidence that the decline in migration in areas closest to the quakes is at least in part due to concurrent declines in households' use of various financial instruments (particularly informal credit and savings). Potential migrants in the most quake-affected areas found it more difficult to obtain financing for migration, causing migration to decline differentially in those areas.

Hypothesis 2: Increased demand for family unity
An unlikely explanation is that the earthquake increases the value placed on family unity: in times of increased stress family members may try to keep the clan together (say, for mutual emotional support). As a result, potential migrants from the most quake-affected areas do not migrate in the period immediately after the quakes. But the demand for family unity should also rise when a family member dies,

and migration (overseas migration in particular) responds *positively* to family deaths (table 2). It is not clear why deaths of family members should qualitatively be very different from an earthquake in raising the demand for family unity.

Hypothesis 3: Increased aid to quake-affected areas

An alternative explanation could be that aid to quake-affected areas was so large in magnitude that it made migration unnecessary. If this were the case, we should observe receipt of aid to be highly correlated with location in the quake-affected areas. I tested this hypothesis by estimating the main regression equation where the dependent variable is an indicator for receiving nonzero aid from sources outside the household due to the earthquakes or other negative events in 2001. The variation in aid receipt within departments does not seem highly correlated with location in the two areas most affected by the quakes: when including department fixed effects in the regression, the coefficients on the quake distance indicators are not statistically significantly different from zero. By contrast, within departments, actual damage suffered is predictive of aid. These same conclusions hold when replacing the dependent variable with the amount of aid received and the logarithm of aid received. (Regressions not reported due to space constraints, but available from the author on request.)

Within-department variation in aid receipt depends on actual damage suffered, and not merely location in the two areas closest to the quakes. Therefore, variation in aid receipt cannot explain why households in the two most quake-affected areas experienced differential declines in outmigration.

Hypothesis 4: Need for family labor in reconstruction

The fourth alternative explanation is that potential migrants in quake-affected areas stayed home to help in reconstruction, as suggested by Halliday (2006). There is suggestive evidence that this may be going on in part: in table 2, the coefficient on the second-quartile earthquake damage indicator is negative and statistically significant (although the lack of a relationship between migration changes and the other quartiles of earthquake damage is something of a puzzle).

More important, table 2 indicates that inclusion of the quake damage indicators (in column 3) has negligible effect on the coefficients on the quake location variables, which remain negative and highly statistically significant. The differential migration changes are more strongly associated with *location* in quake-affected areas than with household damage suffered. Therefore, increased need for family labor in reconstruction cannot explain the differential decline in migration in quake-affected areas.

Hypothesis 5: Increased income opportunities in quake-affected areas
The final unlikely explanation is that income opportunities actually improved differentially in quake-affected areas (in comparison to areas farther away), and so potential migrants in those areas stayed home instead of migrating. I test this hypothesis by estimating the main regression equation where the dependent variable is the change in the log of household income per worker in the sample households from 2000 to 2002. (Regressions are not reported due to space constraints, but available from the author on request.)

When department fixed effects are included in the regression, the coefficients on the quake distance indicators are negative (and not statistically significantly different from zero). There is therefore no evidence that within-department improvements in log income per worker are associated with being in the areas most affected by the quakes. The same conclusion holds when the regression controls for initial household characteristics and when the log of total household income is the dependent variable.

CONCLUSION
In theory, when financial markets are imperfect and when migration involves a fixed cost, the impact of economic shocks on migration can depend on the extent to which shocks are common across households. When shocks are *idiosyncratic*, they are likely to raise migration,

as households send members away to replace lost income or meet increased consumption needs. But *aggregate* shocks can actually lead to *less* migration if such shared shocks lead to breakdowns in the local financial markets that typically finance migration.

This paper presents empirical evidence from a rural household panel in El Salvador that idiosyncratic and aggregate shocks do have opposite effects on migration. When households experience idiosyncratic shocks (a death of family member), they become more likely to have close relatives who are migrants. The net effect of the death of family members on migration is the sum of a large increase in overseas migration and a slight decline in internal (domestic) migration.

But when households are more exposed to aggregate shocks (when they are closer to the epicenters of the massive 2001 earthquakes), they become less likely to have migrant relatives. Analysis of a nationally representative cross-sectional household survey conducted by the government of El Salvador finds similar results: the fraction of households with members who are overseas migrants falls differentially in areas closer to the quake epicenters. To minimize initial differences between shocked and unshocked households, identification of the impact of the quakes relies on assessing how changes in migration are associated with exposure to the quakes among households within the same geographic region (within El Salvador's 14 administrative departments). The estimated negative relationship almost certainly reflects the causal impact of the earthquakes: among households located in the same department, no corresponding migration changes occur in the pre-shock period, and households closer to the quakes do not differ on average from those farther from the quakes in important initial household characteristics.

The evidence is strongly suggestive that the differential decline in migration in areas closest to the quake is in part explained by breakdowns in the various methods by which migration is financed, in particular informal and formal loans. Differential declines in migration in quake-affected areas are accompanied by substantial declines in households' formal and informal granted credit. By contrast, I present empirical evidence that the differential decline in migration in the most quake-affected areas cannot be explained by increases in the demand for family unity, aid to affected areas, the need for family labor in reconstruction, or income opportunities.

To the extent that residents of developed countries are concerned that natural disasters, civil war, or other aggregate shocks in developing countries will lead to increased migrant flows to the rich world, this paper provides evidence that may alleviate such fears: increased difficulty in obtaining migration finance is likely to blunt the impact of such shocks on outmigration. The other side of the coin, of course, is that economic development in poor countries could actually *raise* outmigration in some cases, if economic development is accompanied by the expansion of credit instruments that finance migration.

NOTES

1. I have benefited from discussions with Becky Blank, John DiNardo, Ricardo Hausmann, Jim Levinsohn, Sharon Maccini, Justin McCrary, Kaivan Munshi, Una Okonkwo Osili, and Anna Paulson, and several participants in seminars. Jose Berrospide and Joshua Congdon-Martin have provided excellent research assistance. I am extremely grateful to the staff at the Department of Economic and Social Studies, FUSADES (especially Anabella de Palomo, Margarita Sanfeliu and Mauricio Shi) for their invaluable assistance.

2. By contrast, total world population has grown only 49 percent over the same period.

3. Author's estimates from the year 2001 round of U.S. government's Census 2000 Supplementary Survey (C2SS), and 1990 U.S. Census (IPUMS 1 percent sample). Both these figures are likely to be biased downwards due to under-reporting of illegal migrants.

4. Existing research does suggest that *internal* (domestic) migration plays a role in pooling risk within extended families. Rosenzweig and Stark (1989) argue that village-to-village migration in rural India serves an insurance function, as households with more spatially distributed daughters have smoother consumption. Paulson and Miller (2000)

find in a cross-section of Thai households that remittance receipts from internal migrants are larger in areas where rainfall is currently below the local average. No study in this vein has used data on cross-border migration.

5. For example, Hoddinott (1994) and Adams (1993).

6. As I discuss in the empirical section, using deaths in the family as an idiosyncratic shock is not immune from econometric problems. In particular, some deaths may be anticipated (and so would not truly be shocks), and remittances sent by migrants can keep ill or dying people alive (reverse causation). Both these factors should lead to downward bias, so that the estimated impact of estimated impact of deaths on migration is a *lower bound* of the true causal impact.

7. Author's calculation from the year 2001 round of US government's Census 2000 Supplementary Survey (C2SS).

8. From anecdotal sources, the going rate for hiring a *coyote* to arrange one's journey to the United States prior to the 2001 terrorist attacks was approximately $3,000, and has since roughly doubled.

9. Internal (domestic) migration is considerably less well-documented. The rural household dataset used in the empirical analysis (described below) is not designed to be nationally representative, but it does indicate that internal migration is less common than overseas migration: 12 percent of households in early 2000 reported having close relatives (but not necessarily household members) who were internal migrants; by comparison, 32 percent reported having close relatives overseas.

10. These figures are from the government of El Salvador's Encuesta de Hogares de Propositos Multiples (EHPM).

11. Or, equivalently when the panel consists of just two time periods, estimation using first-differenced variables.

12. The survey does a careful job of following households that move internally within El Salvador, reducing attrition dramatically: only 24 out of 696 households drop out of the sample between these two survey years. One additional household is not included in the analysis because its municipality code (0214) is misrecorded: it does not corre-

spond with any municipality in El Salvador. This leaves a sample size of 671 households.

13. Because surveyed households are typically some distance from one another, there is likely to be little double-counting of migrants.

14. I use a smaller radius for distance to the second earthquake, because it was less powerful than the first one.

15. This will be equivalent to estimating a panel regression with two periods and including household-level fixed effects and year effects.

16. The quake distance indicators only vary at the municipality level, because distances to epicenters are measured from a household's municipal city hall.

17. The departments with internal variation in the quake indicators are Sonsonate, Chalatenango, La Libertad, San Salvador, Cuscatlan, Cabanas, Usulutan, and San Miguel. It will turn out to be important to identify the quake's impact from *within*-department variation, since there were *between*-department trends in the pre-period (1998-2000) analogous to those found in the study period (2000-2002).

18. As argued by Halliday (2006) in this same context.

19. In Ahuachapan, Santa Ana, Morazan, and La Union, there are no surveyed households in the two areas closest to the quakes. In La Paz and San Vicente departments, all surveyed households are in the "Near quakes" area.

20. In columns 4, 5, and 6, these differences are statistically significantly different from zero at conventional levels.

21. Figures can add up to more than 100 percent within columns because migrants can have used more than one source of financing.

22. The log of a variable is taken to be zero when the value of the variable is zero before taking logs. Missing values of the savings variable were replaced with zero in 36 households.

23. If a noncoresident relative dies in 1999, a household may make transfers to that relative's household (and report it in the 2000 survey), but then might not make transfers afterwards. This would generate a negative relationship between 1999 deaths and the change in reported transfers between the 2000 and 2002 surveys.

24. A concern might be that the interactions with indicators for initial use of financial instruments might simply reflect the impact of omitted variables (such as socioeconomic status) rather than initial access to financial markets. But the coefficients on the interaction terms in table 3 remain similar in size and statistical significance when additional interaction terms are included between the shocks and a set of indicators for the household's initial per capita income quartile and head's education.

REFERENCES

Adams, Jr., R. H. "The Economic and Demographic Determinants of International Migration in Rural Egypt." *Journal of Development Studies* 30:1 (October 1993): 146-167.

Cox-Edwards, A., and M. Ureta. "International Migration, Remittances, and Schooling: Evidence from El Salvador." *Journal of Development Economics* 72:2 (December 2003): 429-461.

Fafchamps, M., and S. Lund. "Risk-sharing Networks in Rural Philippines." *Journal of Development Economics* 71:2 (August 2003): 261-287.

Fafchamps, M., C. Udry, and K. Czukas. "Drought and Saving in West Africa: Are Livestock a Buffer Stock?" *Journal of Development Economics* 55:2 (April 1998): 273-305.

Halliday, T. "Migration, Risk, and Liquidity Constraints in El Salvador." *Economic Development and Cultural Change* 54:4 (July 2006): 893-925.

Hanson, G., and A. Spilimbergo. "Illegal Immigration, Border Enforcement, and Relative Wages: Evidence from Apprehensions at the US-Mexico Border." *American Economic Review* 89:5 (December 1999): 1337-1357.

Hatton, T., and J. Williamson. "Demographic and Economic Pressure on Emigration out of Africa." *Scandinavian Journal of Economics* 105:3 (September 2003): 465-486.

Hoddinott, J. "A Model of Migration and Remittances Applied to Western Kenya." *Oxford Economic Papers* 46:3 (July 1994): 459-476.

Ligon, E., J. Thomas, and T. Worall. "Informal Insurance Arrangements with Limited Commitment: Theory and Evidence from Village

Economies." *Review of Economic Studies* 69:1 (January 2002): 209-244.

Lim, Y., and R. M. Townsend. "General Equilibrium Models of Financial Systems: Theory and Measurement in Village Economies." *Review of Economic Dynamics* 1:1 (January 1998): 58-118.

Mayda, A. M. "International Migration: A Panel Data Analysis of Economic and Non-Economic Determinants." IZA Discussion Papers 1590 (May 2005): 1-41.

Morduch, J. "Risk, Production, and Saving: Theory and Evidence from Indian Villages." Mimeo, Harvard University, 1993.

Naciones Unidas: Comisiùn Econùmica para America Latina y el Caribe: Sede Subregional en Mexico. "El Salvador: Evaluacion del Terremoto del Martes 13 de Febrero de 2001." Mexico: United Nations, 2001.

Paulson, A. "Insurance Motives for Migration: Evidence from Thailand." Diss. Northwestern University, 2000.

Paxson, C. "Using Weather Variability to Estimate the Response of Savings to Transitory Income in Thailand." *American Economic Review* 82:1 (March 1992): 15-33.

Rosenzweig, M., and O. Stark. "Consumption Smoothing, Migration, and Marriage: Evidence from Rural India." *Journal of Political Economy* 97:4 (August 1989): 905-926.

Rosenzweig, M., and K. Wolpin. "Credit Market Constraints, Consumption Smoothing and the Accumulation of Durable Production Assets in Low-Income Countries: Investments in Bullocks in India." *Journal of Political Economy* 101:2 (April 1993): 223-244.

Townsend, R. M. "Risk and Insurance in Village India." *Econometrica* 62:3 (May 1994): 539-591.

Udry, C. "Risk and Insurance in a Rural Credit Market: An Empirical Investigation in Northern Nigeria." *Review of Economic Studies* 61:3 (July 1994): 495-526.

——. "Risk and Saving in Northern Nigeria." *American Economic Review* 85:5 (December 1995): 1287-1300.

United Nations. Department of Economic and Social Affairs. Population Division. *International Migration Report 2002.* New York: United Nations, 2002.

William R. Morrish
After the Storm: Rebuilding Cities upon Reflexive Infrastructure

> Disasters don't just destroy lives; they mock them.
> —Susan Neiman (2005)

IN THE LAST TWENTY YEARS, I HAVE TAKEN PART IN RECOVERY AND rebuilding efforts following the1993 Mississippi River floods, the 9/11 World Trade Center attack, and Hurricane Katrina and the levee collapse in New Orleans. Walking into the pit at Ground Zero or through the flood-ravaged neighborhoods of New Orleans, I have felt the heavy truth of Susan Neiman's words and seen it etched in residents' faces and scarred oak trees. I have witnessed the eerie silence as people, birds, and all other signs of life disappeared in the darkness as the city struggled without power, water, or the security of streetlights.

I now see these places as historic classrooms, their ashes and muddied family albums are powerful testaments to the value and vulnerabilities of every city in America. A disaster's swift currents not only alter the familiar topological contours of the distressed community; they also reveal major gaps in civic practices and social justice, surprising changes in local culture and ecologies, and a swarm of unsettling questions about the viability of the entire civil infrastructure network.

When a tsunami, hurricane, or major earthquake strikes a city and metropolitan landscape, the winds, storm surges, and tremors immediately strip away the veneer of everyday life, uncovering the hidden fragility of local life-support systems such as water supply, waste disposal, flood control, telecommunications, public health, and personal mobility—to name just a few. System weaknesses usually are matters of public record long before disaster strikes, but the decision to tackle the tough political and financial issues that come with each upgrade is routinely deferred "to another day" for the sake of budget deficits and political expediency. In the grim aftermath of the storm, responders discover that the day of reckoning has arrived. On top of the chaos and hardship of disaster recovery, the city now faces multiple system failures intensified by prior neglect. Urgent rebuilding demands have to compete with long-overdue infrastructure reconstruction. Meanwhile, besieged residents cope with added risks such as cholera and other water-borne diseases, which seem unimaginable in modern-day America.

In their book, *The Resilient City, How Modern Cities Recover from Disaster*, the editors Lawrence J. Vale and Thomas J. Campanella summarize the publication's urban case studies with a concluding chapter: "Axioms of Resilience." They list 12 activities that cycle through an evolving process of recovery, reconstruction, and rebuilding. As the disaster recovery chart found in their volume illustrates, it is a lengthy process requiring great focus and endurance for any city to successfully navigate. The chart provides an important visual framework that helps describe what happened to New Orleans in the wake of Katrina.

On August 29, 2005, the annual Gulf hurricane event turned into a massive urban disaster and human tragedy. Hurricane Katrina's Category 3 winds and subsequent tidal surge overwhelmed the region's patchwork of protective levees. In two days, 80 percent of the city was under water. Floodwater crushed water and sewer lines and inundated pump, fire, police, and public health stations. Oil and toxic chemicals, mixed with fecal material, turned the water into a dangerous brew that seeped into building walls and lingered in the yards of homes. Meanwhile, 75 percent of the city's celebrated oak and magnolia tree canopy, which protected residents from summer heat and eased stormwater runoff for over a century, was wiped out by wind and saltwater intrusion. Most of the region's hospitals and emerging biotechnology centers were isolated by floodwater. Lacking access to power or dry cooling air, heat and humidity generated mold and bacterial growth throughout the buildings. Today, most remain empty, uninhabitable, requiring complete demolition. The disaster further exposed clumsy leadership at all levels of government, a balkanized and inept emergency preparedness organization, and an extensive map of disenfranchised citizens living on the edge of or outside access to basic city services.

These were just some of the preconditions that created a domino-like cascade of breaches and failures and magnified a comparatively routine Category 3 hurricane into a Category 5 catastrophe. The net result was that governance crumpled, the social safety net dissolved, critical municipal systems stopped working, and nearly 1,500 people died needlessly. The devastation of New Orleans was so complete that it was as if the horizontal line of the disaster recovery chart simply vanished and the city was left without basic civil gravity.

Infrastructure failure is now a daily fact of life in New Orleans. Utility providers struggle to keep aging systems in service—a task made much harder by the lack of steady power supply. Residents live with constant service interruptions, questionable water quality, unreliable sanitation, and skyrocketing utility bills. They also have learned that their heroic efforts to rebuild homes and small businesses are not enough to bring New Orleans back to life; they still need the foundation of reliable municipal services accessible to and supportive of all residents. New Orleans' continuing inability to make tangible progress on infrastructure renewal has undermined its economic recovery and the ability of ordinary citizens to return, rebuild, and realistically hope for a better future. If the trend continues, the city may become an even more segregated, fragmented, and vulnerable place than it is right now.

While catastrophic failure on this scale is mercifully rare in the United States, the event still serves as a potent symbol of the havoc caused by long-standing neglect of the public realm in New Orleans and elsewhere (Connery, 2008). It vividly illustrates the risks and complexity we face to rebuild infrastructure systems in ways that will address past shortcomings but also meet new challenges posed by the disruptive shifts in economic, demographic, and environmental conditions under way across the nation. The required remedies and recipes will not be found in the default codes of traditional urban renewal and reconstruction; we must study the insights revealed by Katrina and fundamentally rethink the role of infrastructure in our private and collective lives and begin to create new models for more robust, resilient, and sustainable systems and cities.

There are three critical insights that this storm revealed.

1. *Long before Katrina arrived, another storm had been quietly brewing—out of sight, out of mind, and mostly underground.*

New Orleans' basic public infrastructure had been on a steady starvation diet for decades. A declining tax base, erratic lines of authority among public agencies, and a rich legacy of corruption all conspired to deprive the system of critically needed maintenance and investment capital. The city could barely keep up with emergency repairs and court-ordered environmental upgrades, much less respond to the steady demands for ad hoc improvements to lure new development and jobs. In a nutshell, the city tried to squeeze as much service out of ragged outdated networks for as long as it could without taking stock of more strategic capital needs and investment priorities or the heavy odds that its piecemeal actions—to avert crises or cater to powerful private interests—merely accelerated overall system decline. In the end, New Orleans was the first city in modern US history to suffer a sweeping catastrophe due in large measure to public sector myopia and basic human denial.

Though the lights in the French Quarter came back on soon after the Katrina swept through the delta, the rest of New Orleans would wait for months to get power. Entergy, one of the nation's largest nuclear power generators, sustained $1 billion in storm-related damage; its local subsidiary—Entergy New Orleans, Inc.—filed for bankruptcy just three weeks after the hurricane made landfall (Brinkley, 2007). The company could survive the immediate financial loss but not the long-term threat of a sharply reduced customer base in the greater New Orleans region. Ultimately, Entergy and other private sector utility providers proved to be as ill prepared for disaster as the public agencies; they simply counted on insurance coverage and the government to bail them out (Klein, 2007; Little, 2006). Anyone who now lives or works in New Orleans has become accustomed to erratic service, systemwide brown-outs, giant rate increases, and gloomy prospects for recovery.

2. Besides the apparent weaknesses of local institutions and infrastructure, Katrina revealed layers of reckless policies and feckless development decisions that had steered the city of New Orleans in self-defeating directions for more than 30 years.

One of the most notorious examples could be seen in the management of the city's vital levee system. The patchwork of local public authorities responsible for this task began to pay more attention to private real estate development than public safety and levee protection (Brinkley, 2006). Like most other American cities, the city fought hard to attract major development projects, such as mixed-use commercial centers, high-income housing, casinos, and professional sport facilities. The levee boards' special district taxing authority provided a handy vehicle to finance some of the costly improvements demanded by developers as a precondition for private investment. While precious tax dollars underpinned private gains, the prevailing public myth was that these projects would yield large tax revenues to invest in sorely needed infrastructure improvements throughout the community. Unfortunately, none of the "trickle-down" benefits promised to the neighborhoods and the working-class families who support these developments ever materialized.

At a more basic level, civic leaders—both public and private sector—and citizens in New Orleans showed little taste for crossing traditional cultural and institutional barriers to advance community-wide planning, development, and emergency preparedness. Moreover, there was no leadership or serious political and economic incentives to encourage the city to join forces with its metropolitan neighbors to strengthen the protective ecological systems in the region and to collaborate on less glamorous issues such as water, power, sewer, waste, and transportation improvements.

Since Katrina, political and media attention to infrastructure has focused mainly on their construction of protective levees and design emergency evacuation systems for residents without cars. Remarkably little attention had been paid to vital services, such as drinking water that underpin the daily lives of all working families. Where many regions of the country are facing drought, water quality is a primary concern today in New Orleans. The drinking water supply comes from the Mississippi River, which is constantly under threat from the residues of upriver chemical plants and pesticides used in the midwest farm belt. As a former resident of New Orleans, I can attest that local water quality and reliability has been less than ideal for many years. City residents who can afford filtered water have typically used local water only for washing and gardening.

The integrity of the whole water supply system is also in jeopardy. In the evening, you can stand in one of New Orleans' great working-class neighborhoods and see the gaudy lights of the French Quarter—the so-called real New Orleans promoted by the tourist industry. Turn the other direction and you are apt to see a visual reminder of its fragile foundation: water spouting from the street and across the sidewalk. The city's 3,200-mile network of water and sewer pipelines, which was in wretched shape long before Katrina, suffered serious additional damage from the massive load of floodwater (up to 10 feet deep) that lingered for 18 days in many parts of the city. The New Orleans Sewerage and Water Board currently pumps 120 million gallons of water into this crumbling system everyday but loses more than 50 million gallons due to leaks before it ever reaches residents (a noteworthy improvement compared to a loss rate of 80 million gallons reported by the *Times-Picayune* in 2006). Meanwhile, the ongoing threat of pump failure—due to power outages, mechanical breakdowns, or additional storm damage—can lead to a severe loss in pressure and widespread water contamination since raw sewage and other pollutants can swiftly back up into the water system through the leaks and shut the system down for weeks. (*USA Today*, 2007)

In the past, it was mainly low-income families who had to worry about the quality and reliability of the public drinking water supply. Today the issue matters to everyone on the street and has become a major factor in the decision by middle-class families and businesses to remain in (or return to) New Orleans—on par with the collapse of the local public school system before Katrina. Poor households also endure extra hardships due to lead connector pipes, damaged home plumbing, and the disproportionate pressure of rising water rates on skintight budgets. Failure to pay these rates can jettison ordinary tax-paying working-class families into second-class citizenship and third-world living conditions—if and when their water service is disconnected.

3. The disaster's historic forces revealed stark transformations in the urban economic environment and the form and function of the region's protective ecological processes.

After any disaster, the common desire of civic leaders and citizens is to quickly restore their city back to its familiar precondition map. This might be possible after a big storm that merely knocks down power lines or rips shingles from house roofs but in the aftermath of historic events such as Hurricane Katrina or 9/11, the cultural and physical landscape is fundamentally and irrevocably altered. Ecologists call this type of change "succession," where one type of ecological habitat evolves into a completely different habitat—such as when an open grassy field changes into a wood lot. The new landscape demands an entirely different operating system to support its vitality.

Many understand the idea of ecological succession as a slow process of natural change. In fact, we are active agents in cultivating this process to suit our needs as long as we have time to manage and accommodate the progressive changes. In contrast, disasters are swift and decisive in their impact on the local cultural and physical ecology. They leave behind a huge list of "change" issues that can overwhelm local governance capacity and paralyze residents. In the case of New Orleans, the power of Hurricane Katrina and the weakness of its protective systems nearly undermined its landmark institutions and upended the norms of everyday life.

Until Katrina, everyday life—in economic and ecological terms—was epitomized by the city's nickname, "The Big Easy." Its economic symbol was a perpetual Mardi Gras party in the French Quarter. The nickname was created more than a century ago by musicians who came to New Orleans from all over the world to seek easy gigs and a chance to jam with greats like Jelly Roll Morton, King Oliver, and Louis Armstrong. Today, The Big Easy is a brand logo laminated onto tourist t-shirts.

Once a diversified economy based on energy, finance, and trade, pre-Katrina New Orleans had been reduced to a monoculture tied to tourism, entertainment, and convention trade shows. Shipping and refining moved upriver to major barge terminals. The once industrious waterfront became a backdrop for expensive condos and flashy hotel casinos serving up big portions of lackluster food prepared in giant service kitchens. Meanwhile, many of the great local chefs and musicians who brewed up all the inventive recipes, unique cuisines, and exhilarating music that made the city famous, quietly moved onto new venues in less dangerous and more culturally cosmopolitan cities. When gumbo can be bought in a box with freeze-dried ingredients, culinary art no longer seemed essential to the city's economic vitality.

Several months after Katrina, local business leaders admitted during national radio interviews that they had not seen the city's economy grow so small and economically segregated in nearly 50 years. The casinos, conventions, and tourists were returning but represented only a thin shell of urban vitality. People who live in New Orleans' neighborhoods still find it extremely hard to restart businesses, locate needed services, or get access to basic health care. Service workers face a severe shortage of affordable housing; many are forced to sleep in their cars or commute great distances to their jobs. In many ways, the city now operates like Las Vegas, where thousands of low-income workers toil invisibly behind the bright lights to maintain the Strip's sacred simulacrum.

New Orleans' urban ecology is framed by two natural systems: the Mississippi River and the urban forest canopy of live oaks. Both reveal the complex water regime that defines life in the city well beyond the channels, lakes, and levees. When the storm clouds cleared after Katrina, satellite photos revealed that the storm surge had stripped away 50 years of tidal grassland and trees (when compared with normal rates of decay in the wetlands of the river delta). A hundred years ago the city of New Orleans had 50 miles of wetlands separating it from the Gulf of Mexico; now in places, it has only 25. For every 2.7 miles of marshes/swampland that disappeared, there was a corresponding increase of one foot of storm surge (Brinkley, 2006).

Katrina's deadly storm surges gave us a detailed picture of the new risks and vulnerabilities facing New Orleans neighborhoods in future storms; they also upended a lot of simplistic notions about "high ground vs. low ground." Metropolitan New Orleans is a mosaic of five different drainage basins, which are urbanized sub-watersheds (Eskew, Morrish, and Schwartz, 2007). Katrina demonstrated that each of these basins has unique flood exposure conditions and that city topography is more complex and dynamic than previously assumed; in fact, the city is floating on a wet urban landscape surrounded by a massive wet Mississippi River delta landscape. Hence, the basis for New Orleans' stability, safety, and survival does not rest on high ground—instead, it depends entirely on the continuous gardening and tending of both landscapes. The silt, mud, and water that pour through the bayous, underground conduits, canals, along curb gutters or in the main channel of the Mississippi River are all part of the same gigantic watershed that drains off all the fluids of the nation's vast midsection. On the river, change is the only constant.

We take for granted that our cities are rooted on solid economic foundations and supported by benevolent environments, yet many float on conditions as fragile and uncertain as those in New Orleans. They may not have abundant blue water nearby to remind them of their vulnerability, but the basic circumstances are often the same: faltering infrastructure, aging and/or diminishing population, waning tax base, severe weather events, declining resources, and the growing realization that time is not on their side. Cities that neglect the care of their basic economic and ecological footings set themselves up for swift and radical changes like those witnessed in the aftermath of Katrina.

What is the remedy?

> The logics of ecology, culture, economics, politics and civil society exist side by side, [they] cannot be reduced or collapsed into one another. Rather each must be independently decoded and grasped in its interdependencies (Beck, 2000).

The words of Munich University sociologist Ulrich Beck set the terms for a radically different thinking process and societal baseline from which to rebuild our city infrastructure. Any design methodology or development outcome needs to start with an understanding of modern-day global challenges—such as climate and demographic change, cultural differences, and economic dislocation and disparities. The conventional logic of civil infrastructure engineering, which has emphasized single functions, separate projects, traditional institutional silos, and uniform codes, now must be replaced by integrated design and development processes that increase interconnectedness and adjust to unpredictable risks.

Drawing inspiration from the tenets of sustainability, reflexive modernization is less concerned with expanding the resource base and more with re-evaluating and redeploying the resources already is use.

The word "reflexive" implies three concepts to help reshape the traditional view of infrastructure. These include:

1. Infrastructure as a cultural repository of memories and future hopes;
2. Infrastructure as interdependent services and support systems that form the threads of the local safety net; and
3. Infrastructure as a set of reciprocal transactions between civic

authorities that promote the sustenance and equitable distribution of the local common wealth.

CULTURAL REPOSITORY

In every century, anyone who planned only for necessity did not even achieve what was necessary. Humanity had need of an emotional relationship to its dwelling places; it demanded aesthetic uplift, a creative culture that could lend more than polish to the everyday.

—Wolfgang Braunfels, *Urban Design in Western Europe: Regime and Architecture, 900-1900* (1988).

Infrastructure is a mirror that reflects our civic values, cultural identity, and collective hopes for a better future. Transportation, water, power, sewer, and waste systems represent an extraordinary collection of public assets and investments. Yet, as users we rarely grasp their crucial value to our daily lives or the collective toll of our individual demands for services. Their components are buried underground, hidden behind drab paint and chain-link fences, or relegated to the poor end of town. On the other hand, when we designed the Golden Gate Bridge spanning the entrance to San Francisco Bay or New York City's Central Park with its gracious reservoirs and intracity arterial roadways, we reaped long-term economic benefits and created world-class landmarks that are celebrated by local and global citizens alike.

Before we can effectively rebuild our aging infrastructure, we must first rekindle public awareness of its central role in our collective existence. Its functional and aesthetic values determine the vitality of the urban landscape that adjoins all of our cherished homes, schools, businesses, and institutions. Natural systems and utility networks need to become integral and interdependent parts of that urban landscape. As prolonged droughts threaten many regions of the world, we may begin to witness cities competing for global prominence on the basis of their stewardship of the local water resources rather than building the tallest skyscraper.

In the words of the late *New York Times* architecture critic Herbert Muschamp, "Instead of burying a city's vital organs out of sight, design could visualize a place for them on the cultural landscape. Into sight, into mind" (Muschamp, 1994).

After a disaster, the affected communities often have the full attention of the nation. People want to help. While most cities have emergency plans to ensure their survival and reduce the event's terrible impacts, few have procedures in place to capitalize on the surge of disaster funds and social equity being offered to aid victims. Most of these donations are dispersed quickly with little opportunity to leverage any of this extraordinary outpouring of public generosity to help create a more sustainable, equitable and less vulnerable infrastructure foundation.

In the United States, the hard work of maintaining infrastructure is never glamorous, well funded, or appreciated until a crucial system fails. We occasionally see workmen in bright orange safety jackets climbing down into manholes to repair communication, water, or power lines out of sight. Sustainable building and landscape design takes those daily routines and celebrates them as major formal, functional, and symbolic acts that gives shape and structure to the living and working environment, increasing productivity and conviviality. Sustainability's key design and development idea is to transform maintenance into a public activity that enriches the everyday routines of public spaces, buildings, and landscapes.

Reflexive and resilient infrastructure systems cannot be created through technological innovation alone; they require a fully engaged citizenry with a strong sense of shared purpose. Likewise, public agencies or private companies cannot engineer the renewal of damaged systems; they need supportive citizens and customers. Active citizen participation is fundamental to daily operation of sustainable infrastructure.

The Netherlands has taken its pervasive problem of living below sea level and devised an innovative comprehensive cultural and ecological approach to the design of climate protection and community infrastructure. The nation's hydrologic system is backbone to its basic public realm, from civic spaces to schoolyards. In the last decade it has transformed protective infrastructure network, creating a global hydrological attraction supporting new neighborhoods and a diverse urban economy. Their approach is to turn the nation's "risky" relationship with the sea into a transparent urban landscape where seawall and other vital protection systems and water regimes become parks, bicycle corridors, iconic bridges, and forests of modern wind turbines that visibly link every residential home, neighborhood, and business. These connections serve as daily reminders of the critical importance of these investments and the need for continuing public maintenance and vigilance. In the Netherlands, infrastructure resilience is based on an informed and actively engaged public citizenry, linked to a sophisticated network of advanced technological monitoring and sensors.

Developing resilient infrastructure begins with collecting a wide range set of data, translating that data into visual material that is accessible to the community so they can respond—either through individual efforts or as collective activities to support sustainable operations. Before the hurricane, access to good data, maps, and aerial images of New Orleans was haphazard at best and typically impossible for general public use. The city lacked the staffing, funding, and impetus to develop a comprehensive digital picture of its cultural and ecological conditions. The disaster highlighted this shortcoming. Governmental and nongovernmental grants have radically changed the local information scene. City officials, neighborhood organizations, academic institutions, and citizens now have direct access to robust body of information. This has empowered New Orleans' nongovernmental organizations with information and mapping capabilities to address precondition issues such as toxic soils and housing inequity and also to monitor recovery and rebuilding efforts.

Unfortunately, future strategies for rebuilding local infrastructure are being held behind closed doors of local utility officials working with the US Army Corps of Engineers, federal and state agencies, and consulting engineering firms. This activity has produced mistrust, insecurity, and legitimate fears that the same old patchwork of separate silos and special interests will prevail.

SAFETY NET

Citizens in New Orleans who are struggling to revitalize their homes and neighborhoods understand that simply patching the same old parts back together will not yield trust worthy results. Likewise, the renewal of the city's devastated infrastructure needs much more than the customary "patch and pray" approach to individual public works improvements. Since Katrina, various federal, state and local leaders, FEMA contractors, and big developers have all tried to resurrect various parts of New Orleans without serious thought about the relationship of those parts to each other or the impact of these separate actions on the long-term cultural, economic and ecological life of the city. Local infrastructure providers continue to lumber along in isolation without the benefit of progressive civic vision and leadership or adequate resources—just as they did before Katrina.

New Orleans' future economic viability and security still needs a public works network that is fully legible and accountable to all citizens who depend on the safety net of their services. Without this assurance, many people feel that they cannot take the risk to stay and build a life in New Orleans. Every infrastructure investment should reinforce and vividly highlight the physical and cultural connections all of the city's neighborhoods and residents and the surrounding delta wetlands whose natural resources sustain them all.

The traditional approach to infrastructure vulnerability and recovery is to harden defenses and focus recovery primarily on repair of big public works. The term "resilience" demands the development of a distributed infrastructure that enables citizens to operate more independently, sustain themselves during service disruptions, and assist the recharge of the larger systems upon return to normal conditions. In this way citizens become the first responders and more active and effective agents in recovery and the revival of the local economy.

In this finer-grained approach to infrastructure, every new urban structure or landscape modification becomes an opportunity and responsibility to add needed value to system capacity and reduce its negative impacts. Recovery and safety can be greatly enhanced by many small lights and services instead of none. In a volatile world of changing climate and the potential for cascading infrastructure failures, the investment in sustainable distributed infrastructure will have a direct and substantial return for communities and businesses by enabling them to rebound more quickly after disasters and stay competitive in the global marketplace. The costs of being shut down for more than a few days or weeks can be catastrophic. For example, in post-Katrina interviews, local business leaders described the swift hemorrhage of top researchers and staff to other cities after New Orleans' major hospitals and biotech firms were flooded and destroyed.

A more reflexive and modern urban infrastructure seeks to build reciprocal relationships between the center, branches, and ends of all of its respective systems. As an example, heating and cooling systems in state-the-art green office buildings now include thousands of small electronic sensors that are embedded in the skin of the building and monitored by a central control computer. During the day as the sun tracks across the sky, the sensors make continuous small adjustments in internal temperature and airflow. The recognition that a building is not just a box but also a mosaic of changing thermal subsurfaces has yielded new design approaches that lower energy costs and increase the productivity and well-being of building inhabitants. Every component— such as lighting or plumbing systems—is vital links of an increasingly integrated network that supports energy efficiency, alternative energy generation, water conservation, public safety, and specific environmental needs of individual tenants.

Likewise, the infrastructure systems that support such buildings and the entire human-made landscape should also serve multiple goals. Besides their functional values, these varied systems can become cultural utilities and civilizing amenities that strengthen neighborhoods, job growth, and local ecological systems.

Sustainable infrastructure design requires the integration of natural ecological processes into local "structural" systems. This means that infrastructure systems cannot be designed from the premise that "one size fits all urban situations." Public sector agencies and private utilities need to reach across their propriety service district boundaries to calculate baselines and combined strategies. Power companies and urban water supply companies need to balance their demands for local water supplies with other critical needs to support healthy neighborhood streams and a cooling urban tree canopy, which help to reduce heat island effect and power demands. Power companies must also work in tandem with transportation agencies to reduce traffic congestion and air pollution; we cannot refresh our work places with open windows and local breezes if the air outside is increasingly polluted.

When the architecture of buildings, landscapes, and cities begins to incorporate natural systems into design and operation, all of these elements can operate as capillaries in a major infrastructure network to continuously provide water, air, energy, communication, transportation, and waste services to meet user demands with the least waste or cost to the environment.

For example, hurricane-force winds stripped off the roofs of many New Orleans homes. Instead of simply replacing roofs with asphalt shingles in the customary hip roof shape, solar voltaic shingles and/or solar water heating systems could be used instead to create roofs that are energy generators. A citywide application of this idea would help residents reduce home energy bills, provide emergency energy to local citizens during the annual hurricane season, reduce overall metropolitan energy demands, and jumpstart an emerging green industry with enormous job potential. In this way, end-users also become "generators" to support overall civic supply needs and incrementally build a comprehensive and redundant safety network of civic infrastructure.

SHARING THE COMMONWEALTH

Katrina . . . illustrated the failure of infrastructure planning to incorporate non-structural alternatives. Wetlands were developed and, as a result, could not performtheir natural function of absorbing surge water flows (Everett and Landy, 2005).

In a highly connected a global society, the word "redundancy" has become a key concept in infrastructure design as a means to reduce system vulnerabilities and risks of failure. Our daily existence and protection from extreme events such as hurricanes or major power outages depend on the ability to switch over to backup or parallel networks when the main systems fail.

To convert our cities into healthier, safer, and more productive and livable places, we need to see infrastructure as a second nature, an artificial urban landscape evolving with natural processes to serve the community and underscore their collective existence (Jackson, 1986; Cronon, 1992). Infrastructure that derives its form, function, and operation from a synthesis of natural and cultural processes represents a more sustainable set of systems and services with the potential of backup resources to absorb the impact of natural or human-made disasters. Redundancy is learning how to use landscape ecologies as a parallel system in dialogue with our built protective lines by adding and enriching local ecologies and by reducing harmful global pollutants. In this way, urban tree forests and tidal wetlands can be seen as critical components of a city's water supply, treatment, and protection system.

In New Orleans, the surrounding deltaic wetlands serve as the first line of defense to protect the city from the devastating impact of storm surges. Each mile of wetland reduces the height of a storm surge by one foot with a corresponding decrease in the required height and width of constructed earthen levees. These natural buffers also provide a nursery for its robust local seafood industry. But the traditional planning and engineering processes still view wetlands as peripheral to the levees and other structural elements of the formal urban flood protection system. In the engineering lexicon, natural and cultural systems are known as "nonstructural alternatives." Many engineers view their use as evidence of weaknesses in the preferred engineered solution. Others in the land development and construction fields are more openly hostile since nonstructural solutions may significantly reduce the scale and profitability of certain projects.

New Orleans' dramatic loss of canopy trees after Katrina is not unique; in the last 25 years, Washington, D.C. has lost over 60 percent of its tree canopy, exposing city residents to increased heat, stormwater flooding, and neighborhood decline. In cities that are exposed to heavy summer downpours, the presence of a thick "green canopy" of assorted trees is another critical extension of the local stormwater management system. Without them, pipes become quickly overwhelmed, causing local flooding. The trees' canopies catch rainfall in their leaves and branches, slowing the water as it falls to the ground. Tree roots absorb water and protect neighborhoods from wind damage.

The destruction of the urban canopy is rarely ever regarded as a major urban infrastructure issue, even though numerous scientific studies demonstrate the cost effectiveness of healthy tree canopies for reducing water pollution, air pollution, children's illnesses, and neighborhood crime. However, in both New Orleans and Washington, D.C, community-based organizations such as Replant New Orleans and the Casey Tree Fund have taken up this critical issue. Specifically, the Casey Tree Fund has created a citywide GIS-based urban tree inventory and trained local youth to monitor and care for old and newly planted trees in their neighborhoods. Meanwhile, community groups in Sacramento, California have begun an aggressive campaign for a citywide "infrastructure" project to add thousands of trees on public and private property to enhance the city's skyline, reduce the heat island effect in the summer, and generally promote a more amenable civic environment.

Most urban water supply and treatment facilities tend to follow generic designs with little adaptation to local cultural or ecological conditions. Specific site conditions or topography that complicate design intentions are simply "corrected" (with lots of bulldozing) to conform to prevailing technology standards, resulting in steep increases in projects costs, energy and other resource demands, and unintended environmental impacts. Yet, conventional engineering wisdom still maintains that mixing structural and nonstructural systems into hybrid and custom tailored solutions is too costly to build and operate—without considering the full spectrum of hidden costs caused by one-size-fits-all solutions.

The key lesson is that natural system and ecological processes are both "structural" components of sustainable infrastructure. Whether they are constructed from concrete and steel or consist of roots, leaves, and mudflats, they can be organized to reinforce each other and provide the capacity to flex with constant environmental changes. The products from this type of design development can be tailored not only to meet the specific local needs and site conditions but also to educate users on how to maintain and use their system through its entire life cycle. Once the project is open and running, the development's design performance standards become the baseline for maintaining, upgrading, and altering the system to future circumstances.

TOWARD SUSTAINABLE DESIGN

"Sustainability" has become a global term that refers to a host of development policies and financing, design, and implementation strategies that attempt to reduce the impact of climate change, ecological destruction, megacity sprawl, social inequity, and the overutilization of scarce human and natural resources. Sustainable design demonstrations throughout the globe have introduced a burst of new cultural diverse ideas and new technologies that have integrated natural systems to create more livable metropolitan cities and regions. They also raise several important questions: How will these individual public and private investments in green systems eventually coalesce in support of the collective needs of society? Will these new investments become the catalyst for a wide-ranging exploration of new innovations and diverse interpretations or simply a strait jacket of conforming standards?

Campaigns for "green objects" and green imperatives do not automatically add up to sustainable design and development. The process demands a much more comprehensive approach and continuing effort to integrate built and natural systems in ways that create reflexive landscapes. It is a messy process that requires close attention to human ecologies as well as the built and natural systems that support them. Above all, it needs an open environment that constantly reinvents itself and creates new ideas that engage local and global audiences.

This process reminds me of the hard work required to create a great bowl of New Orleans gumbo—the rich concoction of local and global seasonings and seafood, chicken, and other regional protein and starches that is stirred, simmered, tasted, and poured over hot rice and has captured a worldwide audience. First you make a roux — the combination of flour and fat that is the heart of this dish. The process demands patience and steady stirring to turn these raw materials into a clear and usable sauce. To make gumbo, chefs learn to blend contrasting flavors that are reflective of each unique locale. Tasting or analyzing gumbo recipes, one can read New Orleans complex cultural and ecological history drawn from local, regional, and global sources. This local stew has close relatives around the world, including bouillabaisse in the Mediterranean or pho in Vietnam.

Just as in gumbo, the life-giving force of sustainable design resides in diversity and creative freedom. The process demands a steady stream of new ideas, interactions, and information from the region and the world, a broad-based collaborative process to aid understanding of complex local problems and inspire designers to dream up innovative solutions and critically test these in the real world. Most may fail; some might just be transformative. In this way, infrastructure can begin to shed its stodgy image and attract the best minds and new resources to help the nation confront the need to renew aging systems and shift away from out-dated technologies. As Nancy Connery has written:

> With this new knowledge, imaginative designers [experts and local citizens] suddenly have a huge incentive to invent "game changing" innovations to transform current obsta-

cles into competitive [and cooperative] opportunities that create new wealth, protect resources, inspire the public and overturn the longstanding stranglehold of status quo technologies (Connery, 2008).

REFERENCES

Beck, Ulrich, *What Is Globalization?* Oxford: Polity, 2000.

Braunfels, Wolfgang. *Urban Design in Western Europe: Regime and Architecture, 900-1900.* Trans. Kenneth J. Northcott. Chicago: University of Chicago Press, 1988.

Brinkley, Douglas. *The Great Deluge: Hurricane Katrina, New Orleans, and the Mississippi Gulf Coast.* New York: William Morrow, 2006.

Connery, Nancy R, "Development of the Next Generation: U.S. Infrastructure Systems: A Framework for National Policy." Commentary. *Public Works Management and Policy.* Thousand Oaks, Calif.: Sage Publications, January 2008.

Cronon, William. *Nature's Metropolis: Chicago and the Great West.* New York: Norton, 1992.

Dyson, Michael Eric. *Come Hell of High Water: Hurricane Katrina and the Color of Disaster.* New York: Basic Civitas Books, 2006.

Everett, E., and B. Landy. *Public Works, Public Wealth: New Directions for America's Infrastructure.* Washington. D.C.: Center for Strategic and International Studies, 2005.

Grant, Albert, and Andrew Lemer, eds. *In Our Own Backyard: Principles for Effective Improvement of the Nation's Infrastructure.* Committee on Infrastructure, National Research Council. Washington, D.C.: National Academy Press, 1993.

Jackson, Jonathan Brinckerhoff. *Discovering the Vernacular Landscape.* New Haven: Yale University Press, 1986.

Kirk, Patricia. "Rebuilding the Nation's Urban Foundation." *Multi-Family Trends* (January/February 2006).

Little, Richard, G. "Controlling Cascading Failure: Understanding the Vulnerabilities of Interconnected Infrastructures." *Journal of Urban Technology* (April 2002).

Little, Richard G. *"Time for an Infrastructure Overhaul."* Urban Land (August 2007).

Miara, John. *"Footing the Bill for Infrastructure."* Multi-Family Trends (January/February 2007).

Moss, Timothy, Simon Guy, and Simon Marvin, Simon, eds. *Urban Infrastructure in Transition: Networks, Buildings, Plans.* London: Earthscan, 2001.

Muschamp, Herbert. "When Is a Roof Not a Roof?" *New York Times,* April 10, 1994.

Neiman, Susan. "The Moral Cataclysm." *New York Times Magazine,* January 16, 2005.

Perrow, Charles. *The Next Catastrophe: Reducing Our Vulnerabilities to Natural, Industrial, and Terrorist Disasters.* Princeton: Princeton University Press, 2007.

Potter, Hillary, ed. *Racing the Storm: Racial Implications and Lessons Learned from Hurricane Katrina.* Lanham, Md.: Lexington Books, 2007.

Roettger, Betsy, ed. "Building after Katrina: Visions for the Gulf Coast." *Urgent Matters.* Vol. 2. Charlottesville: University of Virginia School of Architecture, 2007

Schwartz, Fred, Allen Eskew, and William Morrish. *District 3 and District 4 Plans.* New Orleans: Unified New Orleans Planning Report, 2007.

West, Cornell. "Learning to Talk Race." *New York Times Magazine,* August 2, 1992: 24-26.

Robert J. Ursano, Carol
S. Fullerton, and Artin
Terhakopian

Disasters and Health: Distress, Disorders, and Disaster Behaviors in Communities, Neighborhoods, and Nations

DISASTERS ARE OF TWO MAJOR TYPES: NATURAL AND HUMAN-MADE. Human-made disasters result from human error, such as technological accidents, and intentional human acts, such as terrorism. Overall, human-made disasters cause more frequent and more persistent psychiatric symptoms and distress (for review see Norris et al., 2002). However, this distinction is difficult to make. The etiology and consequences of natural disasters can be the result of human behaviors. For example, the damage caused by an earthquake can be intensified by poor construction. Similarly, humans may contribute to the damage and destruction caused by natural disasters through poor land management that increase the probability of floods. Interpersonal violence between individuals or groups such as assault, war, and terrorism is in many ways the most disturbing traumatic experience. A review of over 60,000 disaster victims found 67 percent of those exposed to mass violence were severely impaired compared with 39 percent of those exposed to technological disasters and 34 percent of those exposed to natural disasters (Norris et al., 2002).

THE NATURE OF DISASTERS AND THE DISASTER COMMUNITY

Disasters overwhelm local resources and threaten the safety and functioning of communities. With the advent of new technology, disasters are witnessed in real time around the globe. Disaster communities can be overwhelmed by the media and people offering assistance. The normal routine of the community is altered not just by the disaster but by the influx of strangers, which affects normal social supports, straining and disrupting community functioning—the important elements in helping communities return to "normal" functioning.

Disaster impacts that includes threat to life, destruction of property and society, as well as the stress events in the recovery environment, are related to the degree of psychiatric morbidity (Noji, 1997). Disruption of the community and workplace increases distress, health risk behaviors, and risk of posttraumatic stress disorders (PTSD). In the immediate aftermath of a disaster or terrorist attack, individuals and communities may respond in adaptive, effective ways or they may make fear-based decisions, resulting in unhelpful behaviors. Knowledge of an individual's and community's resilience and vulnerability before a disaster as well as understanding the specific community's psychological responses enables leaders and medical experts to talk to the public, to promote resilient healthy behaviors, sustain the social fabric of the community, and facilitate recovery (Ursano et al., 2003; Institute of Medicine, 2003). The adaptive capacities of individuals and groups within a community are variable and need to be understood before a crisis in order to target needs effectively after disaster. For example, community embeddedness—the degree to which one belongs to and is connected in one's neighborhood and community—may be both a risk factor and a protective factor after community level disasters (Sampson, 2003; Sampson et al., 1997).

The economic impacts of disasters are substantial. Loss of a job is a major postevent predictor of negative psychiatric outcome (Galea et al., 2002; Nandi et al., 2004). These effects can be seen at the macro level—for example, in a dip in consumer confidence, which occurred during and after the sniper attacks in the Washington, D.C. area in October 2002. Terrorism in particular targets the social capital of the nation—a nation's cohesion, values, and ability to function. Economic impacts after terrorism may be substantial even with little destruction due to changed expectations and faith in leadership and community. Counterterrorism and national continuity are crucially dependent upon our having effective interventions to sustain the psychological, behavioral, and social function of the nation and its citizens.

Economic behaviors and decisions are affected both by the characteristics of a disaster and by the psychological and behavioral responses to the disaster of individuals and the community. For example, after Hurricane Katrina in the United States or the terrorist attacks on cities that have taken place around the world, decisions and behaviors related to travel, home purchase, food consumption, and medical care visits were altered by changes in availability, and also by changes in perceived safety, and optimism about the future. Threats and hoaxes, a common part of terrorism, also carry with them economic costs and consequences. The local or national economy may see altered savings, insurance, and investment, as well as changes in work attendance and productivity or disrupted transportation, communication and energy networks.

There are phases of community disaster response beginning early after the disaster with a sense of cohesion and a "honeymoon" of working together. Later, disillusionment, mistrust, and anger are common. Following major disasters it is not uncommon for rumors to develop and be circulated within the community that focus on the circumstances leading up to the event and the state or government response.

Sometimes there is a heightened state of fear. Over time, anger often emerges in communities. Typically, there is a focus on accountability or blame, resulting in a search for someone who was responsible for a lack of preparation or inadequate response. Community leaders such as mayors, police and fire chiefs are often targets of these feelings. Scapegoating can be an especially destructive process when directed at those who already hold themselves responsible, even if there was nothing further they could have done to prevent adverse outcomes. In addition, nations and communities experience ongoing hypervigilance and a sense of lost safety while trying to establish normality in their lives.

There are many milestones of a disaster which both affect the community and may offer opportunities for recovery. Outpourings of sympathy for the dead, injured, and their friends and families can be expected and are not uncommon. There are the normal rituals associated with burying the dead. Later, energy and planning goes into creating appropriate memorials. Memorialization has the potential to cause harm as well as to do good. There may be disagreement about the design and placement of monuments. Careful thought should go into design and placement of memorials. If a monument is situated too prominently so that community members cannot avoid encountering it, the memorial may heighten intrusive recollections and interfere with the resolution of grief reactions. Impromptu memorials of flowers, photographs, and memorabilia are frequently erected. It is important to distinguish between this type of spontaneous memoralization, such as the candles and photos after 9/11, and more formalized and planned memorials. Churches and synagogues play an important role in assisting communities' search for meaning from such tragedy and in assisting in the grief process. Anniversaries of the disaster (for example, those taking place one year after) often stimulate renewed grief but can be important markers of moving on with one's life.

The risk of psychiatric morbidity is greatest in those with high perceived threat to life, low controllability, lack of predictability, high loss, injury, the possibility that the disaster will recur, and exposure to the dead and the grotesque. Disasters with a high degree of community destruction and those in developing countries are associated with worse outcomes. Terrorism can be distinguished from other natural and human-made disasters by the characteristic extensive fear, loss of confidence in institutions, unpredictability, and pervasive experience of loss of safety (Fullerton et al., 2003).

MENTAL HEALTH AND DISASTER BEHAVIOR

Mental health and community needs after catastrophic disasters are substantial. Four to seven months after Hurricane Katrina in the United States, in the highest impact area (the city of New Orleans), 49.6 percent reported nightmares and 8 percent reported these nightmares were occurring nearly every night (Kessler et al., 2006). Similarly, 58.2 percent reported being more jumpy or easily startled, and 79.4 percent reported being more irritable or angry. Because the National Comorbidity Replication study had surveyed the mental health of the Katrina disaster region before the hurricane struck, we know that the rates of mental disorder had doubled six months after Katrina, from about 15 percent to 30 percent. (Galea et al., 2007; Kessler et al., 2008). In New York City after the terrorist attacks of September 11, 2001, 7.5 percent of lower Manhattan had probable PTSD (Galea et al., 2002). Nearly one-third of people with the highest levels of exposure (for example, 37 percent of those in the buildings or 30 percent of the injured) had PTSD. Rates of PTSD decreased to 0.6 percent six months later.

Individual resilience (Bonanno et al., 2006) and posttraumatic growth (Linley and Joseph, 2004) are common after disasters. Communities can function effectively after disasters based on social capital, economics, information and communication, and community competences (Norris et al., 2008). In fact, the majority of people exposed to disasters do well. The effects of traumatic events are not exclusively bad with many individuals reporting growth. For example, after Hurricane Katrina, 88.5 percent of the disaster-impacted population reported that their experiences with the hurricane helped them develop a deeper sense of meaning or purpose in life (Kessler et al., 2006). The majority (89.3 percent) and 81 percent of the highest impacted area (the city of New Orleans) reported they would be better able to cope with future life stressors following their experience of Hurricane Katrina. Understanding the range of trajectories of response—resilience, distress, illness, recovery—is an important longitudinal perspective on disaster-exposed individuals and communities. For some, however, the outcome can be psychiatric disorders, distress, or health risk behaviors such as an increase in alcohol or tobacco use. PTSD is not uncommon following many traumatic events, from terrorism to motor vehicle accidents to industrial explosions. In its acute form, PTSD may be more like the common cold, experienced at some time in one's life by nearly all. However, when it persists, it can be debilitating and require psychotherapeutic and/or pharmacological intervention.

In recent years we have learned a great deal about PTSD and its public health implications. PTSD is a disorder of forgetting perhaps even more than of remembering. It is the inability to forget that leads to the pathology and suffering in PTSD. Forgetting is a critical component of recovery. Of course, if we could not "forget," our brains would rapidly be cluttered with information and observations and perhaps more limited in cognitive control functions for other activities.

Disaster behavior—how one acts at the time of impact of a disaster—also affects morbidity and at times mortality. Studies of evacuation from the World Trade Center towers in 1993 after a terrorist truck bomb showed that those evacuating in groups greater than 20 took more than six minutes longer to decide to evacuate (Aguirre et al., 1998). In addition, the more people knew each other in the group, the longer the group took to initiate evacuation. After the 9/11 attacks, rather than leave the disaster area, victims from the twin towers tended to congregate at the site (Gershon et al., 2004). Overdedication to one's group can also lead firefighters, police, and other first responders to needlessly risk their lives. In pandemics, or after a bioterrorism attack, adherence to medical recommendations is a lifesaving behavior.

Psychological First Aid (PFA) is an evidence-informed approach designed to reduce the initial distress in the immediate aftermath of traumatic events and to foster adaptive functioning in children, adolescents, adults, and families (Hobfoll et al., 2007). The primary principles of early PFA for individual care are safety, calming, connectedness, efficacy (ability and belief that one can cope/respond), and optimism. Application of these principles is the present state of the art for early intervention.

Children are at risk both from their own exposure and that of their caregivers. The effect of depression and PTSD in caregivers on their children is only beginning to be examined but certainly includes less awareness of the child's needs and therefore altered parenting. Children with direct exposures or who have had a caregiver killed or injured have special needs.

The elderly have substantial practical needs that can go unaddressed when social services disappear. From finding a new grocery store to obtaining medication or transportation for renal dialysis, social service outreach is critical for this group. Similarly, for all chronic medical illnesses, including chronic mental illness, loss of critically important medications and loss of care provider availability can greatly increase morbidity and mortality.

The homeless, who form an integral part of large urban communities, are often forgotten in public health planning for terrorist, bioterrorist, and other disaster events. During a terrorist attack, bioterrorism, or natural disaster, the homeless may be difficult to reach or reluctant to comply with public health outreach programs such as vaccination or quarantine, shelter in place, and evacuation. Behaviors such as not coming to homeless shelters can put the homeless at risk of not receiving health interventions, which not only affects them but has the potential of spreading diseases to the general population. Policy planning for disaster and future research is critical to an effective public health response and addressing barriers to health care in this vulnerable and often forgotten group when disaster strikes.

DISASTER PREPAREDNESS, RESPONSE AND RECOVERY, AND SOCIAL EPIDEMIOLOGY

The importance of individual and community behaviors related to social disadvantage and other social inequalities calls for an examination of social epidemiology concepts and methods in disaster preparedness and response. Berkman and Kawachi (2000) defined social epidemiology as the study of social distribution and determinants of health. Most behaviors are not randomly distributed in a population but in fact group according to various communities, neighborhoods, and familial and work relationships.

Group behavior is determined not only by its composition but also by the context and interaction of group members. In gauging a society's ability to weather pandemic influenza or a massive hurricane, we naturally think of the poor's high risk of exposure to a virus or to the worst of flooding and winds. However, we must also consider in disaster planning and risk models the inability to maintain hand washing because of lack of water or soap and the inability of those exposed to evacuate from the wind and flood waters due to lack of transportation or access. Following Hurricane Katrina, about half of those who did not evacuate chose not to, and half could not because they did not have transportation or a means to leave.

Socioeconomic position is likely to have a significant influence on who survives a pandemic by the way it allows a family to purchase protective masks, access prophylactic medications, or have enough reserved food and supplies to shelter in place, leading to a socially determined distribution of disaster behavior opportunity. Socioeconomic position also influences who survives a hurricane. The associations may not be unlike those that placed women traveling in Third Class on the *Titanic* at 20 times the likelihood of drowning compared to women in First Class.

Individual-level allostatic load and social context models help clarify the pathways through which social conditions determine health outcomes. These models also contribute to our understanding of how social conditions influence the success or failure of disaster behaviors (for example, evacuation, sheltering in place, hand washing) and health effects. The risk of harm from a disaster to an individual cannot be divorced from the risk of harm to the population to which the individual belongs.

One of the pillars of public health is social justice. The unfair or unequal treatment of anyone affected by a disaster or terrorist event can unravel an entire disaster response system. In preparing minority populations for disasters, the consequences of everyday wear and tear of all too common discrimination erodes the trust of minority populations toward the system (government, organizations in charge of preparedness, and disaster response personnel) and can instill a sense of oppression and helplessness. Both of these endanger the necessary creativity, improvisation, cohesion, and sharing that may be necessary to coping postdisaster. Low levels of trust correlate strikingly with low levels of trust and confidence in public institutions (Brehm and Rahn, 1997). For communities in which terrorism is endemic—drug gangs and neighborhood shootings—postdisaster trust can be difficult to sustain.

Disasters disrupt employment and economic resources. Communities that experience job loss see greater excess mortality and morbidity. This excess mortality is largely in the form of suicides, accidents, violent deaths, and alcohol-related deaths (Kasl and Jones, 2000). This can be an expected component of catastrophic disasters. The morbidity accompanying job loss, even without a disaster, is likely to involve depression and a myriad of distress symptoms including somatic/physical symptoms that can be difficult to separate from physical health problems. Hence, postdisaster response plans where jobs are lost must include planning for unemployment benefits, job training, local-hire reconstruction programs, and vocational rehabilitation efforts.

Life acquires a sense of coherence, meaningfulness, and interdependence through contact with friends and family and participation in work and voluntary activities. Because coherence and meaningfulness as well as employment and volunteerism are linked with good health (Berkman and Glass, 2000), disaster response programs must promote and enable contact among friends and relatives, volunteerism, and work side by side with other more conventional programs such as medication refill. A social organizational approach to disaster preparedness that enhances the collective efficacy—individuals working together (Kawachi and Berkman, 2000; Sampson et al., 1997)—and social capital—levels of interpersonal trust and norms of reciprocity and mutual aid (Coleman, 1990; Putnam, 1993)—may be one of the best approaches to preparing for disasters and terrorism.

From a resource perspective, postdisaster interventions focus on quickly replacing valued community resources (Hobfoll and Lilly, 1993). Postdisaster losses occur on multiple ecological levels, including family, organization, and community. The Conservation of Resources (COR) theory posits that people strive to obtain and protect resources (Hobfoll, 1989). In the aftermath of disasters, personal and material resource losses are related to survival, and can result in high levels of distress. In a recent large-scale study of terrorism in Israel, psychosocial resources and psychosocial resource loss and gain were significantly related to exposure to terrorism, greater PTSD, and depressive symptoms (Hobfoll et al., 2006). Organizations such as employee assistance programs, schools, and churches with existing relationships in the community play important roles after terrorism in particular (Institute of Medicine, 2003). These organizations are also well positioned to provide information and support to individuals with specific concerns or in need of additional support, thus greatly enhancing the effectiveness of the overall response. Predisaster planning and education puts individuals and communities in a better position to use their existing infrastructures by shielding within their own communities rather than to engage in spontaneous evacuations to more vulnerable environments (Saathoff and Everly, 2002).

CONCLUSION

Over time, the resilience of individuals and communities is the expected response to a disaster. But for some the effects can be severe and lasting. Experiencing an altered sense of safety, increased fear and arousal, and concern for the future affects not only those who may develop mental health problems but also those who continue to work and care for their families and loved ones. Consequence management for mental health—fostering resilience, decreasing and treating disorders, and responding to health risk behaviors—requires preparing, responding, and focusing on mitigation of disaster effects and recovery. For those directly exposed and those indirectly affected, the additional burdens of lost supports and increased demands is an ongoing part of disaster recovery. Importantly, in the aftermath of large-scale disasters such as the Asian tsunami of 2004 that affected thousands, early identification of individuals at risk for developing psychiatric disorders from those experiencing transient distress is key to delivering effective treatment. How the psychological and behavioral response to a disaster is managed may be the defining factor in the ability of a community to recover.

Interventions require rapid, effective, and sustained mobilization of resources (Ursano and Friedman, 2006). Sustaining the social fabric of the community and facilitating recovery depends on leadership's knowledge of a community's resilience and vulnerabilities as well as an understanding of the distress, disorder, and health risk behavioral responses to the event (Institute of Medicine, 2003; Raphael and Wooding, 2004). A coordinated systems approach across the medical care, public health, and emergency response system is necessary to meet the mental health care needs of a disaster region.

REFERENCES

Aguirre, B. E., D. Wenger, and G. Vigo. "A Test of the Emergent Norm Theory of Collective Behavior." *Sociological Forum* 13 (1998): 301-320.

Berkman, L. F., and T. Glass. "Social Integration, Social Networks, Social Support and Health." *Social Epidemiology*. Eds. L. F. Berkman and I. Kawachi. Oxford: Oxford University Press, 2000.

Bonanno, G. A., S. Galea, A. Bucciarelli, and D. Vlahov. "Psychological Resilience after Disaster: New York City in the Aftermath of the September 11th Terrorist Attack." *Psychological Science* 17 (2006): 181-186.

Coleman, J.S. *Foundations of Social Theory*. Cambridge: Harvard University Press, 1990.

Fullerton, C. S., R. J. Ursano, A. E. Norwood, and H. C. Holloway. "Trauma, Terrorism, and Disaster." *Terrorism and Disaster. Individual and Community Mental Health Interventions*. Eds. R. J. Ursano, C. S. Fullerton, and A. E. Norwood. Cambridge: Cambridge University Press, 2003.

Galea, S., C. R. Brewin, M. Gruber, R. T. Jones, D. W. King, L. A. King, R. J. McNally, R. J. Ursano, M. Petukhova, and R. Kessler. "Exposure to Hurricane-Related Stressors and Mental Illness after Katrina." *Archives of General Psychiatry* 64 (2007): 1427-1434.

Galea, S., J. Ahern, H. Resnick, D. Kilpartick, M. Bucuvalas, J. Gold, and D. Valahov. "Psychological Sequelae of the September 11 Terrorist Attacks in New York City." *New England Journal of Medicine* 346 (2002): 982-987.

Gershon, R., E. Hogan, K. A. Qureshi, and L. Doll. "Preliminary Results from the World Trade Center Evacuation Study—New York City." *MMWR: Morbidity and Mortality Weekly Reports* 53 (2004): 815-817.

Grayson, J. P. "Reported Illness after CGE Closure." *Canadian Journal of Public Health* 80 (1989):16-19.

Hobfoll, S. E. "Conservation of Resources. A New Attempt at Conceptualizing Stress." *American Psychologist* 44 (1989): 513-524.

Hobfoll, S. E., D. Canetti-Nisim, and R.J. Johnson. "Exposure to Terrorism, Stress-related Mental Health Symptoms, and Defensive Coping among Jews and Arabs in Israel." *Journal of Consulting and Clinical Psychology* 74 (2006): 207-218.

Hobfoll, S., and R. Lilly. "Resource Conservation as a Strategy for Community Psychology." *Journal of Community Psychology* 21 (1993): 128-148.

Hobfoll, S., P. Watson, C. C. Bell, R. A. Bryant, M. J. Brymer, M. J. Friedman, M. Friedman, B. P. R. Gersons, J. de Jong, C. M. Layne, S. Maguen, Y. Neria, A. E. Norwood, R. S. Pynoos, D. Reissman, J. I. Ruzek, A. Y. Shalev, Z. Solomon, A. M. Steinberg, R. J. Ursano. "Five Essential Elements of Immediate and Mid-term Mass Trauma Intervention: Empirical Evidence." *Psychiatry: Interpersonal and Biological Processes* 70:4 (2007): 283-315.

Institute of Medicine (IOM). *Preparing for the Psychological Consequences of Terrorism: A Public Health Strategy.* Washington, D.C.: National Academies of Science, National Academies Press, 2003.

Kasl, S. V., and B. A. Jones. "The Impact of Job Loss and Retirement on Health." *Social Epidemiology.* Eds. L. F. Berkman and I. Kawachi. Oxford: Oxford University Press, 2000.

Kawachi, I., and L. F. Berkman. "Socal Cohesion, Social Capital and Health." *Social Epidemiology.* Eds. L. F. Berkman and I. Kawachi. Oxford: Oxford University Press, 2000.

———. "Social Ties and Mental Health." *Journal of Urban Health* 78 (2001): 458-467.

Kessler, R. C., S. Galea, M. J. Gruber, N. A. Sampson, R. J. Ursano, S. Wessely. "Trends in Mental Illness and Suicidality after Hurricane Katrina." *Molecular Psychiatry* 13 (2008): 374-384.

Linley, P. A., and S. Joseph. "Positive Change Following Trauma and Adversity: A Review." *Journal of Traumatic Stress* 17 (2004): 11-21.

Nandi, A., S. Galea, M. Tracy, J. Ahern, H. Resnick, R. Gershon, and D. Vlahov. "Job Loss, Unemployment, Work Stress, Job Satisfaction, and the Persistence of Posttraumatic Stress Disorder One Year after the September 11 Attacks." *Journal of Occupational and Environmental Medicine* 46 (2004): 1057-1064.

Noji, E. K., ed. *The Public Health Consequences of Disasters.* New York: Oxford University Press, 1997.

Norris, F. H., M. J. Friedman, P. J. Watson, C. M. Byrne, E. Diaz, and K. Kaniasty. "60,000 Disaster Victims Speak, Part I. An Empirical Review of the Empirical Literature: 1981-2001." *Psychiatry* 65 (2002): 207-239.

Norris, F. H., S. P. Stevens, B. Pfefferbaum, K. F. Wyche, R. L. Pfefferbaum. "Community Resilience as a Metaphor, Theory, Set of Capacities and Strategy for Disaster Readiness." *American Journal of Community Psychology* 41 (2008):127-150.

Putnam, R. D. *Making Democracy Work: Civic Traditions in Modern Italy.* Princeton: Princeton University Press, 1993.

Raphael, B., and S. Wooding. "Early Mental Health Interventions for

Traumatic Loss in Adults." *Early Intervention for Trauma and Traumatic Loss*. Eds. B. T. Litz. New York: Guilford Press, 2004.

Saathoff, G., and G. S. Everly Jr. "Psychological Challenges of Bioterror: Containing Contagion." *International Journal of Emergency Mental Health* 4 (2002): 245-252.

Sampson, R. J. "The Neighborhood Context of Well-being." *Perspectives in Biology and Medicine* 46 (2003) S53-S64.

Sampson, R. J., S. W. Raudenbush, and F. Earls. "Neighborhoods and Violent crime: A Multilevel Study of Collective Efficacy." *Science* 277 (1997): 918-924.

Ursano, R. J., and M.J. Friedman. "Mental Health and Behavioral Interventions for Victims of Disasters and Mass Violence: Systems, Caring, Planning, and Needs." *Interventions Following Mass Violence and Disasters: Strategies for Mental Health Practice*. Eds. E. C. Ritchie, P. J. Watson, and M. J. Friedman. New York: Guilford Press, 2006.

Ursano, R. J., A. E. Norwood, C. S. Fullerton, H. C. Holloway, and M. Hall. "Terrorism with Weapons of Mass Destruction: Chemical, Biological, Nuclear, Radiological, and Explosive Agents." *Trauma and Disaster: Responses and Management*. Eds. R. J. Ursano, A. E. Norwood. Arlington, Virg.: American Psychiatric Press, 2003.

Journal of Environmental Systems

Editor: Sheldon J. Reaven
Associate Editor: Jeffrey B. Gillow
Managing Editor: Carole Rose

The knowledge of environmental, energy, and waste problems is burgeoning individual disciplines. There are lively, continuing disagreements among environmental professionals as to the basic theories, concepts, methods of analysis, and values that most fruitfully explore environmental issues and systems. We continue to discover the bewildering complexities of environmental systems themselves, and find that they cannot be understood within the confines of individual fields of science and engineering. It becomes ever more evident that environmental problems can be understood only in the context of their social, economic and regulatory "environments."

READERSHIP

In more than 40 countries, *JES* is read by engineers, scientists, business executives, government officials, and others involved in areas relevant to environmental systems. Leading subscribers are from the areas of: recycling and waste management; policy analysis and risk analysis; energy/resource modeling and environmental impact assessment; environmental health and safety; architecture and urban studies; civil engineering, transportation, and public utilities (energy and water); ecology and environmental engineering; law and economics; anthropology and psychology, science and technology studies.

AIMS AND SCOPE

The *Journal* defines environmental problems as systems in which complex natural phenomena affect, and are affected by, the human world of economics, regulation and law, culture, behavior, and public perceptions. The *Journal* is where environmental professionals from many disciplines exchange ideas on, and devise solutions to problems in waste management; energy and resources; and local and global water, land, and air pollution.

SUBSCRIPTION INFORMATION
Sold by volume only (4 issues yearly)
Print ISSN: 0047-2433; Online ISSN: 1541-3802
Institutional Rate: $300.00 + $11.00 postage & handling U.S. and Canada; $20.00 elsewhere
Complimentary sample issue available upon request

BAYWOOD PUBLISHING COMPANY, INC.
26 Austin Avenue, PO Box 337, Amityville, NY 11701
call (631) 691-1270 • fax (631) 691-1770 • toll-free orderline (800) 638-7819
e-mail: baywood@baywood.com • website: http://baywood.com

HELP SUPPORT

THE JOURNAL DONATION PROJECT

Begun in 1990 with the collapse of the Soviet Union, the Journal Donation Project (JDP), a *Social Research*, initiative, is an international library assistance program that assists in the rebuilding of major research and teaching libraries in countries that have fallen victim to political and economic deprivation. Through the provision of current subscriptions drawn from over 2,000 of the most important English-language scholarly, professional and current events journals, the JDP has helped to develop significant journal archives at over 300 libraries in 30 countries. The Project has grown substantially over the years, due to the generosity of donors. Gifts from individuals, families, corporate matching programs, grant-giving foundations, and others are deeply appreciated.

Donors may wish to make a one-time donation, pledge an annual gift, give in honor of or in memory of a loved one, or designate monies for a specific project/geographic location. All donations are tax deductible.

To learn how you can help support the JDP, please contact:

Professor Arien Mack, Project Organizer and Director
New School University, Journal Donation Project
65 Fifth Avenue
New York, NY 10003
Tel: 212 229 5789
Fax: 212 229 5476
Email: jdp@newschool.edu
Website: www.newschool.edu/centers/jdp

Notes on Contributors

ELLIOT ARONSON is Professor Emeritus at the University of California, Santa Cruz. Author of *The Social Animal* (2008, 10 ed.) and *Mistakes Were Made (But Not By Me)* (2007), among others, he is the recipient of distinguished research awards from the American Association for the Advancement of Science, the American Psychological Association, and the Association of Scientific Psychology.

REID BASHER, Senior Coordinator of the Inter-Agency and Policy Coordination Unit in the UN International Strategy for Disaster Reduction, studies the interaction of science, policy, and applications practice concerning climate risk and disasters, early warning and the management of seasonal variability, and adaptation to climate change.

ROBERT D. BULLARD is the Edmund Asa Ware Distinguished Professor of Sociology and Director of the Environmental Justice Resource Center at Clark Atlanta University. He is the author of 14 books, most recently *Deadly Waiting Game Beyond Hurricane Katrina: Government Response, Unnatural Disasters, and African Americans* (forthcoming 2009).

LEE CLARKE is Associate Professor of Sociology at Rutgers University. He is author of *Acceptable Risk?* (1989), *Mission Improbable* (1999) and *Worst Cases: Terror & Catastrophe in the Popular Imagination*

(2006). He is currently writing about problems of science, warnings, and political engagement.

CAROL S. FULLERTON is Research Professor in the Department of Psychiatry at the Uniformed Services University of the Health Sciences, Bethesda, Maryland. The author of numerous articles and several books on individual and community response to disaster and trauma, she is also the Scientific Director of the Center for the Study of Traumatic Stress.

RONALD KASSIMIR, an expert on contemporary African politics and religion, is Associate Provost at The New School. His work has appeared in many journals and periodicals, and he is the coeditor of *Youth Activism: An International Encyclopedia* (2005); *Intervention and Transnationalism in Africa* (2002); and *Youth, Globalization, and Law* (2007).

HOWARD KUNREUTHER is the Cecilia Yen Koo Professor of Decision Sciences and Public Policy at the Wharton School, University of Pennsylvania, and Codirector of the Wharton Risk Management and Decision Processes Center. His most recent book, *At War with the Weather* (coauthored with Michel-Kerjan), is forthcoming from MIT Press in 2009.

ERWANN MICHEL-KERJAN is Managing Director of the Wharton

Risk Management and Decision Processes Center at the University of Pennsylvania and coeditor of *Seeds of Disaster, Roots of Response: How Private Action Can Reduce Public Vulnerability* (2006). His most recent book, *At War with the Weather* (coauthored with Kunreuther), is forthcoming from MIT Press in 2009.

WILLIAM MORRISH is Elwood R. Quesada Professor of Architecture, Landscape Architecture and Urban and Environmental Planning, at the School of Architecture, University of Virginia. Author of *Civilizing Terrains: Mountains, Mounds and Mesas* (2004), he is currently writing a book on lessons learned from rebuilding after Katrina.

JOHN C. MUTTER is Professor in the Departments of Earth and Environmental Sciences and of International and Public Affairs, Director of Graduate Studies for the doctorate in sustainable development and Director of the Fellows program for the Earth Institute at Columbia University. He studies the relationship between natural systems and human well-being with particular focus on extreme events and the vulnerability of poor societies.

MICHAEL OPPPENHEIMER is Albert G. Milbank Professor of Geosciences and International Affairs and the Director of the Program in Science, Technology, and Environmental Policy at Princeton University.

CHARLES PERROW, Professor Emeritus of Sociology at Yale University, is the author of over sixty articles and six books, including *Normal Accidents: Living with High-Risk Technologies* (1984, rev 1999) and *The Next Catastrophe: Reducing Our Vulnerabilities to Natural, Industrial, and Terrorist Disasters* (2007).

ENRICO L. QUARANTELLI is Founding Director of the Disaster Research Center and Professor Emeritus in the Department of Sociology and Criminal Justice at the University of Delaware. His current research includes such topics as future social trends in disasters and catastrophes and theoretical problems of conceptualizing disasters.

IRWIN REDLENER is Professor of Clinical Population and Family Health and Director of the National Center for Disaster Preparedness at the Columbia University Mailman School of Public Health. He is also President and cofounder of the Children's Health Fund. He is the author of *Americans At Risk: Why We Are Not Prepared For Megadisasters and What We Can Do Now* (2006).

NICHOLAS SCOPPETTA has been New York City's Fire Commissioner since December 30, 2001. He is a former Deputy Mayor for Criminal Justice;